Civil Actions for Uncivilized Acts

Civil Actions for UNCIVILIZED ACTS

The Adjudicative Jurisdiction of Common Law Courts in Transnational Human Rights Proceedings

François Larocque

IRWIN LAW

Civil Actions for Uncivilized Acts: The Adjudicative Jurisdiction of Common Law Courts in Transnational Human Rights Proceedings

Published in 2010 by
Irwin Law Inc.
Suite 206
14 Duncan Street
Toronto, ON
M5H 3G8

www.irwinlaw.com

ISBN: 978-1-55221-187-8
e-book ISBN: 978-1-55221-206-6

Cataloguing in Publication available from Library and Archives Canada

The publisher acknowledges the financial support of the Government of Canada through the Book Publishing Industry Development Program (BPIDP) for its publishing activities.

We acknowledge the assistance of the OMDC Book Fund, an initiative of Ontario Media Development Corporation.

Printed and bound in Canada.

1 2 3 4 5 14 13 12 11 10

Summary Table of Contents

Detailed Table of Contents

Foreword

International criminal prosecutions, be they in the various *ad hoc* international criminal tribunals or the International Criminal Court, have become a permanent feature of international law. They express the public and collective opprobrium of most peoples and states against those acts—such as genocide, war crimes, crimes against humanity, and torture—that threaten our collective peace and security. That being the case, it is sometimes easy to forget that international crimes also have a private face; that of the survivors and the victims. At international law, the criminal prohibitions of genocide and torture are consubstantial with the corresponding human right to life and the right to be free from torture. Yet survivors, victims, and their families are typically relegated to the margins of the public processes of international criminal accountability. This is where the development of transnational human rights litigation proves so compelling.

Human rights are meaningless if they cannot be claimed and enforced. In many countries, national courts are playing an increasingly important role in interpreting and applying international norms protecting the population, frequently with life-saving impact, as part of the overarching international legal and social mobilization for human rights accountability and the global fight against impunity. Indeed, the complementarity principle on which the *Rome Statute* is premised specifically establishes the primary role of national courts in this respect.

Rightly or wrongly, the rapid and robust expansion of international criminal law since Nuremberg has monopolized the attention of legal scholars who have documented and analyzed these developments. Few however have paid sustained attention to the potential of civil actions to supplement the functions of international criminal law as protector of the vital interests of the international community and of the rule of law. In this respect, François Larocque's detailed analysis of the jurisdiction of national courts to adjudicate civil claims for extraterritorial human rights violations is an important, timely, and distinctive contribution.

This book is important not only because of the dearth of scholarly literature on transnational human rights litigation writ large, but also because it presents the phenomenon (quite properly in my view) as a complementary part of, rather than as an alternative to, existing institutions and processes of international justice. Corporate liability for extraterritorial human rights abuses is a case in point. The Honourable Justice Ian Binnie once noted that existing "governance gaps provide the permissive environment for wrongful acts by companies of all kinds without adequate sanctioning or reparation."[1] Transnational human rights litigation can potentially bridge this gap in a manner that international criminal law cannot, thereby providing survivors and victims with an opportunity and a forum to bring legitimate human rights claims.

This book is timely because the prospect of civil redress for violations of international human rights norms is increasingly debated in the courts and legislatures all over the world. The Canadian Parliament is currently considering draft legislation that would create a civil cause of action and bar illegitimate immunity claims in proceedings for grave breaches of peremptory norms of international law such as torture, genocide, crimes against humanity, and terrorism.[2] Also, the

1 Cristin Schmitz, "Binnie Calls for Corporate Accountability" *The Lawyers Weekly* (29 August 2008), online: www.lawyersweekly.ca/index.php?section=article&articleid=745.

2 See Bill C-35, *An Act to Deter Terrorism and to Amend the State Immunity Act*, 2d Sess., 40th Parl., 2009 (second reading 30 October 2009); and Bill C-483, *An Act to amend the State Immunity Act (genocide, crimes against humanity, war crimes or torture)*, 2nd Sess., 40th Parl., 2009 (Mr. Cotler, first reading 26 November 2009).

International Court of Justice is presently seized of a dispute between Italy and Germany on the appropriate limits of state immunity in civil actions for war crimes.[3] Similarly, the European Court of Human Rights will soon determine whether the United Kingdom's state immunity legislation is compatible with the *European Human Rights Convention* in the context of civil actions for torture committed abroad,[4] thereby revisiting its ruling in *Al-Adsani* where, by narrowest of margins (9:8), the Grand Chamber held that the peremptory prohibition of torture did not supersede the policy objectives of state immunity.[5] Clearly, the law in this area is in a state of flux.

Finally, the book is distinctive because it focuses on the particular adjudicative tradition of the common law. This is a pragmatic choice for the author. The extensive and ever growing body of US caselaw under the *Alien Tort Claims Act* and its related statutes lends itself well to analogies with the burgeoning experience in Canada and the United Kingdom. In developing their unique jurisprudence, US courts have self-consciously channelled the historical function of the common law judge as a declarer of law and righter of wrongs. Larocque's account of this phenomenon is illuminating and, as far as I can ascertain, wholly original. When conceived as a modern function of the historical "duty of the [judiciary] to say what the law is,"[6] the judicial task of translating international human rights violations into actionable wrongs (or torts) at common law takes on a new yet familiar meaning.

On whatever side one falls with respect to the overall desirability of transnational human rights litigation — a debate that can no longer be avoided — Larocque's work will serve to enrich the discussion. This book will appeal to a wide readership of scholars, public policy makers, lawyers, and judges, and to those who engage with the challenging enterprise of giving effect to human rights and of ensuring that law prevails over tyranny and abuse.

Louise Arbour
President and CEO of International Crisis Group

3 *Jurisdictional Immunities of the State (Germany v. Italy)*, International Court of Justice, General List No. 143, Order of 6 July 2010.

4 *Jones v. United Kingdom* and *Mitchell & Ors v. United Kingdom*, European Court of Human Rights, Application Numbers 34356/06 and 40528/06.

5 *Al-Adsani v. United Kingdom* (2002), 34 E.H.R.R. 273, [2001] E.C.H.R. 761.

6 *Marbury v. Madison*, 5 U.S. 137 at 177 (1803).

Preface

This is a book on the adjudicative jurisdiction of US, UK, and Canadian courts in transnational human rights proceedings, that is, civil lawsuits for extraterritorial violations of international norms protecting the human person. In the United States, foreign nationals have sought civil redress from multinational corporations, foreign state functionaries and sovereign states through a unique legislative framework composed of the *Alien Tort Claims Act* (*ATCA*), the *Torture Victim Protection Act* (*TVPA*), and certain amendments to the *Foreign Sovereign Immunities Act* (*FSIA*). On the basis of these statutes and the common law, US federal courts have asserted jurisdiction over civil claims for such extraterritorial human rights violations as torture, genocide, and crimes against humanity. The question that this book intends to answer is whether UK and Canadian courts can do the same in the absence of US-style legislation.

The book is largely based on my doctoral research in law at the University of Cambridge. When I applied to the Ph.D. program in Cambridge in the fall of 2001, transnational human rights litigation outside the United States remained a mere theoretical possibility. In Canada and the United Kingdom there had been only one case where foreign plaintiffs had sought civil redress for extraterritorial human rights violations; both cases had been dismissed on jurisdictional grounds. The Canadian case involved a Somali family who tried to sue the Canadian government and members of its armed forces in 1999 in connection with the torture and murder of a young boy by five Canadian peacekeepers. In an unreported decision, the case was dismissed for lack of standing and other procedural grounds.[1] Though the accused soldiers were eventually found guilty under Canadian criminal law, no further civil lawsuits were brought in connection to those events. The English case involved a Kuwaiti national who sued his government for torture committed in Kuwait. The claim was dismissed on the basis of the *State Immunity Act, 1978*. The Court of Appeal confirmed that decision and the House of Lords denied leave to appeal in 1996; the consistency of that decision was subsequently upheld, by the narrowest of margins, by the European Court of Human Rights.[2] With such a thin jurisprudential record, I wondered whether I would have enough material to fuel three years of doctoral research.

The European Court of Human Rights' decision in *Al-Adsani* in late 2001 was the first of many important developments. Others included the Ontario Superior Court of Justice's decision in *Bouzari*, the International Court of Justice's decision in the *Arrest Warrant* case, and the Second Circuit's opinion in *Unocal*, all of which were issued in 2002. Since that time, Canada and the UK have seen several new civil claims for extraterritorial human rights violations, including two important appellate court decisions. These, combined with the constant stream of US jurisprudence — including most notably, the first US Supreme Court analysis of the *Alien Tort Claims Act* in 2004 — have altered the situation in terms of available material, whatever conclusions may be drawn as to the substance. One of the trappings of novelty is unpredictability. The dynamism of this topic continued well beyond the completion of my doctorate, and provided important new legal developments, including relevant decisions from the House of Lords and the Supreme Court of Canada, the Maher Arar Inquiry, and the tabling in both the UK and Canadian Parliaments of draft legislation akin to the United

1 *Rage and Samow (Litigation Guardian of) v. Canada (A.G.)* (6 July 1999), Ottawa, 99-CV-9387 (Ont. Ct. Gen. Div.).

2 *Al-Adsani v. Kuwait* (1995), 103 I.L.R. 420 (Q.B.), aff'd (1996), 107 I.L.R. 536 (C.A.), leave to appeal to H.L. refused. See also *Al-Adsani v. United Kingdom*, no. 35763/97, [2001] E.C.H.R. 761, 34 E.H.R.R. 273.

States *TVPA* and *FSIA*. These developments, as well as others relating to the ever-evolving US position, have been integrated in this book.

The book is structured in three parts. Part I, entitled "Transnational Human Rights Litigation in Context," consists of three chapters. Chapter 1 establishes the terminological and conceptual boundaries of the study by defining the terms "transnational," "human rights," and "litigation." Chapter 2 is devoted to the history and judicial application of the *Alien Tort Claims Act* (*ATCA*), the 1789 statute that grants federal courts the jurisdiction to adjudicate civil claims for violations of the "law of nations," and that is at the heart of the US transnational human rights litigation phenomenon. Chapter 3 examines *ATCA*'s companion statute, the *Torture Victim Protection Act* (*TVPA*), as well as the other means by which US courts assert jurisdiction in transnational human rights cases. The US experience is described in detail and assessed on its own terms, and it is often referred to in subsequent chapters on a comparative basis.

Part II, entitled "Jurisdictional Issues," contains four chapters, each aimed at working out the technical legal feasibility of US-style transnational human rights litigation in the UK and Canada having regard to four important issues. In these chapters, Canadian and English jurisprudence and doctrine are analyzed with reference to their US equivalents and the requirements of international law. Chapter 4 examines the historical foundations and contemporary implications of one of transnational human rights litigation's working premises, namely, that customary international law forms part of the common law, which may in turn provide plaintiffs with a cause of action with regard to well-established and accepted norms. Chapter 5 inquires whether and to what extent transnational human rights claims can be reconciled with traditional rules of jurisdiction, choice of law, and justiciability. Chapters 6 and 7, for their part, are discussions of the particular issues that arise in connection to the doctrine of *forum non conveniens* and state immunity, respectively.

Part III, "Synthesis," provides an overall assessment of transnational human rights litigation. Drawing on the preceding chapters, it seeks to achieve two things. First, it attempts to analyze and situate the particular adjudicative mode that is engaged by transnational human rights litigation in the wider common law judicial tradition. Second, the relative costs and benefits of transnational human rights litigation are weighed within the general context of international law enforcement, in an argument emphasising its complementarity with international criminal law. While certain features of US transnational human rights litigation are inconsistent with international law, there exists a range of circumstances in which civil jurisdiction over extraterritorial human rights violations can be asserted constructively and in a manner that is not inconsistent with international law, in particular against locally based corporations. In effect, where personal jurisdiction exists, *ATCA* disables respondents from arguing that their conduct—though in violation of basic human rights standards—was lawful or authorized under the *lex loci* or is non-justiciable. These are roles proper to international law. Further, insofar as US transnational human rights litigation practice cannot simply be ignored and is showing no sign of disappearing, it is worth asking whether and on what basis analogous processes could profitably be established in other jurisdictions.

Transnational human rights litigation raises many issues that were deliberately left out of this book or that receive only incidental treatment, such as the execution of judgments. The scope of this book reflects the current stage of transnational human rights litigation outside the United States and its emphasis on adjudicative jurisdiction. It covers the law as it stood in spring 2010. As transnational human rights litigation continues to evolve, and I expect it will, it is my hope that additional issues will be discussed in future editions of this book.

François Larocque
University of Ottawa
Faculty of Law
September 2010

Acknowledgments

This book is derived from my doctoral dissertation at the University of Cambridge, which was brought to fruition thanks to the watchful guidance and encouragement of my two supervisors, Professors James Crawford and Philip Allott. I am very grateful to both of them.

The ideas and arguments in this book were inspired, forged, tested, and honed through discussions and conversations with numerous colleagues all over the world who continue to humble me with their generosity and brilliance. I am especially indebted to Fannie Lafontaine, Matt Eisenbrandt, and Stephen Pitel for their comments and revisions of parts of this book, and to my dear colleagues at the University of Ottawa, Faculty of Law.

I could not have completed this project without the unwavering encouragement and support of my wonderful friends and family. This long list includes my parents Gilles and Suzanne; my siblings and their spouses Yves, Monica, Brigitte, Robert, Jean, Ruth, Dominique, Steve, Serge, and Melissa; my extended family Claude, Bernadette, Germaine, and Ferdinand; and my dear friends Mark, Sarah, Fannie, Nathalie, Penny, Lauren, Erika, David, Catherine, Jason, Ciara, Tyler, Brad, Stéphane, Danny, and Benoît.

Finally, I wish to thank Anne, my partner in life, work, and play. Words simply cannot wield the extent of my gratitude for her love.

To Houshang Bouzari, Maher Arar, Zahra Kazemi, and to all those who have suffered the indignity of torture and who, in life and in death, still wait for justice.

part one

Transnational Human Rights Litigation in Context

CHAPTER ONE

Transnational Human Rights Litigation

"It is the object of definition to determine the nature or meaning or signification of a thing; in other words, definition is the formal attempt to answer the question, 'What is it?'"

—W.L. Davidson[1]

A Paraguayan family sues the Asuncion chief of police in US federal courts for torturing and killing their son in Paraguay.[2] A group of Israeli nationals sues Libya and the Palestine Liberation Organization in Washington DC for the bombing of a civilian bus in Israel.[3] Residents from the Indian city of Bhopal sue a US corporation in New York after a toxic cloud escapes from a factory killing over 2,000 people.[4] In Manhattan, a group of Croats and Muslims from Bosnia-Herzegovina sues the self-proclaimed president of an unrecognized State for masterminding a campaign of forced impregnation, torture, and genocide carried out by Serb military forces.[5] A Kuwaiti pilot sues his government in London alleging that he was tortured by Kuwaiti State officials at the behest of a relative of the Emir of Kuwait.[6] A US national sues the Islamic Republic of Iran

1 William Leslie Davidson, *The Logic of Definition Explained and Applied* (London: Longmans, Green & Co. 1885) at 32.

2 *Filártiga v. Peña-Irala*, 630 F.2d 876 (2d Cir. 1980).

3 *Tel-Oren v. Libyan Arab Republic*, 726 F.2d 774 (D.C. Cir. 1984).

4 *Re Union Carbide Corp. Gas Plant Disaster at Bhopal, India in December 1984*, 634 F. Supp. 842 (S.D.N.Y. 1986).

5 *Kadić v. Karadzić*, 70 F.3d 232 (2d Cir. 1995).

6 *Al-Adsani v. Kuwait* (1995), 103 I.L.R. 420 (Q.B.), aff'd (1996), 107 I.L.R. 536 (C.A.) [*Al-Adsani*].

for their alleged role in the death of his daughter in a suicide bombing attack by Shaqaqui terrorists in Israel.[7] An Iranian national sues his government in Toronto claiming to have been tortured by police officers in Teheran.[8] A Sudanese Presbyterian church sues a Canadian-based multinational corporation in US courts alleging their participation in acts of genocide and forced labour in Sudan.[9] A Canadian man joins a lawsuit in the UK against Saudi Arabia and Saudi officials alleging he and three other Britons were tortured whilst in Saudi custody.[10]

These are examples of transnational human rights litigation, which can broadly be defined as civil proceedings in the courts of one State in respect of claims for human rights violations that occurred in another State.[11] Put differently, in such cases, individuals or groups attempt to obtain civil redress in the national courts of one State in respect of internationally unlawful conduct perpetrated in a foreign country. The aim of this introductory chapter is to develop this skeletal definition and to outline the terminological and conceptual boundaries of this study on the civil jurisdiction of US, English, and Canadian national courts to adjudicate transnational human rights claims.

7 *Flatow v. Islamic Republic of Iran*, 999 F. Supp. 1 (D.C. Cir. 1998).

8 *Bouzari et al. v. Islamic Republic of Iran*, [2002] O.J. No. 1624, aff'd (2004), 71 O.R. (3d) 675 (C.A.) [*Bouzari*].

9 *Presbyterian Church of Sudan v. Talisman Energy Inc.*, 244 F. Supp. 2d 289 (S.D.N.Y. 2003).

10 *Jones v. Saudi Arabia*,[2004] EWCA Civ 1394 [*Jones* 2004] being the joint appeal from *Jones v. Saudi Arabia*, Case No. A2 2003/2155 [*Jones* 2003] and *Mitchell v. Al-Dali*, Case No. A2 2004/0489 [*Mitchell*]. The Court of Appeal's decision was reversed in part by [2006] UKHL 26 [*Jones* 2006].

11 The expression "transnational human rights litigation" is preferred since it most accurately describes the phenomenon under study. Other synonymous but somewhat equivocal labels include "transnational public law litigation" (see, for example, Harold Koh, "Transnational Public Law Litigation" (1991) 100 Yale L.J. 2347 [Koh]) and "international human rights litigation" (see, for example, Beth Stephens *et al.*, *International Human Rights Litigation in US Courts* (The Hague: Brill, 2008)). Though the expression had previously appeared in the literature (see, for example, Ryan Goodman, "Congressional Support for Customary Human Rights as Federal Common Law" (1998) 4 ILSA J. Int'l & Comp. L. 455), the tag "transnational human rights litigation" was bolstered by the publication of Craig Scott, ed., *Torture as Tort: Comparative Perspectives on the Development of Transnational Human Rights Litigation* (Oxford: Hart, 2001). See also generally Sarah Joseph, *Corporations and Transnational Human Rights Litigation* (Oxford: Hart, 2004).

A. TRANSNATIONAL

It appears that the adjective "transnational" was first used by Norman Angell in *The Fruits of Victory* (1921), the sequel to his most famous work, *The Great Illusion* (1911), in describing the European economy of the pre–First World War era.[12] But it was Philip Jessup who, in his 1956 Storrs lectures, first used it to designate a particular category of law. Jessup called transnational law "the law applicable to the complex interrelated world community, which may be described as beginning with the individual and reaching on up to the so-called 'family of nations' or 'society of States.'"[13] As used by Jessup, the concept of transnational law blurs inherited lines of thinking between national law and international law, between public law and private law, and between distinct constitutional, legal, and societal systems — and does so deliberately. It encompasses "all law which regulates actions or events that transcend national frontiers. Both public and private international law are included, as are other rules which do not wholly fit into such standard categories."[14] In addition to its broad normative content, transnational law encompasses a wide group of actors, including states, organizations, corporations, individuals as well as political, ethnic, and religious groups.[15]

This understanding of "transnational law" as a dynamic normative system created by and applying to a vast array of participants is not very different from certain conceptions of international law.[16] The problem, as Jessup notes, is that the term "*international law* is misleading since it suggests that one is concerned only with the relations of one nation (or State) to other nations (or States)."[17] In this sense, Jessup's "transnational law" closely resembles the classic concept of the "law of nations" which Jeremy Bentham virtually eradicated from

---

12 Norman Angell, *The Fruits of Victory: A Sequel to The Great Illusion* (London: Collins, 1921). See also Norman Angell, *The Great Illusion*, (London: William Heinemann, 1910).

13 Philip Jessup, *Transnational Law* (New Haven: Yale University Press, 1956) at 1 [Jessup].

14 *Ibid.* at 2.

15 *Ibid.* at 3.

16 See, generally, Philip Allott, *Eunomia: New Order for a New World* (Oxford: Oxford University Press, 1990); Rosalyn Higgins, *Problems and Process: International Law and How We Use It* (Oxford: Clarendon Press, 1994) [Higgins].

17 Jessup, above note 13 at 1.

legal literature and language.[18] The "law of nations" is defined in William Blackstone's *Commentaries* as:

> . . . a system of rules, deducible by natural reason, and established by universal consent among the civilized inhabitants of the world; in order to decide all disputes, to regulate all ceremonies and civilities, and to insure the observance of justice and good faith, in that intercourse which must frequently occur between two or more independent states, and the individuals belonging to each . . .[19]

Blackstone's understanding of the "law of nations" was that of a body of law that concerned not only states, but also individuals. Blackstone's theory formed an integral part of the law of the land, and, like Jessup's transnational law, blurred the lines between domestic and non-domestic law. Blackstone continued:

> . . . the law of nations (wherever any question arises which is properly the object of its jurisdiction) is here adopted in its full extent by the common law, and is held to be a part of the law of the land. And those acts of parliament, which have from time to time been made to enforce this universal law, or to facilitate the execution of its decisions, are not to be considered as introductive of any new rule, but merely as declaratory of the old fundamental constitutions of the kingdom; without which it must cease to be a part of the civilized world.[20]

Moreover, the law of nations included many branches of law that, in addition to the transactions between sovereign states, also applied to what would today be considered private international disputes:

> Thus in mercantile questions, such as bills of exchange and the like; in all marine causes, relating to freight, average, demurrage, insurances, bottomry, and others of a similar nature; the law merchant, which is a branch of the law of nations, is regularly and constantly adhered to. So too in all disputes relating to prizes, to shipwrecks, to hostages, and ransom bills, there is no other rule of decision but this great universal law.[21]

---

18 Mark Weston Janis, "Jeremy Bentham and the Fashioning of 'International Law'" (1984) 78 A.J.I.L. 405 at 416; Koh, above note 11 at 2351.

19 William Blackstone, *Commentaries on the Laws of England*, vol. 4 (Oxford: Clarendon, 1769) at 66 [Blackstone].

20 *Ibid.* at 67.

21 *Ibid.* at 67.

With respect to its components, its areas of operation and participants, Blackstone's law of nations, like Jessup's transnational law, "involved a far more hybrid and pluralistic body of law than is currently the case in mainstream international legal thought."[22]

When Bentham coined the term "international law" in his *Introduction to the Principles of Morals and Legislation* (1789), he explicitly intended his expression to replace the "law of nations." In the final chapter of his *Principles*, Bentham distinguished between internal and international jurisprudence. In a footnote to the word "international," he wrote:

> The word *international* it must be acknowledged is a new one; though it is hoped, sufficiently analogous and intelligible. It is calculated to express, in a more significant way, the branch of the law which goes commonly under the name of the *law of nations:* an appellation so uncharacteristic that, were it not for the force of custom, it would seem rather to refer to internal jurisprudence.[23]

Bentham's "international law" was not as extensive as Blackstone's "law of nations." It did not include any participant other than sovereign states and it applied exclusively to the relationship and transactions between them.

> Now as to any transactions which may take place between individuals who are subjects of different states, these are regulated by the internal laws, and decided upon by the internal tribunals, of the one or the other of those states: . . . . There remain then the mutual transactions between sovereigns, as such, for the subject of that branch of jurisprudence which may be properly and exclusively termed *international.*[24]

Of course, Bentham's reclassification was tremendously successful. His label "international law" has endured, even though its content today — which includes, for certain purposes at least, individuals, organizations, and corporations and which extends to international criminal law and international human rights — is more aligned with Blackstone's law of nations. It is this discrepancy between *definiendum*

22 Craig Scott, "Remarks: The *Alien Tort Claims Act* under Attack" (2004) 98 A.S.I.L. Proceedings 58 at 60.

23 Jeremy Bentham, *An Introduction to the Principles of Morals and Legislation* (1789; reprint, James Henderson Burns & Herbert Lionel, eds., Aldolphus Hart, London: Athelone Press, 1970) at 296.

24 *Ibid.*

and *definiens* that Jessup sought to remedy by proposing the expression "transnational law." Thus, in the context of transnational human rights litigation, the word "transnational" invokes the plurality of localities, legal norms, and actors that may come into play in a given claim.

B. HUMAN RIGHTS

Another defining aspect of the type of proceedings under study in this book is the particular nature of the legal rights that claimants seek to vindicate, namely, human rights. More precisely, transnational human rights litigation is concerned with the enforcement of international norms protecting the human person. Brownlie argues that "there is no such entity as International Human Rights Law,"[25] human rights form a broad area of concern and related issues may arise in a variety of international legal contexts. Of course, there is nothing inherently international (or transnational) about the right to be free from torture or the right to a fair and impartial trial. National and international legal systems can make provisions to safeguard these rights through their respective processes, though no one system can claim to be the original source or sole protector of human rights. Though human rights are legal rights,[26] that is, rights *enforced by law*, it is humanness, or rather, the perceived inherent worth or dignity of the human person that is the basis for the rights. Collectively, we regard human beings as intrinsically worthy of respect and, when threatened, of protection. Many international human rights instruments emphasize the essential relationship between dignity and human rights.[27] For example, principle VII of the *Helsinki Final Act* states that human rights and freedoms "derive from the inherent dignity of the human person."[28]

While the concept of dignity affords very limited insight into the legal scope of human rights,[29] it seems to represent a widely shared

25 Ian Brownlie, *Principles of Public International Law*, 6th ed. (Oxford: Oxford University Press, 2003) at 530 [Brownlie].

26 Higgins, above note 16 at 96.

27 See *Charter of the United Nations*, Preamble; *Universal Declaration of Human Rights*, Preamble and art. 1; *International Covenant on Civil and Political Rights*, art. 10; *American Convention on Human Rights*, art. 5; *International Covenant on Economic, Social and Cultural Rights*, art.13.

28 *Helsinki Final Act*, ppl. VII.

29 But see Oscar Schachter, "Human Dignity as a Normative Concept" (1983) 77 A.J.I.L. 848 at 848–54.

paradigm of the international community. Most nations appear to agree with the idea that human rights are immanent insofar as they are linked to the human person's inherent dignity. In this sense, the prevailing account of human rights at international law appears to be broadly aligned with the idea of natural rights.[30] However, to posit dignity as the source of human rights inevitably leads one to query about the source of human dignity itself. Where does humanity's sense of inherent worth come from? Religion might suggest that human dignity is a reflection of God's presence in Her creation.[31] Sociobiology might suggest that dignity finds its roots deep within the cells of the human organism as a socialized expression of self-preservation. Whatever the suggestion, nobody seems to get it quite right, and one wonders if anyone ever will. Beyond dignity, the human rights discourse seems to leave the path of reason to wade in the deep waters of visceral emotion and rhetoric. At their core, human rights simply appear irrational, not frivolous or absurd, but incapable of being fully determined by reasoned analysis. As posited by one commentator, it is possibly the groundlessness or indeterminacy of human rights that gives them their normative sway.[32]

Whatever their ultimate basis, some human rights have been made into law and transnational human rights litigation is concerned with

30 Of course, the concept of natural rights does not enjoy universal consensus. See Jeremy Bentham, "Anarchical Fallacies: Being an Examination of the Declaration of Rights Issued During the French Revolution" in John Bowring, ed., *Works of Jeremy Bentham*, vol. 2 (Edinburgh: William Tait, 1843) at 501, where Bentham decries: "Natural rights is simple nonsense: natural and imprescriptible rights, rhetorical nonsense, — nonsense upon stilts."

31 Natural rights, historically, were often equated with "God-given" rights, as stated for example in the US *Declaration of Independence* (1776): "We hold these truths to be self-evident, that all men are created equal, that they are endowed by their Creator with certain unalienable Rights, that among these are Life, Liberty and the Pursuit of Happiness." Certain authors link the "sacred" nature of the human person to various religious traditions that claim humans were created in the image of God. For example, in Judaeo-Christian religion, it is held that "God created Man in his image. In the image of God He created him. Male and female He created them." (Gen. 1:27) It is also written that "Rich and poor have a common bond: the Lord is the maker of them all." (Prov. 22:2) Islam also equates the sanctity of the human person to God's act of creation. For example, Al *Qu'ran* 6:151 commands: "Take not life, which God hath made sacred, except by way of justice and law." See J. Wronka, *Human Rights and Social Policy in the 21st Century*, rev. ed. (Lanham, MD: University Press of America, 1998) at 36–48.

32 Martii Koskenniemi, "The Pull of the Mainstream" (1990) 88 Mich. L. Rev. 1946 at 1962.

the enforcement of that law through the civil jurisdiction of national courts. Though many international legal instruments purporting to define and protect human rights exist, transnational human rights litigation has largely involved the enforcement of customary international norms. This appears to be so largely for two reasons. The first reason has to do with the non-self-executing character of treaties. In dualist systems like the US, UK, and Canada, international treaties remain unenforceable until they are implemented in domestic law. The second reason has to do with the wording of the US statute under which most transnational human rights claims have been brought thus far. The *Alien Tort Claims Act* (*ATCA*) provides federal courts with jurisdiction over "any civil action by an alien for a tort only, committed in violation of the law of nations."[33] In the United States, as in Canada, the law of nations includes customary norms, which, by virtue of the principle of incorporation, can be made actionable through the common law. The principle of incorporation will be discussed at length in Chapter 4.

Though there is ongoing uncertainty as to the content of the customary international law of human rights, there is substantial consensus among states and commentators that the prohibitions against genocide; slavery; extrajudicial killing, torture or other cruel, inhuman, or degrading treatment; prolonged arbitrary detention; systematic racial discrimination; war crimes; and crimes against humanity form part of customary international law.[34] Moreover, many customary international human rights norms are understood to have attained the status of peremptory norms of international law (*jus cogens*).[35]

That transnational human rights claims are usually[36] articulated within contemporary international human rights paradigms and not

33 28 U.S.C. § 1350.

34 American Law Institute, *Restatement of the Law Third: The Foreign Relations Law of the United States* (St. Paul, MN: American Law Institute, 1987) at § 702; Brownlie, above note 25 at 537. See also Theodor Meron, *Human Rights and Humanitarian Norms as Customary Law* (Oxford: Clarendon Press, 1989).

35 Alexander Orakhelashvili, *The Effects of Peremptory Norms in International Law* (Oxford: Oxford University Press, 2006) at 50–66.

36 Claims are sometimes brought jointly under international human rights law and municipal tort law. See, for example, *Mehinović v. Vucković*, 198 F.Supp. 2d 1322 (N.D. Ga. 2002), where the plaintiff sued for torture and arbitrary detention as defined at international law and in tort for battery and false imprisonment under the laws of the state of Georgia.

within classical tort categories is noteworthy. What is the significance and consequence of framing a complaint for torture at international law instead of merely claiming damages for the tort of battery in respect of the same wrongful acts? Could violations of the human right to be free from arbitrary detention not be captured by the common law tort of false imprisonment? Why sue for genocide and extrajudicial killing and not simply for wrongful death? In the United States, the answers to these questions lie in the language of the statute that grants federal courts jurisdiction in such matters. The *Alien Tort Claims Act* directs federal courts to adjudicate "any civil action by an alien for a tort only, committed in violation of the law of nations or treaty of the United States."[37] The characterization of the alleged wrong as a "violation of the law of nations" is a threshold requirement under *ATCA*; foreign plaintiffs could not invoke the statute if they merely alleged garden-variety torts, even if the conduct described is the same. Other reasons have also been advanced for rejecting municipal tort law as the basis for transnational human rights claims. First, it is thought that municipal tort categories would inadequately address the complex factual matrix of most claims brought under *ATCA*. Second, by not tying *ATCA* to overlapping or analogous tort categories, federal courts can develop a uniform response to international law violations, which, as it will be seen in the following chapter, was an important reason federal courts were granted jurisdiction over such actions in the first place. Finally, it is suggested that classic common law torts do not express the gravity and opprobrium that international human rights violations carry, or their focus on the gravest breaches of human dignity.[38]

Most of these reasons, save perhaps the last, flow from the particularities of the US legal system, that is, either from the specific terms of *ATCA* or from the constitutional mandate of the federal judiciary. A question thus arises: do the same factors apply to countries such as Canada or the UK that possess no legislation equivalent to *ATCA*? Should civil claims for extraterritorial torture be framed as human

---

37 28 U.S.C. §1350.

38 *Xuncax v. Gramajo*, 886 F. Supp. 162 at 182–83 (D. Mass. 1995). See also François Larocque, "The Tort of Torture" (2009) 17 Tort Law Review 158; Sandra Raponi "Grounding a Cause of Action for Torture in Transnational Law" in Scott, ed., *Torture as Tort*, above note 11 at 373; and E. Hyland, "International Human Rights Law and the Tort of Torture: What Possibility for Canada" in Scott, ed., *Torture as Tort*, above note 11 at 401.

right violations or municipal torts in those countries? Why would a litigant suing in Canada or the UK ground his or her claim in the international norm prohibiting torture rather than Canadian or English tort law? The Canadian cases on record offer little guidance in this respect. In one case, a torture victim sought damages for assault and loss of income.[39] In two other cases, the courts appear to have accepted that a civil action could be brought for torture as defined at international law without attempting to link the international definition of that wrong to any domestic tort concept.[40] The British cases are no more illuminating. While they all relate at their core to allegations of torture as defined at international law, one claim was made for battery and negligence,[41] while another was brought for "assault and battery, trespass to the person, torture and unlawful imprisonment."[42] None of the Canadian and British cases disclose an attempt on the part of counsel or judges to distinguish between torts and human rights violations. Did the courts simply assume that a new nominate tort of "extraterritorial torture" grounded in the international law could be fashioned or did they simply believe it to be within their mandate to enforce international norms protecting the human person qua human rights? The many references to various international sources and principles in the submissions of counsel and in the courts' reasons for judgment support this second hypothesis, though one cannot draw any definitive conclusion in the absence of more explicit reasoning on this point.

The consequences of such characterizations on the adjudicative jurisdiction of the court and the justiciability of the claims will be discussed elsewhere in this book.[43] For the purposes of this introductory chapter, it is sufficient to observe that transnational human rights cases in the US have largely been framed in reference to international norms protecting the human person, while the Canadian and British experience is variable.

39 *Saleh v. United Arab Emirates* (2003), 15 C.C.L.T. (3d) 231 (Ont. S.C.J.).

40 *Bouzari*, above note 8; *Arar v. Syrian Arab Republic*, (2005), 28 C.R. (6th) 187 (Ont. S.C.J.) [*Arar*].

41 *Jones* 2003, above note 10.

42 *Mitchell*, above note 10.

43 See Chapter 2, Section D(5)(c) and Chapter 5, Section B.

C. LITIGATION

The final terminological component to be discussed is "litigation," that is, the adversarial legal process by which claims, rights, and responsibilities are determined in a court of law. As has been noted above, transnational human rights litigation refers to civil, as opposed to criminal, proceedings. It is usual for anti-social conduct to give rise simultaneously to both criminal and civil liability. Reckless driving, environmental damage, assault, fraud, and unlawful detention are examples of injurious behaviours capable of attracting both criminal and civil responsibility. The reason for this *dédoublement* of legal means is rooted in the proposition that the effects of certain harmful conduct are felt both publicly and privately. Publicly, the community has a clear and pressing interest in deterring reckless driving or fraud because such crimes are harmful to the community as a whole. Privately, the victim of an automobile accident has an interest in the loss of income and life enjoyment that may result from his or her injuries. Accordingly, the law employs distinct juridical methods and standards to determine the liability of the offender and to restore the injured parties, although the relation between concurrent criminal and civil liability is an issue dealt with in different ways in different national systems.

Transnational human rights litigation involves domestic civil proceedings in respect of breaches of norms protecting the human person derived for the most part from customary and conventional human rights norms (including the *International Covenant on Civil and Political Rights*), international criminal law (including those norms included in the *Statute of the International Criminal Court*), and humanitarian law (including the *Geneva Conventions*). Its proponents argue that international crimes such as torture, genocide, war crimes, and crimes against humanity entail, or at least *should* entail, an effective right to sue wrongdoers and obtain a civil remedy by virtue of their incorporation into the law of the land, a right which international law generally does not afford at the international level. This remains unsettled, at least outside the United States. In that country, courts have taken the position that international crimes may give rise to commensurate civil causes of action at common law provided the international norms in question are sufficiently well established and defined. As noted earlier, the jurisdiction of US courts to adjudicate such internationally derived tort claims is provided by statute.[44] Canada and the United Kingdom for their part have no similar jurisdictional legislation and the courts of those countries have only obliquely opined that international wrongs may give rise to domestic civil liability. In 2009, the Quebec Superior Court noted for instance that, "[a] war crime is an indictable offence. As such, it is an imperative rule of conduct that implicitly circumscribes an elementary norm of prudence, the violation of which constitutes a civil fault pursuant to art. 1457 [of the *Civil Code of Quebec*]."[45]

The House of Lords held in 2006 that customary international crimes are not directly triable in national courts on the basis that Parliament alone possesses the authority to define criminal offences and that new judicially recognized crimes are no longer admissible.[46] The Australian Federal Court reached a similar conclusion in 1999.[47] This has not always been so and contrary opinions exist.[48] It is by no means clear that the reasons barring the direct enforcement of international crimes at domestic law—in particular the proposition that new crimes may only be created by Parliament—exclude the recognition of internationally-derived torts. By contrast the historical practice of the Admiralty shows that English courts have some experience in recognizing and enforcing international norms in the exercise of civil jurisdiction. Civil rights and liabilities in proceedings for salvage and collisions were determined by a species of international law (in Blackstone's sense), yet English courts freely administered and enforced that law as part of their civil jurisdiction.[49] The case can be put more force-

44 28 U.S.C. §1350. See, generally, Chapters 2 & 3.

45 *Bil'in (Village Council) v. Green Park International Inc.*, 2009 QCCS 4151 at para. 175. The civil actionability of international wrongs was also apparently assumed in *Mack v. Canada (Attorney General)*, (2002), 60 O.R. (3d) 737 (C.A.), where plaintiffs alleged that Canada's laws that unfairly taxed the entrance of Chinese immigrants until 1947 violated the customary international prohibition against racial discrimination. While the court ultimately found that no such customary norm existed in the 1940s, it appears to have assumed that violations of customary law were actionable in Canadian courts.

46 *R. v. Jones and Milling*, 2006 UKHL 16 at para. 23.

47 *Nulyarimma v. Thompson* (1999), 165 A.L.R. 621 (F.C.A.) [*Nulyarimma*].

48 *R. v. Bow Street Metropolitan Stipendiary Magistrate, ex parte Pinochet (No. 3)*, [1999] 2 W.L.R. 827 at 912 (H.L.), Lord Millett; *Nulyarimm*, *ibid.* at paras. 136–86, Merkel J; Roger O'Keefe, "Customary International Crimes in English Courts" (2001) 72 Brit.Y.B. Int'l L. 293 at 335.

49 Edward Stanley Roscoe, *The Admiralty Jurisdiction and Practice of the High Court of Justice*, 5th ed. by Geoffrey Hutchinson (London: Sweet & Maxwell, 1931) at 66–120 and 126–86.

fully still in respect of the law of prize, which, though entirely based on international law, gave rise to enforceable rights in English courts.[50] Lord Stowell repeatedly remarked that the prize court was "properly and directly a court of the law of nations."[51] But notwithstanding the historical practice of the courts of Admiralty, it remains the case that the jurisdiction of national courts to derive civil causes of action from modern international human rights violations has not been firmly established in countries such as Canada and the United Kingdom.

Even if international crimes and human rights breaches may properly ground domestic claims for civil remedies, another question arises: to which civil remedy are victims entitled and by which means can they seek it? As noted above, transnational human rights litigation are civil lawsuits aimed at obtaining civil redress (usually financial compensation) for victims, but trials are not the only available process,[52] nor is compensation the only possible type of reparation. International and domestic law recognize other forms of remedies that may be applicable to human rights victims, such as restitution, rehabilitation, satisfaction, and guarantees of non-repetition.[53] These may be obtained, together with compensation, through non-adversarial public processes such as diplomatic channels or commissions of inquiry. In 2007, Canadian citizen Maher Arar obtained a formal apology from the Canadian government and an $11 million (CDN) compensatory settlement following the recommendations of a judicial inquiry into the events that lead

50 Edward Stanley Roscoe, *A History of the English Prize Court* (London: Lloyd's, 1924) at 1. The author notes that "the legal character of the English Prize Court, when it had grown to maturity, was partly due to the fact that the tribunal was not only a court for the decisions of questions as to prize in time of war, but also a court of law for the settlement of maritime disputes between individuals, whether British or foreign."

51 *The Washington Packet* (1799), 2 C. Rob. 77 at 189. See also *The Santa Cruz* (1798), 1 E.P.C. 39.

52 One author explores the possibility of using arbitration to settle transnational human rights claims: Antonin I. Pribetic, *Litigation or Arbitration? Forum Selection and Arbitration Clauses and the Prospects for Adjudicating International Human Rights Claims in Canada* (6 November 2009), online: http://ssrn.com/abstract=1501191.

53 *Basic Principles and Guidelines on the Right to a Remedy and Reparation for Victims of Gross Violations of International Human Rights Law and Serious Violations of International Humanitarian Law*, GA/RES/60/147, Annex , para. 18, U.N. Doc. A/Res/60/147 (2005). See also Commission on Human Rights, *The Right to Restitution, Compensation and Rehabilitation for Victims of Gross Violations of Human Rights and Fundamental Freedoms*, Special Rapporteur C. Bassiouni, E/CN.4/2000/62, 18 January 2000 at 10.

to his 2002 deportation to Syria where he was detained and tortured.[54] This result is to be contrasted with Arar's failed litigation in relation to the same events. His lawsuit against US State officials in the Eastern District Court of New York[55] and his claim against Syria in the Ontario Superior Court of Justice were both dismissed.[56]

Ultimately, the question whether violations of international norms protecting the human person give rise to domestic civil liability leads to another question: who has jurisdiction to decide? Or, as Jessup put it, "the fundamental question is to determine which national authorities may deal effectively with which transnational situations — effectively in the sense that authorities of other states will recognize that that exercise of authority is reasonable and will therefore give effect to judgments or refrain from protests through diplomatic channels."[57] The transnational human rights litigation enterprise posits that national courts may, in certain circumstances, exercise their civil jurisdiction over claims for violations of international norms protecting the human person. This study will examine that proposition in the context of the common law courts of the United States, Canada, and the United Kingdom.

---

54 Hon. Justice D. O'Connor, *New Review Mechanisms for the RCMP's National Security Activities*, Report of the Commission of Inquiry in the Actions of Canadian Officials in Relation to Maher Arar (Ottawa, 2006), online: www.sirc-csars.gc.ca/pdfs/cm_arar_rcmpgrc-eng.pdf.

55 *Arar v. Ashcroft*, 414 F. Supp. 2d 250 (E.D.N.Y. 2006), aff'd 532 F.3d 157 (2d Cir. 2008).

56 *Arar*, above note 40.

57 Jessup, above note 13 at 70.

CHAPTER TWO

The *Alien Tort Claims Act*

"As a moth is drawn to a light, so is a litigant drawn to the United States."

—Lord Denning MR[1]

A. INTRODUCTION

On 29 March 1976 Americo Norberto Peña-Irala, the Inspector General of Police in Asuncíon, Paraguay, kidnapped seventeen-year-old Joelito Filártiga and tortured him to death. That afternoon, police officers brought Joelito's sister, Dolly, to Peña's home where she was confronted with her brother's mutilated body. As she fled in horror, Peña shouted out to her: "Here you have what you have been looking for for so long and what you deserve. Now shut up!" The Filártigas believe that Joelito was tortured in retaliation for his family's political opposition to the government of Paraguay. Criminal proceedings were commenced in Paraguay against a member of the Peña household who confessed to the crimes, but the man was never convicted or sentenced. Two years later, in 1978, Peña settled in Brooklyn, New York. Upon learning of his presence in the country, Dolly Filártiga, who was living in Washington, DC, at the time, commenced civil proceedings against her brother's torturer in the Eastern District Court of New York. The action, it was pleaded, arose under a little-known and rarely invoked statute, 28 U.S.C. § 1350, "the U.N. Charter; the Universal

1 *Smith Kline & French Laboratories v. Bloch*, [1982] 1 W.L.R. 730 at 733.

Declaration on Human Rights; the U.N. Declaration Against Torture; the American Declaration of the Rights and Duties of Man; and other pertinent declarations, documents and practices constituting the customary international law of human rights and the law of nations."[2] Section 28 U.S.C. § 1350, the *Alien Tort Claims Act* (*ATCA*), provides district courts with "original jurisdiction of any civil action by an alien for a tort only, committed in violation of the law of nations or a treaty of the United States."[3] The trial judge held that no jurisdiction existed where a Paraguayan state official is alleged to have committed a violation of international law in respect of another Paraguayan national. In dismissing the claim, the trial judge stated he was bound by 2nd Circuit precedent directing the narrow construction of the "law of nations" under *ATCA*. It was held in *Dreyfus v. Von Finck* that violations of the law of nations "do not occur when the aggrieved parties are nationals of the acting state."[4] The Filártiga family appealed. In a watershed decision, the Court of Appeals for the Second Circuit reversed the trial judge's ruling, holding "that deliberate torture perpetrated under colour of official authority violates universally accepted norms of international law of human rights, regardless of the nationality of the parties. Thus, whenever an alleged torturer is found and served with process by an alien within our borders, § 1350 provides federal jurisdiction."[5]

The court made several important determinations that have become axioms of transnational human rights litigation. First, it reiterated a long-held principle of the Anglo-American legal tradition, that the "law of nations" forms part of the law of the land and that judges could ascertain the content of that law "by consulting the works of the jurists, writing professedly on public law; or by the general usage and practice of nations; or by judicial decisions recognizing and enforcing that law."[6] Second, the court endorsed an organic and evolving model of international law. In applying *ATCA*, "courts must interpret

2 *Filártiga v. Peña-Irala*, 79 Civ. 917 (E.D.N.Y.), Complaint, para. 4. The complaint and other pleadings are available on the Project DIANA website, online: http://avalon.law.yale.edu/diana/13june.asp.

3 28 U.S.C. § 1350.

4 *Dreyfus v. Von Finck*, 534 F.2d 24 at 31 (2d Cir. 1976).

5 *Filártiga v. Peña-Irala*, 630 F.2d 876 at 878 (2d Cir. 1980) [*Filártiga*].

6 *Ibid.* at 880, quoting *United States v. Smith*, 18 U.S. 153 at 160–61(1820) [*Smith*] and *The Paquete Habana*, 175 U.S. 677 at 700 (1900).

international law not as it was in 1789, but as it has evolved and exists among the nations of the world today."[7] Third, after taking notice of state practice, judicial opinions and the writings of jurists, the court concluded that "official torture is now prohibited by the law of nations. That prohibition is clear and unambiguous and admits no distinction between the treatment of aliens and citizens."[8] The court went on to overrule its holding in *Dreyfus* that a state's treatment of its own citizens could not form the object of international legal scrutiny, characterizing that decision as being "out of tune" with current reality. Fourth, the court held that *ATCA* does not create new rights for plaintiffs, but rather mandates US federal courts to adjudicate disputes surrounding existing and emerging rights and liabilities at international law.[9] The basic premise of *ATCA*, indeed of transnational human rights litigation, is the meaningful involvement of national courts in the enforcement of international norms protecting the human person.[10]

The *Filártiga* decision has been called transnational law's *Brown v. Board of Education*.[11] Regardless of whether one agrees with this comparison, *Filártiga* represents a novel interpretation of a unique statute, and an important pronouncement on the domestic reception and application of international norms protecting the human person. *Filártiga* marks the beginning of transnational human rights litigation, a phenomenon that — for better or for worse — has yet to be fully duplicated outside the United States. In that country, however, the phenomenon has become a distinct area of legal practice. Hundreds of claims have been filed under *ATCA* since 1980. In 1991, Congress enacted the *Torture Victim Protection Act* (*TVPA*), which extended *ATCA* jurisdiction to US nationals in specific circumstances, a move that can only be described as supportive of the general policy of opening US courts to survivors of human rights violations. Congressional commitment to transnational human rights litigation is perhaps most strikingly evinced by amendments to the *Foreign Sovereign Immunities Act* (*FSIA*) allowing US citizens to sue certain designated sovereign states with regards to certain designated human rights violations. For its part, executive

7 *Ibid.* at 881.
8 *Ibid.* at 884.
9 *Ibid.* at 887.
10 *Ibid.* at 890.
11 Harold H. Koh "Transnational Public Law Litigation" (1991) 100 Yale L.J. 2347 at 2366.

support for transnational human rights litigation appears to shift with the political winds. The Carter administration filed an *amicus* brief in *Filártiga* supporting an expansive reading of *ATCA*, calling for a more active role of the federal judiciary in redressing international human rights violations.[12] By contrast, the first Bush administration remained apprehensive of the effects that such litigation could have on foreign policy and urged the courts to adopt a far more restrictive view of *ATCA*.[13] Nevertheless, President Bush did not exercise his veto when Congress enacted the *TVPA* into law in 1992. Ten years later, the executive launched another attack on *ATCA* in the *Unocal* litigation, inviting the court to overrule nearly twenty years of jurisprudence and restrict *ATCA* to eighteenth century violations of international law.[14] But though courts remain mindful of the policy concerns raised by the executive, they have generally declined to attenuate the holding in *Filártiga* and continue to assert jurisdiction over civil proceedings for extraterritorial human rights violations through a myriad of means.

This is the first of two chapters examining the existing legislative framework, of which *ATCA* and *TVPA* form the centrepiece, through which US courts have taken jurisdiction over certain transnational human rights claims. Because of their particular importance and specificity, *ATCA* and *TVPA* will receive more detailed treatment. Other jurisdictional grounds are discussed in the following chapter: these are the *Foreign Sovereign Immunities Act* (*FSIA*), federal question jurisdiction, diversity jurisdiction, and state law. The purpose of these chapters is to outline the rationale underlying US adjudicative jurisdiction in civil proceedings for extraterritorial human rights violations. As the United States is so far the only nation to have legislatively opened its courts to victims of human rights violations seeking to enforce public and humanitarian international law through civil litigation, it is important to understand how and why such jurisdiction is assumed in order to determine whether such a model can or should be reproduced elsewhere.

The present chapter is devoted to *ATCA*, a terse statute that has produced a considerable body of jurisprudence, legal literature, and legislation. As will be seen in the next chapter, the *TVPA* and certain

12 The Carter administration *amicus* brief is available at 19 I.L.M. 585 (1984).

13 *Trajano v. Marcos*, 978 F.2d 493 (9th Cir. 1992) [*Trajano*].

14 *Doe v. Unocal Corporation*, 395 F.3d 932 (9th Cir. 2002).

recent amendments to the *FSIA* can be regarded as companion legislation to *ATCA*. Despite the addition of these more specialized statutes however, *ATCA* remains the most frequently sustained jurisdictional footing in transnational human rights claims. This chapter contains three sections. The first section situates *ATCA* within the US constitutional framework. The second section investigates the historical reasons for its enactment. The third section traces its substantive contours and analyzes how federal courts have interpreted it.

B. CONSTITUTIONAL FOUNDATIONS

The jurisdiction of federal courts in proceedings for violations of international law is rooted in Article III of the Constitution of the United States. Article III provides for the creation of a federal judiciary (§ 1) and defines its subject-matter jurisdiction, in part, as follows:

> §2 The judicial power shall extend to all cases, in law and equity, *arising under this Constitution, the laws of the United States, and treaties* made, or which shall be made, under their authority; — to all cases affecting ambassadors, other public ministers and consuls; — to all cases of admiralty and maritime jurisdiction; — to controversies to which the United States shall be a party; — to controversies between two or more states; — between a state and citizens of another state; — between citizens of different states; — between citizens of the same state claiming lands under grants of different states, and between a state, or the citizens thereof, and foreign states, citizens or subjects [emphasis added].[15]

Under the first clause of Article III § 2, federal courts are generally empowered, subject to the limits imposed by Congress and other requirements of justiciability, to adjudicate all matters "arising under" the Constitution, the laws, and treaties of the United States. In the words of the Supreme Court, the first clause extends the national judiciary's authority to all claims in which federal law "forms an ingredient."[16] Jurisdiction over claims based in customary international law, though not expressly provided for, is implied by the words "laws of the United States," which encompass both statutes and common law. US courts

15 U.S. Const. art. III, § 2.

16 *Osborn v. Bank of the United States*, 22 U.S. (9 Wheat.) 738 at 823 (1824).

have held that customary law is part of the common law and cases arising under the former are cognizable through the latter. While it is a shared feature among common law jurisdictions, such as the UK and Canada, the incorporation of the law of nations into the common law takes on a particular significance in the United States. Indeed, pursuant to Article IV § 2 of the Constitution (the so-called "supremacy clause"), the "laws of the United States," which include international treaties and custom, are declared to be the "supreme law of the land" and trump inconsistent state law.[17] Thus, all federal norms being equally supreme subject to the Constitution, conflicts between international and domestic law are resolved following the last-in-time rule, whereby a new statute, for instance, supplants a prior inconsistent treaty.[18] The proposition, however, that new customary norms of international law may supersede prior legislation remains unsettled and controversial.[19]

Federal courts do not assert jurisdiction on the bare terms of the Constitution but rather following the express statutory authorizations of Congress listed under Title 28 of the *US Code*. The Constitution is the jurisdictional benchmark of the national judiciary in that every congressional grant of authority must derive from and comply with one of the heads of judicial power contained in Article III § 2. The *ATCA*, for instance, is generally understood to be an exercise of "arising under" jurisdiction as described above.[20] As Judge Kaufman noted in *Filártiga*, "the constitutional basis for the Alien Tort Statute is the law of nations, which has always been part of the federal common law."[21] For its part, the *TVPA* grant of authority flows jointly from the "arising under" and alienage clauses of Article III § 2 insofar as that cause of action extends to both foreign nationals and US citizens.[22]

17 *United States v. Belmont*, 301 U.S. 324 (1937); American Law Institute, *Restatement of the Law (3d) of Foreign Relations Law of the United States* (St. Paul, MN: American Law Institute, 1988) at § 111(1) [Restatement].

18 *Whitney v. Robertson*, 124 U.S. 190 at 194 (1888).

19 Curtis A. Bradley & Jack L. Goldsmith, "Customary International Law as Federal Common Law: A Critique of the Modern Position" (1997) 110 Harv. L. Rev. 816; Restatement, above note 17 at § 115, comment d.

20 Anne-Marie Burley, "The Alien Tort Statute and the Judiciary Act of 1789: A Badge of Honor" (1989) 83 A.J.I.L. 461 [Burley]; *Filártiga*, above note 5 at 886; *Alvarez-Machain v. United States*, 331 F.3d 604 at 612 (9th Cir. 2003) [*Alvarez-Machain* 2003].

21 *Filártiga*, above note 5 at 885.

22 The first clause of art. III, § 2 of the US Constitution, the so-called diversity clause, authorizes federal jurisdiction over suits between a citizen of a state and a "citizen or subject of a foreign state."

C. HISTORICAL RATIONALE FOR *ATCA*

Before *Filártiga*, *ATCA* was rarely invoked, much less sustained as a jurisdictional footing for civil proceedings.[23] Between 1789 and 1980, courts asserted jurisdiction under the *ATCA* only three times.[24] While curial reluctance towards *ATCA* can be attributed in part to the factual specificity of the particular cases in which the statute was invoked (extraterritorial torture had never been alleged under the *ATCA* before *Filártiga*), it can also be linked to judicial unfamiliarity with the statute. Little was known about its origins and intended scope. In a now famous dictum, Judge Friendly once compared "this old but little used section [to] a kind of legal Lohengrin . . . no one seems to know whence it came."[25] Responding to judicial complaints regarding the historical obscurity of *ATCA*,[26] scholars have searched through the legislative history of the first *Judiciary Act*, constitutional debates, the Founders' papers, early caselaw, and congressional proceedings hoping to discover what *ATCA* was meant to achieve.[27] No direct evidence of the statute's intended scope has been found. Instead, what has emerged is a clearer understanding of the legal, political, and philosophical context

---

23 *ATCA* was invoked twenty-one times between 1789 and the *Filártiga* case, above note 5, in 1980. See K. Randall, "Federal Jurisdiction over International Law Claims: Inquiries into the Alien Tort Statute" (1985) 18 N.Y.U. J. Int'l L. & Pol. 1 at 4 [Randall].

24 *Moxon v. The Fanny*, 17 F. Cas. 942 (D. Pa. 1793); *Bolchos v. Darrell*, 3 F. Cas. 810 (D. S.C. 1795) (both admiralty cases); *Adra v. Clift*, 195 F. Supp. 857 (D.C. MD. 1961) (child custody dispute involving fraudulent passports) [*Adra*].

25 *IIT v. Vencap, Ltd.*, 519 F.2nd 1001 at 1015 (2d Cir. 1975) [*IIT*].

26 In *Tel-Oren v. Libyan Arab Republic*, 726 F.2d 774 at 812 (D.C. Cir. 1984), [*Tel-Oren*], Judge Bork noted that "historical research has not yet disclosed what section 1350 was intended to accomplish." He further states at 823: "The meaning and application of section 1350 will have to await clarification elsewhere. Since [it] appears to be generating an increasing amount of litigation, it is to be hoped that clarification will not be long delayed."

27 See most notably Jeffrey Blum & Ralph Steinhardt, "Federal Jurisdiction over International Human Rights Claims: The Alien Tort Claims Act after *Filártiga v. Peña-Irala*" (1981) 22 Harv. Int'l L.J. 53 [Blum & Steinhardt]; Randall, above note 23; William R. Casto, "The Federal Courts' Protective Jurisdiction over Torts Committed in Violation of the Law of Nations" (1986) 18 Conn. L. Rev. 467 [Casto]; Anthony D'Amato, "The Alien Tort Statute and the Founding of the Constitution" (1988) 82 A.J.I.L. 62 [D'Amato]; Burley, above note 20; Joseph M. Sweeney, "A Tort Only in Violation of the Law of Nations" (1995) 18 Hast. Int'l & Comp. L. Rev. 445; William S. Dodge, "The Historical Origins of the Alien Tort Statute: A Response to 'Originalists'" (1996) 19 Hast. Int'l & Comp. L. Rev. 221 [Dodge].

in which *ATCA* was enacted. On the basis of this scholarship, it will be argued that *ATCA* reflected a general concern for the security of the nascent United States of America and expressed the convictions of the Framers with regards to the duties of statehood and membership in the community of nations. This *esprit d'internationalité*[28] was very much in the minds of the Framers at the time *ATCA* was drafted.

1) The Letter of the Law

The provision referred to as *ATCA* was initially a clause of § 9 of the first *Judiciary Act*, which established the federal district courts (§ 3), the circuit courts (§ 4), and the Supreme Court (§ 1).[29] The jurisdiction of each court is delineated in §§ 9, 11, and 13, respectively, and can be schematized as follows:

District courts (§ 9)

- Exclusive jurisdiction over "all crimes and offences that shall be cognizable under the authority of the United States, committed within their respective districts, or upon the high seas";
- Exclusive jurisdiction over "all civil causes of admiralty and maritime jurisdiction";
- Exclusive jurisdiction over "all seizures on land, or other waters than as aforesaid, made, and of all suits for penalties and forfeitures incurred, under the laws of the United States";
- Concurrent jurisdiction with state and circuit courts over proceedings "where an alien sues for a tort only in violation of the law of nations or a treaty of the United States"; and
- Exclusive jurisdiction over "all suits against consuls or vice-consuls."

28 That is, the "spirit that taught nations and races to follow certain common principles not only in their mutual relations but also in their domestic legislation." Martii Koskenniemi, *The Gentle Civilizer of Nations* (Cambridge: Cambridge University Press, 2001) at 13. Though Koskenniemi was referring to "*l'esprit d'internationalité*" that animated international lawyers of the second half of the nineteenth century, that sentiment, it will be argued, was also very much alive in the eighteenth century.

29 *An Act to Establish the Judicial Courts of the United States*, 1789, c. 20, 1 Stat. 73. The Supreme Court had in fact been created by art. III § 1 of the Constitution, which also empowered Congress to create other federal courts as needed. See Charles Warren, "New Light on the History of the Federal Judiciary Act of 1789" (1923) 37 Harv. L. Rev. 49.

Circuit courts (§ 11)

- Concurrent jurisdiction over all civil claims where the amount-in-controversy exceeds $500, involving an alien or citizens of the United States;
- Exclusive jurisdiction over "all crimes and offences cognizable under the authority of the United States, except where this act otherwise provides, or the laws of the United States shall otherwise direct"; and
- Concurrent jurisdiction over the crimes and offences cognizable by the district courts.

Supreme Court (§ 13)

- Exclusive jurisdiction over all civil cases where a state is a party, except between a state and its citizens and between a state and citizens of other states;
- Concurrent jurisdiction in civil causes between states and aliens;
- Exclusive jurisdiction over proceedings against "ambassadors, or other public ministers, or their domestics, or domestic servants, as a court of law can have or exercise consistently with the law of nations";
- Original, "but not exclusive jurisdiction of all suits brought by ambassadors, or other public ministers, or in which a consul, or vice consul, shall be a party"; and
- Appellate jurisdiction from the circuit and state courts.

ATCA is the fourth clause of § 9 and provides that the district courts "shall have cognizance, concurrent with the courts of the several states, or the circuit courts, as the case may be, of all causes where an alien sues for a tort only in violation of the law of nations or a treaty of the United States." The language of the provision changed in the 1878 revision to read as follows: "The district courts shall have jurisdiction . . . of all suits brought by any alien for a tort only in violation of the law of nations, or of a treaty of the United States."[30] The 1911 revision added the word "original" and displaced a comma, resulting in the following formulation: "The district courts shall have original jurisdiction . . . of all suits brought by any alien for a tort only, in violation of the law of nations or of a treaty of the United States."[31] The deletion in both revisions of the words "concurrent with the courts of the several States" signals the adoption of a simplified legislative drafting approach, not a grant of exclusive federal jurisdiction. After

30 1878, Rev. Stat. § 563.

31 Act of March 3, 1911, c. 231, § 24, 36 Stat. 1087.

the 1878 revision, all instances of exclusive federal jurisdiction were consolidated under one section.[32]

Finally, following the 1948 revision, *ATCA* was further changed by replacing the words "law suit" with "civil action" and by adding the word "committed."[33] Accordingly, *ATCA*, now § 1350 under Title 28 of the *United States Code*, reads as follows:

> The district courts shall have original jurisdiction of any civil action by an alien for a tort only, committed in violation of the law of nations or a treaty of the United States.

The practice of consolidating instances of exclusive federal jurisdiction under one section has been abandoned, with Congress now specifying exclusivity of jurisdiction on a section-by-section basis. Today, with regards to § 1350 actions, the jurisdiction of the district courts remains, as originally enacted, concurrent with that of the state courts, which are courts of general jurisdiction.

2) The Spirit of the Law

The jurisdictional grant contained in *ATCA* is just one instance of the federal courts' jurisdiction over foreigners and matters of international concern. Prior to the enactment of the *Judiciary Act*, indeed prior to the adoption of the US Constitution, the Federalists pushed for the creation of a national judiciary empowered to adjudicate proceedings involving foreigners and foreign states.[34] The Federalists believed the international jurisdiction of federal courts to be an essential tenet of the central government's constitutional power over foreign affairs, a power that required uniformity of policy and execution. As Madison wrote: "If we are to be one nation in any respect, it clearly ought to be in respect to other nations."[35] And so, pursuant to the constitutional

32 See § 711 and § 256 of the 1878 and 1911 revisions respectively.

33 28 U.S.C. § 1350.

34 Alexander Hamilton, James Madison, & John Jay, *The Federalist Papers* (New York: J. and M. Lean, 1788; reprint, New York: Oxford University Press, 2008) No. 80 (Madison) at 388–93 [*The Federalist Papers*]. James Madison describes the powers of the would-be federal judiciary as extending to cases involving: (1) federal statutes, (2) the Constitution, (3) the federal government, (4) the constituent states and foreign nations, (5) the high seas, and (6) cases where recourse to state courts is deemed improper.

35 *Ibid.*, No. 42 (Madison) at 208.

division of powers, Congress was empowered to "define and punish piracies and felonies committed in the high seas, and offences against the law of nations" (Article I § 8) while the President was empowered to make treaties and appoint ambassadors, ministers, and consuls (Article II § 2).[36] Finally, Article III § 2 defined the federal judicial power as extending "to all cases, in law and equity, arising under this Constitution, the laws of the United States, and treaties made, or which shall be made, under their authority; — to all cases affecting ambassadors, other public ministers and consuls; — to all cases of admiralty and maritime jurisdiction; . . . — to controversies . . . between a state, or the citizens thereof, and foreign states, citizens or subjects."[37] In accordance with the constitutional mandate of Article III, Congress enacted the *Judiciary Act*, which established the international jurisdiction of the federal courts. More precisely, as outlined above, the district courts were given jurisdiction over claims brought by aliens and in proceedings against consuls and vice-consuls (§ 9), the circuit courts received jurisdiction over civil claims involving aliens where the amount-in-controversy exceeded $500 (§ 11), whereas the Supreme Court had jurisdiction in claims involving ambassadors (§ 13).[38] *ATCA* is thus more properly approached not as an extraordinary, singular jurisdictional grant, but rather as part of a more general objective of empowering federal courts to adjudicate matters of international interest.

To understand the perceived necessity of establishing a national judiciary competent over foreign persons and affairs is to gain insight into the spirit that animated the *Judiciary Act* in general and *ATCA* in particular. In this regard, three theories are examined. The first two (the denial of justice and the diplomatic protection theories) are variants of the wider proposition that *ATCA* "was an important part of the national security interest in 1789."[39] As John Jay insisted, "it is of high importance to the peace of America that she observe the laws of nations."[40] Violations of international law were understood by eighteenth century lawyers as one of the just causes of war and it was reasoned that conflicts could best be avoided by the creation of a national

36 U.S. Const. art. I, § 8 and art. II, § 2.
37 U.S. Const. art. III, § 2.
38 U.S. Const. art. III, §§ 9, 11, and 13.
39 D'Amato, above note 27 at 65.
40 *The Federalist Papers*, above note 34, No. 3 (Jay) at 19.

judiciary in which "treaties, as well as the laws of nations, [would] always be expounded in one sense and executed in the same manner, whereas adjudications of the same points and questions, in thirteen states, . . . [would] not always accord or be consistent."[41] Thus, *ATCA* can be understood as part of a concerted effort to protect the fledgling Union against the threat of war by ensuring the even interpretation and application of international law.[42] The third theory, without denying the first two, also supposes *ATCA* to be premised on the necessity for the US to abide by international legal standards, but for different reasons. If international law was observed by the United States, it was not only to avoid the wrath of foreign powers, but also because the duties of statehood so commanded. Under this view, the international jurisdiction of federal courts — including the authority granted under *ATCA* — is understood as responding to the highest aspirations and ideals of eighteenth century political culture, namely the cosmopolitan precepts of law, duty, and honour.

a) Denial of Justice Theory

Beyond concerns of embroiling the young Union in conflicts with foreign powers on account of violations of international obligations, the Framers also feared reprisals for the domestic mistreatment of foreign nationals. An important concern was the possibility that aliens might be denied access to state courts, or worse, bear the brunt of an unfair trial. Eighteenth century state courts were often parochial in focus, insensitive to foreign affairs, and "notoriously biased against foreigners."[43] Such a denial of justice, the Framers worried, could amount to a *casus belli*, a danger that *ATCA* would have lessened by creating an alternative forum in the more internationally minded federal courts for claims involving aliens.

---

41 Emer de Vattel, *Le Droit des gens ou Principes de la loi naturelle* (Paris: Librairie de Guillaumin et Cie, 1863) Liv. III, c. 3 at § 37 [Vattel].

42 The US Supreme Court agreed that the *Judiciary Act* reflects "a concern for uniformity in this country's dealings with foreign nations and . . . a desire to give matters of international significance to the jurisdiction of federal institutions." *Banco Nacional de Cuba v. Sabbatino*, 376 U.S. 398 (1964).

43 D'Amato, above note 27 at 65. Tocqueville's assessment is consonant: "En faisant appliquer les lois de l'Union par les tribunaux des états particuliers, on livrait donc la nation, non seulement à des juges étrangers, mais encore à des juges partiaux." See Alexis de Tocqueville, *De la démocratie en Amérique* (1835, 1840; reprint, Eduardo Nolla, ed., Paris: Vrin, 1990) at 110.

Proponents of the denial of justice theory generally refer to Hamilton's classic essay in the *Federalist Papers* entitled *The Powers of the Judiciary* in which Publius describes the categories of cases that should, for the good of the Union, fall to the federal courts.

> The Union will undoubtedly be answerable to foreign powers for the conduct of its members. And the responsibility for an injury ought ever to be accompanied with the faculty of preventing it. As the denial or perversion of justice by the sentences of courts, as well as in any other manner, is with reason classed among the just causes of war, it will follow that the federal judiciary ought to have cognizance of all causes in which the citizens of other countries are concerned. This is not less essential to the preservation of the public faith, than to the security of the public tranquillity.[44]

Hamilton reasoned that "the peace of the whole ought not to be left at the disposal of a part" and since "so great a proportion of the cases in which foreigners are parties involve national questions . . . it is by far most safe and most expedient to refer all those in which they are concerned to the national tribunals."[45]

Despite having found considerable support from commentators,[46] the denial of justice theory and Hamilton's essay ultimately fail to account for the specific wording and scope of *ATCA*. Indeed, as Burley observed, Hamilton was not defending § 9 of the *Judiciary Act* but rather was expounding the merits of Article III of the Constitution, particularly the so-called alienage provision of the diversity clause.[47] But under the *Judiciary Act*, alienage jurisdiction was ultimately attributed to the circuit courts pursuant to § 11, not the district courts to which the *ATCA* applied. Even if one considers both § 9 and § 11 as implements of a Federalist legislative package aimed at keeping internationally sensitive cases in the federal judiciary, important gaps remain which would have left many cases involving aliens to be adjudicated in state courts.

44 *The Federalist Papers*, above note 34, No. 80 (Hamilton) at 389.

45 *Ibid.*

46 Supporting denial of justice theory: *Amici Curiae* in *Trajano*, see David Cole *et al.*, "Interpreting the Alien Tort Statute: Amicus Curiae Memorandum of International Scholars and Practitioners in *Trajano v. Marcos*" (1988) 12 Hast. Int'l & Comp. L. Rev. 1 at 15 (list of agreeing commentators); D'Amato, above note 27 at 64–65; Randall, above note 23 at 21–22; Casto, above note 27 at 521–22.

47 Burley, above note 20 at 465.

First, with regards to § 11, the $500 amount-in-controversy threshold would have presented a very high bar in 1789. As Casto's research indicates, during the period in which the *Judiciary Act* was drafted, there is no record of damages ever being awarded in excess of $340, with most judgments being for less than $100.[48] Second, § 9 also presents important limitations by granting district courts jurisdiction only in proceedings where aliens are *plaintiffs*, yet, clearly, foreigners would have equally risked being denied justice as *defendants*, if not more so. Finally, the subject-matter restrictions of § 9—"tort only in violation of the law of nations or a treaty of the United States"—prevented district courts from adjudicating what would have been the most frequent (and potentially explosive) controversies of the day: commercial disputes.[49] Given its relative exclusivity, it is difficult to see how *ATCA*'s primary purpose would have been to address Federalist concerns of preventing denials of justice when the bulk of cases involving aliens would have fallen to state courts. In short, while the provision would have likely assuaged the Federalists' fears by granting foreigners a measure of access to federal courts, its specific terms seem to suggest that *ATCA* was meant to achieve another purpose.

b) Diplomatic Protection Theory

A second theory posits *ATCA* as a means of ensuring the protection of the rights and privileges of ambassadors. Judge Bork advanced this interpretation of § 9 of the *Judiciary Act* in his concurrence in *Tel-Oren*.[50] He speculated that the words "tort . . . in violation of the law of nations" could refer to Blackstone's enumeration of crimes against the international order, namely, (1) the violation of safe-conducts; (2) infringement of the right of ambassadors; and (3) piracy.[51] If these are the "torts" the drafters of the *Judiciary Act* had in mind in enacting *ATCA*, Judge Bork argued, then suits under the provision should not be allowed for offences that eighteenth century international law did not recognize, such as torture. Ultimately, Judge Bork opined that in the absence of firm evidence with regards to the aims of *ATCA*, the provision should

48 Casto, above note 27 at 497, n. 168.

49 Burley, above note 20 at 467. Eighteenth century lawyers distinguished claims arising in tort and contract. See William Blackstone, *Commentaries on the Laws of England* vol. 3 (Oxford: Clarendon, 1765–69) at 117 [Blackstone].

50 *Tel-Oren*, above note 26 at 813–16.

51 *Ibid.* at 814. See Blackstone, above note 49 vol. 4 at 68.

receive a narrow interpretation. "When courts lack such evidence," he stated, "to construe is to legislate, to act in the dark, and hence to do many things that, it is virtually certain, Congress did not intend."[52]

Despite Judge Bork's misgivings, the diplomatic protection theory is not without historical merit. Indeed, in the years preceding the enactment of *ATCA*, two incidents of assaults on foreign dignitaries would have most likely caused the enforcement of ambassadorial rights to be on the minds of the legislative drafters. The first event, mentioned in passing by Judge Bork,[53] occurred in England in 1708 and involved Count Mattueof, the ambassador to London of Czar Peter the Great, who, after having been detained and "roughed-up" by his English creditors, demanded of Queen Anne that "a severe corporal punishment be inflicted" upon his assailants.[54] At that time, the assault on the ambassador was tantamount to a common law misdemeanour and attracted only non-capital punishment, a sanction that fell short of appeasing the dishonoured ambassador. Czar Peter intervened on behalf of his emissary and requested that the criminals be put to death, and further intimated that, "on failure of satisfaction worthy of, and equivalent to the injured Honour," his Czarish Majesty might be "compelled to obtain it by way of Reprisal."[55] Parliament responded with the enactment of the *Diplomatic Privileges Act, 1708*, which codified the customary privileges of ambassadors and ensured that any further such violations would be appropriately tried and punished.[56] The Mattueof Incident was well known and sparked considerable commentary.[57] Accordingly, Judge Bork hypothesized, "if this was indeed the incident the Convention considered in allocating to Congress the power to 'define and punish offences against the Law of Nations' it may be that the

---

52 *Ibid.* above note 26 at 815.

53 William Winslow Crosskey, *Politics and the Constitution in the History of the United States* (Chicago: Chicago University Press, 1953) at 459 [Crosskey].

54 *Ibid.* at 460.

55 *Ibid.* at 461.

56 *Diplomatic Privileges Act, 1708* (U.K.), 7 Anne c. 12. The statute provided, *inter alia*, further violations of ambassador's rights would be tried by the Kingdom's highest judicial authorities, namely the Lord Chancellor, the Chief Justice of the Queen's Bench, and the Chief Justice of the Common Pleas, who were granted full discretion with regards to the severity of the ensuing corporal punishment.

57 Crosskey, above note 53 at 462. Lord Mansfield comments on the Mattueof Incident in *Triquet v. Bath* (1764), 3 Burr. 1478 at 1480 and *Heathfield v. Chilton* (1767), 4 Burr. 2015 at 2016; Blackstone, above note 49 vol. 4 at 70–71.

First Congress, sensitive to the international ramifications of denying ambassadors redress, enacted [*ATCA*] to give ambassadors the option of bringing tort actions in federal courts as well as in state courts."[58]

The second event is the 1784 *cause célèbre* known as the Marbois Affair. This case concerned a French nobleman, Chevalier De Longchamps, who physically assaulted the consul general of France to the United States, Francis Barbé-Marbois, in Philadelphia. De Longchamps was found guilty by the Supreme Court of Pennsylvania of violating international law, which the court expressly recognized as being part of state law. As Casto noted, "the Marbois Affair was a national sensation" and as evidenced by their correspondence, "attracted the concern of virtually every public figure in America," including Washington, Franklin, Jefferson, Madison, Jay and Adams.[59] Though the controversy had been appropriately dealt with in Pennsylvania, nothing ensured that other state courts would be as internationally minded in the future. Above all, the Marbois Affair highlighted Congress' inability to prevent and respond to such violations of international law, its input being limited in that case to a resolution "highly approving" the state court's decision.[60] At the opening of the Constitutional Convention in Philadelphia in 1787, the Marbois Affair was very likely still fresh in the minds of the delegates. When he introduced his "Virginia Plan" at the outset of the Convention, Edmund Randolph emphasized that the confederation of states "could not cause infractions of treaties or of the Law of Nations to be punished" and that "particular states might by their conduct provoke war."[61] Likewise, later during the Convention, James Madison, in motivating his rejection of the "New Jersey Plan," stated:

> Will it prevent those violations of the Law of Nations & Treaties which, if not prevented, must involve us in the calamities of foreign wars? The tendency of the states to these violations has been manifested in sundry instances . . . . Hitherto indulgence has been shewn to us. This

58 *Tel-Oren*, above note 26 at 815; Crosskey, above note 53 at 463.

59 Casto, above note 27 at 492–94.

60 *Ibid.*

61 United States Constitutional Convention, *The Records of the Federal Convention of 1787*, vol. 1 (1787; reprint, Max Farrand, ed., New Haven: Yale University Press, 1966) at 19 (Randolph, 29 May 1787). Randolph's insistence on vesting jurisdiction of international matters in the Federal government most likely stems from the states' failure to respond to the 1781 resolution, of which he was the principal author. See Section C(3), below in this chapter.

> cannot be the permanent disposition of foreign nations. A rupture with other powers is among the greatest national calamities.[62]

In this light, the diplomatic protection theory clearly emerges as a variation of the denial of justice theory. Indeed, if the ill treatment of "ordinary" foreigners could result in grave international embarrassment, then judicial unfairness to ambassadors would most assuredly present the worse kind of peril. By opening the district courts to the injured representatives of foreign sovereigns, *ATCA* would have helped to avert such crises.

Despite its historical plausibility, the diplomatic protection theory ultimately fails to explain the specificity of *ATCA* as a grant of *civil* jurisdiction for violations of international law. Firstly, according to Blackstone, infringements of the rights of ambassadors were crimes, that is, one of the rare offences against the law of nations that could "be the object of the *criminal law* of any particular state."[63] Both the Mattueof and Marbois Affairs were restricted to issues of criminal liability. In the words of M'Kean CJ, De Longchamps was "guilty of a crime against the world."[64] Surely, if Blackstone, Mattueof, and Marbois impressed anything upon the Framers, it is that assaults upon ambassadors were serious crimes to be "animadvert[ed] upon . . . with becoming severity."[65] Accordingly, the Constitutional Convention ensured that US Congress would have the authority to "define and punish . . . offences against the law of Nations" (Article I § 8). Congress then translated this authority to both district and circuit courts by granting them jurisdiction over "crimes and offences cognizable under the authority of the United States."[66] This being so, the proposition that the civil jurisdiction created under *ATCA* was intended by the Framers to prevent and punish crimes committed against ambassadors fails to convince.

---

62 *Ibid.*, vol. 1 at 316 (Madison, 19 June 1787). Madison's speech was manifestly inspired by Blackstone who, in his *Commentaries*, above note 49 vol. 4 at 68, warned that a sovereign who fails to punish offences against the law of nations "draws upon his community the calamities of foreign wars."

63 Blackstone, above note 49, vol. 4 at 68.

64 *Respublica v. De Longchamps*, 1 U.S. 111 at 116 (Sup. Ct. Pa. 1784) [*De Longchamps*].

65 Blackstone, above note 49, vol. 4 at 68. Blackstone's "animadversion" language was used by Congress in its 1781 resolution (Section C(3), below in this chapter) and by M'Kean CJ in sentencing De Longchamps (*Ibid.* at 117).

66 *Judiciary Act of 1789*, §§ 9 and 11.

The theory seems even less probable when one considers the surrounding provisions of the *Judiciary Act*. Under another clause of § 9, the district courts were given exclusive jurisdictions over "consuls and vice-consuls." More importantly, under § 13, the Supreme Court had exclusive jurisdiction of "proceedings against ambassadors, or other public ministers, or their domestic, domestic servants" and original (but not exclusive) jurisdiction of "all suits brought by ambassadors, or other public ministers, or in which a consul, or vice consul shall be a party."[67] In short, as Burley observed, "all foreign plenipotentiaries worth worrying about were provided for by name, quite liberally at that. They could bring any type of action, under state, federal or international law, with no amount-in-controversy requirement—all in a setting befitting their honoured status."[68] If the purpose of *ATCA* was to give ambassadors a forum to enforce their legal privileges, then it was clearly redundant. Where the drafters of the *Judiciary Act* intended to secure federal jurisdiction over foreign dignitaries, they did so unequivocally by expressly mentioning the words "ambassadors," "public ministers," "consuls and vice-consuls." By contrast, *ATCA* refers only to generic "aliens." Given that violations of ambassadorial rights were crimes, not torts, and that ambassadors were well provided for in other parts of the *Judiciary Act*,[69] it would seem that *ATCA* was meant to achieve something other than the protection of diplomats.

c) Dutiful Compliance and Enforcement Theory

Another way of approaching *ATCA* is as an implementation of what the Framers understood to be the duty of the United States: to comply with and enforce international law. Burley first suggested this high-minded conception of *ATCA*, which has the merit of not reducing the "international" provisions of the *Judiciary Act* to mere expressions of

67 *Ibid.* § 13.

68 Burley, above note 20 at 473. By allowing ambassadors to have direct access to the Supreme Court, Congress was probably emulating the English *Diplomatic Privileges Act, 1708*, which provided that crimes against ambassadors would be tried by the three highest judicial officials in the land. Publius also agreed that as "immediate representatives of their sovereigns" ambassadors are entitled "in the first instance to the highest judicatory of the nation": *The Federalist Papers*, above note 30, No. 81 (Hamilton) at 398.

69 Also, Congress would enact in 1790, in imitation of the English *Diplomatic Privileges Act, 1708*, a statute which voided all writs and processes against ambassadors: Act of 15 April 1790, c. 9; 1 Stat. 112 at 117.

some Hobbesian "consequentialist calculus,"[70] where international law is complied with out of fear and in the interest of national security. While the Framers were most certainly concerned with the avoidance of wars in the early years of the Union, to maintain that it was their only priority is almost certainly overly simplistic. A more balanced view of *ATCA* is one that, without negating the national security benefits afforded by the statute, situates it in the prevailing philosophical and political context of its time. Under this view, if international law was to be complied with and enforced it was not solely to avoid foreign reprisals, but also, as a matter of national honour, to fulfil the duties of statehood.

If only for this reason, a brief sketch of the intellectual and philosophical climate in the United States at the end of the eighteenth century is warranted. It was a time of great social change, of revolution of ideas and political systems, first in the North American British colonies, then in France. Law was the lens through which new societies founded on liberty and equality were envisioned. "Excepting only the ideals of religion, there were probably no ideals of such impact upon the minds of men as the ideals of law. Leaders in law had a knowledge of contemporary legal thought and of the great legal systems which has rarely been equalled since."[71] Many of the Framers were lawyers of "enviable learning" as such that, "whenever in terms or by implication they spoke or wrote with reference to the Law of Nations, they were indulging no mere flights of hopeful rhetoric. They were as realistic as Lord Mansfield, as practical as the examples of Blackstone."[72] As Marshall CJ stated: "we must suppose that the Framers of our constitution were intimately acquainted with the writings of those wise and learned men, whose treatises on the laws of nature and nations have guided public opinion."[73] Though the erudition of the Framers has been well documented,[74] one need not look further than the resolution of

70 Burley, above note 20 at 486.

71 Edwin D. Dickinson, "The Law of Nations as Part of the National Law of the United States" (1952) 101 U. Pa. L. Rev. 26 at 34 [Dickinson].

72 *Ibid.* at 35–36.

73 *Ogden v. Saunders*, 25 U.S. 213 at 353–54 (1827) (citing Vattel and others on international obligation).

74 Jesse S. Reeves, "The Influence of the Law of Nature upon International Law in the United States" (1909) 3 A.J.I.L 547 [Reeves]; Dennis R. Nolan, "Sir William Blackstone and the New American Republic: A Study of Intellectual Impact"

Congress authorizing the purchase of books for its library to appreciate the breadth of the prevailing intellectual culture. Madison sat on the committee charged with drawing "a list of books proper for the use of Congress," a list containing well in excess of 250 titles, including among others, the works of Grotius, Pufendorf, Burlamaqui, Montesquieu, Wolff, Vattel, Blackstone, Hobbes, Hume, and Locke.[75]

Among international legal writers, Emer de Vattel's influence dominated.[76] According to Reeves, "at the time of the American Revolution the work of Vattel was the latest and most popular if not the most authoritative of the Continental writers . . . . Possibly after the Revolution Vattel is quoted more frequently than his predecessors."[77] The historical records contain many high endorsements of Vattel's work by influential statesmen. Franklin, thanking Dumas for gifting him his edition of *Le droit des gens*, wrote: "It came to us in good season, when the circumstances of a rising State make it necessary frequently to consult the law of nations. Accordingly that copy, which I kept . . . has been continually in the hands of the members of our Congress."[78] Hamilton held Vattel to be "perhaps the most accurate and approved of the writers of the Law of Nations."[79] When commenting on United States foreign policy, Jefferson reportedly said: "we will not assume the exclusive right of saying what the law and usage is. Let us appeal to enlightened and disinterested judges. None is more so than Vattel."[80] Given Vattel's great influence on the Framers, it is perhaps not entirely irrelevant to read *ATCA* through the Vattelian looking glass, particularly in outlining the perceived scope of international duties and obligations.

(1976) 51 N.Y.U. L. Rev. 731; Julian S. Waterman, "Thomas Jefferson and Blackstone's Commentaries" (1933) 27 Ill. L. Rev. 629.

75 Worthington C. Ford *et al.*, eds., *JCC, 1774–1789* (Washington, DC: 1904–37), 24:83–92.

76 Daniel George Lang, *Foreign Policy in the Early Republic* (Baton Rouge: Louisiana State University Press, 1985) at 1–33 [Lang].

77 Reeves, above note 74 at 549. An electronic search of the *Journals of the Continental Congress*, *Farrand's Reports*, *Eliott's Debates*, and of the *Letters of the Delegates* confirm that during the period before the enactment of the *Judiciary Act*, Vattel was mentioned and cited more often than any other writer on international law.

78 Franklin to Dumas, 9 December 1775, Smith, Paul H., *et al.*, eds., *Letters of Delegates to Congress, 1774–1789.*, 25 volumes (Washington, DC: Library of Congress, 1976–2000) 2:466.

79 Lang, above note 76 at 11.

80 *Ibid.*

For Vattel, obligations were an essential concomitant of statehood and of membership in the community of nations. He distinguished four kinds of obligations: (1) *necessary* (internal duties owed by the state to itself pursuant to the law of nature); (2) *voluntary* (self-imposed duties owed to others out of conscience); (3) *conventional*; and (4) *customary* (both arbitrary external obligations born respectively from express and tacit consent).[81] An important thread running through the Vattelian obligations theory is the fulfilment of duties as a matter of reason and conscience. If the web of obligations that make up the law of nations is to remain taut, it is by the inner pull of each nation's moral imperative. Even the supreme duty of states to themselves is ultimately subject to this higher code. Vattel wrote: «*les devoirs envers soi-même l'emportant incontestablement sur les devoirs envers autrui, une Nation se doit premièrement & préférablement à elle-même tout ce qu'elle peut faire pour son bon bonheur et sa perfection. (Je dis ce qu'elle* peut, *non pas seulement* physiquement, *mais aussi* moralement, *c'est-à-dire ce qu'elle peut faire légitimement, avec justice & bonnêteté).*»[82] Or, stated more succinctly: «*Le Droit n'est d'autre chose qu*'une faculté morale d'agir, *c'est-à-dire de faire ce qui est moralement possible, ce qui est bien & conforme à nos devoirs.*»[83] Therefore, to abide by the law of nations is, where possible, to simultaneously fulfil both necessary and voluntary obligations, to answer the competing calls of self-preservation and morality, and to reconcile self-interest with the interest of the other or the community.

Indeed, the fulfilment of state obligations by the harmonizing of self-interested prudential concerns and moral imperatives is so complete in the Vattelian system that both motives become nearly undistinguishable. By disregarding their engagements and solemn promises to others, states only attract dire consequences upon themselves, Vattel warned. «*Plus de sûreté, plus de commerce entre les hommes, s'ils ne se croient point obligés de garder la foi, de tenir la parole. Cette obligation est donc aussi nécessaire et indubitable, entre les Nations . . . pour maintenir l'ordre & la paix dans leur Société.*»[84] By respecting their obligations to others, states *ipso facto* fulfilled their duties to themselves. This is not so merely because Vattel inextricably linked individual states and the community they

81 Vattel, above note 41, Préliminaires, §§ 7–28.

82 *Ibid.*, Préliminaires at §§ 14 and 21.

83 *Ibid.*, Préliminaires § 3 and Liv. II, c. 4 at § 49.

84 *Ibid.*, Liv. II, c. 12 at § 163.

form,[85] but rather more pragmatically, because of the political benefits that derive from keeping one's word. Indeed, «*rien n'est si glorieux au Prince et à la Nation, que la réputation d'une fidélité inviolable à sa parole.*»[86] For Vattel, virtue is always its own reward. Good reputation and national honour, though clearly secondary benefits in his opinion, were also not negligible. In one of his most poetic passages, referring with nostalgic admiration to the teachings of Cicero, Vattel dreamed aloud: «*Et pourquoi n'espérerions-nous pas de trouver encore parmi ceux qui gouvernent, quelques Sages, convaincus de cette grande vérité, que la Vertu, même pour les Souverains, pour les Corps Politiques, est le chemin le plus assuré de la prospérité & du bonheur?*»[87] He continued: «*Il est au moins un fruit que l'on peut attendre des saines Maximes hautement publiées, c'est qu'elles contraignent ceux-là même qui les goûtent le moins à garder quelque mesure, pour ne pas se perdre entièrement de réputation.*»[88]

Vattel's view of international law abidingness was not lost on the statesmen and jurists of the early republic who, at every turn, formulated and defended US law and foreign policy in terms of self-interest, legal and moral duty, and national honour. For example:

- During the War of Independence, after US naval forces captured Spanish neutral property in 1779, the Continental Congress, by resolution, recorded its pledge to the European powers that "they will cause the law of nations to be most strictly observed" and after due trial, "cause reparation to be made in such manner as to do ample justice and vindicate the honour and dignity of the Spanish flag." Congress agreed these measures were "necessary for the preservation of the general peace of the United States."[89]
- Likewise, in *Respublica v. De Longchamps* (1784), citing Vattel at nearly every page of his decision, Chief Justice M'Kean explained the court's sentence in the following terms: "You, then, have been guilty of an atrocious violation of the law of nations . . . . And it is now the interest as well as the duty of the government to animadvert upon your conduct with a becoming severity—such a severity as may tend to reform yourself, to deter others from the commission of

85 *Ibid.*, Préliminaires, §§ 10–11.

86 *Ibid.*, Liv. II, c. 12 at § 163.

87 *Ibid.*, Liv. II, c. 1 at § 1.

88 *Ibid.*

89 *JCC, 1774–1789*, above note 75 at 635:36.

the like crime, preserve the honour of the state and maintain peace with our great and good ally, and the whole world."[90]

- In his Inaugural Speech in 1789, President Washington declared that ". . . the foundations of our national policy will be laid in the pure and immutable principles of private morality, and the pre-eminence of free government be exemplified by all the attributes which can win the affections of its citizens, and command the respect of the world."[91]
- When war broke out in Europe following the French Revolution, Washington announced the United States' 1793 neutrality policy in the following terms: "Whereas it appears that a state of war exists between Austria, Prussia, Sardinia, Great Britain, and the United Netherlands, of the one part, and France on the other; and the duty and interest of the United States require, that they should with sincerity and good faith adopt and pursue a conduct friendly and impartial toward the belligerent Powers." Washington goes on to exhort all Americans to respect the law of nations.[92]
- Charging the grand jury in the trial of Gideon Henfield in 1793, Chief Justice Jay advised that "the peace, prosperity and reputation of the United States, will always greatly depend on their fidelity to their engagements; and every virtuous citizen . . . will concur in observing and executing them with honour and good faith; and that whether they be made with nations respectable and important, or with nations weak and inconsiderable, our obligation to keep our faith results from our having pledged it."[93]
- In *Chisholm v. Georgia*, Chief Justice Jay further stated that the United States, "by taking a place among the nations of the earth, become amenable to the laws of nations; and it was their interest as well as their duty to provide, that those laws should be respected and obeyed."[94]
- Using clear Vattelian language, Hamilton defended Article 10 of the 1794 Jay Treaty, which prevented the sequestration and confiscation

90 *De Longchamps*, above note 64 at 117.

91 Inaugural Speech of President Washington, 30 April 1789, American State Papers: Foreign Affairs, 1:9–10 at 10.

92 Proclamation of Neutrality, 3 December 1793, American State Papers: Foreign Affairs, 1:140.

93 *Trial of Gideon Henfield*, 11 F. Cas. 1099 (C.C.D. Pa. 1793); see Burley, above note 20 at 483.

94 *Chisholm v. Georgia*, 2 U.S. 419 at 474 (1793).

of private debts and monies as a means of reprisal: "I derive the vindication of the article from a higher source: from the natural or necessary law of nations, from the eternal principles of morality and good faith."[95]

- In his Farewell Address (1796), Washington urged his compatriots to

> Observe good faith and justice towards all nations; cultivate peace and harmony with all. Religion and morality enjoin this conduct; and can it be, that good policy does not equally enjoin it? It will be worthy of a free, enlightened, and at no distant period, a great nation, to give to mankind the magnanimous and too novel example of a people always guided by an exalted justice and benevolence. Who can doubt that, in the course of time and things, the fruits of such a plan would richly repay any temporary advantages which might be lost by a steady adherence to it? Can it be that Providence has not connected the permanent felicity of a nation with its virtue? The experiment, at least, is recommended by every sentiment which ennobles human nature.[96]

The historical documents and the early case law contain many such executive, legislative, and judicial pronouncements, linking US foreign policy to the highest philosophical and moral ideals of the eighteenth century. They are not just "flights of hopeful rhetoric"[97] but expressions of the ideological heritage of the United States, of the prevailing *esprit d'internationnalité* of the time. The newly independent United States was eager to be recognized as a just and honourable state and thus enacted measures to ensure national compliance with international law. It did so not only to protect its own interests but also out of a profound sense of moral obligation and duty.

3) *ATCA*'s Probable Precursor

So it is that the Framers were deeply concerned with the United States' compliance with the law of nations and its even application throughout the Union. This concern, it is argued, was motivated as much by

95 19 Hamilton Papers 329 at 342. Cited in Burley, above note 20 at 483.

96 Farewell Address of President Washington, 17 September 1796, American State Papers: Foreign Affairs, 1: 34–38 at 36–37.

97 Dickinson, above note 71 at 35–36.

the apprehension of the consequence of non-compliance as by a rich understanding of the duties of statehood as a matter of virtue and national honour. To ensure that international law would be respected and enforced in the United States, the Framers made constitutional provisions for the creation of a federal judiciary to which all internationally sensitive matters would be entrusted. This was the genesis of the *Judiciary Act* and *ATCA*. However, while this general narrative of the events, attitudes, and sensitivities of the time might broadly explain the international jurisdiction of federal courts, it stops short of providing a satisfactory justification for the specificity of *ATCA* as a grant of civil jurisdiction over "torts" committed "in violation of the law of nations." As outlined above, Blackstone and the Framers considered violations of international law by individuals to be crimes, not torts. The jurisdiction of the various federal courts over ambassadors and diplomats, in conjunction with the civil alienage jurisdiction of the circuit courts, would have covered nearly all bases and provided a wide range of judicial options in dealing with delicate international controversies. Why then did Congress feel the need to pass the specific provisions of *ATCA*? The answer to this question likely lies between the lines of a pre-*Judiciary Act* resolution of Congress that some scholars believe to be the direct ancestor of *ATCA*.

A little-known resolution passed by the Continental Congress in November 1781 has been identified as the probable ancestor of *ATCA* insofar as it refers explicitly to the enforcement of the law of nations by way of civil proceedings.[98] The resolution begins by summarizing the findings of a congressional committee "appointed to prepare a recommendation to the states to enact laws for punishing infractions of the laws of nations."[99] Recall that the unsatisfactory manner in which state courts applied international law constituted an important impetus for the creation of the federal judiciary. Indeed, the committee found "that the scheme of criminal justice in the several states does not sufficiently comprehend offences against the law of nations."[100] Congress accordingly resolved, visibly inspired by Blackstone's list of international crimes:

98 Casto, above note 27 at 491; Burley, above note 20 at 476.
99 *JCC*, 1774–1789, above note 75 at 21:1136.
100 *Ibid.*

> That it be recommended to the legislatures of the several states to provide expeditious, exemplary and adequate punishment:
>
> *First.* For the violation of safe conducts or passports . . .
>
> *Secondly.* For the commission of acts of hostility against such as are in amity, league or truce with the United States, or who are within the same, under a general implied safe conduct:
>
> *Thirdly.* For the infractions of the immunities of ambassadors and other public ministers, authorized and received as such by the United States . . .
>
> *Fourthly.* For infractions of treaties and conventions to which the United States are a party.[101]

While Congress viewed the preceding as those "offences against the law of nations which are most obvious," it went further in its second resolve by urging the several states to empower their courts to punish those "offences against the law of nations not contained in the foregoing enumeration."[102] Then, in its final resolution, Congress moved that "it be farther recommended to authorize suits to be instituted for damages by the party injured, and for compensation to the United States for damage sustained by them from an injury done to a foreign power by a citizen."[103]

That the 1781 resolution is the probable ancestor of *ATCA* is supported by their formal and substantive similarities. First, as mentioned above, both the resolution and the *Judiciary Act* were born from the Federalist concern that the law of nations ought to be respected and its violations punished. Second, both the resolution and *ATCA* are open-ended in scope. Where the resolution encourages state courts to punish all international crimes, including, "those not contained in the foregoing enumeration," *ATCA* grants jurisdiction over unspeci-

101 *Ibid.* at 1136–37.

102 *Ibid.* at 1137. If the resolution is taken to be the ancestor of the *ATCA*, then the open-ended reference to other crimes tends to negate the view of Judge Bork in *Tel-Oren*, above note 26, that international crimes in the eighteenth century were limited to Blackstone's enumeration.

103 The second clause of the final resolve referring to compensation owed to the United States is better understood with reference to the findings of the congressional committee. It noted: "That as instances may occur, in which, for the avoidance of war, it may be expedient to repair out of the public treasury injuries recommitted by individuals, and the property of the innocent be exposed to reprisal, the author of those injuries should compensate the damage out of his private fortune." *Ibid.* at 1136.

fied torts in violation of the law of nations. Third, and most importantly, both the final clause of the 1781 resolution and *ATCA* authorize the commencement of civil proceedings for violations of the law of nations as a complement to criminal prosecutions. As Burley noted, "this was an entirely logical addition, implicitly recognizing that justice under the law of nations could require making the victim whole as well as punishing the transgressor."[104] The final clause recommends the authorization of "suits to be instituted for damages by the party injured." Using consonant but more specific language, *ATCA* provides jurisdiction "where an alien sues for a tort." The eighteenth century understanding of *torts* included "actions for trespasses, nuisances, assaults, defamatory words, and the like."[105]

With the exception of Connecticut,[106] the states never responded to the recommendations of the 1781 resolution,[107] which likely strengthened the Framers in their belief that any hope for the uniform application of international law in the Union rested in a federal judiciary. Ultimately, the Constitution and the *Judiciary Act* implemented every recommendation of the 1781 resolution, ensuring that the majority of controversies involving foreign nationals or the law of nations could be adjudicated in the federal courts, in either criminal or civil proceedings. The Supreme Court has acknowledged the probable link between the 1781 resolution and *ATCA*.[108]

D. ELEMENTS OF *ATCA* JURISDICTION

Today, *ATCA* is codified at 28 U.S.C. § 1350, and provides that "[t]he district courts shall have original jurisdiction of any civil action by an alien for a tort only, committed in violation of the law of nations

104 Burley, above note 20 at 477.

105 Blackstone, above note 49 vol. 3 at 117.

106 In 1782, Connecticut passed *An Act to Prevent Infractions Against the Law of Nations* criminalizing an open-ended list of offences and providing limited civil remedies to injured foreign states. See Dodge, above note 27 at 228.

107 Casto, above note 27 at 491. Casto cites a letter from Francis Dana to Elbridge Gerry, dated 28 June 1784, in which Dana lamented the states' failure to act upon the 1781 resolution: "Recommendations of this sort, though important in themselves, are too often laid aside by the Legislatures, till they are forgotten." Paul H. Smith *et al.*, eds., *Letters of Delegates to Congress, 1774–1789*, 25 volumes (Washington, DC: Library of Congress, 1976–2000) 21:702.

108 *Sosa v. Alvarez-Machain*, 542 U.S. 692 at 716–17 (2004) [*Sosa*].

or a treaty of the United States." Each constituent element will be discussed in turn.

1) *ATCA* Is a Jurisdictional Grant Only

In the early post-*Filártiga* jurisprudence and literature, there lingered a debate about whether *ATCA* provided plaintiffs with a cause of action, in addition to explicitly granting the district courts with jurisdiction over civil actions for violations of international law. A plaintiff is said to have a cause of action if she belongs to "the class of litigants that may, as a matter of law, appropriately invoke the power of the court."[109] In *Filártiga*, the question whether *ATCA* provided a cause of action was a non-issue. Judge Kaufman and his colleagues unanimously held that "international law confers fundamental rights upon all people vis-à-vis their own governments," including the right to be free from official torture.[110] It is this "recognized legal right" — the customary international right to be free from official torture — that entitled the Filártiga family to seek relief through *ATCA*, which explicitly empowers the federal courts to grant such relief. The Second Circuit stated that *ATCA* should be construed "not as granting new rights to aliens, but simply as opening the federal courts for adjudication of the rights already recognized by international law."[111]

In *Tel-Oren*, Judge Bork disagreed with the 2nd Circuit's reading of *ATCA*, emphasizing that it is solely a jurisdictional grant, and does not create new causes of action. In *Tel-Oren*, plaintiffs alleged violations of various international treaties, namely the Geneva Conventions and the United Nations Charter.[112] Since neither the terms of the treaties nor the implementing legislation explicitly granted a cause of action in case of breaches, Judge Bork held that the plaintiffs could not sue. He stated that "it is essential that there be an explicit grant of a cause of action [by Congress] before a private plaintiff be allowed to enforce principles of international law in a federal tribunal."[113] In his view, to read *ATCA* as providing plaintiffs with a right to seek a remedy for

109 *Davis v. Passman*, 442 U.S. 228 at 237–40 (1979); *Tel-Oren*, above note 26 at 801.
110 *Filártiga*, above note 5 at 884.
111 *Ibid.* at 888.
112 *Tel-Oren*, above note 26 at 808–9.
113 *Ibid.* at 801.

breaches of treaty obligations in the absence of an explicit statutory conferral of such a right contravenes the constitutional requirement that international agreements be implemented by the legislature. In his view, the Second Circuit's interpretation of *ATCA* renders, by judicial *fiat*, "all United States treaties effectively self-executing."[114] Moreover, Judge Bork continued, insofar as *ATCA* mentions both treaties and the law of nations, the *Filártiga* reasoning would "authorize tort suits for the vindication of any international legal right," whether based in treaty or customary law.[115] In his view, by opening their doors to foreign litigants and foreign disputes, federal courts would overstep their constitutional role and improperly interfere in matters of international sensitivity that are best left to the political branches of the State. Judge Bork summed up his misgivings as follows:

> A statute whose original meaning is hidden from us and yet which, if its words are read incautiously with modern assumptions in mind, is capable of plunging our nation into foreign conflicts, ought to be approached by the judiciary with great circumspection. It will not do simply to assert that the statutory phrase, the "law of nations," whatever it may have meant in 1789, must be read today as incorporating all the modern rules of international law and giving aliens private causes of action for violations of those rules. It will not do because the result is contrary not only to what we know of the framers' general purposes in this area but contrary as well to the appropriate, indeed the constitutional, role of courts with respect to foreign affairs.[116]

Very little was known about the historical background of *ATCA* in 1984. In an effort to fill the historical void, Judge Bork advanced his own theory of what the statute was meant to accomplish and concluded that *ATCA* establishes federal civil jurisdiction with respect solely to the three international crimes recognized in 1789: piracy, passport violations, and infringement of ambassadorial rights.[117] In short, on the basis of separation of powers, judicial policy, and hermeneutic preferences, Judge Bork opined that the term "law of nations" ought not to be read to include present day offences and should most certainly not

114 *Ibid.* at 812.
115 *Ibid.*
116 *Ibid.*
117 *Ibid.* at 813.

be understood to grant a cause of action to individuals in relation to extraterritorial human rights violations.

Courts and commentators have generally disagreed with Judge Bork.[118] Except in his own D.C. Circuit where the question remained unsettled until the Supreme Court's 2004 decision in *Sosa*,[119] every judicial circuit of the United States that considered the matter had held *ATCA* to provide federal courts with jurisdiction and plaintiffs with a cause of action.[120] For some, the "violation" language of *ATCA* implies the concomitant right of plaintiffs to seek redress, without the need "to invoke a separate enabling statute."[121] For others, the enactment of the *TVPA* amounts to congressional approval of the *Filártiga* reading of *ATCA*.[122] Indeed upon passing the *TVPA*, the Judicial Committee for the Senate stated: "The TVPA would establish an unambiguous and modern basis for a cause of action that has been successfully maintained under an existing law, section 1350 of the *Judiciary Act* of 1789 (the *Alien Tort Claims Act*), which permits Federal district courts to hear claims by aliens for torts committed in violation of the law of nations."[123]

In 2004 the Supreme Court apparently settled the debate. The Court rejected the view that *ATCA* was a mere jurisdictional grant to be activated with subsequent enactments of specific causes of action.

118 D'Amato, above note 27; Virginia A. Melvin, "*Tel-Oren v. Libyan Arab Republic*: Redefining the Alien Tort Claims Act" (1985) 70 Minn. L. Rev. 211. But see *Jones v. Petty Ray Geophysical Geosource Inc.*, 722 F. Supp. 343 (Tex. S.D. 1989).

119 *Al-Odah v. United States*, 321 F.3d 1134 (D.C. Cir. 2003). But see *contra*, *Burnett v. Al Baraka Investment and Development Corp.*, 274 F. Supp. 2d 86 (D.C.C. 2003) [*Burnett*].

120 *Handel v. Artukovic*, 601 F. Supp. 1421 (C.D. Cal. 1985) [*Handel*]; *Forti v. Suarez-Mason*, 672 F. Supp. 1531 (N.D. Cal. 1987) [*Forti*]; *Paul v. Avril*, 901 F. Supp. 330 (S.D. Fla. 1994) [*Paul*]; *Hilao v. Estate of Ferdinand Marcos*, 25 F.3d 1467 (9th Cir. 1994) [*Hilao 1994*]; *Xuncax v. Gramajo*, 886 F. Supp. 162 (D. Mass. 1995) [*Xuncax*]; *Kadić v. Karadzić*, 866 F. Supp. 734 (S.D.N.Y. 1994); *Abebe-Jiri v. Negewo*, 72 F.3d 844 (11th Cir. 1996) [*Abebe-Jiri 1996*]; *Beanal v. Freeport-McMoran Inc.*, 969 F. Supp. 362 (E.D. La. 1997) [*Beanal*]; *Iwanowa v. Ford Motor Co.*, 67 F. Supp. 2d 424 (D.N.J. 1999) [*Iwanowa*]; *Doe v. Unocal Corp.*, No. 00-56603, 2002 (9th Cir. 2002) [*Unocal 2002*]; *Papa v. United States*, 281 F.3d 1004 (9th Cir. 2002) [*Papa*]; *Presbyterian Church of Sudan v. Talisman Energy Inc.*, 244 F. Supp. 2d 289 (S.D.N.Y. 2003) [*Talisman 2003*]; *Burnett*, *ibid.*; *Alvarez-Machain*, above note 20.

121 *Kadić* , *ibid.* at 241; *Abebe-Jiri*, *ibid.* at 848. See also *Handel*, *ibid.*; *Forti*, *ibid.*; *Paul*, *ibid.*

122 *Cabello (Estate) v. Fernandez-Larios*, 157 F. Supp. 2d 1345 (S.D. Fla. 2001) [*Cabello*]; *Abebe-Jira*, above note 120.

123 Senate Committee on the Judiciary, *Report on the Torture Victim Protection Act*, 102d Cong., 1st Sess., 1991, S. Rep. No. 102-249, reprinted in Beth Stephens *et al.*, *International Human Rights Litigation in US Courts*, 2d ed. (Leiden: Martinus Nijhoff, 2008) at 568–84 [Stephens 2008].

It stated: "the First Congress did not pass [*ATCA*] as a jurisdictional convenience to be placed on the shelf for use by a future Congress . . . to make some element of the law of nations actionable for the benefit of foreigners. The anxieties of the preconstitutional period cannot be ignored easily enough to think that the statute was not meant to have a practical effect."[124] The Court continued, partially vindicating Judge Bork, "Congress intended [*ATCA*] to furnish jurisdiction for a relatively modest set of actions alleging violations of the law of nations," referring explicitly to the three eighteenth century paradigmatic offences of piracy, violations of safe conducts, and offences against ambassadors.[125] As a matter of first principles of Anglo-American legal tradition, it was as axiomatic in the eighteenth century as it is today that the "law of nations" forms part of the law of the land.[126] As such, it would not have occurred to the First Congress to create a separate federal cause of action for "torts in violation of the law of nations" as "the law of nations" was considered to be part and parcel of the common law, which afforded both the right to sue and the jurisdiction to adjudicate. Indeed, in the eighteenth century, tort actions were understood as proceedings "whereby a man claims a satisfaction in damages for some injury done to his person or property."[127] No statutory cause of action was required for torts as the right to sue was conferred by the common law. As Blackstone noted, "wherever the common law gives a right or prohibits an injury, it also gives a remedy by action."[128]

2) Forum for *ATCA* Claims

The *Alien Tort Claims Act* grants federal district courts jurisdiction over civil actions for violations of international law. Since the dissolution of the federal circuit courts in 1912, the district courts serve as the main trial venues of the federal judiciary, having jurisdiction over the vast majority of federal proceedings, both civil and criminal. Though *ATCA* speaks only of district courts, it should be noted that state courts also have original jurisdiction over *ATCA*-style transnational human rights

124 *Sosa*, above note 108 at 719.
125 *Ibid.*
126 Blackstone, above note 49, vol. 4 at 67; See also Chapter 4, Section B(1).
127 *Ibid.*, vol. 3 at 117.
128 *Ibid.*, vol. 3 at 123.

claims pursuant to their general jurisdiction over all civil and criminal matters.[129]

3) *ATCA* Plaintiffs

Only "aliens" may bring *ATCA* claims; that is, "any person not a citizen or national of the United States."[130] The exclusion of US nationals from the ambit of *ATCA* provided much of the impetus for the *TVPA*, which extends a similar cause of action to all victims of torture or extrajudicial killing, regardless of nationality. Aliens suing under *ATCA* must be able to show so-called "Article III standing," which requires (1) that "the plaintiff must have suffered an 'injury in fact'"; (2) that "there must be a causal connection between the injury and the conduct complained of"; and (3) that the injury is likely to be "redressed by a favorable decision."[131]

It has been held that "alien" groups and associations may also bring *ATCA* claims, either on their own behalf or on behalf of their members, provided sufficient evidence of injury is preliminarily shown.[132] In *Islamic Salvation Front* (1998), the Rassemblement Algérien de Femmes Démocrates, a non-governmental human rights organization of Algerian women, was given standing to join the claim of eight anonymous plaintiffs. More recently, in allowing a trade union to bring an *ATCA* claim against a US mining corporation, the Northern District Court of Alabama warily stated:

> this court is uncomfortable about permitting a trade union to sue under the *ATCA* and *TVPA*, particularly because neither statute addresses this issue and the legislative history does not indicate Congress' intent. Indeed, the court questions whether allowing the union to proceed will stretch the outer reaches of the *ATCA*. However, the court finds that SINTRAMIENERGETICA has alleged a cognizable injury, sufficient to have direct standing under ordinary circumstances.[133]

---

129 See Chapter 3, Section E(4).

130 8 U.S.C. § 1101(a)(3).

131 *Lujan v. Defenders of Wildlife*, 504 U.S. 555 at 561 (1992).

132 *Doe v. Islamic Salvation Front*, 993 F. Supp. 3 at 10 (D.D.C. 1998) [*Islamic Salvation Front*].

133 *Rodriguez (Estate) v. Drummond Co. Inc.*, 256 F. Supp. 2d 1250 at 1259 (N.D. Ala. 2003) [*Rodriguez Estate*].

ATCA plaintiffs therefore stand as an exception to "the general rule that non-resident aliens have no standing to sue in United States courts"[134] insofar as their standing is explicitly provided for by federal statute. Non-resident aliens may also sue in US courts if the *res* of the action is situated the United States or if they are apprehended abroad and extradited to the United States for prosecution.[135] Also, as illustrated by the proceedings brought by Guantanamo Bay detainees, non-resident aliens also have standing to bring certain constitutional challenges, such as *habeas corpus*.[136]

4) Claims under *ATCA*

As a threshold matter, it must be established that the claim concerns a "violation of the law of nations or a treaty of the United States." In US courts, the law of nations "may be ascertained by consulting the works of jurists, writing professedly on public law; or by the general usage and practice of nations; or by judicial decisions recognizing and enforcing that law."[137] Courts have applied various standards in determining whether impugned conduct amounts to a "violation of the law of nations" for *ATCA* purposes.[138] In a pre-*Filártiga ATCA* decision, Judge Friendly opined that "a violation of the law of nations arises only when there has been a violation by one or more individuals of those standards, rules or customs (a) affecting the relationship between states or between an individual and a foreign state, and (b) used by those states for their common good and/or in dealings *inter se*."[139] In *Filártiga*, Judge Kaufman held *ATCA* claims to be restricted to violations of "well established, universally recognized norms of international law" as opposed to mere "idiosyncratic legal rules."[140] Courts of the Second Circuit consistently apply the *Filártiga* standard.[141] Another test, which has met with the general approval of the Ninth Circuit, is the requirement that the

134 *Berlin Democratic Club v. Rumsfeld*, 410 F. Supp. 144 at 152 (D.D.C. 1976) [*Berlin Democratic Club*]; *Doe v. Exxon Mobile Corporation*, 2009 U.S. Dist. LEXIS 90237 (D.D.C. 2009) [*Exxon 2009*].

135 *Berlin Democratic Club*, *ibid.* at 152; *Exxon 2009*, *ibid.* at 7.

136 *Boumediene v. Bush*, 128 S. Ct. 2229 at 2262 (2008).

137 *Smith*, above note 6 at 160–61.

138 Stephens 2008, above note 123 at 48–50.

139 *IIT*, above note 25 at 1075.

140 *Filártiga*, above note 5 at 881 and 888.

141 See, for example, *Kadić*, above note 120 at 239; *Talisman 2003*, above note 120 at 304.

impugned acts contravene "universal, definable and obligatory" international norms, that is, norms that are "characterized by universal consensus in the international community as to their binding status and content."[142] Commentators of the *Filártiga* decision first devised this test in an early effort to identify other violations of international law that could eventually give rise to *ATCA* litigation.[143] Substantively speaking however, despite differences in formulation, both tests are indistinguishable, converging as they do on the clearest and most widely accepted norms of international law. The courts of the Eleventh Circuit have applied both standards interchangeably.[144] For its part, the D.C. Circuit has expressed a preference for the "universal, definable and obligatory" test and noted that *ATCA* jurisdiction should be restricted to "a handful of heinous actions."[145]

One scholar has suggested a *jus cogens* threshold, requiring the impugned conduct to be a violation of peremptory norms in order to be actionable under *ATCA*.[146] This view is based partly on an ambiguous dictum from a single judge in an early phase of the *Unocal* litigation. The court stated: "While the Ninth Circuit has not expressly held that only *jus cogens* norms are actionable, the Circuit's holding in *Estate II* that actionable violations are only those that are specific, universal, and obligatory is consistent with this interpretation."[147] Aside from this dictum, there is little evidence to support the contention that *ATCA* jurisdiction is only triggered by violations of peremptory norms. While federal courts agree that *jus cogens* violations are a sufficient

142 *Forti*, above note 120 at 1540; *Hilao* 1994, above note 120 at 1475 ("Actionable violations of international law must be of a norm that is specific, universal, and obligatory."); *Beanal*, above note 120 at 370 ("To be recognized as an international tort under 1350, the alleged violation must be definable, obligatory (rather than hortatory), and universally condemned"). See also *Unocal 2002*, above note 120 at 27; *Papa*, above note 120 at 1013; *Alvarez-Machain*, above note 20 at 612.

143 Blum & Steinhardt, above note 27 at 87–89. The article was cited by the court in *Forti*, above note 120, which was the first judicial instance to use the "universal, definable and obligatory" language.

144 See, for example, *Abebe-Jiri*, above note 120, following the 9th Circuit test; *Rodriguez Estate*, above note 133, following the Second Circuit criterion; and *Mehinović v. Vucković*, 198 F. Supp. 2d 1322 (N.D. Ga. 2002) [*Mehinović*], applying both tests.

145 *Tel-Oren*, above note 26 at 781. See also *Al-Odah*, above note 119 at 1146: "The meaning of § 1350 has been an open question in our court . . . [and] has not been decided."

146 William S. Dodge, "Which Torts in Violation of the Law of Nations?" (2001) 24 Hastings Int'l & Comp. L. Rev. 351 at 354.

147 *Doe v. Unocal Corp.*, 110 F. Supp. 2d 1294 at 1304 (C.D. Cal. 2000) [*Unocal 2000*].

basis for *ATCA* jurisdiction, none have gone so far as to make them a necessary condition. In *Talisman*, Judge Schwartz observed: "while *jus cogens* violations are actionable under the *ATCA*, a *jus cogens* violation is not required. Under the *ATCA*, any violation of a specific, universal and obligatory international norm is actionable, whether it is *jus cogens* or not."[148] In *Alvarez-Machain*, the Court of Appeals for the Ninth Circuit, sitting *en banc*, explicitly rejected the application of a *jus cogens* threshold, noting that in so doing, it was "guided by the language of the statute."[149] Similarly, in *Flores*, the Second Circuit rejected the importation of an egregiousness standard, whereby only "shockingly egregious" violations of international law would be actionable under the *ATCA*. Such an evaluation of the severity of the breach, the court reasoned, would be inconsistent with the statute's language and would cause jurisdiction to be determined on the basis of "the consciences and sensibilities of individual judges" rather than on established norms of international law.[150] In so holding, the court was forced to qualify previous dicta from an earlier decision in which it dismissed the *ATCA* claim of a Colombian national against the New York State Lottery (NYSL). In that case, the plaintiff alleged that she was illegally deprived of her property by the NYSL's policy of paying winnings over ten years, rather than in one lump sum. In dismissing the "unusually frivolous" claim, the court stated that *ATCA* "applies only to shockingly egregious violations of universally recognized principles of international law."[151] In *Flores*, the court disassociated itself from its previous statement and held that, "no matter how shocking or egregious an action, it does not provide the basis for a claim under the *ATCA* unless it violates customary international law" or a treaty of the United States.[152]

In *Sosa* (2004), the Supreme Court approved of the standards developed by the Second and Ninth Circuits and emphasised that only

148 *Talisman 2003*, above note 120 at 306; *Mehinović*, above note 144 at 1344; *Unocal 2002*, above note 120 at 29.

149 *Alverez-Machain 2003*, above note 20 at 613.

150 *Flores v. Southern Peru Copper Corp.*, 343 F.3d 140 at 159–60 (2d Cir. 2003) [*Flores*].

151 *Zapata v. Quinn*, 707 F.2d 691 at 692 (2d Cir. 1983). See also *De Wit v. KLM Royal Dutch Airlines NV*, 570 F. Supp. 613 at 618 (S.D.N.Y 1983) (action for breach of contract and employment dismissal deemed not to present necessary "extraordinary circumstances" for *ATCA* purposes); *Jogi v. Piland*, 131 F. Supp. 2d 1024 at 1027 (C.D. Ill. 2001) [*Jogi*] (following *Zapata* and improperly applying an egregiousness threshold).

152 *Flores*, above note 150 at 159.

those international norms that enjoy a high level of specificity and acceptance are made actionable under *ATCA*. Without adopting a *jus cogens* threshold, the Court stated:

> Whatever the ultimate criteria for accepting a cause of action subject to jurisdiction under § 1350, we are persuaded that federal courts should not recognize private claims under federal common law for violations of any international law norm with less definite content and acceptance among civilized nations than the historical paradigms familiar when § 1350 was enacted [i.e., piracy, assault upon ambassadors, and passport violations] . . . . This limit upon judicial recognition is generally consistent with the reasoning of many of the courts and judges who faced the issue before it reached this Court.[153]

The Court further added that "the determination whether a norm is sufficiently definite to support a cause of action should (and, indeed, inevitably must) involve an element of judgment about the practical consequences of making that cause available to litigants in the federal courts."[154]

Therefore, to be actionable under *ATCA*, the impugned conduct must contravene well-established, highly defined, and widely accepted international norms. In accordance with this standard, the *Filártiga* court found torture to fall within the ambit of *ATCA* given the international consensus surrounding its prohibition. That holding has since been followed in numerous cases.[155] Prior to *Sosa* (2004), courts had identified a number of other violations of international law that trigger *ATCA* jurisdiction, including passport fraud,[156] racial

153 *Sosa*, above note 108 at 732.

154 *Ibid.* Unfortunately, the court did not expand on specific "practical consequences." Stephens argues that such an assessment is already built into the new stringent standard articulated in *Sosa*, and that no additional analysis is required: *Stephens 2008*, above note 123 at 56–57. If by "practical consequences" the court meant the potential effect specific proceedings might have on foreign relations or on judicial resources, then it is argued that such prudential assessments are best left to be resolved on a case-by-case basis as part of well-established doctrines such as the political question doctrine and *forum non conveniens*. See Chapters 5 and 6.

155 See, for example, *Filártiga*, above note 5; *Forti*, above note 120; *Paul*, above note 120; *Xuncax*, above note 120; *Kadić*, above note 120; *Abebe-Jiri*, above note 120; *Wiwa v. Royal Dutch Petroleum Co.*, 226 F.3d 88 (2d Cir. 2000) [*Wiwa 2000*]; *Tachiona v. Mugabe*, 169 F. Supp. 2d 259 (S.D.N.Y. 2001) [*Tachiona 2001*].

156 See, for example, *Adra*, above note 24.

discrimination,[157] kidnapping,[158] slavery,[159] unpaid forced labour,[160] disappearance,[161] aircraft high-jacking,[162] extrajudicial killing,[163] war crimes,[164] crimes against humanity,[165] and genocide.[166] Though some courts had found arbitrary detention to be sufficiently well defined at international law for *ATCA* purposes,[167] the Supreme Court held in *Sosa* that "a single illegal detention of less than a day, followed by the transfer of custody to lawful authorities and a prompt arraignment, violates no norm of customary international law so well defined as to support the creation of a federal remedy."[168]

By the same token, courts have declined to assert *ATCA* jurisdiction over certain wrongs that failed to meet the requisite level of widespread acceptance and definition. For instance, in *IIT v. Vencap*, an action by a Luxemburgish investment trust for fraud, conversion, and corporate waste, Judge Friendly dismissed the *ATCA* claim holding that the prohibition of theft by every nation did not cause the norm to be incorporated into the law of nations.[169] Expropriation[170] and violations of the right to free speech[171] were also non-justiciable under *ATCA* for lack of international consensus as to their normative contours. *ATCA* claims in relation to environmental damage have also consistently been dismissed for analogous reasons.[172] Similarly, the right to health

157 See, for example, *Sarei v. Rio Tinto plc*, 221 F. Supp. 2d 1116 (C.D. Cal. 2002) [*Sarei 2002*]; *Kadić*, above note 120.

158 See, for example, *Trajano*, above note 13.

159 See, for example, *Tel-Oren*, above note 26.

160 See, for example, *Iwanowa*, above note 120.

161 See, for example, *Forti v. Suarez-Mason*, 694 F. Supp. 707 (N.D. Cal. 1988) [*Forti II*].

162 See, for example, *Burnett*, above note 119.

163 See, for example, *Forti*, above note 120; *Beanal v. Freeport-McMoran Inc.*, 197 F.3d 161 (5th Cir. 1999) [*Beanal 1999*].

164 See, for example, *Handel*, above note 120; *Kadić*, above note 120; *Sarei 2002*, above note 157.

165 *Kadić*, above note 120; *Wiwa 2000*, above note 155.

166 See, for example, *Kadić*, above note 120; *Beanal 1999*, above note 155; *Mehinović*, above note 144.

167 See, for example, *Forti*, above note 120; *Eastman Kodak Co. v. Kavlin SA./Carbello v. Kavlin SA*, 978 F. Supp. 1078 (S.D. Fla. 1997); *Martinez v. City of Los Angeles*, 141 F.3d 1373 (9th Cir. 1998).

168 *Sosa*, above note 108 at 738.

169 *IIT*, above note 25 at 1015. See also *Arndt v. UBS, AG*, 342 F. Supp. 2d 132 (E.D.N.Y. 2004).

170 *De Sanchez v. Banco Central de Nicaragua*, 770 F.2d 1385 (5th Cir. 1985).

171 *Guinto v. Marcos*, 654 F. Supp. 276 (S.D. Cal. 1986).

172 *Jota v. Texaco Inc.*, 157 F.3d 153 (2d Cir. 1998) [*Jota*]; *Beanal 1999*, above note 163; *Sarei 2002*, above note 157. See also, generally, Stephens 2008, above note 123 at 205–8.

and the right to sustainable development were deemed insufficiently determinate to be actionable under *ATCA*.[173] For its part, forced prison labour was distinguished from forced labour and slavery, respectively, and was found not to be proscribed at international law and therefore not actionable under *ATCA*.[174]

Generally, since *Filártiga*, US courts have made reasonably fair assessments of what acts contravene international law for *ATCA* purposes, though some characterizations remain questionable. Police failure to advise a foreign national upon his arrest of his right to contact his consulate did not trigger *ATCA* jurisdiction, despite amounting to a violation of a treaty of the United States, i.e., the *Vienna Convention on Consular Relations*.[175] In 1984, the D.C. Circuit Court held "terrorism" not to be actionable under *ATCA* because it did "not believe that under current law terrorist attacks amount to law of nations violations,"[176] a conclusion that must probably be qualified after 11 September 2001.[177] Currently, US nationals may bring civil claims against terrorists and their supporters under the *Anti-terrorism Act*[178] and under new amendments to the *Foreign Sovereign Immunities Act* (*FSIA*).[179] Foreign nationals have also filed lawsuits under the *ATCA* in relation to the attacks on the World Trade Center and other terrorist attacks outside the US.[180]

Sosa can be said to have generally endorsed the *Filártiga* paradigm, but it did so conservatively. While holding that the doors of the common law were still open to the judicial incorporation of new actionable international norms, "subject to vigilant doorkeeping"[181] by federal courts, the court did not articulate a specific test or bright line by which actionable international wrongs could be identified. Instead, the

---

173 *Flores*, above note 150.

174 *Bao Ge v. Li Peng*, 201 F. Supp. 2d 14 (D.D.C. 2000) [*Bao Ge*].

175 *Jogi*, above note 151.

176 *Tel-Oren*, above note 26 at 795.

177 *Burnett*, above note 119; John Norton Moore, ed., *Civil Litigation against Terrorism* (Durham, NC: Carolina Academic Press, 2004).

178 The *Anti-terrorism Act* provides that "Any national of the United States injured in his or her person, property, or business by reason of an act of international terrorism, or his or her estate, survivors, or heirs, may sue therefor in any appropriate district court of the United States . . . " See 18 U.S.C. § 2333.

179 28 U.S.C. § 1605(a)(7). See discussion Chapter 3, Section E(1).

180 *Burnett*, above note 119; *Mwani v. Bin Laden*, 417 F.3d 1 (D.C. Cir. 2005) (*ATCA* suit again Al Qaeda and Osama bin Laden in relation to the 1998 attacks on the US embassy in Kenya.)

181 *Sosa*, above note 108 at 729.

majority merely cited in apparent approval the *Filártiga* and Ninth Circuit standards discussed above and restricted the recognition of new internationally derived causes of actions to violations of norms possessing comparatively as much definite content as Blackstone's list of eighteenth century crimes. As post-*Sosa* cases show, however, this standard is proving generally unhelpful and is producing peculiar results.[182]

The post-*Sosa* malaise can be illustrated with reference to two cases. The first is *Aldana v. Del Monte* (2005),[183] a decision in the ongoing proceedings against the Del Monte Corporation in relation to alleged human rights abuses in Guatemala. Specifically, the plaintiffs alleged that corporate officials directly ordered the kidnapping, detention, and torture of trade union representatives. This conduct, the plaintiffs alleged, amounted to violations of the international rights to be free from torture; arbitrary detention; and cruel, inhumane, and degrading treatment; as well as of the right to associate and organize. The Southern District court of Florida had dismissed the claims in 2003 because of the poor evidentiary record and the plaintiff's failure to show that the alleged misconduct amounted to violations of international law.[184] On appeal, the Eleventh Circuit affirmed and reversed in part, upholding the claims for torture, but dismissing the claims in relation to the right to associate and organize and cruel, inhumane, and degrading treatment. With respect to this last holding, the court held that the international prohibition against cruel, inhumane, and degrading treatment did not possess the normative specificity *Sosa* requires to be actionable under *ATCA*. The court acknowledged that its holding was contrary to at least two pre-*Sosa* district court decisions that found cruel, inhuman, or degrading treatment to be sufficiently

182 See, for example, Beth Stephens, "*Sosa v. Alvarez-Machain*: The Door is Still Ajar for Human Rights Litigation in U.S. Courts" (2004) 70 Brooklyn L. Rev. 533; Zachary S. Kahn, "How Far is the 'Door Ajar': Whether Rape as Torture is Actionable under the *Alien Tort Statute* after *Sosa*" (2006) 12 Cardozo J.L. & Gender 685; Carolyn A. D'Amore, "*Sosa v. Alvarez-Machain* and the *Alien Tort Statute*: How Wide Has the Door to Human Rights Litigation Been Left Open?" (2006) 39 Akron L. Rev. 593; Igor Fuks, "*Sosa v. Alvarez-Machain* and the Future of *ATCA* Litigation: Examining Bonded Labor Claims and Corporate Liability" (2006) 106 Colum. L. Rev. 112.

183 *Aldana v. Del Monte Fresh Produce, N.A., Inc.*, 416 F.3d 1242 at 1247 (11th Cir. 2005) [*Aldana 2005*].

184 *Aldana v. Fresh Del Monte Produce, Inc.*, 305 F. Supp. 2d 1285 (S.D. Fla., 2003) [*Aldana 2003*].

well-defined at international law to give rise to civil liability under the Alien Tort Statute (ATS).[185] Surprisingly, the Court of Appeal for the Eleventh Circuit distinguished those cases on the basis of their reliance on the *International Covenant on Civil and Political Rights* (ICCPR), which *Sosa* found did not "create obligations enforceable in the federal courts."[186]

The grounds invoked by the court to distinguish the relevant precedents from the case before it are more than a little suspect. While both the *Mehinović* and *Cabello* courts cited the ICCPR as evidence of the well-established and well-defined nature of the international norms at issue in those claims, neither case turned solely on that treaty. In both cases, the courts looked to a variety of international legal sources to assess the validity of the plaintiffs' claims, including customary international law and a number of multilateral treaties. It was disingenuous and arguably an error of law to zero-in as the *Aldana* court did on a single feature of the pre-*Sosa* precedents instead of engaging with their merits in light of the *Sosa* standard.

The decision in *Aldana* not to recognize cruel, inhumane, and degrading treatment as actionable under the ATS is symptomatic of the post-*Sosa* malaise. While the *Sosa* standard leaves admittedly much to be desired in terms of clarity, it did generally endorse the stringent threshold established in *Filártiga* and its progeny, namely that § 1350's reach ought to be limited to "a handful of heinous actions — each of which violates definable, universal and obligatory norms."[187] That being so, it is difficult to imagine another international norm as "definable, universal and obligatory" as the prohibition against cruel, inhumane and degrading treatment, particularly in light of that norm's connection to the prohibition against torture in the *Convention against Torture*.[188] Nevertheless, in 2006, a majority of the Court of Appeal for the Eleventh Circuit, sitting *en banc*, upheld the 2005 decision and denied a

185 *Mehinović*, above note 144; *Cabello*, above note 122 at 1361.

186 *Sosa*, above note 108 at 735.

187 *Ibid*. at 732, quoting Judge Ewards, concurring, in *Tel-Oren*, above note 26 at 781. The court also referred to the decisions in *Filártiga*, above note 5 at 888 and *Hilao, 1994*, above note 120 at 1475, holding that actionable violations of international law must be of a norm that is "specific, universal, and obligatory."

188 *Convention against Torture and other Cruel, Inhuman or Degrading Treatment or Punishment*, 10 December 1984, UN Doc. A/39/51 (1985), 465 U.N.T.S. 85.

rehearing of the case on this point.[189] Judge Barkett dissented in strong terms, citing scores of weighty authorities — caselaw, multilateral treaties, resolutions, and doctrinal writing — evincing the well-established and well-defined nature of the prohibition against cruel, inhumane or degrading treatment.[190] Taking the view that the majority misapprehended the *Sosa* standard, Judge Barkett stated:

> Had the panel followed the required *Sosa* analysis, it would have seen that *the specific content requirement of* Sosa *is not one of categorical specificity* — it does not require defining every possible instance of cruel, inhuman, or degrading treatment or punishment, but rather compels a determination of whether the facts alleged in a particular situation sit within the universal prohibition against cruel, inhuman, or degrading treatment or punishment [emphasis added].

Judge Barkett's dissent represents an earnest attempt to distil the *Sosa* standard into a workable approach, something the majority of the *en banc* court and the 2005 panel failed to do. That being said, holding that *Sosa* requires something less than "categorical specificity" in defining the content of an actionable international norm does not provide much additional guidance. Indeed, determining "whether the facts alleged in a particular situation sit within [a given] universal prohibition" is not the same as comparatively assessing the specificity of the norm at issue to the historical eighteenth century paradigms of piracy, assault upon ambassadors, and violations of safe conducts, which is clearly the task entailed by the *Sosa* standard. In any event, the dissent in *Aldana* strikingly highlights *Sosa*'s shortcomings.

The other case is *Kiobel v. Royal Dutch Petroleum* (2006), where Nigerian plaintiffs sued Royal Dutch Petroleum (RDP) in relation to alleged environmental and human rights abuses stemming from the corporation's activities in the Niger delta.[191] The complaint lists seven counts of international human rights breaches on the part of RDP, namely (1) extrajudicial killing; (2) crimes against humanity; (3) torture and cruel, inhuman or degrading treatment; (4) arbitrary arrest and detention; (5) violations of the rights to life, liberty, security and association; (6) forced exile; and (7) property destruction. The defendant

189 *Aldana v. Del Monte Fresh Produce, N.A., Inc.*, 452 F.3d 1284 (11th Cir. 2006).
190 *Ibid.* at 1284–89.
191 *Kiobel v. Royal Dutch Petroleum Co.*, 02 Civ. 7618 (KMW) (HPB) (S.D.N.Y. 2006) [*Kiobel*].

moved to strike the claims, arguing that they fell short of the standard set in *Sosa*. Before discussing the effect of the Supreme Court's decision on the plaintiffs' claims, Judge Wood reminded herself that, prior to *Sosa*, the controlling precedent in her circuit was *Filártiga*, which "set a high bar for holding that a rule occupies the status of well-settled international law such that a district court may exercise jurisdiction under the *ATCA*."[192] Judge Wood articulated the *Filártiga* threshold as follows: "It is only where the nations of the world have demonstrated that the wrong is of mutual, and not merely several, concern, by means of express international accords, that a wrong generally recognized becomes an international law violation within the meaning of the statute."[193]

Turning to the post-*Sosa* state of the law, the court found the Supreme Court's decision to be confusing, stating that it "provided little guidance concerning which acts give rise to an *ATCA* claim."[194] It then proceeded to highlight the ambiguities in *Sosa* by comparing it to *Filártiga*. The court's reasoning on this point is worth reproducing in its entirety.

> Certain language in the *Sosa* opinion suggests that the Court intended to signal its rejection of the broad scope of *ATCA* jurisdiction asserted by the Second Circuit in *Filártiga*. The *Sosa* Court permits *ATCA* jurisdiction only where the norm violated has the same definite content and acceptance among civilized nations as "the historical paradigms familiar when § 1350 was enacted," 542 U.S. at 732; the *Filártiga* court had suggested that *ATCA* jurisdiction is broader—the norm violated need only have commanded the "general assent of civilized nations, 630 F.2d at 881."
>
> Other language in *Sosa* suggests that *Sosa* endorses the reasoning employed in *Filártiga*. See 542 U.S. at 732 ("This limit upon judicial recognition is generally consistent with the reasoning of many of the courts and judges who faced the issue before it reached this Court. See *Filártiga*."); *id*. at 731 ("The position we take today has been assumed by some federal courts for 24 years, ever since the Second Circuit decided *Filártiga*.")

192 *Ibid*. at 460.
193 *Ibid*., quoting *Filártiga*, above note 5 at 888.
194 *Ibid*. at 462.

> The general language cited above is, however, *dicta*. The holding in *Sosa* is very narrow: "It is enough to hold that a single detention of less than a day, followed by the transfer of custody to lawful authorities and a prompt arraignment, violates no norm of customary international law so well defined as to support the creation of a federal remedy." *Id.* at 738.
>
> In light of *Sosa*'s ambiguities, it would be inappropriate for a district court to assume that *Filártiga*'s view of the scope of *ATCA* jurisdiction no longer controls. The Court therefore analyzes Plaintiffs' claims on the assumption that the *Filártiga* holding controls, and will dismiss claims only where they clearly run afoul of *Sosa*.[195]

In short, Judge Wood found the *Sosa* standard to be so unhelpful that, rather than attempting to unpack the ruling, she confined it to its own facts and resorted to the more familiar *Filártiga* standard as if it were still the controlling precedent. It was perhaps not unreasonable to proceed in this manner given *Filártiga*'s vintage and *Sosa*'s ambiguity, but it is nevertheless an odd way to treat a Supreme Court decision. In any event, the court went on to determine the actionability of the plaintiffs' claims by looking to Second Circuit precedents for guidance — mostly *Talisman* (2003)[196] and *Wiwa* (2002)[197] — and paying merely occasional lip service to *Sosa*. Ultimately, the court upheld the claims in relation to crimes against humanity, torture, and arbitrary detention as being sufficiently well defined at international law to ground an ATS action, but dismissed the claims for extrajudicial killing; violations to the rights to life, liberty, security, and association; forced exile; and property destruction for the opposite reasons.

The decision in *Kiobel* is illustrative of the dissatisfaction *Sosa* produced from the outset.[198] In one of the first post-*Sosa* decisions, *South African Apartheid Litigation* (2004), the court commented:

> While it would have been unquestionably preferable for the lower federal courts if the Supreme Court had created a bright-line rule that limited the [*ATCA*] to those violations of international law clearly recognized at the time of its enactment, the Supreme Court left the

195 *Kiobel*, above note 191 at 563.

196 *Talisman 2003*, above note 120 at 320–21.

197 *Wiwa v. Royal Dutch Petroleum*, No. 96 Civ. 8386 (KMW) (S.D.N.Y. 2002) [*Wiwa 2002*].

198 See also *Aldana 2005*, above note 183.

> door at least slightly ajar for the federal courts to apply that statute to a narrow and limited class of international law violations beyond those well-recognized at that time.[199]

That approach, the court continued, "relegated to the lower courts the task of grappling with and determining what offences against international law fit within that narrow class of offences."[200] As *Kiobel* shows, it is a task that is proving more difficult than the Supreme Court itself seems to have anticipated and that can perhaps be undertaken most beneficially with the support of the authoritative standards developed before *Sosa*. According to Stephens, the universal, obligatory and definable test will likely "continue to offer useful guidance and precedential support for future [*ATCA*] claims."[201]

5) *ATCA* Defendants

The identity of the defendant determines both the personal and subject-matter jurisdiction of the federal courts in the context of *ATCA* proceedings. First, *ratione personae*, federal courts cannot assert *ATCA* jurisdiction over foreign states; the *FSIA* is "the sole basis for obtaining jurisdiction over foreign states" in US courts.[202] Incumbent heads-of-state are also immune.[203] The *Alien Tort Claims Act* only permits civil actions against individual state officials[204] and non-state actors such as multinational corporations[205] and political organizations.[206] Second, *ratione materiae*, the identity of the defendant determines the characterization and justiciability of certain conduct as torts committed "in

---

199 *In re S. African Apartheid Litigation*, 346 F. Supp. 2d 538 at 547 (S.D.N.Y. 2004) [*In re S. African Apartheid Litigation*]. The first post-*Sosa* case was *Doe v. Saravia*, 348 F. Supp. 2d 1112 (E.D. Cal. 2004), which was issued five days before *In re S. African Apartheid Litigation*.

200 *In re S. African Apartheid Litigation*, *ibid*.

201 Stephens 2008, above note 123 at 59.

202 *Argentine Republic v. Amerada Hess Shipping Corp.*, 488 U.S. 428 at 434 (1989).

203 *Tachiona v. United States*, 386 F.3d 205 (2d Cir. 2004) [*Tachiona II*]; *Wei Ye v. Jiang Zemin*, 383 F.3d 620 (7th Cir. 2004); *Tachiona 2001*, above note 155; *Lafontant v. Aristide*, 844 F. Supp. 128 (E.D.N.Y. 1994); Stephens 2008, above note 123 at 374.

204 See, for example, *Filártiga*, above note 5.

205 See, for example, *Jota*, above note 172; *Unocal*, above note 120; *Talisman 2003*, above note 120.

206 See, for example, *Islamic Salvation Front*, above note 132; *Tachiona 2001*, above note 155.

violation of the law of nations" because certain violations of international law—such as torture and extrajudicial killing—by definition require a measure of state action. Accordingly, a torture claim against the Palestine Liberation Organization (PLO) was dismissed on the basis that the PLO "is not a recognized State, and it does not act under colour of any recognized state's law" and therefore could not have engaged in internationally proscribed "official or State-initiated torture."[207] Contrarily to the *TVPA*, *ATCA* does not explicitly require the plaintiffs to show that the defendant was a state official or otherwise acted under the colour of law or public authority.[208] However, depending on the nature of the claim itself, the plaintiff may have to prove state involvement in the impugned conduct.[209] As mentioned above, it is official torture that is prohibited at international law. Accordingly, an *ATCA* claim for torture unavoidably implies the burden of establishing some form of state participation or acquiescence in the torture. It is only in this limited sense that one may speak of "ATCA's state action requirement."[210]

State involvement is neither formally nor substantively required by *ATCA*. All that is needed is a violation of international law. Courts have recognized that private parties (or non-state actors) are capable of contravening international law without the involvement of states or their officials. Pirates are the paradigmatic private violators of international law. "A pirate is one who roves the sea in an armed vessel without any commission or passport from any prince or sovereign state, solely on his own authority, and for the purpose of seizing by force, and appropriating to himself without discrimination, every vessel he may meet."[211] As such, "they are in the law *hostes humani generis*, enemies, not of one nation, or of one sort of people only, but of all mankind. They are outlawed, as I may say, by the laws of all nations; that is, out of the protection of all princes, and of all laws whatsoever."[212] Likewise, the assault upon the person of an ambassador or diplomatic envoy has long been considered "an atrocious violation of the law of

207 *Tel-Oren*, above note 26 at 791 and 795.

208 See discussion Chapter 3, Section C(3)(iii).

209 *Jama v. United States Immigration and Naturalization Service*, 22 F. Supp. 2d 353 at 362 (D.N.J. 1998).

210 *Wiwa 2002*, above note 197 at 9.

211 *Smith*, above note 6 at 162.

212 *Ibid*. at 163.

nations" and criminals were correspondingly held individually accountable.[213] In the wake of WW II, the trials at Nuremberg and Tokyo further developed the notion that war criminals and *génocidaires* could personally be held responsible for their actions, regardless of state involvement.[214] In *Kadić*, the Second Circuit extended this principle and recognized the civil liability of non-state actors under *ATCA* for genocide and war crimes. In addition, the *Kadić* court held that torture and extrajudicial killing—crimes that usually require state involvement to be considered violations of the law of nations—were also actionable under *ATCA* when "committed in pursuit of genocide and war crimes."[215] In addition to piracy, assaults on diplomatic envoys, genocide, war crimes, torture, and extrajudicial killing committed in furtherance of genocide or war crimes, state involvement need not be shown in *ATCA* claims against non-state actors alleging slavery,[216] forced labour,[217] kidnapping,[218] and terrorism.[219]

a) *ATCA* and Non-State Actors

As noted above, one of the main characteristics of *ATCA* litigation is the statutory requirement of grounding claims in international law. This requirement in turn has direct bearing on who can be sued under the *ATCA*, for it is only those persons to whom international law applies who are capable of committing actionable transgressions. Obviously, there is no question that international law applies to states and their instrumentalities and that international "torts" committed by state actors are cognizable by US federal courts under § 1350, subject to the specificity of the violated international norm and relevant doctrines of immunity and justiciability.[220] Less obvious however is the extent to which international law is binding upon non-state actors, such as private persons and multinational corporations (MNCs).

213 *De Longchamps*, above note 64 at 117.

214 *Kadić*, above note 120 at 240–44; *Talisman 2003*, above note 112 at 308–19; Ian Brownlie, *Principles of Public International Law*, 6th ed (Oxford: Oxford University Press, 2003) at 559–75 [Brownlie].

215 *Kadić*, above note 120 at 243–44; *Beanal*, above note 120 at 371.

216 *Tel-Oren*, above note 26.

217 *Unocal*, above note 120.

218 *Islamic Salvation Front*, above note 132.

219 *Burnett*, above note 119.

220 *Sosa*, above note 108.

At the time *ATCA* was adopted, international law was understood as binding upon both state and non-state actors, albeit in a more limited sense in the case of the latter. Individuals incurred international responsibility for certain acts committed in their private capacity, including piracy, slavery, and assaults upon ambassadors. Not surprisingly, then, the justiciability of private violations of international law under *ATCA* was recognized from the outset. In 1795, when an American slave trader and French privateers plundered a British colony in Sierra Leone, US Attorney General Bradford responded to the protests of the British ambassador by advising that a civil remedy could be obtained in US courts under *ATCA* against the pirates.[221] However, while violations of specific international norms by individuals appear to have caused few problems, the civil liability of "juristic persons" under *ATCA* met with initial judicial hesitancy.

In *Tel-Oren*, an *ATCA* case against the Palestine Liberation Organization, Judge Edwards queried whether in 1984 international law prohibition of torture applied to non-state actors. Noting the gradual attrition of "the general principle of statism," the nineteenth century view that international rights and duties were for states alone, Judge Edwards remained cautious: "While I have little doubt that the trend in international law is toward a more expansive allocation of rights and obligations to entities other than States, I decline to read section 1350 to cover torture by non-State actors."[222] In *Carmichael v. United Technologies* (1988), the Court of Appeal for the Fifth Circuit queried whether private parties are capable, either on the own or with state actors, of violating the "law of nations" for *ATCA* purposes.[223] In that case, a British national sought redress from several Saudi Arabian corporations whom he alleged supported Saudi State officials in detaining and torturing him. While the court ultimately did not have to decide the issue — it dismissed the claim for improper service and failure to plead sufficient facts — it nevertheless offered its opinion:

> We will also only assume, because it is unnecessary to decide, that the *Alien Tort Statute* does confer subject matter jurisdiction over pri-

221 1 Op. Att'y Gen. 57 at 59 (1795).

222 *Tel-Oren*, above note 26 at 794–95.

223 *Carmichael v. United Technologies Corp.*, 835 F.2d 109 (5th Cir. 1988) [*Carmichael*].

vate parties who conspire in, or aid and abet, official acts of torture by one nation against the citizens of another nation.[224]

Remnants of the statist paradigm persisted during the first part of the 1990s. In *Trajano*, one of the decisions in the *ATCA* litigation against former Philippines President Ferdinand Marcos, the Court of Appeal for the Ninth Circuit rejected the view that purely private actors are capable of bearing international legal liabilities. Without much discussion, the court stated: "Only individuals who have acted under official authority or under colour of such authority may violate international law."[225]

It was the 1995 decision in *Kadić* that displaced the notion that international law binds exclusively state actors for *ATCA* purposes. In that case, Muslim-Croat plaintiffs sued Radovan Karadzić, the leader of Bosnian-Serb insurgent forces and so-called president of the unrecognized Bosnian-Serb republic. In this leadership capacity, Karadzić was alleged to have organized and directed systematic torture, genocide, and war crimes, including summary execution, rape, and forced impregnation. Chief among the many issues raised in the case was whether *ATCA* granted the court jurisdiction over Karadzić *qua* non-state actor. In perhaps the most expansive reading of *ATCA* since *Filártiga*, the *Kadić* court unanimously held that the statute properly conferred jurisdiction in proceedings against non-state actors where international law itself defines the norm at issue as applicable to private persons, such as the prohibition of genocide[226] and war crimes.[227] What is more, the court found that *ATCA* extends jurisdiction over private persons in relation to international offences containing a state-action element (e.g., torture and summary execution) where such offences are perpetrated in the course of genocide or war crimes or, alternatively, when perpetrated in concert with, or with support from, state actors.[228]

---

224 *Ibid.* at 113–14.

225 *Trajano*, above note 13 at 501–2.

226 Article 4 of the *Genocide Convention* provides that "persons committing genocide . . . shall be punished, whether they are constitutionally responsible rulers, public officials or private individuals." See *Convention on the Prevention and Punishment of the Crime of Genocide*, 78 U.N.T.S. 277 entered into force for the United States 23 February 1989.

227 The offences described at the common art. 3 of the *Geneva Conventions* apply to all parties to a conflict, including insurgents. *Geneva Convention Relative to the Treatment of Prisoners of War*, art. 3, Aug. 12, 1949, 75 U.N.T.S. 135.

228 *Kadić*, above note 120 at 239–45.

b) Multinational Corporations

The ruling in *Kadić* inaugurated the second generation of *ATCA* litigation, broadening the class of potential defendants to include non-state actors, including MNCs. Since *Kadić* there have been dozens of *ATCA* claims brought against MNCs, several of which have been dismissed on either substantive[229] or procedural[230] grounds, some have been settled,[231]

229 Examples of cases that were dismissed because the complaint did not allege the required "tort committed in violation of the law of nations." Note that some of these claims have since been refiled on alternative grounds: *Hamid v. Price Waterhouse*, 51 F.3d 1411 (9th Cir. 1995); *Beanal 1999*, above note 163; *Bao Ge*, above note 174; *Mendonca v. Tidewater Inc.*, 159 F. Supp. 2d 299 (E.D. La 2001); *Aldana 2003*, above note 184; *Flores*, above note 150; *Maugein v. Newmont Mining Corp.*, 298 F. Supp. 2d 1124 (D. Colo. 2004); *In re S. African Apartheid Litigation*, above note 199; *Presbyterian Church of Sudan v. Talisman Energy Inc.*, 582 F.3d 244 (2d Cir. 2009) [*Talisman 2009*].

230 Examples of cases that were dismissed on procedural grounds, note that some of these have since been refiled: *Carmichael*, above note 223 (improper service and deficient record); *Iwanowa*, above note 120 (*ATCA* claims barred by settlement treaties, statute of limitation, comity and political question doctrine); *Bano v. Union Carbide Corp.*, 2000 U.S. Dist. LEXIS 12326 (S.D.N.Y. 2000) (foreign settlement order barred US proceedings); *Aguinda v. Texaco, Inc.*, 303 F.3d 470 (2d Cir. 2001) (Ecuador deemed more appropriate forum); *In Re: WWII Era Japanese Forced Labor Litigation*, 164 F. Supp. 2d 1160 (N.D. Cal. 2001) (*TVPA*'s analogous ten-year limitations period barred *ATCA* claims); *In Re: WWII Era Japanese Forced Labor Litigation*, 164 F. Supp. 2d 1153 (N.D. Cal. 2001) [*In Re: WWII Era Japanese Forced Labor Litigation II*] (*Treaty of Peace with Japan*, 8 September 1951, 3 U.S.T. 3169, T.I.A.S. No. 2490, barred claims by Filipino plaintiffs).

231 Notable settlements include *Abdullahi v. Pfizer Inc*: In April 2009, after an adverse appellate hearing, Pfizer agreed to pay $150 million to the plaintiffs in settlement of their *ATCA* claim alleging that the company conducted illegal and nonconsensual drug trials on Nigerian children, (2009) 103 A.J.I.L. 592 at 592–93. In June 2009, Shell settled its lawsuit with Nigerian plaintiffs in *Wiwa v. Shell*, an *ATCA* claim alleging corporate complicity in the death of environmental activists. Shell agreed to pay $15.5 million in compensation to the victim's families and to pay the plaintiffs' litigation costs, (2009) 103 A.J.I.L. 592 at 593. In March 2005, the parties in *Doe v. Unocal* reached a settlement. Though the monetary terms remain confidential, the parties issued the following joint statement on 21 March 2005: "The parties to several lawsuits related to Unocal's energy investment in the Yadana gas pipeline project in Myanmar/Burma announced today that they have settled their suits. Although the terms are confidential, the settlement will compensate plaintiffs and provide funds enabling plaintiffs and their representatives to develop programs to improve living conditions, health care and education and protect the rights of people from the pipeline region. These initiatives will provide substantial assistance to people who may have suffered hardships in the region. Unocal reaffirms its principle that the company respects human rights in all of its activities and commits to enhance its educational programs to further this principle. Plaintiffs and their representatives reaffirm their commitment to protecting human rights." Online: www.earthrights.org/legal/final-settlement-reached-doe-v-unocal.

and many are still ongoing at the time of writing.[232] As far as can be ascertained, only two *ATCA* complaints against MNCs have been resolved on the merits.[233]

Since the Second World War, MNCs have emerged as powerful entities, wielding considerable financial and political influence on the economies and peoples of the world.[234] Through the ever-accelerating flow of goods, capital, and communications across national boundaries and the corresponding liberalization of world markets — the historical phenomenon generically called "globalization" — MNCs have expanded their operations and increased their wealth to levels surpassing those of many states. In 2009, for instance, General Electric generated sales worth in excess of US$182.5 billion and held assets valued at well over US$797 billion,[235] that is, considerably more than the gross domestic product of Finland.[236] MNCs engage in a diverse range of commercial activities, including agriculture, pharmaceutics, biotechnology, telecommunications, media, banking and finance, oil and gas, aerospace and defence, manufacturing and transportation, and, in so doing, profoundly affect the lives of human communities everywhere. The commercial activities of MNCs have, for the most part, improved the quality

232 Notable ongoing suits include *Sarei 2002*, above note 157 (filed in 2000); *Arias v. DynCorp.*, Case No. 01-1908, D.C.C. (filed in 2001); *Sinaltrainal v. Coca-Cola*, Case No. 01-3208-CIV-MARTINEZ/DUBE, S.D. Fla. (filed in 2001); *Khulumani v. Barclays*, Case No. 05-2141-cv, 05-2326-cv, S.D.N.Y (filed in 2002); *Mujica v. Occidental Petroleum*, Case No. CV 03-2860 WJR (JWJx), C.D. Cal. (filed in 2003); and *Saleh v. Titan*, Case No. 04CV1143 R (NLS), S.D. Cal. (filed 2004).

233 *Rodriguez Estate v. Drummond*: On 26 July 2007, after six years of litigation, a jury acquitted Drummond on surviving *ATCA* claims in relation to the death of Colombia union leaders; see Kyle Whitmire, "Alabama Company is Exonerated in Murders at Colombian Mine" *New York Times* (27 July 2007), online: www.nytimes.com/2007/07/27/business/27drummond.html?ex=1343275200&en=b0dc4c8b43c02282&ei=5124&partner=permalink&exprod=permalink; *Bowoto v. Chevron*: On 1 December 2008, after a four-week trial and eight and a half years of litigation, the jury returned a verdict for defendants on claims for torture, extrajudicial killing, and crimes against humanity. See Steven E.F. Brown, "Jury Acquits Chevron in Nigeria Case" *San Francisco Business Times* (1 December 2008), online: http://sanfrancisco.bizjournals.com/sanfrancisco/stories/2008/12/01/daily18.html.

234 Detlev F. Vagts, "The Multinational Enterprise: A New Challenge for Transnational Law" (1970) 83 Harv. L. Rev. 739 at 746.

235 See *Forbes Global 2000 Rank*. Online: www.forbes.com/lists/2009/18/global-09_The-Global-2000_Rank.html.

236 In 2009, Finland's GDP was US$182.6 billion. See *CIA World Factbook*. Online: https://www.cia.gov/library/publications/the-world-factbook/geos/fi.html.

of life of Western consumers and states, providing employment, goods, services, and general prosperity. In developing nations however, where MNCs often operate, the economic and social benefits of their activities are sometimes overshadowed by their proximity to grave human rights violations. Multinational corporations have been accused of interfering with democratic rights and the right to self-determination by bribing state officials, funding political campaigns, and financially and materially supporting civil wars and *coups d'états*.[237] Moreover, since the 1990s, MNCs have faced charges of violating rights to life, limb, and liberty, as allegations of substantial environmental damage, substandard work-safety conditions, and mistreatment and intimidation of workers have surfaced in several developing nations. The most egregious allegations of human rights abuses arise in situations of "militarized commerce," that is, where security forces (often provided by the host state) are used to guard corporate installations or supervise work progress in remote areas.[238] In such cases, some MNCs have been charged of committing or aiding and abetting slave labour, forced displacements, disappearances, torture, and extrajudicial killings.[239]

It can be argued that MNCs form an incoherent legal category in light of the definitional difficulties that arise from the many distinctions that can be drawn on the basis of corporate structure, ownership, coordination, control, nationality, or domicile. Nevertheless it is the case that they find themselves embroiled in a remarkably busy branch of *ATCA* litigation. Human rights advocates have turned to domestic courts and civil litigation in an attempt to obtain some form of redress for victims of alleged human rights violations. Of course, their ability to sue MNCs for alleged breaches of international norms largely depends on the extent those norms can be said to create obligations for MNCs. In *ATCA* proceedings against MNCs, not only must the alleged tort relate to a norm possessing the required specificity, the rule

237 For instance, *IIT*, above note 25, has been linked to the overthrowing of the Allende government in Chile. See Sarah Joseph, *Corporations and Transnational Human Rights Litigation* (Oxford: Hart, 2004) at 76 [Joseph]; Nicola Jägers, *Corporate Human Rights Obligations: In Search of Accountability* (Antwerp: Intersentia, 2002) at 120 [Jägers].

238 Craig Forcese, "*ATCA*'s Achilles Heel: Corporate Complicity, International Law and the *Alien Tort Claims Act*" (2001) 26 Yale J. Int'l L. 487 [Forcese].

239 See, for example, *Doe v. Unocal Corp. et al.*, 963 F. Supp. 880 (C.D. Cal. 1997) [*Unocal 1997*]; *Talisman 2003*, above note 120.

must also be one that international law itself recognizes as capable of being breached by non-state actors. Unfortunately, the Supreme Court did not address this issue in any detail in *Sosa*.[240] Thus, for the moment, the *Kadić* line of cases still stand for the proposition that international law extends liability to private actors for *ATCA* purposes with regards to a handful of crimes of universal concern, including piracy, slavery, genocide, and crimes against humanity.[241] According to *Kadić* and its progeny, *ATCA* jurisdiction arises with regards to these crimes regardless of whether they were committed by public officials or private parties. Moreover, courts have held that atrocities such as torture or extrajudicial killings (i.e., offences that contain an element of state involvement) are also actionable under *ATCA* without regard to state action if they were committed in pursuit of genocide, war crimes, or forced labour.[242]

Whether one agrees with these determinations largely depends on the view one takes of the international legal personality of MNCs. The scholarship on this issue is divided. According to Brownlie, corporations enjoy, in principle, no legal personality at international law.[243] Rather, the concept of corporate personhood is countenanced by international law as forming part of the "rules generally accepted by municipal legal systems."[244] In other words, international law recognizes the legal personality of corporations to the same extent as the states themselves. While Shaw leaves the question open,[245] Dupuy takes the view that corporations have a temporary personal status, to the extent of their ability to assert rights under certain dispute settlement mechanisms.[246] For their part, Kinley and Tadaki conclude that, "it is possible to invest in [MNCs] sufficient international personality as to bear obligations, as much as to exercise their rights."[247]

---

240 *Sosa*, above note 108 at 733, n. 20.

241 *Kadić*, above note 120 at 239–41.

242 *Ibid.*, at 244; *Unocal*, above note 120 at 32.

243 Brownlie, above note 214 at 65.

244 *Barcelona Traction, Light & Power Co. (Second Phase) (Belgium v. Spain)*, 1970 I.C.J. Rep. 3 at § 50.

245 Malcolm N. Shaw, *International Law*, 5th ed. (Cambridge: Cambridge University Press, 2003) at 255.

246 Pierre-Marie Dupuy, "L'unité de l'ordre juridique international: Cours general de droit international public" (2002) 297 R.C.A.D.I. 105 at 105.

247 David Kinley & Junko Tadaki, "From Talk to Walk: The Emergence of Human Rights Responsibilities for Corporations at International Law" (2004) 44 Va. J.

For Clapham, this debate will remain unproductive as long as the emphasis remains on international personality rather than international capacity, that is, the capacity to bear rights and to fulfil obligations. He argues:

> . . . references to the subjects of international law are obviously misleading. Conflating the question of subjectivity with the concepts of international legal personality and international capacity has prevented a clear appreciation of the fact that non-State actors can bear international rights and obligations (even where they have no State-like characteristics or pretensions).[248]

Under this view, the extent to which an entity can be said to benefit from rights and owe and fulfil obligations at international law is not exclusively a function of the classic attributes of statehood — sovereignty, equality, independence — but increasingly a function of the manner in which different entities participate and interact on the international plane. In this respect, there is no doubt that corporations have become important "participants" in the international legal order.[249]

Multinational corporations interact with states and international institutions in different ways. For instance, corporations are the beneficiaries of internationally enforceable rights, such as those conferred by so-called internationalized contracts. Concluded between corporations and sovereign states, internationalized contracts usually take the form of land concessions and economic development agreements in which justiciable rights and duties are conferred.[250] Also, the international rules governing foreign investment protect the rights of corporations in respect of expropriation, compensation, and non-discriminatory treatment. These rights are firmly entrenched in customary international law.[251] Second, international treaties regularly include corporations in the definition of "persons" on whom obligations are imposed, for instance in the area of environmental protec-

---

Int'l L. 931 at 947. [Kinley & Tadaki]

248 Andrew Clapham, *Human Rights Obligations of Non-State Actors* (Oxford: Oxford University Press, 2006) [Clapham] at 80.

249 Rosalyn Higgins, *Problems and Process: International Law and How We Use It* (Oxford: Clarendon Press, 1994) at 50.

250 James N. Hyde, "Economic Development Agreements" (1962-I) 105 Rec. des Cours 267.

251 Jägers, above note 237 at 28.

tion.[252] Moreover, several international codes of conduct, so-called "soft law," address the ethical and human rights duties of corporations.[253] Another frequently made argument in support of the proposition that corporations enjoy a limited international subjectivity is their recognized right and ability to make and defend international claims. As proponents of this view point out,[254] several international institutions expressly grant corporations *jus standi* before their tribunals, including the World Bank's ICSID,[255] NAFTA's dispute settlement process[256] and UNCLOS' Seabed Dispute Chamber.[257] In addition, corporations have standing to bring claims before certain human rights tribunals, most notably the Inter-American[258] and European[259] Courts of Human Rights. Of course, it could be rebutted that if MNCs have standing before certain international institutions, it is because they fall within a wider class of persons and that none of the aforementioned mechanisms treat corporations differently from individuals.

Whatever international legal capacity MNCs may be said to possess is limited in important respects. Most notably, corporations do not directly participate in the process of international lawmaking. Internationalized contracts are not treaties and corporate practice will not lead to the creation of customary norms. Rather, as participants on the international scene, corporations exert a correspondingly limited — though increasingly more important — impact on international lawmaking. In the courses of treaty negotiations, states may come under pressure to pursue engagements that favour the interests of their

252 See, for example, art. 2(6) of the *Convention on Civil Liability for Damage Resulting from Activities Dangerous to the Environment*, 21 June 1993, E.T.S. No. 150. See also art. 1(2) of the IMO's *International Convention on Civil Liability for Oil Pollution Damage*, 29 November 1969, entered into force 19 June 1975, 973 U.N.T.S. 3. See Jägers, above note 237 at c. 4, for an extensive discussion of the human rights obligations of MNCs.

253 See, generally, Kinley & Tadaki, above note 247.

254 Clapham, above note 248 at 81.

255 *Convention on the Settlement of Investment Disputes between States and Nationals of other States*, 18 March 1965, 4 I.L.M. 524, art. 25(1).

256 *North American Free Trade Agreement*, 17 December 1992, Can. T.S. 1994 No. 2, 32 I.L.M. 289 and 605 (entered into force 1 January 1994) c. 11.

257 *United Nations Convention on the Law of the Sea*, 10 December 1982, 1833 U.N.T.S. 397, Part XI, art. 187.

258 *American Convention on Human Rights*, 22 November 1969, O.A.S.T.S. No. 36, 1144 U.N.T.S. 123, (entered into force 18 July 1978) art. 44.

259 *Convention for the Protection of Human Rights and Fundamental Freedoms*, 4 November 1950, E.T.S. No. 5, 213 U.N.T.S. 221 (entered into force 3 September 1953) art. 34.

corporate nationals, the *General Agreement on Tariffs and Trade* (GATT), and the Kyoto Accord being among the most conspicuous examples. Corporations also may influence the evolution of customary norms through the mechanism of diplomatic protection. As Byers points out, "many of the obligations which States have in respect of individuals and corporations in international law exist, through the concept of diplomatic protection, as obligations to other States."[260] When taking up the claims of their corporate nationals, states engage in practice that, if sufficiently maintained, could lead to the emergence of new customary norms.

Whether corporations ought to be considered subjects, objects, or participants in the international legal order remains controversial and, ultimately, is of limited importance in the context of transnational human rights litigation. The international personhood of MNCs is irrelevant in home state civil actions because corporations, like any national, must obey the laws in force in their home jurisdiction. Accordingly, to the extent most human rights violations are convertible into private torts under the law of the home state a plaintiff need not plead the peremptoriness or international character of the wrong to make his or her case, as was done for example in the UK asbestos cases.[261]

The putative international personality of corporations and the application of international norms protecting the human person to MNCs take on a different significance however in the context of US *ATCA* litigation where corporate conduct is examined in light of international law. As noted above, plaintiffs suing MNCs under *ATCA* must not only plead a violation of the law of nations, but must necessarily limit their claims to those international norms capable of being breached by private actors. However, in light of the orthodox view and despite the position taken by US courts since *Kadić*, it is difficult to conclude that corporations are bound by general human rights norms as international law currently stands. If this indeed is the case, then all *ATCA* claims alleging that corporations have directly violated international norms — such as *Unocal*, *Talisman*, and *Sarei* — are simply

260 Michael Byers, "Decisions of British Courts during 1999" (1999) 70 Brit. Y.B. Int'l L. 277 at 80.

261 *Connelly v. R.T.Z. Corporation Plc.*, [1998] A.C. 854 (H.L.) and *Lubbe and Others and Cape Plc. and Related Appeals*, [2000] 4 All E.R. 268 (H.L.). For a Canadian example, see *Recherches Internationales Québec v. Cambior Inc.*, [1998] Q.J. No. 2554 at para. 98 (Sup. Ct.).

unfounded. Hopefully, the US Supreme Court will offer some guidance on this most important issue sooner rather than later. Alternatively, the difficulty of claiming direct violations of international law may be circumvented in two ways. First, plaintiffs may bring regular civil actions against corporations, alleging garden-variety torts instead of international law violations under *ATCA*.[262] Second, because many international human rights norms are defined as containing an element of state action, such as the prohibition against torture, *ATCA* litigation involving MNCs may alternatively proceed on theories of state-corporate complicity.

c) Corporate Complicity under *ATCA*

As noted above, the *Kadić* court held that in proceedings against private parties where offences containing an element of state-action are alleged (e.g., torture, rape, or extrajudicial killing), *ATCA* jurisdiction may attach where the private party is shown to have acted under the colour of law or can be considered a state-actor. State action is generally found where a private party conspires, aids and abets, or otherwise acts in complicity with a state-actor. The *Kadić* court pointed to "the 'colour of law' jurisprudence of 42 U.S.C. § 1983 [as] a relevant guide to whether a defendant has engaged in official action for purposes of jurisdiction under [*ATCA*]."[263] Section 1983 of title 42 of the *United States Code* is the cornerstone of US civil liberties jurisprudence, creating a cause of action against any person acting under the colour of authority of the federal government or that of the several states and who deprives another person of their constitutional rights. US courts have developed four different context-specific standards to determine whether a private party can be deemed to have acted under the "colour of law" within the meaning of § 1983.[264] First, under the "public function" test, private action may constitute state action "if the State dele-

262 In *Unocal*, above note 120, for instance, plaintiffs sued in California state courts for negligence, wrongful death, battery, false imprisonment, intentional and negligent infliction of emotional distress, and conversion. See Joseph, above note 237 at 68–71. See also *In Re: Union Carbide Corp. Gas Plant Disaster at Bhopal, India in December 1984*, 634 F. Supp. 842 (S.D.N.Y. 1986); *Sequihua v. Texaco Inc.*, 847 F. Supp. 61 (S.D. Tx. 1994); *Aquinda v. Texaco Inc.*, 945 F. Supp. 625 (S.D.N.Y. 1996).

263 *Kadić*, above note 120 at 245.

264 *Lugar v. Edmondson Oil Co. Inc.*, 457 U.S. 922 at 939 (1982). See Forcese, above note 238 at 504; Andrew Ridenour, "*Doe v. Unocal Corp.*, Apples and Oranges: Why Courts Should Use International Standards to Determine Liability for Violation of the

gates to a private party a function traditionally exclusively reserved to the State."[265] Second, under the "compulsion" test, state action is found where a private party is compelled or coerced by the state to act.[266] Third, under the "nexus" text, state action exists in situations where the relational nexus between the state and the private actor is such that "the action of the latter may fairly be treated as that of the State itself."[267] Finally, under the "joint action" test, state action is found where the state and private party "acted in concert in effecting a particular deprivation of constitutional rights."[268]

It is this last standard — the "joint action test" — that federal courts have most consistently applied in determining whether MNCs have acted under the colour law for *ATCA* purposes.[269] In *Wiwa*, the court agreed that "the relevant test in this case is the 'joint action' test, under which private actors are considered State actors if they are 'wilful participant[s] in joint action with the State or its agents.'"[270] In addition to the willingness of private actors to act jointly with the State, the "joint action" test also takes into account the nature and quality of the cooperation itself. The *Wiwa* court held that "where there is a 'substantial degree of cooperative action' between the State and private actors in effecting the deprivation of rights, State action is present."[271] In that case, the plaintiffs alleged that Royal Dutch-Shell and Nigeria coordinated the campaign to suppress the Ogoni people, that the corporation provided the Nigerian military with boats and helicopters to facilitate attacks on Ogoni villages, that the corporation bribed witnesses to falsify their testimony against Saro-Wiwa and paid the military to respond violently to Ogoni complaints concerning oil spills. The court was satisfied that the alleged relationship between

---

Law of Nations under the *Alien Tort Claims Act*" (2001) 9 Tul. J. Int'l & Comp. L. 581 at 591 [Ridenour].

265 *Gallagher v. "Neil Young Freedom Concert,"* 49 F.3d 1442 at 1456 (10th Cir. 1995) [*Gallagher*].

266 *Adickes v. S.H. Kress & Co.*, 398 U.S. 144 at 170 (1970).

267 *Jackson v. Metropolitan Edison Co.*, 419 U.S. 345 at 351 (1974).

268 *Gallagher*, above note 265 at 1453.

269 See, for example, *Forti*, above note 120 at 1546; *Kadić*, above note 120 at 245; *Beanal*, above note 120 at 374–80; *Bigio v. The Coca-Cola Co.*, 239 F.3d 440 at 448 (2d Cir. 2001); *Unocal 2000*, above note 147 at 890-91; *Bao Ge*, above note 174 at 22; *Wiwa 2002*, above note 197 at 40; *Talisman 2003*, above note 120 at 328.

270 *Wiwa 2002*, above note 197 at 40, citing *Dennis v. Sparks*, 449 U.S. 24 at 27 (1980).

271 *Wiwa 2002*, *ibid.* at 40–42, citing *Unocal 2000*, above note 147 at 891.

the MNC and Nigeria, if proven, would constitute "wilful participation" and "substantial cooperative action" within the meaning of the "joint action" test.

In 2002, some courts began applying international criminal standards of complicity to *ATCA* cases in addition to, or in lieu of, the domestic standards suggested in *Kadić*.[272] The first application of international criminal law to corporate complicity was *Unocal*. The court found that recent decisions by the International Criminal Tribunal for the Former Yugoslavia (ICTY) and the International Criminal Tribunal for Rwanda (ICTR) were "especially helpful" for ascertaining the international law standard for aiding and abetting as it pertains to *ATCA*.[273] With particular reference to the *Furundzija* and *Tadić* cases and the discussion therein surrounding the constitutive *actus reus* and *mens rea* of aiding and abetting, the court devised a "slight modified *Furundzija* standard" for *ATCA* purposes. In the Ninth Circuit, corporate complicity is actionable under *ATCA* if the defendant MNC is shown to have provided "knowing practical assistance or encouragement that has a substantial effect on the perpetration of the crime."[274] The court in *Talisman* (2003) also derived substantive standards of complicity from ICTY caselaw and adopted a standard similar to the *Unocal* test. In that case, the court was satisfied the plaintiffs had an arguable case that "Talisman aided and abetted or conspired with Sudan to commit various violations of the law of nations . . . . [that] Talisman worked with Sudan to carry out acts of 'ethnic cleansing'; that Talisman encouraged Sudan to do so; and that Talisman provided material support to Sudan, knowing that such support would be used in carrying out such unlawful acts."[275] The court in *Talisman* (2006) also referred to international criminal standards of complicity, but found there was insufficient evidence to support the plaintiffs' claims.[276]

The choice of legal standards by which state action and complicity ought to be assessed is yet another unresolved issue of *ATCA* litigation. There had been substantial speculation in the early phases of

272 *Mehinović*, above note 144 at 1355; *Cabello (Estate) v. Fernandez-Larios*, 205 F. Supp. 2d 1325 at 1333 (S.D. Fla 2002); *Unocal 2002*, above note 120 at 45.

273 *Unocal 2002*, *ibid.*

274 *Ibid.* at 49–50.

275 *Talisman 2003*, above note 120 at 321–24.

276 *Presbyterian Church of Sudan v. Talisman Energy Inc.*, 453 F. Supp. 2d 633 at 668 (S.D.N.Y 2006) [*Talisman 2006*].

the litigation about whether *ATCA* cases should turn on international or domestic substantive law. The *Xuncax* court for instance took the view that international law should properly provide the substantive standards for deciding *ATCA* cases.[277] In *Tel-Oren*, Judge Ewards opined that the US rules of decision should govern,[278] while the *Trajano* court, relying on *lex loci delicti*, applied Philippines tort rules.[279] After *Kadić*, with courts applying § 1983 jurisprudence to decide whether a private party had engaged in state action, it appeared as though the issue had been resolved in favour of US domestic law. However, the application of international criminal standards of complicity in *Unocal*, and Judge Reinhardt's dissent on this point, clearly indicates that the debate is still very much a live one. The majority in *Unocal* justified its position in the following terms:

> Application of international law — rather than the law of Myanmar, California state law, or our federal common law — is also favoured by a consideration of the factors listed in the *Restatement (Second) of Conflict of Laws* § 6 (1969). First, "the needs of the . . . international system" are better served by applying international rather than national law. Second, "the relevant policies of the forum" cannot be ascertained by referring — as the concurrence does — to one out-of-circuit decision which happens to favour federal common law and ignoring other decisions which have favoured other law, including international law . . . . Third, regarding "the protection of justified expectations," the "certainty, predictability and uniformity of result," and the "ease in the determination and application of the law to be applied," we note that the standard we adopt today from an admittedly recent case nevertheless goes back at least to the Nuremberg trials and is similar to that of the *Restatement (Second) of Torts* . . . . Finally, "the basic policy underlying the particular field of law" is to provide tort remedies for violations of international law. This goal is furthered by the application of international law, even when the international law in question is criminal law but is similar to domestic tort law, as discussed in the next paragraph. We conclude

277 *Xuncax*, above note 120 at 180–83.
278 *Tel-Oren*, above note 26 at 782.
279 *Trajano*, above note 13 at 503.

> that given the record in the present case, application of international law is appropriate.[280]

For his part, Judge Reinhardt would have applied "traditional civil tort principles embodied in federal common law."[281] When resolving ancillary issues raised by federal grants of jurisdiction or causes of action, courts have traditionally turned to federal common law to fill the gaps, particularly when the statute in question implements a particular policy of the US.[282] In Judge Reinhardt's opinion, "it is precisely in order to implement the policies underlying Congress's decision to make the violation of international law a federal tort, that it is necessary to flesh out the statute and apply federal common law."[283] For Judge Reinhardt, the benefit of the vast experience of the common law is lost when federal courts apply, as did the majority, "undeveloped principles of international law promulgated by a recently-constituted *ad hoc* international tribunal."[284] He was fortified in his view by the nature of the particular issue to be resolved in *Unocal*, that is, the question of when and how third-party liability arises. Complicity, Judge Reinhardt stated,

> is not an issue of such rarity, so seldom broached and so puzzling that our domestic law offers inadequate guidance and we are compelled to look elsewhere. The fact that some of the acts at issue here may have taken place abroad does not militate in favour of applying international law; transnational matters are litigated in federal court, using federal legal standards, more and more frequently as the pace of globalization grows ever more rapid. Nor is there any reason to apply international law to the question of third-party liability simply because international law applies to the substantive violation; as discussed above, federal common law is properly invoked when the statute at issue leaves an ancillary question unanswered, regardless of the nature of the statute. In short, federal common law principles provide the traditional and time-tested method of filling in the interstices and resolving the type of ancillary legal questions presented by this case.[285]

280 *Unocal 2002*, above note 120 at 41–42.
281 *Ibid.* at 90.
282 *Ibid.* at 93.
283 *Ibid.* at 94.
284 *Ibid.* at 97.
285 *Ibid.* at 95.

Judge Reinhardt's position is suspect in light of *Sosa*, which points to international law as the governing law for *ATCA* purposes.[286] Certain commentators have taken the view that the application of domestic standards in civil proceedings concerning violations of international law is inappropriate and that US courts should assess state action and complicity in light of international law.[287] One of the main reasons invoked for preferring international norms in the specific context of complicity is that the international criminal standard of "aiding and abetting" outlined in *Furundzija* and *Tadić* is broader than the "joint action" test under § 1983.[288] The adoption of international criminal law standards in *ATCA* litigation, it is argued, would thus cast the net of accountability over a wider range of state-corporate co-operative action. Another reason for favouring international law, as advanced by the court in *Xuncax*, is the perceived inability of domestic norms to reflect the moral and legal gravity of international human rights violations, and the risk of reducing such crimes as genocide and torture to mere "garden-variety municipal torts."[289]

The problem however is that there is no perfectly transposable international equivalent to domestic rules. International law does not possess a concept of private civil liability, much less a concept of complicit civil liability.[290] That being said, international law does contain special rules governing the attribution of third-party conduct to states, as developed under the regime of state responsibility.[291] However, as suggested by Forcese, for the rules of attribution of state responsibility to apply in *ATCA* proceedings like *Unocal*, courts must be "prepared to adopt and invert the roles of the relevant parties" so to attribute the conduct of the State to the MNC, rather than vice versa.[292] Another

286 *Sosa*, above note 108 at 725.

287 See generally Ridenour, above note 264; Forcese, above note 238.

288 Forcese, *ibid.* at 507–10; Ridenour, above note 264 at 592.

289 *Xuncax*, above note 120 at 183.

290 See *Case Concerning the Application of the Convention on the Prevention and Punishment of the Crime of Genocide (Bosnia and Herzegovina v. Serbia and Montenegro)*, 26 February 2007, General List No. 91, I.C.J. Rep. 2007, Judgment at part IV. [*Bosnian Genocide Case*].

291 See arts. 4–11 of the ILC *Draft Articles on the Responsibility of States for Internationally Wrongful Acts*, UN GAOR, 56th Sess, Supp No 10, p. 43, UN Doc A/56/10 (2001) [*Articles on State Responsibility*]; James Crawford, *The International Law Commission's Articles on State Responsibility: Introduction, Text and Commentaries* (Cambridge: Cambridge University Press, 2002) at 91–123 [Crawford].

292 Forcese, above note 238 at 510.

option would be to borrow the international law of state responsibility's "aid and assist" standard in *ATCA* proceedings where complicity is alleged.[293] However, as the ICTY's decision in *Tadić* illustrates, the rules of state responsibility do not necessarily lend themselves to every context. In that case, the ICTY declined to apply the "effective control" standard devised by the International Court of Justice (ICJ) in the *Military and Paramilitary Activities Case* to determine whether or not an armed conflict is international, formulating instead its own standard of "overall control."[294] Likewise, in the *Bosnian Genocide Case*, the ICJ found the ICTY's "overall control" test to be "unsuitable" for the task of determining whether or not a state is to be held responsible for the conduct of persons acting on its behalf.[295] It thus appears that even within the international sphere there are no ready-made solutions for problems that arise in different contexts.

In the particular context of civil litigation under *ATCA*, the better approach is surely the creation of legal standards by reference or analogy to existing rules of international criminal law, as exemplified by the "modified *Furundzija*" test in *Unocal*. Another example is *Talisman* (2006), where the court stated that "to show that a defendant aided and abetted a violation of international law, an [*ATCA*] plaintiff must show: (1) that the principal violated international law; (2) that the defendant knew of the specific violation; (3) that the defendant acted with the intent to assist that violation, that is, the defendant specifically directed his acts to assist in the specific violation; (4) that the defendant's acts had a substantial effect upon the success of the criminal venture; and (5) that the defendant was aware that the Acts assisted the specific violation.[296] It is interesting to note that, while Judge Cote cited *Tadić* and *Furundzija* as authority, the standard she formulated is more aligned with the concept of "aiding and abetting" for purposes of state responsibility, requiring as it does high degrees of specific intention to aid and abet in the commission of a specific act.[297] While this standard is arguably more stringent than that required by the

293 *Articles on State Responsibility*, above note 291, art. 16; Crawford, above note 291 at 149.

294 *Prosecutor v. Tadić*, I.C.T.Y., IT-94-1-A, 38 I.L.M. 1518 at paras. 124–45 (1999) [*Tadić*].

295 *Bosnian Genocide Case*, above note 290 at paras. 402–6.

296 *Talisman 2006*, above note 276 at 668.

297 *Articles on State Responsibility*, above note 291, art. 16; Crawford, above note 291 at 149.

ICTY cases Judge Cote cited as authority — in *Tadić*, assistance that "indirectly and substantially affected the commission" of an offence was deemed sufficient to support aider and abetter liability[298] — it nevertheless illustrates the willingness of US courts to consult international law in determining complicity under *ATCA*.[299] The Second Circuit upheld Judge Cote's approach in 2009 and affirmed her dismissal of the claim against Talisman.[300]

6) Procedural Issues under *ATCA*

a) Service and Presence

Pursuant to the *Federal Rules of Civil Procedure*, service of process establishes jurisdiction over the person of the defendant.[301] This is relatively straightforward when the defendant is a US national residing in one of the eleven judicial districts. In such cases, service may be affected personally or in the manner prescribed by the law of the state in which the federal district court is situated.[302] The Federal rules also allow plaintiffs to initiate a lawsuit against persons temporarily present in the US — so-called transient or "tag" jurisdiction — as was the case in *Kadić* where Radovan Karadzić was served in New York whilst visiting the United Nations.[303] For their part, domestic and foreign corporations may be served by delivering a copy of the summons and the complaint with an officer or director of the corporation.[304] Personal jurisdiction can either be general or specific. A federal court may exercise general jurisdiction over any defendant who "could be subjected to the jurisdiction of a court of general jurisdiction in the state in which

298 *Tadić*, above note 294.

299 Judge Cote nevertheless referred to US criminal law to shore up her reliance on international criminal standards, noting that "the international law of aiding and abetting liability closely parallels federal criminal law. Under federal law, a prosecutor must show the presence of two separate mental elements: knowledge and intent. Criminal culpability exists under federal law where it is shown that 'the defendant knew of the crime, and that the defendant acted with the intent to contribute to the success of the underlying crime.'" See *Talisman 2006*, above note 276 at 668.

300 *Presbyterian Church of Sudan v. Talisman Energy, Inc.*, 582 F.3d 244 (2d Cir. 2009).

301 Fed. R. Civ. P. 4(k)(1).

302 Fed. R. Civ. P. 4(e)(1).

303 *Kadić*, above note 120; Fed. R. Civ. P. 4(e)(2) permits service upon a person physically present in a judicial district.

304 Fed. R. Civ. P. 4(h).

the district court is located."[305] Courts apply a "minimum contacts" test to evaluate the sufficiency of the defendant's ties with the forum. If the defendant's activities in the judicial district are "substantial, continuous and systematic, general jurisdiction is available; in other words, the foreign defendant is subject to suit even on matters unrelated to his or her contacts to the forum."[306] By contrast, specific jurisdiction can be exercised over a foreign defendant only if his or her ties with the forum give rise to the cause of action before the court. Specifically, it must shown (1) that the foreign defendant's sought to avail himself of the advantages of doing business in the forum; (2) that the claim arises out of the defendant's activities in the forum; (3) that the assertion of specific personal jurisdiction is reasonable.[307] In *Unocal*, the district court declined to assert specific jurisdiction over the French corporation Total because no evidence could be shown that the activities of its California subsidiaries gave rise to the human rights violations in Myanmar. As observed by Stephens, the rules governing specific jurisdiction are "surprisingly complex and vary among the 50 states."[308] Accordingly, *ATCA* claims involving corporations are typically based on the broader principle of general personal jurisdiction.

The cases against Talisman and Royal Dutch-Shell, both brought in New York, underscore the salience of state rules on general jurisdictional in the context of *ATCA* claims against foreign corporations. Pursuant to New York rules of court, foreign corporations are subject to the general personal jurisdiction of state courts if they are "doing business" in the state.[309] Though now codified, the "doing business" rule was established by jurisprudence. In New York it has been long held that "a corporation is 'doing business' and is therefore 'present' in New York and subject to personal jurisdiction with respect to any cause of action, related or unrelated to the New York contacts, if it does business in New York 'not occasionally or casually, but with a

305 Fed. R. Civ. P. 4(k)(1)(A).

306 *John Doe I v. Unocal Corp.*, 27 F. Supp. 2d 1174 at 1184 (C.D. Cal. 1998) [*Unocal 1998*], citing *Perkins v. Benguet Consolidated Mining Co.*, 342 U.S. 437 at 444 (1952).

307 *Unocal 1998*, *ibid.* at 1125; citing *Gordy v. Daily News L.P.*, 95 F.3d 829 at 831–32 (9th Cir. 1996).

308 Beth Stephens, "Corporate Accountability: International Human Rights Litigation against Corporations in US Courts" in Menno T. Kamminga & Saman Zia-Zarifi, eds., *Liability of Multinational Corporations under International Law* (The Hague: Kluwer Law International, 2000) at 221.

309 N.Y. C.P.L.R. § 301 .

fair measure of permanence and continuity.'" [310] Phrased differently, the standard requires the plaintiff to show that a foreign corporate defendant is engaged in "continuous, permanent, and substantial activity in New York."[311] Courts must accordingly enquire into the nature and sufficiency of the contacts between the corporation and the jurisdiction to determine whether it is engaged in "continuous, permanent, and substantial activity."[312] Relevant contacts include the existence of an office in the jurisdiction, the active solicitation of business, the presence of property, and the presence of employees or agents in the jurisdiction.[313] In *Wiwa*, Royal Dutch-Shell was found to be "doing business" in New York because it listed its shares on the New York Stock Exchange (NYSE) and maintained an investor relations office in New York City.[314] Similarly, in *Talisman*, the listing of shares on the NYSE and the active presence in the district of a wholly-owned subsidiary, Fortuna Inc., sufficed to establish that Talisman was "doing business" in New York for personal jurisdiction purposes.[315]

That general personal jurisdiction can be obtained over a parent corporation through one of its subsidiaries warrants comment. It could be objected that taking jurisdiction in such circumstances conflicts with an important objective of incorporation, namely, the isolation of liability through the creation of distinct juristic persons, and contravenes due process notions of fair play. It does neither. A court's assertion of personal jurisdiction over a parent corporation through a subsidiary does not, of itself, amount to a finding of liability with regards to either the parent or subsidiary. Rather, it is a judicial determination that, in light of the particular relationship between the two entities and the circumstances of the case, it is both reasonable and expedient to sue the parent corporation in the subsidiary's district. Under New York law, "personal jurisdiction over a foreign corporation can be established on the basis of its subsidiary's presence in the state

310 *Hoffritz For Cutlery Inc. v. Amajac Ltd.*, 763 F.2d 55 at 58 (2d Cir. 1985), citing *Tauza v. Susquehanna Coal* Co., 220 N.Y. 259 at 267 (1917).

311 *Landoil Resources Corp. v. Alexander & Alexander Services Inc.*, 918 F.2d 1039 at 1043 (2d Cir. 1991).

312 *Ibid.*

313 *Presbytarian Church of Sudan v. Talisman Energy Inc. and Republic of Sudan*, 2004 US Dist. LEXIS 17030 at 4 (S.D.N.Y. 2004) [*Talisman 2004*].

314 *Wiwa 2000*, above note 155 at 93–95.

315 *Talisman 2003*, above note 120 at 329–30.

by demonstrating that the subsidiary is a "mere department" of the parent corporation.[316] To determine whether a subsidiary is a "mere department," four factors are considered:

> (1) common ownership of the parent and subsidiary, (2) the financial dependency of the subsidiary on the parent, (3) the degree to which the parent corporation interferes in the selection and assignment of the subsidiary's executive personnel and fails to observe corporate formalities, and (4) the degree of control over the marketing and operational policies of the subsidiary exercised by the parent.[317]

In *Talisman*, Fortuna Inc. was deemed a "mere department" of Talisman to the extent that it was wholly owned and solely funded by Talisman, that Fortuna's Board of Directors was composed entirely of Talisman directors and that Talisman exercised considerable control over Fortuna's operations.

Once the subsidiary is shown to be a "mere department" of the parent corporation, it must then be ascertained whether the assertion of jurisdiction complies with federal requirements of fair play and substantial justice. This enquiry entails a second, wider assessment of the contacts between the defendant, the claim, and the forum, an enquiry similar to that of *forum non conveniens*.[318] As stated by the court in *Talisman*, "in assessing whether the exercise of jurisdiction comports with notions of fair play and substantial justice, courts examine five factors: (1) the burden that the exercise of jurisdiction will impose on the defendant; (2) the interests of the forum state in adjudicating the case; (3) the plaintiff's interest in obtaining convenient and effective relief; (4) the interstate judicial system's interest in obtaining the most efficient resolution of the controversy; and (5) the shared interest of the states in furthering substantive social policies."[319] Evoking the reasons of its 2003 ruling on *forum non conveniens*,[320] the court held in 2004 that the maintenance of personal jurisdiction was consistent with principles of fair play and substantial justice. It was satisfied that "the burden on [Talisman] is substantially outweighed by the plaintiff's interest

316 *Talisman 2004*, above note 313 at 4.

317 *Ibid.* at 5, citing *Jazini v. Nissan Motor Co., Ltd.*, 148 F.3d 181 at 184 (2d Cir. 1998).

318 See Chapter 6.

319 *Talisman 2004*, above note 313 at 5, n. 2.

320 *Talisman 2003*, above note 120 at 338–41.

in obtaining relief, and that the United States has a strong interest in vindicating violations of established human rights. New York also has an interest in ensuring that companies doing business in the state adhere to recognized norms of international law."[321]

b) Limitation Period

Because *ATCA* is silent on such matters as limitations periods and exhaustion of local remedies, procedural limits were fashioned by the courts by analogical reference to comparable legislation. As the Supreme Court directed, when a statute does not provide a statute of limitations, courts should not "assume that Congress intended that there be no time limit on actions at all; rather, [the] task is to 'borrow' the most suitable statute or other rule of timeliness from . . . the most closely analogous statute of limitations."[322] The most analogous statute to *ATCA* is of course the *TVPA*, which is codified as an annotation to 28 U.S. § 1350. Thus, since the enactment of the *TVPA*, courts have generally borrowed that statute's ten-year limitations period and applied it to *ATCA* claims.[323] In *Xuncax*, however, the court held the plaintiff's action to be admissible under both the terms of the *TVPA* and Massachusetts state law.[324] Despite the ruling in *Xuncax*, the use of state legislation to determine the applicable statute of limitations in the context of *ATCA* claims is clearly inappropriate. The Supreme Court specifically instructed federal courts not to borrow state law "when a rule from elsewhere in federal law clearly provides a closer analogy than available state statutes, and when the federal policies at stake and the practicalities of litigation make that rule a significantly more appropriate vehicle for interstitial lawmaking."[325]

---

321 *Talisman 2004*, above note 313 at 6.

322 *DelCostello v Int'l Brotherhood of Teamsters*, 462 U.S. 151 at 158 (1983) [*DelCostello*].

323 *Cabiri v. Assasie-Gyimah*, 921 F. Supp. 1189 at 1195 (S.D.N.Y. 1996) [*Cabiri*]; *Iwanowa*, above note 120 at 462; *In Re: WWII Japanese Forced Labor Litigation II*, above note 230 at 1180; *Wiwa 2002*, above note 197 at 62; *Papa*, above note 120 at 101; *Arce v. Garcia*, 434 F.3d 1254 at 1261–62 (11th Cir. 2006); *Van Tu v. Koster*, 364 F.3d 1196 at 1199 (10th Cir. 2004).

324 *Xuncax*, above note 120 at 192–93.

325 *DelCostello*, above note 322 at 172.

c) Exhaustion of Local Remedies

With regards to the exhaustion of local remedies, courts have held *ATCA* claims to be subject to the requirement that plaintiffs exhaust adequate and available local remedies before seeking redress in the United States.[326] Though this requirement is not explicitly contained in § 1350, it too, like the statute of limitations, has been borrowed from the *TVPA*. The *TVPA*'s exhaustion provisions will be discussed in the next chapter. However, as the court in *Sarei* (2002) noted, "no court has imposed an exhaustion requirement in a case brought exclusively under the ATCA. Rather, all alien tort actions in which exhaustion of remedies has been addressed have involved claims pleaded [jointly] under the TVPA."[327] The *Sarei* court declined to "borrow" the *TVPA*'s exhaustion element, holding that, under the bare terms of *ATCA*, plaintiffs need not "demonstrate that they have exhausted local remedies, or that doing so would be futile, in order to state a claim under the ATCA."[328] Through the *TVPA*, Congress explicitly established the exhaustion of local remedies as a precondition to asserting jurisdiction in civil actions for torture and extrajudicial killing. Accordingly, the court reasoned, civil actions for *all other* violations of international law should not be subjected to an exhaustion requirement. The parties objected, and the court acknowledged, that the exhaustion of local remedies is a well-established feature of international law.[329] Nevertheless, in the court's opinion, "ATCA does not adopt wholesale all principles of international law . . . . Because it is a creature of domestic law, the ATCA need not impose the same conditions on a plaintiff's right to sue as international law or the domestic law of other nations."[330]

In *Sarei* (2007), a divided Ninth Circuit Court provided the most sustained and scholarly discussion to date of the issue of whether an exhaustion requirement ought to be grafted into *ATCA*. The majority held that it would be "inappropriate, given the lack of clear direction from Congress (either in 1789 or when it revisited the issue in 1991), and with only an aside in a footnote on the issue from the Supreme

---

326 *Xuncax*, above note 120 at 178; *Hilao v. Estate of Ferdinand Marcos*, 103 F.3d 767 at 778 (9th Cir. 1996); *Alomang v. Freeport-McMoran Inc.*, 1996 U.S. Dist. LEXIS 15908 at 3 (E.D. La. 1996); *Cabiri*, above note 323 at 1197.

327 *Sarei 2002*, above note 157 at 1133.

328 *Ibid.* at 1139.

329 *Ibid.* at 1138.

330 *Ibid.* at 1139.

Court [in *Sosa*], now to superimpose on our circuit's existing ATCA jurisprudence an exhaustion requirement where none has been required before."[331] After reviewing an extensive range of international and domestic legal sources, dissenting Judge Bybee came to the opposite conclusion on grounds of comity and respect for foreign legal processes. He stated: "In my view, international law requires exhaustion of local remedies as a condition to bringing an international cause of action in a foreign tribunal. Even if international law did not so require exhaustion, I would, as an exercise in discretion, require it as a matter of our domestic law."[332]

Because it considered the issue sufficiently important, the Court of Appeal for the Ninth Circuit granted an application for rehearing *en banc* and vacated the 2007 decision.[333] In 2008, a plurality of the eleven-judge panel reversed the 2007 decision, holding that in most cases judicial prudence required the subjection of *ATCA* claims to an exhaustion of local remedies rule.[334] Writing for the majority, Judge McKeown noted that the issue of the applicability of the exhaustion rule was best decided not on the basis of a comparison between *ATCA* and the *TPVA*, but more straightforwardly as a stand alone prudential principle. This approach, the majority reasoned, not only relieved the court of the task of deciding whether Congress intended the *TVPA* exhaustion clause to apply to *ATCA* claims, but also permitted the court to avoid the even thornier "jurisprudential debate remaining in the wake of *Sosa*: whether exhaustion is a substantive norm of international law, to which the 'requirement of clear definition' applies; or if it is nonsubstantive, what source of law—federal common law or international law—illuminates its content."[335] Judge McKeown went on to observe that

> in [*ATCA*] adjudication, the United States courts are *not* international tribunals. With this in mind, the appropriateness of applying prudential exhaustion to some [*ATCA*] cases only gains force; if exhaustion

331 *Sarei v. Rio Tinto plc*, 487 F.3d 1193 at 1099 (9th Cir. 2007) [*Sarei 2007*]. Interestingly, in that case, Judge Stephen M. Schwebel of the International Court of Justice filed an *amicus* brief supporting the position that *ATCA* ought to be subjected to an exhaustion requirement.

332 *Ibid*. at 1101.

333 *Sarei 2007*, above note 331.

334 *Sarei v. Rio Tinto, plc*, 550 F.3d 822 (9th Cir. 2008).

335 *Ibid*. at 828.

> is considered essential to the smooth operation of international tribunals whose jurisdiction is established only through explicit consent from other sovereigns, then it is all the more significant in the absence of such explicit consent to jurisdiction.[336]

The majority then proposed a framework for determining the appropriateness of requiring the exhaustion of local remedies. First, the defendant bears the burden to plead and justify the exhaustion requirement, including the availability of local remedies, a presumption that can subsequently be rebutted by the plaintiff by showing the futility of exhaustion. Second, to satisfy the exhaustion rule, "it is not sufficient that a plaintiff merely initiate a suit, but rather, the plaintiff must obtain a final decision of the highest court in the hierarchy of courts in the legal system at issue, or show that the state of the law or availability of remedies would make further appeal futile."[337] Third, the effectiveness of the local remedy is to be assessed in light of its utility to the petitioner, its timeliness and enforceability. Thus, if a US court is not convinced that an effective remedy could have been obtained in the foreign jurisdiction, it should not abstain from exercising its jurisdiction under *ATCA*. The concurring judges held the exhaustion rule to be mandated by *ATCA*,[338] while the dissenting judges would have excluded the rule altogether.[339]

The proposition that a state may determine the admissibility of foreign claims in its courts is unexceptionable. However, in a jurisdiction where international law forms part of the law of the land, the 2007 decision and 2008 dissents in *Sarei* are arguably at odds with basic tenets of international law. The exhaustion of local remedies rule is "an important principle of international customary law."[340] Insofar as *ATCA* claims derive from international customary law and in keeping with the canon that statutes ought to be construed, where possible, in conformity with international law,[341] it can be argued that *ATCA* claims should properly be subject to an exhaustion of local remedies require-

336 *Ibid.* at 830.
337 *Ibid.* at 832.
338 *Ibid.* at 833–40, Judge Bea; and at 840–41, Judge Kleinfeld.
339 *Ibid.* at 837–41, Judge Ikuta; and at 841–46, Judge Reinhardt.
340 *Case on Elettronica Sicula S.p.A (ELSI) (United States v. Italy)*, [1989] I.C.J. Rep. 15 at para. 50; Crawford, above note 291 at 265.
341 *Murray v. Schooner Charming Betsy*, 6 U.S. 64 (1804).

ment. In its *amicus* brief in *Sosa*, the European Commission argued in favour of a broad principle of transnational civil jurisdiction "predicated on a showing that there was no reasonable prospect of redress in either a State exercising jurisdiction on a traditional basis or through an international mechanism."[342] It may equally be argued, on the other hand, that little would be gained by requiring the exhaustion of local remedies in *ATCA* cases since the doctrine's underlying goals are largely addressed by other domestic prudential doctrines such as *forum non conveniens*. Both the local remedies and *forum non conveniens* doctrines seek to strike a balance between preventing denials of justice and ensuring that claims are determined by the most appropriate decider.[343] The Supreme Court in *Sosa* hinted in a footnote that it might settle this "in an appropriate case."[344]

Other procedural issues affect *ATCA* jurisdiction. In cases that potentially compromise US foreign relations, courts have resorted to certain common law doctrines where claims appear too political or too remote, namely, the political question doctrine, the Act of State doctrine, *forum non conveniens*, and immunity. These will be discussed in Chapters 5, 6, and 7.

342 Brief of *Amicus Curiae* European Commission in *Sosa v. Alvarez-Machain*, 2004 WL 177036 at 24.

343 See, generally, Chapters 4 and 6.

344 *Sosa*, above note 108 at 733, n. 21 and 760, Breyer J concurring.

CHAPTER THREE

The *Torture Victim Protection Act* and other US Jurisdictional Bases

"Congress . . . has not only expressed no disagreement with our view of the proper exercise of the judicial power, but has responded to its most notable instance by enacting legislation supplementing the judicial determination in some detail."

—Justice D.H. Souter[1]

A. INTRODUCTION

In addition to the *Alien Tort Claims Act* (*ATCA*), US federal courts may assert jurisdiction in transnational human rights proceedings on a number of statutory bases. Most notable among these is the *Torture Victim Protection Act* (*TVPA*), enacted in 1992 as companion legislation to *ATCA*[2] and aimed at enhancing its jurisdictional grant by providing an explicit statutory cause of action for torture and extrajudicial killing. Other possible jurisdictional avenues include the *Foreign Sovereign Immunities Act* (28 U.S.C. §§ 1330, 1602–11), so-called federal question jurisdiction (28 U.S.C. § 1331), and so-called diversity jurisdiction (28 U.S.C. § 1332). These jurisdictional grants will be discussed in turn in this chapter. Finally, the inherent jurisdiction of state courts over all civil and criminal controversies will be discussed in relation to transnational human rights litigation.

1 *Sosa v. Alvarez-Machain*, 542 U.S. 692 at 731 (2004) [*Sosa*].

2 Both *ATCA* and *TVPA* are codified at 28 U.S.C. § 1350.

B. THE *TORTURE VICTIM PROTECTION ACT*

The *Torture Victim Protection Act*[3] (*TVPA*) consists of three sections. Section 1 establishes the short title of the Act and § 3 defines the terms "torture" and "extrajudicial killing." The salient provision, § 2, reads as follows:

> SECTION 2. ESTABLISHMENT OF CIVIL ACTION.
>
> (a) LIABILITY—An individual who, under actual or apparent authority, or colour of law, of any foreign nation –
>
> (1) subjects an individual to torture shall, in a civil action, be liable for damages to that individual; or
>
> (2) subjects an individual to extrajudicial killing shall, in a civil action, be liable for damages to the individual's legal representative, or to any person who may be a claimant in an action for wrongful death.
>
> (c) EXHAUSTION OF LOCAL REMEDIES.—A court shall decline to hear a claim under this section if the claimant has not exhausted adequate and available remedies in the place in which the conduct giving rise to the claim occurred.
>
> (d) STATUTE OF LIMITATIONS.—No action shall be maintained under this section unless it is commenced within 10 years after the cause of action arose.[4]

C. ELEMENTS OF JURISDICTION

1) Forum for *TVPA* Claims

The *TVPA* is codified as an annotation to *ATCA* at 28 U.S.C. § 1350, that is, under the legislated heads of jurisdiction of the federal district courts.[5] Accordingly, despite the statute's use of the generic term "court," actions under the *TVPA* are necessarily brought in the federal district courts. That being said, as noted by the Senate Committee

---

3 Pub. L. No. 102-256, 106 Stat. 73 (1992).

4 *Ibid.* at § 2.

5 The position of the section in the overall structure of the US Code is as follows:

Title 28: Judiciary and Judicial Procedure
  Part IV: Jurisdiction and Venue
    Chapter 85: District Courts, Jurisdiction
      § 1350—Aliens' Action in Tort

reviewing the bill before its passing, the *TVPA* does not preclude state courts from adjudicating transnational human rights claims pursuant to their inherent jurisdiction. The Senate Committee observed however: "as a practical matter, state courts are not likely to be inclined or well-suited to consider these cases. International human rights cases predictably raise legal issues — such as interpretations of international law — that are matters of federal common law and within the particular expertise of federal courts."[6] As will be discussed below, despite their inherent authority to do so, state courts rarely assert jurisdiction in transnational human rights cases.[7]

2) Plaintiffs under the *TVPA*

The *TVPA* creates a cause of action for two classes of plaintiffs. First, with regards to torture, § 2(a)(1) permits victims to recover against their torturers. Second, with regards to extrajudicial killing, pursuant to § 2(a)(2), a cause of action lies with the deceased victim's "legal representatives" or "any person who may be a claimant in an action for wrongful death." The Senate Committee specified in its report that the term "legal representative" was specifically intended "to include situations in which the executor or executrix of the decedent's estate is suing."[8] In *Wiwa*, the plaintiffs included a British citizen suing as "legal representative" of the estate of a deceased torture victim under § 2(a)(1). The defendant moved to dismiss the claim brought by the legal representative on the grounds that, on its bare terms, § 2(a)(1) allows only torture victims to sue, not their representatives. The court declined to follow this interpretation, as it would result in denying a remedy in the most egregious torture cases, that is, torture that causes the victim to die or to become legally incompetent. As the court noted, such a result would "thwart the purpose of the TVPA to redress and, hence, deter torture."[9]

---

6 Senate Report Accompanying Bill S-313, S. Rep. 102-249 (1991) [*TVPA* Senate Report], in Beth Stephens *et al.*, *International Human Rights Litigation in US Courts*, 2d ed. (Leiden: Martinus Nijhoff Publishers, 2008) at 574 [Stephens 2008].

7 Section E(4), below in this chapter.

8 *TVPA* Senate Report, above note 6 at 575.

9 *Wiwa v. Royal Dutch Petroleum*, No. 96 Civ. 8386 (KMW), 2002 U.S. Dist. Lexis at 3293 at 52–53 (S.D.N.Y. 2002) [*Wiwa 2002*].

One of the notable features of the *TVPA* is its inclusion of US citizens as possible plaintiffs under the statute by using the generic term "individual" in § 2. As emphasized by the Senate Committee, the *TVPA* would "enhance the remedy already available under § 1350 in an important respect: while the *Alien Tort Claims Act* provides a remedy to aliens only, the *TVPA* would extend a civil remedy also to US citizens who may have been tortured abroad."[10] In *Arar*, the district court rejected the claim in part on the basis that "U.S. citizens, and only U.S. citizens, are covered by the *TVPA*."[11] Though the Second Circuit affirmed that decision on other grounds, it corrected the court below, noting: "[w]e . . . observe that past holdings of our Court, as well as those of our sister courts of appeals, strongly suggest that *TVPA* actions may in fact be brought by non-U.S. citizens."[12] Noteworthy instances involving US citizens include the *Ortiz*[13] and *Ford*[14] cases, where American missionaries or their executors sought damages for torture and extrajudicial killing that occurred in Guatemala and El Salvador respectively.

3) Claims under the *TVPA*

The *TVPA* creates a cause of action with regards to (i) "torture," (ii) "extrajudicial killing" committed, or (iii) "under actual or apparent authority, or colour of law." Furthermore, the claim cannot proceed unless (iv) "the plaintiff has exhausted adequate and available remedies in which the conduct giving rise to the claim occurred" and (v) "it is commenced within ten years after the cause of action arose."[15] Each of these components will be discussed in turn.

i) *Torture*. The *TVPA*'s definition of torture (§ 3(b)) is modelled on Article 1 of the *Convention Against Torture* (CAT). Using similar wording,

---

10 *TVPA* Senate Report, above note 6 at 572.

11 *Arar v. Ashcroft*, 414 F. Supp. 2d 250 (E.D.N.Y. 2006).

12 *Arar v. Ashcroft*, 532 F.3d 157 at 176, n.13 (2d Cir. 2008). The court cited the following cases as authority for that proposition: *Wiwa v. Royal Dutch Petroleum Co.*, 226 F.3d 88 at 104–5 (2d Cir. 2000); *Kadić v. Karadzić*, 70 F.3d 232 at 236 (2d Cir. 1995) [*Kadić*]; *Arce v. Garcia*, 434 F.3d 1254 at 1257–58 (11th Cir. 2006) [*Garcia*]; *Hilao v. Estate of Marcos*, 103 F.3d 767 at 771 (9th Cir. 1996) [*Hilao 1996*].

13 The case of Dianne Ortiz was tried jointly with the *Xuncax* litigation, *Xuncax v. Gramajo*, 886 F. Supp. 162 (D. Mass. 1995) [*Xuncax*].

14 *Ford Estate v. Garcia*, 289 F.3d 1283 (11th Cir. 2002).

15 Pub. L. No. 102-256, 106 Stat. 73 (1992).

both the *TVPA* and CAT definitions describe torture as the intentional infliction of physical pain or mental suffering for such purposes as obtaining information, punishment or intimidation.

TVPA, § 3(b)

(b) For the purposes of this Act—

(1) the term "torture" means any act, directed against an individual in the offender's custody or physical control, by which severe pain or suffering (other than pain or suffering arising only from or inherent in, or incidental to, lawful sanctions), whether physical or mental, is intentionally inflicted on that individual for such purposes as obtaining from that individual or a third person information or a confession, punishing that individual for an act that individual or a third person has committed or is suspected of having committed, intimidating or coercing that individual or a third person, or for any reason based on discrimination of any kind; and

(2) mental pain or suffering refers to prolonged mental harm caused by or resulting from—

(A) the intentional infliction or threatened infliction of severe physical pain or suffering;

(B) the administration or application, or threatened administration or application, of mind altering substances or other procedures calculated to disrupt profoundly the senses or the personality;

(C) the threat of imminent death; or

(D) the threat that another individual will imminently be subjected to death, severe physical pain or suffering, or the administration or application of mind altering substances or other procedures calculated to disrupt profoundly the senses or personality.

CAT, Article 1

1. For the Purposes of this Convention, torture means any act by which severe pain or suffering, whether physical or mental, is intentionally inflicted on a person for such purposes as obtaining from him or a third person information or a confession, punishing him for an act he or a third person has committed or is suspected of having committed, or intimidating or coercing him or a third person, or for any reason based on discrimination of any kind, when such pain or suffering is inflicted by or at the instigation of or with the consent or acquiescence of a public official or other person acting in an official capacity. It does not include pain or suffering arising only from, inherent in or incidental to lawful sanctions.

Significantly, both definitions exempt from the scope of torture the pain and suffering that might arise from or be inherent in lawful punishment, that is, "sanctions authorized by domestic law or by judicial interpretation of such law."[16] Such sanctions could not go so far however as to defeat the object and purpose the international prohibition of torture. The *TVPA* definition of torture goes further than the CAT in that it defines the meaning of "mental pain or suffering" (§ 3(b)(2)), as "prolonged mental harm" caused by the infliction or threat of infliction of physical pain, of mind altering substances, death or threats that others will be subject to such treatment. The *TVPA* also contains a "custody" requirement that is absent from the CAT.

ii) *Extrajudicial killing.* The *TVPA* defines extrajudicial killing in terms that trace the common Article 3(1)(d) of the *Geneva Conventions.* For *TVPA* purposes, extrajudicial killing is described at § 3(a) as a "deliberated killing not authorized by a previous judgment pronounced by a regularly constituted court affording all the judicial guarantees which are recognized as indispensable by civilized peoples."[17] Perhaps not surprisingly given US policy on capital punishment, the definition goes on to expressly exclude from the scope of the *TVPA* "such killing that, under international law, is lawfully carried out under the authority of a foreign nation." The House of Representatives Judicial Committee was satisfied that the word "deliberated" was sufficient to exclude "killings that lack the requisite extrajudicial intent, such as those caused by a police officer's authorized use of deadly force."[18]

iii) *Under actual or apparent authority, or colour of law.* Pursuant to § 2(a) of the *TVPA*, extraterritorial torture or extrajudicial killings give rise to a cause of action only if such acts are perpetrated "under actual or apparent authority, or colour of law". This phrase, according to the House of Representatives, "makes clear that the plaintiff must establish some governmental involvement in the torture or killing to prove a claim. . . . [It] does not attempt to deal with torture or

16 *TVPA* Senate Report, above note 6 at 572.

17 Pub. L. No. 102-256, 106 Stat. 73 (1992) at § 3.

18 H.R. Rep. No. 367 (1991) [*TVPA* H.R. Report], reprinted in Stephens 2008, above note 6 at 561.

killing by purely private groups."[19] The congressional committees that shouldered the *TVPA* both stated that courts should strive to "give the fullest coverage possible" to the words "apparent authority" and construe them in accordance with the principles of agency law which centres on the plaintiff's subjective and reasonable belief that the defendant was acting under authority.[20] For its part, the expression "colour of law" should be interpreted in a manner consistent with 42 U.S.C. § 1983, the provision that authorizes lawsuits against US officials for the violations of civil and constitutional rights. This approach is consonant with the judicial standard employed in certain *ATCA* claims involving foreign government officials. In *Forti I*, the court held that "claims for tortious conduct of government officials under 28 U.S.C. § 1350 may be analogized to domestic lawsuits brought under 42 U.S.C. § 1983, where plaintiffs must allege both deprivation of a federally protected right and action under colour of state law."[21] US courts have developed four different standards to determine whether individual conduct amounts to state action, and each are applicable to *TVPA* litigation, namely, the "nexus test", the "symbiotic relationship test", the "joint action test" and the "public function test."[22]

iv) *Exhaustion of local remedies.* Section 2(b), directs the court to decline jurisdiction until the plaintiff has "exhausted adequate and available remedies in the place in which the conduct giving rise to the claim occurred." In commenting on this feature of the *TVPA*, the House Committee explained it was designed to ensure that "US courts will not intrude into cases more appropriately handled by courts where the alleged torture or killing occurred. It can also avoid exposing US Courts to unnecessary burdens, and can be expected to encourage the development of meaningful remedies in other countries."[23] The Senate Committee for its part focused on the procedural aspects of the provision, noting that, as matter of international practice, it falls to the defendant to prove that the plaintiff failed to exhaust local remedies. Thereafter, "once the de-

19 *Ibid.* at 565.

20 *TVPA* Senate Report, above note 6 at 577.

21 *Forti v. Suarez-Mason*, 672 F. Supp. 1531 at 1546 (N.D. Cal. 1987) [*Forti 1987*].

22 Stephens 2008, above note 6 at 251–57.

23 *TVPA* H.R. Report, above note 18 at 565–66.

fendant makes a showing of remedies abroad which have not been exhausted, the burden shifts to the plaintiff to rebut by showing that the local remedies were ineffective, unobtainable unduly prolonged, inadequate or obviously futile."[24] Indeed, both the *TVPA* and international law require nothing more than the exhaustion of "adequate and available remedies."[25] The *Xuncax* court interpreted § 2(b) as not being a "prohibitively stringent condition precedent to recovery under the statute."[26] In that case, local remedies were deemed exhausted where criminal proceedings against the defendant in Guatemala had not progressed in several years and national law prevented the initiation of civil proceedings until final judgment is rendered in the criminal proceedings.

v) *Limitation period*. Finally, § 2(c) provides that *TVPA* actions shall not be maintained unless commenced within ten years after the cause of action arose. Though the congressional committees agreed that courts should not adjudicate stale claims, both emphasized the importance of applying equitable tolling principles in calculating the period.[27] For instance the period during which a defendant was immune from lawsuit, or concealed his whereabouts or identity, should be excluded from the limitations period. Likewise, the plaintiff's inability to initiate civil proceedings due to imprisonment also suspends the statute of limitations. In *Arce*, the Eleventh Circuit held that it was "Congress's clear intent that courts toll the [*TVPA*] statute of limitations so long as the defendants are outside the reach of the United States courts."[28] In that case, the plaintiffs commenced proceedings in 1999 against Salvadorian state officials, with respect to torture that allegedly occurred in 1979 and

24 *TVPA* Senate Report, above note 6 at 579; *Hilao 1996*, above note 12 at 778; *Wiwa 2002*, above note 9 at 55–56; *Mehinović v. Vucković*, 198 F. Supp. 2d 1322 at 1347 (N.D. Ga. 2002) [*Mehinović 2002*]; *Sinaltrainal v. Coca-Cola Co.*, 256 F. Supp. 2d 1345 at 1358 (S.D. Fla. 2003) [*Sinaltrainal*]; *Cabello (Estate) v. Fernandez-Larios*, 291 F. Supp. 2d 1360 at 1366 (S.D. Fla. 2003). The *TVPA* exhaustion requirement is consistent with the "prudential exhaustion" principle applied with respect to *ATCA*: *Sarei v. Rio Tinto, plc*, 550 F.3d 822 (9th Cir. 2008).

25 James Crawford, *The International Law Commission's Articles on State Responsibility: Introduction, Text and Commentaries* (Cambridge: Cambridge University Press, 2002) at 246.

26 *Xuncax*, above note 13 at 178.

27 *TVPA* H.R. Report, above note 18 at 566; *TVPA* Senate Report, above note 6 at 580–81.

28 *Garcia*, above note 12.

> 1980. The record supported the conclusion that, until the end of Salvadorian civil war in 1992, the military would have thwarted any efforts to redress the human rights violations it perpetrated. "Evidence of those violations would have been suppressed. Potential witnesses would have been intimidated and perhaps tortured if they came forward. The plaintiffs legitimately feared that their family members and friends remaining in El Salvador would be subject to harsh reprisals and the same brutalities that the plaintiffs suffered."[29] In such circumstances, applying equitable tolling principles, the Circuit held that the limitations period did not start running until the defendants became permanent residents of the United States in 1989.

The ten-year statute of limitations under the *TVPA* has since been extended by analogy to *ATCA* claims.[30] In *Xuncax*, where the claim of one plaintiff arose prior to the *TVPA*'s enactment, the court found the statute to be retroactive. In the court's view, the usual presumption against legislative retroactivity did not apply to the *TVPA*, which it characterized as a jurisdictional statute that affects "the power of the court rather than the rights and obligations of the parties."[31] In addition, a statute is presumed to apply retroactively when it is designed to remedy a "perceived jurisdictional gap" in existing legislation, as does the *TVPA* with regards to *ATCA*.[32]

4) Defendants under the *TVPA*

The *TVPA* has been drafted and interpreted to include an expansive class of potential defendants. Section 2(a) establishes a cause of action against "an individual who, under actual or apparent authority, or colour of law, of any foreign nation" subjects another individual to torture or extrajudicial killing. Firstly, the district courts must have personal jurisdiction over the defendant. In *Kadić*, the defendant Karadzić challenged the jurisdiction of the court on the basis that he was served while visiting New York on UN business. The court dismissed the ob-

29 *Ibid.* at 1263.

30 *In re S. African Apartheid Litigation*, 617 F. Supp. 2d 228 at 288 (S.D.N.Y. 2009); *Garcia*, above note 12 at 1261–62; *Van Tu v. Koster*, 364 F.3d 1196 at 1199 (10th Cir. 2004).

31 *Xuncax*, above note 13 at 177, citing *Landgraf v. USI Film Products*, 511 U.S. 244 (1994).

32 *Ibid.*

jection, ruling that transient physical presence in a district, no matter how brief, is sufficient to establish the jurisdiction of the court over a properly served defendant.[33] Service *ex juris*, or so-called "long arm" jurisdiction, is also possible under the *TVPA* with regards to persons "who could be subjected to the jurisdiction of a court of general jurisdiction in the state in which the district court is located."[34]

The Eastern District Court of Louisiana held, using a plain language interpretation of the *TVPA*, that the term "individual" in § 2(a) did not include corporations. The court found support for its reading in the absence of specific direction on this point from Congress in the legislative materials.[35] The Court of Appeals for the Fifth Circuit affirmed that decision on other grounds and did not discuss the meaning of the word "individual."[36] The opposite conclusion was reached in *Sinaltrainal*. In that case, the court viewed the absence of congressional direction as an indication that the liability of corporations was not excluded under the *TVPA*. "Moreover," the district court continued, "the Supreme Court in *Clinton v. New York* recently held that the term 'individual' is synonymous with 'person,' acknowledging that 'person' often has a broader meaning in the law than in ordinary usage."[37] With this precedent, coupled with the settled interpretation of *ATCA* as permitting claims against corporations,[38] the court held that "had Congress intended to exclude corporations from liability under the TVPA, it could and would have expressly stated so."[39] The inclusion of corporations as defendants under the *TVPA* is consonant with the stated purpose of the *TVPA* extending the *ATCA* cause of action to US plaintiffs. To be sure, it would be odd if the *TVPA* failed to encompass corporate defendants and left US citizens with a narrower remedy than "aliens" under *ATCA* and with fewer defendants from whom to obtain it.

The term "individual" in § 2(a), in the opinion of Congress, makes "crystal clear that foreign states or their entities cannot be sued . . . .

33 *Kadić*, above note 12 at 247. See also *Burnham v. Superior Court of California*, 495 U.S. 604 (1990).

34 Fed. R. Civ. P. 4(k)(1)(A); Stephens 2008, above note 6 at 249, n. 11.

35 *Beanal v. Freeport-McMoran Inc.*, 969 F. Supp. 362 at 381–82 (E.D. La. 1997) [*Beanal* 1997].

36 *Beanal v. Freeport-McMoran Inc.*, 197 F.3d 161 at 169 (5th Cir. 1999).

37 *Sinaltrainal*, above note 24 at 1358; *Clinton v. New York*, 524 U.S. 417 at 428 (1998).

38 See *Presbyterian Church of Sudan v. Talisman Energy Inc.*, 244 F. Supp. 2d 289 (S.D.N.Y. 2003) for an illustrative survey of the cases.

39 *Sinaltrainal*, above note 24 at 1359.

Consequently the *TVPA* is not meant to override the *Foreign Sovereign Immunities Act (FSIA)* of 1976."[40] The *FSIA* thus remains, as held by the Supreme Court in *Amerada Hess*, wholly determinative of the jurisdiction of US courts over foreign states.[41] The Senate Committee further noted that the *TVPA* does nothing to alter head-of-state immunity at common law.[42] Courts declined to exercise personal jurisdiction over Jean-Bertrand Aristide[43] and Robert Mugabe[44] under the *TVPA* on the basis of head-of-state immunity. By contrast, *TVPA* jurisdiction was asserted over Radovan Karadzić, the self-proclaimed president of the Republika Srpska. The court denied Karadzić's immunity claim since Republika Srpska was not a recognized state. In addition to claiming immunity, Karadzić argued that the court lacked jurisdiction since, at the time of service, he was present in New York as an invitee of the United Nations. While the court agreed that the *TVPA* did not supersede diplomatic and consular immunity or that of international organizations, it was satisfied that neither applied since Karadzić was served outside the protected premises of the United Nations.[45]

D. THE PURPOSE AND POLITICS OF THE *TVPA*

The foregoing exposition of the *TVPA* tracked the express language of the statute and the interpretation it has received by Congress and the judiciary. Despite giving rise to some disagreement as to the meaning of certain terms, the *TVPA* has been the object of relative consensus from the outset, at least with regards to its substantive requirements and operation. In clear terms, the *TVPA* permits victims of torture and extrajudicial killing and their families to sue wrongdoers in US district courts, provided certain substantive and procedural requirements are met. Two wider aspects of the *TVPA*, however, warrant further discussion. First, there are particular consequences that flow from the cause of action granted by the *TVPA*, especially with regards to *ATCA*.

---

40 *TVPA* H.R. Report, above note 18 at 576; *TVPA* Senate Report, above note 6 at 566.

41 *Argentine Republic v. Amerada Hess Shipping Corp.*, 488 U.S. 428 (1989) [*Amerada Hess*].

42 *TVPA* Senate Report, above note 6 at 576.

43 *Lafontant v. Aristide*, 844 F. Supp. 128 (E.D.N.Y. 1994).

44 *Tachiona v. Mugabe*, 169 F. Supp. 2d 259 (S.D.N.Y. 2001).

45 *Kadić*, above note 12 at 246–48. See also American Law Institute, *Restatement of the Law (3d) of Foreign Relations Law of the United States* (St. Paul, MN: American Law Institute, 1988) at § 469, n. 8 [*Restatement*].

Second, there is some uncertainty as to the relationship between the *TVPA* and the *Convention Against Torture* (CAT). These issues will be examined in turn.

1) The *TVPA*'s Relationship to *ATCA*

The avowed purpose of the *TVPA* is the creation of a clear cause of action in relation to torture and extrajudicial killing.[46] Accordingly, as some courts have noted, the *TVPA* can be fairly viewed as a direct congressional endorsement of *ATCA* jurisprudence and of the general policy that US courts continue to "serve as forums of redress for violations of international law."[47] The Senate's view on this point is unequivocal:

> The *TVPA* would establish an unambiguous basis for a cause of action that has been successfully maintained under the existing law, section 1350 of title 28 of the U.S. Code . . . . The *TVPA* would . . . enhance the remedy already available under §1350 in an important respect: while [*ATCA*] provides a remedy for aliens only, the *TVPA* would extend a civil remedy also to US citizens who may have tortured abroad. Official torture and summary executions merit special attention in a statute expressly addressed to those practices. At the same time, claims based on torture or summary execution do not exhaust the list of actions that may be appropriately covered by section 1350. Consequently that statute should remain intact.[48]

The *TVPA* is thus meant to supplement *ATCA*, not replace it.[49] Substantively speaking however, the *TVPA* is one-dimensional: while creating a right of action for plaintiffs, the *TVPA* does not grant federal courts jurisdiction over those claims it empowers litigants to bring. Accordingly, courts must look to other statutes to establish their subject-matter jurisdiction over *TVPA* proceedings.

The most relevant jurisdictional grant for *TVPA* purposes is obviously *ATCA*, as was noted by the court in *Sinaltrainal*: "Although the *TVPA* creates a private cause of action for torture and extrajudicial

46 *TVPA* H.R. Report, above note 18 at 564; *TVPA* Senate Report, above note 6 at 571.

47 *Doe v. Islamic Salvation Front*, 993 F. Supp. 3 at 7 (D.C.C. 1998). See also *Sosa*, above note 1 at 731; *Abebe-Jiri v. Negewo*, 72 F.3d 844 at 248 (11th Cir. 1996); *Kadić*, above note 12 at 243.

48 *TVPA* Senate Report, above note 6 at 564.

49 *Sosa*, above note 1 at 731.

killing perpetrated by individuals acting under the colour of law of any foreign nation, it does not confer jurisdiction standing alone. Claims for torture and extrajudicial killing may be entertained only if they fall within the jurisdiction conferred by the *ATCA*."[50] Indeed, as the *TVPA*'s codification under § 1350 indicates, there is a direct symbiotic relationship between the two statutes: while the *TVPA* enhances *ATCA* with its definitions, its statute of limitations and (according to some courts at least[51]) its requirement to exhaust local remedies, *ATCA* lends its jurisdictional grant to the *TVPA*.[52] However, contrary to the *Sinaltrainal* court's assertion, *ATCA* is not the "only" possible jurisdictional footing for *TVPA* claims. Courts have also identified "federal question" jurisdiction under 28 U.S.C. § 1331 as a likely candidate, though no clear advantage is gained by invoking it.[53]

Courts and Congress have said that *ATCA* should remain intact and that "there is no reason to conclude that by enacting the TVPA Congress took away causes of action for torture and extrajudicial killings under § 1350."[54] This is questionable. If *ATCA* can be used in every civil claim involving torture and extrajudicial killing, then arguably, the procedural controls of the *TVPA*—that is, the limitations periods and the requirement to exhaust local remedies—can be circumvented at the court's discretion by invoking *ATCA*, as was apparently done in at least one case. In *Abebe-Jiri v. Negewo*, three Ethiopian women sued a former official of the Dergue regime in relation to their unlawful detention, torture and cruel, inhuman and degrading treatment. In their statement of claim, the plaintiffs based their action on *ATCA*, the *TVPA*, and federal question jurisdiction. The court found the defendant liable on all counts but only on the basis of *ATCA* and federal question jurisdiction.[55] Though it is unclear why the court declined to apply the *TVPA* in relation to the alleged torture, it is possible, as surmised by one commentator, "that the court perceived that it had a choice. Because

---

50 *Sinaltrainal*, above note 24 at 1356–57.

51 See discussion at Chapter 2, Section D(6)(c).

52 *Wiwa 2002*, above note 9 at 10.

53 *Kadić*, above note 12 at 246; *Xuncax*, above note 13 at 178; *Al-Odah v. United States*, 321 F. 3d. 1134 at 1146 (D.C. Cir. 2003). See Section E(2), below in this chapter, for discussion on § 1331.

54 *Beanal 1997*, above note 35 at 380; *TVPA* Senate Report, above note 6 at 259. See also *Kadić*, above note 12 at 241; *Wiwa 2002*, above note 9 at 12.

55 *Abebe-Jiri v. Negewo*, 1993 U.S. Dist. Lexis 21158 at 9 (N.D. Ga. 1993) [*Abebe-Jiri*].

the plaintiffs' claim included international violations in addition to torture, the court may have deemed it to be within its discretion to use ATCA instead of the TVPA."[56] However, had the court applied the *TVPA* as the cause of action, the torture claims would likely have been dismissed, as there was no evidence that the plaintiffs pursued remedies in Ethiopia or that the claim was brought within the prescribed statute of limitations. It is possible that the court would have found that no "adequate" remedy was available or possible in Ethiopia and applied equitable tolling to the statute of limitations in light of the plaintiffs' imprisonment — but it said nothing in this respect. Nevertheless, the point remains: unless the *TVPA* is found to be the exclusive cause of action for torture and extrajudicial killing, the important procedural features of the *TVPA* are negated by maintaining a concurrent cause of action for those wrongs under *ATCA*. While some US judicial circuits apply the *TVPA*'s procedural provisions to *ATCA*, as was discussed in the previous chapter, not all of them do so as a matter of course. Given its specificity and built-in procedural controls, there are strong reasons to prefer the *TVPA* to *ATCA* as the proper vehicle for civil claims in relation to torture and extrajudicial killing in US federal courts.

2) The *TVPA* and the *Convention Against Torture*

House Representative Gus Yatron and Senator Arlen Specter, both from Pennsylvania, unsuccessfully introduced the *TVPA* bill in their respective legislative chambers twice during the Reagan administration and once during the first year of the Bush presidency. Finally, after being reintroduced in the 101st Congress, the Committees on the Judiciary of both chambers recommended that the *TVPA* bill be passed.[57] From the outset, the *TVPA*'s relationship with the CAT caused disagreement between the legislative and executive branches. The CAT entered into force on 27 June 1987 and the US became a signatory on 18 April 1988. On 27 October 1990, the Senate authorized the President to

56 Christopher W. Haffke, "The *Torture Victim Protection Act*: More Symbol Than Substance" (1994) 43 Emory L.J. 1467 at 1484.

57 In the House of Representatives the bill was introduced in October 1987 (H.R. 1417), again in April 1989 (H.R. 1662), and April 1991 (H.R. 2092), finally successfully passing in November 1991. In the Senate, the bill was first introduced in June 1986 (S.2528), again in March 1987 (S.824), September 1989 (S.1629), and January 1991 (S.313), finally successfully passing in March 1992.

ratify the CAT.[58] One year later, in November 1991, the Committees on the Judiciary of both chambers expressed the view that the *TVPA* gave effect to US obligations under the CAT to provide victims of torture with redress and compensation. In its report on the *TVPA*, the House of Representatives noted:

> The [CAT] was signed by the United States on April 18, 1988, and ratified by the US Senate on October 27, 1990. Essentially enforcement-oriented, this Convention obligates state parties to adopt measures to ensure that torturers are held legally accountable for their acts. One such obligation is to provide means of civil redress to victims of torture. Judicial protections against flagrant human rights violations are often least effective in those countries where such abuses are most prevalent . . . . The *Torture Victim Protection Act* (*TVPA*), H.R. 2092, would respond to this situation.[59]

The Senate concurred:

> This legislation will carry out the intent of the *Convention Against Torture and Other Cruel, Inhuman or Degrading Treatment or Punishment*, which was ratified by the US Senate on October 27, 1990. The Convention obligates state parties to adopt measures to ensure that torturers within their territories are held legally accountable for their acts. This legislation will do precisely that—by making sure that torturers and death squads will no longer have a safe haven in the United States.[60]

The Bush Administration opposed the enactment of the *TVPA*. The Departments of State and Justice had both voiced their concerns about one of the *TVPA*'s predecessor bills,[61] arguing that such legislation could provoke retaliatory litigation against US officials and unduly hamper foreign relations.[62] President Bush echoed these sentiments when he signed the *TVPA* into law on 12 March 1992. While generally approving

58 136 Cong. Rec. S17491 (27 October 1990).

59 *TVPA* H.R. Report, above note 18 at 563.

60 *TVPA* Senate Report, above note 6 at 571.

61 *Torture Victim Protection Act of 1989*: Bills H.R. 1662 and S. 1629.

62 *Torture Victim Protection Act of 1989: Hearing on H.R. 1662 and S. 1629 before the Subcommittee on Immigration and Refugee Affairs of the Senate Committee on the Judiciary*, 101st Cong., 2d Sess. (1990) (statements of John McGinnis, Department of Justice and David Stewart, Department of State).

of the "fundamental goals" of the legislation, he repeatedly insisted that the *TVPA* did nothing to implement the CAT:

> I regret that the legislation proposed by the Administration to implement the [CAT] has not yet been enacted . . . . The Senate gave its advice and consent to the Torture Convention on October 27, 1990, but the United States cannot proceed to become a party until the necessary implementing legislation in is in place . . . . I note that H.R. 2092 does not help to implement the Torture Convention and does present a number of potential problems about which the Administration has expressed concern in the past . . . . I again call upon Congress to make a real contribution to the fight against torture by enacting the implementing legislation of the Torture Convention so that we can finally ratify that important treaty.[63]

The *TVPA* was thus passed, with both the executive and legislative branches expressing opposing views with regards to the statute's relationship to the CAT. To resolve what effect, if any, the enactment of the *TVPA* had in relation to the CAT obligations of the United States, it is necessary to bear in mind the particularities of the US treaty making process under the Constitution as well as the particular history of the implementation of the CAT in US law.

Both reports from the Committees on the Judiciary on the *TVPA* claim that the Senate "ratified" the CAT on 27 October 1990. This is inaccurate. As President Bush properly stated upon signing the *TVPA*, the Senate gave its "advice and consent" to ratify; it did not ratify the CAT, nor could it have done so. Ratification, as defined under the *Vienna Convention on the Law of Treaties*, is "the international act so named whereby a State establishes on the international plane its consent to be bound by a treaty."[64] Ratification is an international act that can only be performed by the Executive.[65] For its part, the Senate's "advice and consent" to ratify amounts to the domestic confirmation of the United States' intention to be bound by a treaty. Therefore, while Senate's "advice and consent" remains a constitutional prerequisite to ratification

63 Statement of President George Bush upon signing into law the *Torture Victim Protection Act of 1991*, reprinted in Stephens 2008, above note 6 at 585.

64 *Vienna Convention on the Law of Treaties*, 23 May 1969, 1155 U.N.T.S. 331, art. 2(1)(b).

65 On the international character of ratification, see Anthony Aust, *Modern Treaty Law and Practice* (Cambridge: Cambridge University Press, 2000) at 81.

and domestic implementation, it is to be distinguished from ratification under international law.

As noted above, the Senate gave its "advice and consent" to ratify the CAT in 1990, yet domestic implementation did not occur until 1994. The CAT was partially implemented on 30 April 1994 when Congress amended the *United States Code* and made torture a federal crime.[66] Seven months later, on 20 November 1994, the President ratified the CAT.[67] Given this timeframe and notwithstanding Congress' opinion on the matter, can it be said that the *TVPA* constitutes a domestic implementation of Article 14 obligations to provide civil redress? That question remains unsettled. Timing is not likely an issue: international law does not preclude the domestic implementation of a treaty prior to its ratification.[68] In this sense, the *TVPA* could very well be, as Congress appears to have intended, an early and partial implementation of the CAT. On the other hand, it could be objected that the *TVPA* does not implement Article 14 given the "understanding" that Congress took of that Article when it gave its "advice and consent" to ratify the CAT in 1990. The Senate's authorization to ratify was subject to a series of reservations and understandings. With regards to Article 14, the Senate held that "it is the understanding of the United States that Article 14 requires a State Party to provide a private right of action for damages only for acts of torture committed in territory under the jurisdiction of that State Party."[69] Insofar as the *TVPA* cause of action extends to extraterritorial torture, in addition to torture committed in the United States, it could be argued that the statute does not carry out the intent of Article 14 as that article was "understood" by Congress. On the other hand, states are permitted to implement wider terms than those required by the treaty, provided that in so doing

---

66 *Foreign Relations Authorization Act, Fiscal Years 1994 and 1995*, Pub. L. 103–236, 108 Stat. 464 (1994), § 506. Section 506 is entitled "Torture Convention Implementation." The amendment is a partial implementation of the CAT insofar as it relates solely to the obligation to make torture an offence in US criminal law as provided by arts. 4 & 5 of the CAT. Other obligations under the CAT are not implemented by the 1994 legislation.

67 Depositary Notification, Ratification by the United States of America, *Convention Against Torture and Other Cruel, Inhuman or Degrading Treatment or Punishment*, United Nations, Reference C.N.382.1994.Treaties-6 (27 February 1995).

68 *Salomon v. Commissioners of Customs & Excise*, [1967] 2 Q.B. 116 at 143 (C.A.).

69 Senate Resolution, advising and consenting to ratification of the CAT with reservations and understandings, 136 Cong. Rec. S.17491, § II(3) (27 October 1990).

they are not defeating the treaty's object and purpose.[70] In a report to the Committee on Torture, the United States recognized that "federal law currently provides rights which are potentially broader than those required by Article 14 with respect to obtaining redress for acts of torture occurring outside of United States territory."[71] The Committee praised the US for this feature of its legal system, with specific reference to Article 14.[72]

Another issue with regard to the *TVPA*'s relationship to the CAT is the extent to which the treaty was ultimately implemented in domestic law. The 1994 legislation is a partial implementation of the obligations contained in the CAT insofar as it relates only to Articles 4 and 5, pursuant to which states agree to make torture a crime in their domestic law. The 1994 legislation made torture a criminal offence in federal law. In addition to criminalizing torture, the legislation goes on to expressly exclude the possibility of civil actions: "Nothing . . . in this chapter [shall] be construed as creating any substantive or procedural right enforceable by law by any party in any civil proceeding."[73] Given the silence of the legislative record on this last provision, it is difficult to draw any meaningful conclusions as to its purpose or relation to the *TVPA*. Bearing in mind Congress' view that the *TVPA* carried out the intention of the CAT, it may be that Congress excluded civil remedies in the 1994 implementation of the CAT because it felt that it would have been redundant to provide a civil cause of action for torture since, by that time, civil redress was already available under the *TVPA*.

The *TVPA*'s normative relationship to the CAT matters for at least two reasons. First, if the *TVPA* were connected to the CAT in one way or another, it would constitute important state practice with regards to a vastly under-implemented provision of the CAT (Article 14). So far, the Yukon Territory is the only jurisdiction to have expressly created a civil cause of action pursuant to the CAT in relation to both in-

70 In this case however, it is possible that the *TVPA* cause of action over torture occurring outside the United States strains conformity with established international rules regarding extraterritorial jurisdiction. That issue will be discussed at length in Chapter 5.

71 *Report of the United States of America to the Committee against Torture Under Article 19 of the Convention*, CAT/C/28/Add.5 (15 October 1999) at § 268.

72 Report of the Committee against Torture, 23rd & 24th Sess., A/55/44 (1 January 2000) at § 178(b).

73 18 U.S.C. § 2340B.

tra- and extraterritorial torture committed by its officials.[74] Second, if a connection between the convention and the statute were established, courts could resort to the CAT in interpreting the *TVPA* should an ambiguity ever arise. The connection need not be explicit; indeed, the statute need not even refer to the convention for it to be relevant.[75] Cogent extrinsic evidence that the enactment was intended to carry out the intention of the convention will normally suffice.[76] In this case, their common subject matter and consonant goals, the statements of Congress on the purpose of the *TVPA* in relation to the CAT, coupled with the fact that the *TVPA*'s definition of torture (§ 3(b)) was modelled on that of the CAT, is some evidence in support of the claim that the statute carries out obligations under the convention.

E. OTHER JURISDICTIONAL BASES

In addition to *ATCA* and *TVPA*, US courts have asserted jurisdiction in transnational human rights claims on several other bases. These are the *Foreign Sovereign Immunities Act*, so-called federal question jurisdiction, so-called diversity jurisdiction and state law.

1) *Foreign Sovereign Immunities Act*

Pursuant to 28 U.S.C. § 1330, district courts have "original jurisdiction without regard to amount in controversy of any nonjury civil action against a foreign State . . . as to any claim for relief in *personam* with respect to which the foreign State is not entitled to immunity." The issue of whether a foreign state is entitled to immunity in a given case is resolved in accordance with the provisions codified under 28 U.S.C. §§ 1602–11, referred to also as the *Foreign Sovereign Immunities Act* (*FSIA*). As the Supreme Court emphasized, the *FSIA* "must be applied by the district courts in every action against a foreign sovereign, since subject-matter jurisdiction in any such action depends on the existence of one of the specified exceptions to foreign sovereign immunity."[77] The

74 *Torture Prohibition Act*, S.Y. 1988, c. 26.

75 *Hogg v. Toye & Co. Ltd.*, [1935] 1 Ch. 497 at 520.

76 *Salomon*, above note 68 at 144; Ian Brownlie, *Principles of Public International Law*, 6th ed (Oxford: Oxford University Press, 2003) at 46 [Brownlie].

77 *Verlinden B.V. v. Central Bank of Nigeria*, 461 U.S. 480 at 493 (1983) [*Verlinden*].

FSIA has been held to be the "sole basis for obtaining jurisdiction over foreign states" in US courts.[78] The international law of state immunity, the *FSIA*, and the manner in which these determine the jurisdiction of municipal courts in transnational human rights proceedings will be discussed in greater detail in Chapter 7. An outline of *FSIA* provisions is sufficient for the purposes of the present survey of US jurisdictional bases in transnational human rights cases.

At the time of its enactment in 1976,[79] the *FSIA* marked the first unilateral attempt by a state to codify for itself the principles of restrictive immunity.[80] Section 1604 enunciates the basic rule: "Subject to existing international agreements to which the United States is a party at the time of enactment of this Act a foreign state shall be immune from the jurisdiction of the courts of the United States except," the provision continues, "as provided in §§ 1605 to 1607 of this chapter." For their part, §§ 1605–07 enumerate the categories of cases in which foreign states cannot claim immunity. These include proceedings involving: waiver,[81] commercial activities,[82] property taken in violation of international law,[83] property situated in the US,[84] local torts,[85] arbitrations,[86] extraterritorial torture or terrorism,[87] admiralty law,[88] and counterclaims.[89] If a plaintiff's claim falls within the terms of an enumerated exception, the immunity of the foreign state is denied and the jurisdiction of the court upheld.

The extraterritorial torture and terrorism exception is a recent addition to the *FSIA*'s catalogue of exceptions, having been introduced in 1996 and amended many times since. Before its enactment, virtually all human rights claims against foreign states were dismissed for lack of jurisdiction. Unless the circumstances surrounding the alleged

78 *Amerada Hess*, above note 41 at 434.

79 Pub. L. 94-583, 90 Stat. 2892 (21 October 1976).

80 The *European Convention on State Immunity*, E.T.S. No. 74, the first multilateral treaty on state immunity, was opened for signature in 1972. Eight nations have ratified the convention.

81 28 U.S.C. § 1605(a)(1).

82 28 U.S.C. § 1605(a)(2).

83 28 U.S.C. § 1605(a)(3).

84 28 U.S.C. § 1605(a)(4).

85 28 U.S.C. § 1605(a)(5).

86 28 U.S.C. § 1605(a)(6).

87 28 U.S.C. § 1605(a)(7).

88 28 U.S.C. §§ 1605(b) and (d).

89 28 U.S.C. § 1607.

human rights violations presented a sufficient nexus with the terms of the codified exceptions, such as the commercial activity or local tort provisions, state immunity constituted an insurmountable bar to civil redress. Immunity was denied however in a few notable cases. The Republic of Chile was not entitled to immunity in proceedings involving the murder of a Chilean official in Washington, DC, since the crime occurred on US territory, thus triggering the local tort exception. Given the abhorrent character of the impugned state act, the court in that case further noted: "there is no 'discretion' to perpetrate conduct . . . that is clearly contrary to the precepts of humanity as recognized in both national and international law."[90] Similarly, China was denied immunity in proceedings involving the alleged murder of an American citizen by Chinese officials on US soil.[91] In proceedings alleging torture and expropriation, Argentina was deemed to have waived its immunity when it sought the assistance of US courts to affect service of process in other related proceedings.[92] Under US law, a state is not deemed to have implicitly waived its immunity by perpetrating acts that contravene peremptory norms of international law such as torture and genocide.[93]

Since the adoption of the extraterritorial torture and terrorism exception in 1996, the number of human rights claims against foreign states has substantially increased. In its initial form, § 1605(7) permitted: US citizens to bring a claim for compensatory damages against certain designated foreign states for death or personal injury arising from an act of torture, extrajudicial killing, aircraft sabotage, hostage taking or for supporting such activities, provided the plaintiff afforded the foreign state with a reasonable opportunity to settle the claim through arbitration. The exception has been subject to many controversial amendments since 1996, including the authorization to award punitive damages and provisions allowing plaintiffs to access frozen assets and even certain diplomatic property to satisfy judgments obtained under § 1605(7). These provisions are discussed in Chapter 7.

---

90 *Letelier v. Chile*, 488 F. Supp. 665 at 673 (D.D.C. 1980).

91 *Liu v. The Republic of China*, 892 F.2d 1419 (9th Cir. 1989).

92 *Siderman de Blake v. Republic of Argentina*, 965 F.2d 699 (9th Cir. 1992).

93 *Princz v. Federal Republic of Germany*, 26 F.3d 1166 (D.C. Cir. 1994).

2) Federal Question Jurisdiction

The constitutional grant of authority of federal courts to interpret international law under Article III is to be distinguished from its statutory homologue. Under 28 U.S.C. § 1331, district courts have original but not exclusive jurisdiction "of all civil actions arising under the Constitution, law or treaties of the United States." Though the language of the statute clearly traces that of Article III § 2 of the Constitution, it has consistently received a narrower construction.[94] Federal question jurisdiction is subject to the "well-pleaded complaint" rule pursuant to which federal courts have "jurisdiction to hear, originally or by removal from a state court, only those cases in which a well-pleaded complaint establishes either that federal law creates the cause of action or that the plaintiff's right to relief necessarily depends on resolution of a substantial question of federal law."[95] Accordingly, federal question jurisdiction under § 1331, also sometimes referred to as "arising under" jurisdiction, encompasses all claims to which federal law applies, including federal statutes, international treaties and customary law, insofar as the latter is part of the common law.[96] The interpretation of international law has been held to be a "federal question" for § 1331 purposes.[97] Therefore, inasmuch as international law "arises under" the laws of the United States, § 1331 is said to grant district courts subject-matter jurisdiction in transnational human rights proceedings.

That transnational human rights claims are cognizable as a matter of federal question jurisdiction appears to have been assumed from the outset. In *Filártiga*, the Second Circuit opined that jurisdiction could have been asserted under § 1331 as well as under *ATCA*, but that it preferred the latter in light of that provision's specific relevance to the claim.[98] In *Martinez-Baca*, where the claim was brought by a US citizen who could not avail himself of *ATCA*, the court held that allegations of extraterritorial torture, arbitrary detention and cruel, inhuman, and degrading treatment "[arose] under customary international law [and therefore arose] under the laws of the United States for purposes of fed-

94 *Verlinden*, above note 77 at 495.

95 *Franchise Tax Board v. Construction Laborers Vacation Trust*, 463 U.S. 1 at 13 (1983).

96 *Restatement*, above note 45 at § 111 Reporter's note 4.

97 *Banco Nacional de Cuba v. Sabbatino*, 376 U.S. 398 at 415 (1964) [*Banco Nacional*].

98 *Filártiga v. Peña-Irala*, 630 F.2d 876 at 887 (2d Cir 1980) [*Filártiga*].

eral question jurisdiction."[99] The courts in *Forti*[100] and *Abebe-Jiri*[101] also asserted jurisdiction under both *ATCA* and § 1331. The proposition that federal courts can adjudicate *Filártiga*-type claims on the basis of federal question jurisdiction is not unanimously accepted however. Judges Edwards and Bork in *Tel-Oren*,[102] as well as the courts in *Handel*[103] and *Xuncax*[104] took the view that § 1331 is not a stand-alone jurisdictional grant and that its operation requires the existence of an independent federal cause of action. As stated in *Xuncax*:

> [B]ecause international law is not itself a source of private rights of action — as is, for example, the common law of contracts or torts — a plaintiff's claims for violation of human rights cannot ordinarily "arise under" federal-common-law-cuminternational-law [*sic*] and consequently, §1331 jurisdiction does not extend to such claims.

Therefore, it is argued that in the absence of a distinct cause of action for victims of human rights violations (like the *TVPA*), international law cannot be understood to create one on its own, despite its incorporation in US common law. This view has since caused the Second Circuit — the court that first recognized the possibility of federal question jurisdiction in *Filártiga* — to admit that the applicability of § 1331 in transnational human rights litigation remains "an issue of some uncertainty."[105]

This judicial disagreement appears not to hinge on whether international law creates private rights of action, but whether it does so once incorporated into the common law. One possible response is to ask whether it is proper to distinguish international law from domestic law once it is incorporated. If the law of nations is indeed part of the common law as US courts have consistently held, then the cause of action for human rights violations may be provided by the common law itself.[106] In other words, once adopted into the common law, customary

99 *Martinez-Baca v. Suarez-Mason*, 1988 U.S. Dist. Lexis 19470 (N.D. Cal. 1988).
100 *Forti 1987*, above note 21.
101 *Abebe-Jiri*, above note 55.
102 *Tel-Oren v. Libyan Arab Republic*, 726 F.2d 774 at 779–80, n. 4, Edwards J.; and 811, Bork J. (D.C. Cir. 1984).
103 *Handel v. Artukovic*, 601 F. Supp. 1421 at 1428 (C.D. Cal. 1985).
104 *Xuncax*, above note 13 at 194.
105 *Kadić*, above note 12 at 246.
106 William S. Dodge, "The Historical Origins of the *Alien Tort Statute*: A Response to 'Originalists'" (1996) 19 Hast. Int'l & Comp. L. Rev. 221 at 238.

international human rights are enforceable as any other civil right as a matter of first principles. Arguably, then, following the "well-pleaded-complaint" rule, federal question jurisdiction in *Filártiga*-style cases may be established by alleging the violation of a domestically received international legal norm. Once shown to be part of the common law, the international ascendancy of the right becomes irrelevant and its enforcement can be pursued as a matter of domestic law.

Another (opposite) way of resolving the issue is by questioning the incorporationist view of international law on which proponents of § 1331 rely. Indeed, if customary international law is not directly incorporated into the common law, then international rights are clearly not enforceable in municipal courts without explicit directives from Congress. Bradley and Goldsmith have assiduously defended this view.[107] The proposition that customary international law is part of the "law of the land," in the authors' opinion, is nothing more than an historical assumption with undesirable, undemocratic consequences. In their view, US federal courts lack the jurisdiction to apply customary international law without express constitutional or congressional authorization. As evidence of this, the authors point out that neither the supremacy clause (Article VI) nor Article III § 2 of the Constitution mention customary law, let alone provide for its domestic juridical bindingness. The authors' argument relies on a restrictive reading of *Erie Railroad v. Tompkins* (1938) in which the Supreme Court held:

> Except in matters governed by the Federal Constitution or by acts of Congress, the law to be applied in any case is the law of the state. And whether the law of the state shall be declared by its Legislature in a statute or by its highest court in a decision is not a matter of federal concern. There is no federal general common law.[108]

In other words, US federal courts possess no inherent jurisdiction over the common law and may not apply customary norms without express authorization by Congress. Therefore, the authors argued, in the absence of a federal common law in which customary norms can be

107 Curtis A. Bradley & Jack L. Goldsmith, "Customary International Law as Federal Common Law: A Critique of the Modern Position" (1997) 110 Harv. L. Rev. 815 [Bradley & Goldsmith]. See also Curtis A. Bradley, "Universal Jurisdiction and U.S. Law" (2001) U. Chi. Legal F. 323; Curtis A. Bradley, "The *Alien Tort Statute* and Article III" (2002) 42 Va. J. Int'l L. 587.

108 *Erie Railroad Co. v. Tompkins*, 304 U.S. 64 at 78 (1938).

incorporated, federal courts have no jurisdiction in *Filártiga*-style cases that allege the violation of customary norms since these do not "arise under" federal law within the meaning of § 1331.

Though the wider concerns voiced by Bradley and Goldsmith merit debate (that is, whether the benefits of transnational human rights litigation outweigh its inconveniences[109]), their understanding that US federal courts lack the jurisdiction to administer customary international law is at odds with the historical record. One of the principal purposes for founding the federation of states was precisely the creation of a national judiciary charged with the uniform interpretation and application of international law.[110] Moreover, the incorporationist view of international law has long been a feature of the US legal system.[111] While the Constitution does not expressly state this point, at one time or another, every branch of government has unequivocally expressed the view that international law is part of the "supreme law of the land." In *Banco Nacional de Cuba v. Sabbatino* (a post-*Erie* decision), the Supreme Court stated that the "ordering of our relationship with other members of the international community must be treated exclusively as an aspect of federal law."[112] Likewise, in their joint *amicus* brief filed in *Filártiga*, the Departments of State and Justice agreed: "Customary international law is federal law, to be enunciated by the federal courts."[113] The Senate observed in its report on the *TVPA*: "International human rights cases predictably raise legal issues — such as the interpretation of international law — that are matters of Federal common law and within the particular expertise of Federal courts."[114] Finally, the *Erie* decision is arguably of little help to Bradley and Goldsmith who, according to Koh, overextend its intended application.[115] *Erie* stands for the proposition that the federal government must respect the division of powers and refrain from interfering in the exclu-

109 See Chapter 8, Section C.

110 See Chapter 2, Section C(2)(a).

111 *The Nereide*, 13 U.S. 388 at 423 (1815); *The Paquete Habana*, 175 U.S. 677 at 700 (1900); *Sosa*, above note 1.

112 *Banco Nacional*, above note 97 at 425.

113 Brief of *Amicus Curiae* United States in *Filartíga v. Peña-Irala* (1980) 19 I.L.M. 585 at 606.

114 *TVPA* Senate Report, above note 6 at 574, n. 6.

115 Harold H. Koh, "Is International Law Really State Law?" (1997) 111 Harv. L. Rev. 1824 at 1830.

sive jurisdiction of the several states.[116] It should be recalled that in *Erie*, the court was considering the liability for the injury of a person walking on a railroad, a matter of pure municipal concern. It is unclear why the decision ought to be taken beyond this context. Shortly after *Erie*'s release, Jessup opined that "Mr Justice Brandeis [who wrote the decision] was surely not thinking of international law when he wrote his dictum. Any question of applying international law in our courts involves the foreign relations of the United States and can thus be brought within a federal power."[117]

In 2004, the Supreme Court endorsed Koh's and Jessup's reading of *Erie Railroad* and affirmed the continued incorporation of customary international law into the common law for *ATCA* purposes, but suggested that § 1331 did not necessarily permit similar opportunities.[118] Partially vindicating Bradley and Goldsmith on this point, the Court stated:

> Our position does not, as Justice Scalia suggests, imply that every grant of jurisdiction to a federal court carries with it an opportunity to develop common law (so that the grant of federal-question jurisdiction would be equally as good for our purposes as §1350). Section 1350 was enacted on the congressional understanding that courts would exercise jurisdiction by entertaining some common law claims derived from the law of nations; and we know of no reason to think that federal-question jurisdiction was extended subject to any comparable congressional assumption. Further, our holding today is consistent with the division of responsibilities between federal and state courts after *Erie*, as a more expansive common law power related to 28 U.S.C. §1331 might not be.[119] [Citations omitted.]

While the Court was not specific — the issues in *Sosa* did not require it to address this question — the majority's comments effectively cast doubt on the appropriateness of grounding *Filártiga*-type claims in § 1331's jurisdictional grant. Arguably, deriving new actionable wrongs from customary international law on the basis of a statute that explicitly refers

116 *Ibid.*

117 Philip C. Jessup, "The Doctrine of *Erie Railroad v. Tompkins* Applied to International Law" (1939) 33 A.J.I.L. 740 at 743.

118 *Sosa*, above note 1 at 729–31.

119 *Ibid.* at 731, n. 19.

to the law of nations is different from doing so on the basis of one that does not. For one thing, under *ATCA*, the judicial gaze is focused on international law, thus permitting a measure of appreciation in determining a given norm's actionability at common law. By contrast, § 1331 requires courts to approach the incorporation of customary norms as a *fait accompli*, directing judges to look for customary norms already received within the "laws of the United States." But such distinctions are surely unmanageable, premised as they are on marginally different conceptions of the relationship between common and customary law. Perhaps the most cogent reason for reconsidering the relevance of § 1331 in transnational human rights proceedings, as the Court suggested in *Sosa*, is the proper scope of the authority of federal courts in light of the exigencies of US federalism.[120]

3) Diversity Jurisdiction

Diversity jurisdiction is codified at 28 U.S.C. § 1332, which reads in part as follows:

> §1332(a) The district courts shall have original jurisdiction of all civil actions where the matter in controversy exceeds the sum or value of $75,000, exclusive of interest and costs, and is between—
> (1) citizens of different States;
> (2) citizens of a State and citizens or subjects of a foreign state;
> (3) citizens of different States and in which citizens or subjects of a foreign state are additional parties; . . .

Under the *Judiciary Act* of 1789, diversity jurisdiction was initially vested in the circuit courts pursuant to § 11.[121] After serving as the principal federal trial forum for over a century, the federal circuit courts were abolished in 1911 and diversity jurisdiction transferred to the district courts.[122]

Diversity jurisdiction, also called "alienage jurisdiction," can be asserted when (1) the amount-in-controversy exceeds $75,000 (up from the original $500 of 1789) and (2) a US citizen is party to the proceedings. While the amount-in-controversy criteria is usually not much of

120 *Sosa*, above note 1 at 731.
121 See Chapter 2, Section C(1).
122 36 Stat. 1087, 3 March 1911.

an issue in transnational human rights litigation cases where multi-million-dollar damages are routinely sought, the second criteria—that the case involve a US citizen—is not always met. For example, § 1332 could not have been invoked in *Filártiga* where both the plaintiffs and defendants were foreign nationals. It should be noted however that, for the purposes of the section, "an alien admitted to the United States for permanent residence shall be deemed a citizen of the State in which such alien is domiciled."[123] Accordingly, the nationality requirements of § 1332 would be met in cases involving a permanent resident and foreign national. Diversity was lacking in *De Wit v. KLM* where the plaintiff, a Dutch national residing in New York, though not permanently, sued Netherlands-based KLM Airlines. Despite being a named party to the proceedings, the plaintiff's son, an American citizen, did not provide the required diversity since he was a minor. For diversity purposes, the citizenship of a minor child is deemed to be the same as his parent.[124] By contrast, § 1332 was successfully invoked in an action brought by the estate of a US citizen who was tortured and murdered by rebels involved in the Nicaraguan civil war.[125] Likewise, a California district court had diversity jurisdiction in proceedings where a Mexican national sued the Los Angeles Police Department and the City of Los Angeles for their role in the false arrest and detention of the plaintiffs in Mexico.[126] Finally, § 1332 jurisdiction is possible as between natural persons and corporations, provided there is diversity of nationality. For instance, the Court of Appeals for the Second Circuit held that it had diversity jurisdiction in a claim brought by Canadian citizens against Coca-Cola Co., a Delaware corporation, with regards to its conduct in connection with the illegal nationalization of the plaintiff's property by the Egyptian government in the 1960s.[127] Despite its application to a wide number of factual permutations, diversity jurisdiction is not frequently invoked in transnational human rights litigation compared to more specific provisions like *ATCA* and the *TVPA*.

---

123 28 U.S.C. § 1330(a).

124 *De Wit v. KLM Royal Dutch Airlines NV*, 570 F. Supp. 613 (S.D.N.Y 1983).

125 *Linder v. Portocarrero*, 963 F.2d 332 (11th Cir. 1992).

126 *Martinez v. City of Los Angeles*, 141 F.3d 1373 (9th Cir. 1998).

127 *Bigio v. Coca-Cola Co.*, 239 F.3d 440 (2d Cir. 2001).

4) State Law

The several states of the United States of America are not "states" at international law.[128] They enjoy no recognition of statehood or sovereignty and possess no constitutional powers in matters of foreign affairs. Pursuant to Article I § 10 of the Constitution, the states cannot "keep troops, or ships of war in time of peace, enter into any agreement or compact with another state, or with a foreign power, or engage in war," save with the approval of Congress. As Justice Sutherland once noted, "complete power over international affairs is in the national government and is not and cannot be subject to any curtailment or interference on the part of the several states."[129] This, it will be recalled, was viewed by the Framers as one of the primary *raisons d'être* and salutary features of the Union: internationally the Union ought to speak in one voice, not thirteen, much less fifty.[130] It should be qualified however that the concentration of the power over foreign affairs in the federal government does not alter the general adjudicative authority of state courts, nor do *ATCA* or the *TVPA* pre-empt or displace state tort law.[131] Indeed, the original text of *ATCA* specified that the jurisdiction of the district courts over torts in violation of the law of nations is "concurrent with [that of] the courts of the several states."[132] Today as in 1789, state courts enjoy original jurisdiction over civil and criminal matters, including foreign parties and claims.[133] Moreover, under the doctrine of transitory torts, extraterritorial events and controversies can be adjudicated in state courts, subject to the conflict of laws rules and the Constitution. As Lord Mansfield explained:

> If A becomes indebted to B, or commits a tort upon his person or upon his personal property in Paris, an action in either case may be maintained against A in England, if he is there found . . . . As to

128 *Restatement*, above note 45 at § 1, n. 5.

129 *United States v. Belmont*, 301 U.S. 324 at 331 (1937).

130 See Chapter 2, Section C(2)(a).

131 *Alomang v. Freeport-McMoran Inc.*, 1996 U.S. Dist. Lexis 15908 at 9–12 (E.D. La. 1996) [*Alomang 1996*].

132 See Chapter 2, notes 28–29 and accompanying text.

133 State jurisdiction over international parties and claims is original and concurrent with that of the federal courts. See 28 U.S.C. § 1330 (foreign states), § 1331 (federal question), § 1332 (diversity), § 1350 (alien tort), and § 1367 (supplemental jurisdiction).

> transitory actions, there is not a colour of doubt but that any action which is transitory may be laid in any county in England, though the matter arises beyond the seas.[134]

Likewise, if P tortures F in Paraguay, an action may be maintained against P in the state of New York, if he is found there.

Despite their vast jurisdiction and powers, state courts have not been the fora of choice for transnational human rights cases; they are mostly resorted to only when federal claims have been dismissed.[135] The fact that transnational human rights suits are not always filed in state courts does not make state law entirely irrelevant. Plaintiffs in federal courts sometimes invoke state law in addition to *ATCA* and *TVPA* in relation to the same events. In such cases, federal district courts can exercise supplemental jurisdiction under 28 U.S.C. § 1367 over all attendant state claims that "form part of the same case or controversy under Article III of the United States Constitution."[136] Both federal and state claims must arise from a "common nucleus of operative facts" for supplemental jurisdiction to apply.[137] In *Mehinović*, in addition to *ATCA* jurisdiction, the district court asserted supplemental jurisdiction over the plaintiff's state tort law claims. The court was satisfied that the defendant "committed the following torts under the laws of the State of Georgia: assault and battery, false imprisonment, intentional infliction of emotional distress, and conspiracy to commit those torts."[138]

From time to time, state legislatures have adopted statutes aimed at redressing extraterritorial wrongs or at otherwise securing their foreign interests. For instance, in 1999, California amended its *Code of Civil Procedure* to provide a cause of action for WW II victims of slave or forced labour and permitting the recovery of compensation "from any entity or successor in interest thereof, for whom that labour was

134 *Mostyn v. Fabrigas* (1774), 1 Cowp. 161, cited in *Filártiga*, above note 98 at 885. Judge Kaufman continued: "*Mostyn* came into our law as the original basis for state court jurisdiction over out-of-state torts, *McKenna v. Fisk*, . . . (personal injury suits held transitory); *Dennick v. Railroad Co.* . . . (wrongful death action held transitory), and it has not lost its force in suits to recover for a wrongful death occurring upon foreign soil, *Slater v. Mexican National Railroad Co.*, . . . as long as the conduct complained of was unlawful where performed."

135 Stephens 2008, above note 6 at 121.

136 28 U.S.C. § 1367(a).

137 *United Mine Workers v. Gibbs*, 383 U.S. 715 at 725 (1966).

138 *Mehinović 2002*, above note 24 at 1357.

performed, either directly or through a subsidiary or affiliate."[139] Section 354.6 extended the governing statute of limitations to 2010 and did not restrict the right of action to California residents. That year, over thirty lawsuits were filed in California against Japanese corporations including Mistubishi and Nippon Steel Corporation by victims of forced or slaved labour, many of who were non-US nationals.[140] In 1999, California also enacted the *Holocaust Victim Insurance Relief Act*, codified at § 354.5 of its *Code of Civil Procedure*, allowing state residents to sue in state courts for Holocaust-related life insurance claims. Among other things, the legislation required any insurer doing business in California to disclose information about all policies sold in Europe between 1920 and 1945 upon penalty of revocation of its California business licence. Both amendments were independently challenged and declared to be unconstitutional intrusions upon the federal foreign affairs power.[141] Applying the rule in *Zschernig* (1968),[142] the reviewing courts agreed that the impugned state legislation is likely to produce "more than an incidental effect on foreign affairs," the control over which, in the constitutional division of powers, rests exclusively in the political branches of the national government. Inversely stated, state legislation will not be pre-empted if its effect in matters of foreign relations and policy is merely incidental. In *Garamendi* (2003),[143] the Supreme Court held that § 354.5 specifically infringed upon the President's power over the conduct of foreign policy and undermined concurrent executive initiatives aimed at settling outstanding Holocaust-era claims. However, the court expressly declined to resolve the question whether the doctrine of federal pre-emption applied to all state intrusions in the field of foreign affairs, even in the absence of affirmative federal activity in the subject matter of the impugned state law.

---

139 Cal. Civ. Pro, § 354.6.

140 John Haberstroh, "Comment: In re World War II Era Japanese Forced Labor Litigation and Obstacles to International Human Rights Claims in U.S. Courts" (2003) 10 Asian L.J. 253 at 260.

141 *American Insurance Association v. Garamendi*, 539 U.S. 396 (2003) [*Garamendi*] declaring § 564.5 unconstitutional; *Deutsch v. Turner Corp et al.*, 317 F.3d 1005 (9th Cir. 2003) declaring § 564.6 unconstitutional. See also *In Re: World War II Era Japanese Forced Labor Litigation*, 164 F. Supp. 2d 1160 (N.D. Cal. 2001).

142 *Zschernig v. Miller*, 389 U.S. 429 (1968). Wherein Oregon legislation purporting to limit the inheritance rights of non-resident foreign nationals was held to directly interfere with federal power over foreign relations.

143 Above note 141.

It is unlikely that state courts will be called upon to adjudicate many transnational human rights claims in the future given the specificity of existing federal law, such as *ATCA*, *TVPA*, and the *FSIA* amendments. Federal supplemental jurisdiction under 28 U.S.C. § 1367 and constitutional primacy over matters of international concern, as expressed through the doctrine of pre-emption, will in all likelihood continue to limit state-level incursions, legislative or judicial, into transnational human rights disputes. Ultimately, given the sensitive international issues involved and the historical impetus behind the creation of the national judiciary, the interests of the United States are probably best served by the continued exclusion of the several states from transnational human rights litigation. Judge Kaufman observed in *Filartíga*:

> we note that the foreign relations implications of this and other issues . . . underscores the wisdom of the First Congress in vesting jurisdiction over such claims in the federal district courts through the Alien Tort Statute. Questions of this nature are fraught with implications for the nation as a whole, and therefore should not be left to the potentially varying adjudications of the courts of the fifty states.[144]

F. CONCLUSION ON THE UNITED STATES EXPERIENCE

United States federal courts may adjudicate civil claims for extraterritorial violations of well-established international norms protecting the human person on the basis of *ATCA*, the *TVPA*, and other legislated grants of authority. Except in matters brought under the *TVPA*, the cause of action in such lawsuits is derived from the common law by virtue of that legal tradition's receptiveness to customary international norms. The *TVPA*'s explicit cause of action for torture and extrajudicial killing likely supersedes the common law regarding those specific wrongs, but the common law still operates with respect to other widely recognized norms of international law, such as the prohibitions against war crimes, crimes against humanity, and genocide. Furthermore, in *Sosa* (2004), the US Supreme Court held that under *ATCA* federal courts had the jurisdiction to recognize new common law causes of action for

144 *Filártiga*, above note 98 at 890.

violations of international norms, provided these enjoyed high levels of specificity and acceptance.

A number of observations are warranted at this juncture. First, US-style transnational human rights litigation relies not only on specific legislation, but also on certain features of its legal tradition, namely, the common law's relationship with customary international law and the declarative powers of common law judges. While *ATCA* may be unique to the US, the common law tradition is not. A question thus arises as to whether the courts of other common law countries — such as the UK and Canada — can exercise their civil jurisdiction in *ATCA*-type scenarios on the basis of their shared legal heritage with the United States.

Second, the conception of international law on which *ATCA* jurisdiction historically stands is, in some respects, consistent with current international legal thinking — with regards to the salience of non-state actors and individuals for instance, though it could be remarked that international law made provisions for individuals since at least the eighteenth century. In other respects, some features of US transnational human rights litigation may be regarded as anachronistic, such as its strong reliance on judge-made law and custom, as opposed to positive legal sources. Nevertheless, *ATCA* jurisdiction has been supplemented by Congress and upheld by the Supreme Court, thus affirming the continued relevance of classical doctrine in the United State's increasingly positivistic legal environment. There thus arises a question as to whether or not the UK and Canadian legal systems can, on their own terms, accommodate competing conceptions of international and common law.

Finally, while transnational human rights litigation will be criticised in detail in Parts II and III of this book, it can already be noted at this juncture that the US model strains orthodox understanding of extraterritorial jurisdiction, justiciability, and immunity. On the other hand *ATCA* jurisdiction beneficially offers victims a forum not otherwise available in which to seek justice. In any event, despite criticisms, US transnational human rights litigation is not likely to disappear. Thus, the question is not whether *ATCA* ought to be repealed (it won't be) but rather whether and in what manner transnational human rights litigation can be pursued legitimately and constructively both inside and outside the US.

part two

Jurisdictional Issues

CHAPTER FOUR

Customary International Law and Common Law Courts

"International law is part of our law, and must be ascertained and administered by the courts of justice of appropriate jurisdiction, as often as questions of right depending upon it are duly presented for their determination."

—Justice Gray[1]

A. INTRODUCTION

Whereas previous chapters sought to describe and assess the US experience, the remainder of this book is aimed at working out the legal desirability and feasibility of US-style transnational human rights litigation in the UK and Canada having regard to four jurisdictional issues. Thus Chapter 4 examines the historical foundations and contemporary implications of one of transnational human rights litigation's working premises, namely, that customary international law forms part of the common law, which may in turn provide plaintiffs with a cause of action with respect to breaches of well-established and accepted international norms protecting individuals. Chapter 5 is an inquiry into whether and to what extent transnational human rights claims can be reconciled with traditional rules of jurisdiction, choice of law, and justiciability. Chapters 6 and 7 discuss the particular problems that arise in connection to the doctrines of *forum non conveniens* and state immunity, respectively, given that transnational human rights claims usually implead the foreign state concerned and always involve conduct committed in its territory. In each of these chapters, Canadian

1 *The Paquete Habana*, 175 U.S. 677 at 700 (1900) [*Paquete Habana*].

and English jurisprudence and doctrine are analyzed with reference to their US counterparts and the requirements of international law.

As outlined above, the present chapter examines the proposition that customary international law is part of the law of the land and that common law courts may ascertain, interpret, and apply that law in appropriate cases.[2] The reception of customary norms in the national legal order — referred to here as the principle of incorporation — is a tenet of Anglo-American legal systems. The summary manner in which the rule is often invoked, sometimes without citation of precedent or authorities, underscores its axiomatic character but also makes its analysis somewhat more difficult.[3] Clearly, it is not a self-evident proposition, requiring no formal demonstration of its truth. But the principle's vintage and long line of authoritative support help to explain its widespread present-day judicial acceptance. The historical roots of incorporation need to be explored since the principle constitutes part of the foundation of the transnational human rights litigation phenomenon in the US. The principle has also been raised in Canadian and English cases. Generally speaking, plaintiffs bring civil claims in municipal courts for violations of international norms because it is assumed that those courts possess the authority to administer that body of law. Finally, the implications of incorporation will also be considered with respect to both the municipal judicial task and the wider role national judiciaries are playing in the twenty-first century international legal order.

---

2 Ian Brownlie, *Principles of Public International Law*, 6th ed. (Oxford: Oxford University Press, 2003) at 41–44 [Brownlie]; James Crawford, "Decisions of British Courts during 1976–1977" (1977) 48 Brit. Y.B. Int'l L. 333 at 357–59; Edwin D. Dickinson, "Changing Concepts and the Doctrine of Incorporation" (1932) 26 A.J.I.L. 239 at 239–60 [Dickinson]; Louis Henkin, "International Law as Law in the United States" (1984) 82 Mich. L. Rev. 1555 at 1555–1569 [Henkin]; Hersch Lauterpacht, "Is International Law Part of the Law of England?" in Elihu Lauterpacht, ed., *The Collected Papers of Hersch Lauterpacht*, vol. 2 (Cambridge: Cambridge University Press, 1975) at 537–69 [Lauterpacht]; Gibran van Ert, *Using International Law in Canadian Courts*, 2d ed. (Toronto: Irwin Law, 2008) c. 6 [van Ert]; John Westlake, "Is International Law a Part of the Law of England" (1906) 22 Law Q. Rev. 14 at 14–26 [Westlake].

3 See for example, *Bouzari v. Islamic Republic of Iran* (2004), 71 O.R. (3d) 675 at para. 65 (C.A.) [*Bouzari 2004*]; *Campaign for Nuclear Disarmament v. The Prime Minister*, [2002] EWHC 2759 at para. 23; Rosalyn Higgins, "Dualism in the Face of a Changing Legal Culture" in Mads Andenas & Duncan Fairgrieve, eds., *Judicial Review in International Perspective* (The Hague: Kluwer Law International, 2000) at 19.

B. A BRIEF HISTORY OF INCORPORATION

1) Beginnings

William Blackstone's statement of the principle is not the first but it is among the clearest and most influential. In Book IV (entitled *Of Public Wrongs*) of his *Commentaries*, Blackstone first defined the law of nations as "a system of rules, deducible by natural reason, and established by universal consent among the civilized inhabitants of the world" before going on to discuss the manner of its enforcement at the level of the State.[4] He wrote:

> *[T]he law of nations (wherever any question arises which is properly the object of its jurisdiction) is here adopted in its full extent by the common law, and is held to be part of the law of the land.* And those acts of parliament, which have from time to time been made to enforce this universal law, or to facilitate the execution of its decisions, are not to be considered as introductive of any new rule, but merely as declaratory of the old fundamental constitutions of the kingdom; without which it must cease to be a part of the civilized world.[5]

The non-italicized portion of the passage will be discussed below and is added at this point only to complete the quotation and to introduce the question of legislative transformation of customary norms that arose in the late nineteenth century. For present purposes however, the adoptionist view of incorporation must be analyzed, that is, the view that international law "is here adopted" by the common law.

As Lauterpacht argued, Blackstone's explanation is not a mere "picturesque generalization" but an accurate statement of eighteenth century law by a practicing lawyer.[6] Blackstone was counsel in *Triquet v. Bath* (1764), the first case in which the principle of incorporation is clearly reported. There, Lord Mansfield recalled an earlier case, *Buvot v. Barbuit* (1736), in which he (then Mr. William Murray) served as counsel before Lord Talbot LC who "declared a clear opinion—'That the law of nations, in its full extent was part of the law of England.'" Lord Mansfield continued: "I was counsel in this case, and have a full note

4 William Blackstone, *Commentaries on the Laws of England*, vol. 1 (Oxford: Clarendon Press, 1765–69) at 66–67 [Blackstone].

5 *Ibid.* at 67 [emphasis added].

6 Lauterpacht, above note 2 at 538.

of it. I remember, too, Lord Hardwicke's declaring his opinion to the same effect; and denying that Lord Chief Justice Holt ever had any doubt as the law of nations being part of the law of England, . . . Mr Blackstone's principles are right."[7]

Lord Mansfield evoked the principle of incorporation in subsequent cases. In *Lockwood v. Coysgarne* (1765), he described the *Diplomatic Privileges Act, 1708*, which codified the customary privileges of ambassadors and ensured appropriate punishment for any violation thereof, as "declaratory" of international law and that the "law of the nations was in full force in these kingdoms."[8] He commented again on the statute in *Heathfield v. Chilton* (1767), where he held the privileges of foreign ministers to "depend upon the law of nations, which is part of the common law of England" and that "the law of nations will be carried as far in England as anywhere."[9]

By the time Blackstone published the fourth volume of his *Commentaries* in 1769, the principle of incorporation had become a rule of decision in England. Less clear however is how or why the principle came to be formulated in the first place by Lord Mansfield (or indeed by Lord Talbot in *Barbuit*, if Mansfield's recollection is accurate). Dickinson has argued that the appearance of the doctrine is likely due to changes in legal thinking. Incorporation, he claimed, was for English courts

> . . . a perfectly natural deduction from the theories of national and international law which flourished in the 17th and 18th centuries. All law, national no less than international, was being tested by the standards of what was assumed to be a rational, universal and immutable system. The English courts were developing English national law in harmony, as it was assumed, with right reason and natural justice . . . . International law was not only in harmony with right reason and natural justice, but was a veritable *corpus juris naturalis* in the treaties of the most influential publicists. In an age dominated by such ideas, nothing could have been more plausible than the conclusion that international law formed an integral part of the national law governing matters of international concern.[10]

---

7 *Triquet v. Bath* (1764), 3 Burr. 1478 at 1481 [*Triquet*]. See *Buvot v. Barbuit* (1736), Talb. 281.

8 *Lockwood v. Coysgarne* (1765), 3 Burr. 1676 at 1678. See also Chapter 2, Section C(2)(b).

9 *Heathfield v. Chilton* (1767), 4 Burr. 2015 at 2016 [*Heathfield*].

10 Dickinson, above note 2 at 13.

Of course eighteenth century civil lawyers were versed in natural law and knew their Gentili, Grotius, and Burlamaqui; that was part of their practice in the civil courts and in their advisory work to the Crown. But this does not explain how the law of nations came to be understood as forming part of the English common law, a law historically understood as confined to England and Wales and, for the most part, standing against the civil law. In Lord Mansfield's time, the legal practice of civil lawyers was distinct from that of common lawyers, focused as it was, in terms of international law, on the Admiralty, especially in prize.[11] For its part, the practice of common lawyers generally involved municipal and private law issues. This being said, the common law certainly had natural law characteristics, holding its principles to be discoverable by right reason and conceiving itself as the historical successor to the great legal systems of the past. In Coke's hubristic words, there is

> no knowledge of any Lawes (I speak of humane) so necessary for all estates, and for all causes, concerning goods, lands, or life, as the Common Lawes of England . . . . If the ancient Lawes of this noble Island had not excelled all others, it could not be but some of the severall Conquerors, and Governors thereof; That is to say, the Romanes, Saxons, Danes, or Normans, and specially the Romanes, who, (as they justly may) doe boast of their Civill Lawes, would (as every of them might) have altered or changed the same.[12]

The view that the law of nations formed part of the common law may well have been facilitated by their shared natural law lineage, but Dickinson's hypothesis probably only tells half the story.

As Crawford and others have commented, the notion that the law of nations formed part of the common law in the early eighteenth century is "historically untenable" given that the common law traditionally "defined itself as the law of the land in a literal sense, the law of the Kingdom of England, as contrasted with the law applicable

11 James Crawford, "Public International Law in Twentieth-Century England" in Jack Beatson & Richard Zimmermann, eds., *Jurists Uprooted: German-speaking Emigré Lawyers in Twentieth Century Britain* (Oxford: Oxford University Press, 2004) at 685–86 [Crawford 2004].

12 Sir Edward Coke, "*(Preface) To the Learned Reader*" in Steve Sheppard, ed., *Selected Writings and Speeches of Sir Edward Coke* (Indianapolis: Liberty Fund, 2003) vol. 1 at 39–40.

to foreign places and transactions."[13] Indeed, prior to the seventeenth century, common law courts did not have subject-matter jurisdiction in cases involving international law. Generally speaking, at that time, the judicially administered law of nations extended to the law merchant, conflict of laws, and maritime causes, including prize, piracies, shipwrecks, hostages, and ransom bills, which all belonged to the Admiralty and to the civil lawyers.[14] For its part, the international law of immunities and interstate transactions derived from the royal prerogative and was administered by the King and his Council.[15] During Queen Elizabeth's reign the common lawyers, led by Coke CJ, began their expansionist assault upon the jurisdictions of the Chancery and Admiralty. A detailed account of the jurisdictional battles is too involved to be included here. It is enough for present purposes to note that by the early eighteenth century, the common lawyers had managed to hollow out much of the jurisdiction of the Admiralty and Chancery.[16] If Mansfield and Blackstone were able to declare the law of nations to be part of the common law, it is also likely in part because the common law had been so successful in appropriating for itself a large measure of the jurisdiction of the Admiralty in international matters, leaving it only with special jurisdiction in prize as an area of exclusive competence.

Whatever its origins, the "tradition" that the law of nations formed part of the common law was carried across the Atlantic and became part of the law of the British colonies and, later, of the United States.[17] In *Respublica v. De Longchamps* (1784), the trial that followed the Marbois affair, M'Kean CJ held that the law of nations "in its full extent is part of the law of this state [Pennsylvania], and is to be collected from the practice of different nations and the authority of writers."[18] The works

---

13 Crawford 2004, above note 11 at 686, n. 26. See also Edward Robert Adair, *The Extraterritoriality of Ambassadors in the Sixteenth and Seventeenth Centuries* (London: Longmans, Green, 1929) at 88 and 238–43.

14 Sir William Searle Holdsworth, *A History of English Law*, 7th ed., vol. 1 (London: Sweet & Maxwell, 1956) at 548 [Holdsworth].

15 Lauterpacht, above note 2 at 553.

16 James Oldham, *The Mansfield Manuscripts and the Growth of English Law in the Eighteenth Century*, vol. 2 (Chapel Hill: University of North Carolina Press, 1992) at 657–58; Holdsworth, above note 14, vol. 1 at 559.

17 Henkin, above note 2 at 1555–56.

18 *Respublica v. De Longchamps*, 1 U.S. 111 at 116 (1784). In this passage, M'Kean CJ closely tracks the language of Lord Mansfield. See *Triquet*, above note 7 at 1481.

of Vattel and Blackstone were extremely influential and citations of their principles abound in the historical record of the Constitutional Convention of 1787.[19] In his charge to a grand jury in 1790, Jay CJ instructed that the law of nations was "part of the laws of this, and of every other civilized nation."[20] Similarly, Irdell J charged in 1794: "The Common Law of England, from which our own is derived, fully recognizes the principles of the Law of Nations, and applies them in all cases falling under its jurisdiction, where the nature of the subject requires it."[21] It would be possible to provide further dozens of authorities applying the principle of incorporation in the US, but none as authoritative as Marshall CJ who held that, absent contrary legislation, "the Court is bound by the law of nations, which is part of the law of the land."[22]

a) Transformation and Incorporation

Another view emerged in late nineteenth century English jurisprudence — the transformation doctrine — that conditions the domestic reception of international norms by some overt, formal act of assent, in particular by Parliament. While transformation has largely been discredited for most purposes,[23] it has the merit of emphasising two important considerations concerning the reception of customary international law, namely, the required evidence of the existence of customary norms and respect for the supremacy of Parliament. The case of *Regina v. Keyn* (1876) in the Court for Crown Cases Reserved is usually cited as authority for the doctrine of transformation.[24] A

19 See, generally, Dickinson, above note 2; Julian S. Waterman, "Thomas Jefferson and Blackstone's Commentaries" (1933) 27 Ill. L. Rev. 629; Dennis R. Nolan, "Sir William Blackstone and the New Republic: A Study of Intellectual Impact" (1976) 51 N.Y.U.L. Rev. 731; Stewart Jay, "The Status of the Law of Nations in Early American Law" (1989) 42 Vand. L. Rev. 819 [Jay].

20 *Charge to the Grand Jury for the District of New York* (4 April 1790), cited in Jay, *ibid.* at 825.

21 *Charge to the Grand Jury for the District of South Carolina* (12 May 1794), cited in Jay, *ibid.* at 826.

22 *The Nereide*, 13 U.S. 388 at 423 (1815).

23 *Trendtex Trading Corporation v. Central Bank of Nigeria*, [1977] 2 W.L.R. 356 at 365 (C.A.) [*Trendtex*]. See Brownlie, above note 2 at 44; Lauterpacht, above note 2 at 545–46; van Ert, above note 2 at 189; *R. v. Hape*, 2007 SCC 26 at §34–39 [*Hape*]. But see *R. v. Jones and Milling*, [2006] UKHL 16 [*Jones and Milling*] regarding the reception of customary international crimes.

24 *R. v. Keyn* (1876), 2 Ex. D. 63 [*Keyn*].

thirteen-judge bench had to decide whether English courts had jurisdiction to try a foreigner for manslaughter committed on a foreign ship in the territorial waters of Britain. In a 7–6 decision, the majority held that, in the absence of enabling legislation, English courts had no jurisdiction over the criminal offences of foreigners on a foreign ship outside the realm of England, irrespective of the ship's position in relation to the territorial waters. The minority would have asserted jurisdiction since the offence occurred within what was considered English territory under international law. The judgment of Cockburn CJ and the concurrence of Sir Robert Phillimore starkly illustrate the nineteenth century tension between the struggling natural law tradition (Phillimore was a trained civil lawyer) and the rise of positivism. Sir Robert Phillimore expressly declined to decide the "most grave question" of whether "an Act of Parliament would not be required to empower the Court to exercise jurisdiction"[25] and went on rather to review the authorities of his *maîtres de pensée* — including Grotius, Vattel, and Lord Stowell — holding that neither international or domestic law granted jurisdiction.

Agreeing that English law did not provide guidance, Cockburn CJ reviewed the international law on the matter, specifically requiring evidence that the examined principles "have received the assent of the nations who are to be bound by it. This assent may be express, as by treaty or the acknowledged concurrence of governments, or may be implied from established usage."[26] Cockburn CJ then goes on to state:

> In the absence of proof of assent, as derived from one or other of these sources, no unanimity on the part of theoretical writers would warrant the judicial application of the law on the sole authority of their views or statements. Nor, in my opinion, would the clearest proof of unanimous assent on the part of other nations be sufficient to authorize the tribunals of this country to apply, without an Act of Parliament, what would practically amount to a new law. In so doing we should be unjustifiably usurping the province of the legislature.[27]

In the above passages, Cockburn CJ introduces two considerations that continue to infuse the present day understanding of incorporation,

25 *Ibid.* at 68.
26 *Ibid.* at 202.
27 *Ibid.* at 203.

namely, the evidentiary requirement of establishing the international norm's existence and bindingness and the importance of parliamentary supremacy.

Whether or not Cockburn CJ's reasons generally require international norms to be "transformed" into national law by Parliament remains controversial.[28] As pointed out by O'Keefe, out of the thirteen judges on the panel, he is the only one "to cast doubt on whether, as a matter of principle, the law of nations formed part of the law of England in the absence of legislation — and even then *obiter* and ambiguously."[29] Indeed, the relationship between international and national law was incidental to the central issue of whether criminal jurisdiction could be exercised against foreigners on a foreign vessel in British territorial waters. As Crawford noted, Lindley J's (inaccurately cited) comments on "Lord Mansfield's observations" in *Triquet* (1764) are the only express reference to the principle of incorporation of *Keyn's* case.[30]

In any event, *Keyn's* case was not the last word on the matter. The English position further evolved in the twentieth century towards a more developed view of incorporation.[31] The considerations raised by Cockburn CJ echo through Lord Atkin's oft-quoted dictum in *Chung Chi Cheung v. The King* (1939) in the Privy Council:

> [So far as] the Courts of this country are concerned, international law has no validity save in so far as its principles are accepted and adopted by our own domestic law. There is no external power that imposes its rules upon our own code of substantive law or procedure. The Courts acknowledge the existence of a body of rules which nations accept amongst themselves. On any judicial issue they seek to ascertain what the relevant rule is, and, having found it, they will treat it as incorporated into the domestic law, so far as it is not

28 Lauterpacht, above note 2 at 545–46; Brownlie, above note 2 at 43.

29 Roger O'Keefe, "Customary International Crimes in English Courts" (2001) 72 Brit. Y.B. Int'l L. 293 at 304–5. [O'Keefe]. As noted by the author, Pollock B and Field J concurred in a single sentence.

30 James Crawford, "The Contribution of Professor D.P. O'Connell to the Discipline of International Law" (1980) 51 Brit. Y.B. Int'l L. 1 at 61, n. 2. Lindley J refers, at 91, to "Lord Mansfield's observation in 3 Burr. 1471" that the law of nations formed part of the law of England. The citation should have been 3 Burr. 1478 at 1481.

31 The adoptionist view of incorporation was most notably affirmed in *West Rand Central Gold Mining Co. Ltd. v. The King*, [1905] 2 K.B. 391 at 406; See also *Re Suarez* (1918), 1 Ch. 176; *Engelke v. Musmann*, [1928] A.C. 433 (H.L.).

> inconsistent with rules enacted by statutes or finally declared by their tribunals.[32]

Though Lord Atkin's judgment has been cited as authority for transformation,[33] a careful reading reveals it to be rather supportive of incorporation.[34] Lord Atkin's starting point is the principle of state sovereignty, that is to say, customary international law forms part of English law on English law's own terms. Revisiting the concerns raised by Cockburn CJ in *Keyn*, Lord Atkin specifies that only those customary norms that have been proven or "ascertained" are adopted in the domestic legal order to the extent of their compatibility with statutory law and judicial precedent.

This final proviso—that incorporated customary norms are subject to the rule of *stare decisis*—has since been rejected by the Court of Appeal in *Trendtex Trading Corp. v. Central Bank of Nigeria* (1977) which cemented incorporation's place in English jurisprudence. In a case concerning the emergence in customary law of a commercial exception to State immunity, Lord Denning MR queried whether, and by what means, the exception would form part of English law. After reviewing both schools of thought on the subject, Lord Denning MR and Shaw LJ agreed that customary norms are automatically adopted in the common law, subject only to contrary legislation.[35] "As between the two schools," the Master of Rolls stated, "I now believe the doctrine of incorporation is correct. Otherwise I do not see that our courts could ever recognise a change in the rules of international law . . . . International law does change, and the courts have applied the changes without the aid of any Act of Parliament."[36]

United Kingdom courts continue to affirm the principle of incorporation for most purposes,[37] but the doctrine of transformation has

---

32 *Chung Chi Cheung v. The King*, [1939] A.C. 160 at 167–68 (P.C.) [*Chung Chi Cheung*].

33 See, for example, *Trendtex*, above note 23 at 554.

34 O'Keefe, above note 29 at 306; van Ert, above note 2 at 187–89.

35 *Trendtex*, above note 23 at 552–54, Lord Denning MR; at 577–79, Shaw LJ).

36 *Ibid.* at 554.

37 See for example, *Maclaine Watson & Co. Ltd. v. Department of Trade and Industry*, [1988] 3 W.L.R 1033 at 1089 (C.A.); *J.H. Rayner (Mincing Lane) Ltd. v. Dept. of Trade and Industry*, [1989] Ch. 72 at 207 (C.A.); *Al-Adsani v. Kuwait* (1995), 103 I.L.R. 420 (Q.B.); *R. v. Bow Street Metropolitan Stipendiary Magistrate, ex parte Pinochet (No. 3)*, [2000] 1 A.C. 147 (H.L.) [*Pinochet III*]; *A(FC) & Others v. Secretary of State for the Home Department*, [2005] UKHL 71 at para. 27. See also Shaheed Fatima, *Using International Law in Domestic Courts* (Oxford: Hart, 2005) at 405–10.

been rehabilitated in respect of customary international crimes. In *Jones & Milling* (2006), peace activists were charged with attempting to impede and obstruct the UK's participation in the US-led war in Iraq. The defendants argued that their criminal conduct was legally justified insofar as they were trying to prevent the commission of a greater crime by their government, that is, the international crime of aggression. Accordingly, one of the central questions raised by *Jones & Milling* was "whether the crime of aggression, if established in customary international law, is a crime recognized by or forming part of the domestic criminal law of England and Wales."[38] The Lords upheld the general principle of incorporation[39] but held that if common law judges once enjoyed the power to recognize new offences at common law, it was no longer appropriate for them to do so. The Court went on to conclude that customary international crimes were not directly triable in domestic courts pursuant to the policy that the power to define criminal offences rests solely with Parliament. Lord Mance stated in his concurring speech:

> The expansive former view that the courts had a general residual power to recognize or in effect create new crimes, when the public interest in their view so required, no longer survives: *Knuller (Publishing, Printing and Promotions) Ltd v. Director of Public Prosecutions*, [1973] AC 435. The creation and regulation of crimes is in a modern Parliamentary democracy a matter *par excellence* for Parliament to debate and legislate. Even crimes under public international law can no longer be, if they ever were, the subject of any automatic reception or recognition in domestic law by the courts.[40]

The Federal Court of Australia had reached a similar conclusion in *Tompson v. Nulyarimma* (1999) where individuals sought to enforce the international crime of genocide in domestic courts in relation to the government's treatment of the aboriginal population.

This debate could not have gone far in Canada where the prosecution of criminal offences at common law has been expressly barred in

38 *Jones & Milling*, above note 23 at para. 2.

39 *Ibid.* at para.1, Lord Bingham.

40 *Ibid.* at para.102, Lord Mance; paras. 30–31, Lord Bingham; and paras. 65–66, Lord Hoffman.

the *Criminal Code*.[41] For all other purposes however incorporation is the rule in Canada.[42] The decision in *Fraser-Brace Overseas Corp. v. Saint John (City)* (1958) clarified the Supreme Court's ambiguous position of earlier cases and established the principle that customary norms are directly received in Canadian law without legislative implementation.[43] In deciding whether the US government was immune from taxation in the city of Saint John in relation to certain leaseholds, the Court reviewed the customary law of State immunity. In the leading judgment, citing seminal authorities, Rand J held customary law to be part and parcel of Canadian law: "If in 1767 Lord Mansfield, in *Heathfield v. Chilton* . . . could say, 'The law of nations will be carried as far in England, as any where,' in this country, in the 20th century, in the presence of the United Nations and the multiplicity of impacts with which technical developments have entwined the entire globe, we cannot say any thing less."[44] Rand J expressly rejected transformation in the following terms:

> . . . to say that precedent is now required for every proposed application to matters which differ only in accidentals, that new concrete instances must be left to legislation or convention, would be a virtual repudiation of the concept of inherent adaptability which has maintained the life of the common law, and a retrograde step in evolving the rules of international intercourse. However slowly and meticulously they are to be fashioned they must be permitted to meet the necessities of increasing international involvements.[45]

Canadian courts continue to affirm the principle that customary international law is automatically incorporated in Canadian law, subject to contrary legislation.[46]

---

41 *Criminal Code*, R.S.C. 1985, c. C-46, s. 9: "Notwithstanding anything in this Act or any other Act, no person shall be convicted or discharged under section 730: (a) of an offence at common law."

42 See van Ert, above note 2 at 194–208 for a review of the Canadian authorities. See also François Larocque & Martin Kreuser, « L'incorporation de la coutume internationale en common law canadienne » (2007) 45 Can. Y.B. Int'l L. 173.

43 *Reference re: Exemption of United States Forces from Proceedings in Canadian Criminal Courts*, [1943] S.C.R. 483; *Reference re: Powers of Ottawa (City) and Rockcliff Park*, [1943] S.C.R. 208.

44 *Saint John (City of) v. Fraser-Brace Overseas Corp.*, [1958] S.C.R. 263 at 268–69.

45 *Ibid*. at 269.

46 See for example, *Re Regina and Palacios* (1984), 45 O.R. (2d) 269 at 276 (C.A.); *Bouzari v. Islamic Republic of Iran*, [2002] O.J. No. 1624 at para. 39 (S.C.J.) [*Bouzari 2002*]; *Bouzari 2004*, above note 3 at § 65; *Hape*, above note 23 at paras. 34–39.

Incorporation also remains firmly established in US law. Authoritative twentieth century endorsements of the rule include *The Paquete Habana* (1900)[47] and *Banco Nacional de Cuba* (1964).[48] As the majority of the Supreme Court noted in *Sosa* (2004), "for two centuries we have affirmed that the domestic law of the United States recognizes the law of nations."[49] The minority in *Sosa*, along with certain commentators,[50] took the view that the decision in *Erie Railroad v. Tompkins* (1939) "signalled the end of federal court elaboration and application of the general common law." In that case, the Court held:

> Except in matters governed by the Federal Constitution or by acts of Congress, the law to be applied in any case is the law of the state. And whether the law of the state shall be declared by its Legislature in a statute or by its highest court in a decision is not a matter of federal concern. There is no federal general common law.[51]

In the absence of a federal common law in which customary norms could be incorporated, the *Sosa* minority opined, federal courts cannot take cognizance of international law without explicit legislative authorization. The majority rejected this view and upheld the post-*Erie* understanding that cases involving international law remain the province of federal courts and that customary international norms continue to be judicially discoverable "in a common law way."[52] As it was explained in Chapter 2, the concentration of international matters in the federal courts was a major impetus for the *Judiciary Act 1789* and a foundational tenet of the US federation.[53] In the majority's view, "it would be unreasonable to assume that the First Congress would have expected federal courts to lose all capacity to recognize enforceable international norms simply because the common law might lose some metaphysical cachet on the road to modern realism."[54]

47 *The Paquete Habana*, above note 1 at 700.

48 *Banco Nacional de Cuba v. Sabbatino*, 376 U.S. 398 at 423 (1964) [*Banco Nacional*].

49 *Sosa v. Alvarez-Machain*, 542 U.S. 692 at 729 (2004) [*Sosa*].

50 Curtis A. Bradley & Jack L. Goldsmith, "Customary International Law as Federal Common Law: A Critique of the Modern Position" (1997) 110 Harv. L. Rev. 815.

51 *Erie Railroad Co. v. Tompkins*, 304 U.S. 64 at 78 (1938).

52 *Sosa*, above note 49 at 729; *Banco Nacional*, above note 48 at 425. See also Philip Jessup, "The Doctrine of *Erie Railroad v. Tompkins* Applied to International Law" (1939) 33 A.J.I.L. 740 at 743.

53 See Chapter 2, Section C(2).

54 *Sosa*, above note 49 at 730.

C. THE IMPLICATIONS OF INCORPORATION

Several consequences flow from the incorporation of customary norms into the law of the land. While these relate primarily to the municipal judicial task, they also have considerable bearing on the role national courts are increasingly called to play in the international legal order. The implications of incorporation most relevant to transnational human rights litigation can be grouped in four categories: (1) the extent of incorporation; (2) the domestic applicability of customary norms; (3) customary norms and *stare decisis*; and (4) the international function of national courts in light of incorporation. Each will be discussed in turn.

1) The Extent of Incorporation

One of the most straightforward implications of incorporation is the scope and extent of domestic reception. In short, customary norms are incorporated to their "full extent by the common law."[55] Or, as Justice Gray emphatically put it: "International law, in its widest and most comprehensive sense . . . is part of our law."[56] Whether relating to the state immunity,[57] the privilege of ambassadors,[58] or the permissive heads of criminal jurisdiction,[59] all relevant customary international norms are received in the law of the land. Of course, some issues to which customary law applies simply do not arise in national courts. Questions relating to the use of force for instance are usually directed to the International Court of Justice (ICJ) or arbitral tribunals. Certain international customary international crimes are also incorporated in the common law, but are not necessarily triable.[60] In *Jones & Milling*, Lord Bingham accepted without deciding that war crimes could arguably be added to Blackstone's list of paradigmatic international offences (violations of safe-conducts, infringements of the rights of ambassadors, and piracy) that "would now be triable and punishable under the domestic criminal law of this country irrespective of any domestic statute."[61]

55 Blackstone, above note 4 at 67.
56 *Hilton v. Guyot*, 159 U.S. 113 at 163 (1895).
57 *Trendtex*, above note 23; see Chapter 7.
58 *Heathfield*, above note 9.
59 *Pinochet III*, above note 37; see Chapter 7.
60 *Jones & Milling*, above note 23 at para. 23. See also O'Keefe, above note 29 at 294.
61 *Jones & Milling*, *ibid.* at para. 22. See also Blackstone, above note 4 at 68.

Transnational human rights litigation is largely premised on the domestic reception of customary norms pertaining to the protection of individuals *qua* human rights standards. It is generally accepted that many fundamental principles of human rights protection form part of customary international law.[62] These norms too are received into the law of the land. Through the process of incorporation, as Justice La Forest expressed in biological language, Anglo-American legal systems "are absorbing international legal norms affecting the individual through [their] constitutional pores."[63] In *Sosa*, recalling that US courts have recognized the incorporation of customary law for over two centuries, the majority noted: "it would take some explaining to say now that federal courts must avert their gaze entirely from any international norm intended to protect individuals."[64]

Also implicit in the domestic reception of customary international law is the requirement that the norms at issue be indeed recognized as customary norms. That is to say, the rule must be binding at international law, having crystallized by way of generalized state practice and *opinio juris*. As a rule, national courts take judicial notice of international law.[65] In practice however, parties seeking to avail themselves of a particular norm have the burden of proving its existence. As Justice Story said, courts ascertain the state of international law by consulting "the works of jurists, writing professedly on public law; or by the general usage and practice of nations; or by judicial decisions recognising and enforcing that law."[66] In the context of transnational human rights litigation, US courts have consistently required a high evidentiary threshold in determining whether a given customary norm is to be considered an enforceable part of domestic law.[67] In *Re Marcos' Estate* (1994), the Court of Appeal for the Ninth Circuit held that "actionable violations of international law must be of a norm that is specific, uni-

---

62 *Barcelona Traction, Light & Power Co. (Second Phase) (Belgium v. Spain)*, [1970] I.C.J. Rep. 3 at para. 32. See also Brownlie, above note 2 at 537; Theodor Meron, *Human Rights and Humanitarian Norms as Customary Law* (Oxford: Clarendon Press, 1989).

63 Hon. Justice Gérard V. La Forest, "The Expanding Role of the Supreme Court of Canada in International Law Issues" (1996) 34 Can.Y.B. Int'l L. 89 at 98 [La Forest].

64 *Sosa*, above note 49 at 730.

65 *Halsbury's Laws of England*, 4th ed., vol. 17 (London: Butterworths, 1977) at § 100; Brownlie, above note 2 at 12.

66 *United States v. Smith*, 18 U.S. 153 at 160–61 (1820).

67 See for example, *Filártiga v. Peña-Irala*, 630 F.2d 876 at 881 (2d Cir. 1980) [*Filártiga*]; *Tel-Oren v. Libyan Arab Republic*, 726 F.2d 774 at 781 (D.C. Cir. 1984) [*Tel-Oren*].

versal, and obligatory."[68] At international law, universal adherence is not required for custom to form; substantial uniformity is sufficient.[69] In *Sosa*, the Court upheld the stringent threshold adopted by the lower courts, requiring evidence that actionable customary norms possess at least as much "definite content and acceptance among civilized nations as the historical paradigms familiar when [*ATCA*] was enacted."[70]

2) Domestic Applicability of Customary Norms

Once established at international law, customary norms are *ipso facto* incorporated and become an effective part of national law. Courts apply and give effect to customary law as they would any other rule of law, "as often as questions of right depending upon it are duly presented for their determination."[71] In Westlake's words: "courts must enforce rights given by international law as well as those given by the law of the land in its narrower sense."[72] Accordingly, before the enactment of legislation codifying the customary principle of state immunity, courts applied it as a matter of common law.[73] In 2007, the Supreme Court of Canada stated, "absent an express derogation, the courts may look to prohibitive rules of customary international law to aid in the interpretation of Canadian law and the development of the common law."[74]

While other international norms may well be directly incorporated and applied at common law, customary international crimes must receive the transformative assent of Parliament. Despite Lord Millet's view to the contrary in *Pinochet III*,[75] it is now firmly established that customary international crimes are not directly triable in English courts. One may accordingly wonder about the propriety of recognizing new civil causes of action on the basis of international law, as transnational human rights litigation proposes. Do the policy reasons

68 *Hilao v. Estate of Ferdinand Marcos*, 25 F.3d 1467 at 1475 (9th Cir. 1994).

69 *Asylum Case (Columbia v. Peru)*, Judgment, [1950] I.C.J. Rep. 276 at 276–77; Brownlie, above note 2 at 7.

70 *Sosa*, above note 49 at 732.

71 *The Paquete Habana*, above note 1 at 700.

72 Westlake, above note 2 at 26.

73 *Trendtex*, above note 23; Hazel Fox QC, *The Law of State Immunity* (Oxford: Oxford University Press, 2002) at 112–17.

74 *Hape*, above note 23 at para. 39.

75 *Pinochet III*, above note 37 at 276–77, Lord Millet. See also O'Keefe, above note 29 at 335.

of democratic accountability and legitimacy that counsel against the direct enforcement of international crimes in domestic courts apply *mutatis mutandis* to the recognition of internationally derived torts through the common law? The House of Lords said nothing of the possibility of enforcing international norms through domestic civil actions in *Jones & Milling*, and Lord Hoffman was careful to confine his conclusions to the criminal law.[76] Lord Bingham cited *Sosa* (2004) as an example of an instance where an international norm was not domestically enforced.[77] It will be recalled that in *Sosa* the US Supreme Court found that the prohibition against arbitrary detention lacked sufficient definite content at international law to be actionable under *ATCA*. It is unclear how Lord Bingham felt that *Sosa* was on point: it is not authority in support of the proposition that international norms may not give rise to enforceable rights in domestic courts per se, but rather a decision about the specific requirements of *ATCA*, a statute with no equivalent in the UK. It may be that His Lordship was referring to the specificity of customary norms that is required to make them enforceable.

It is one of the arguments of this book that violations of well-established customary norms may give rise to privately actionable rights at common law. This has been expressly recognized in the US in the unique context of *ATCA* litigation, but it appears that no feature of UK or Canadian law precludes the civil actionability of customary norms in those countries.[78] Clearly, that violations of customary norms may give rise to actionable rights at common law does not automatically follow from incorporation, nor was it an inevitable development in US law. Judge Bork[79] and the minority in *Sosa*[80] certainly would have decided otherwise. But the actionability of customary norms at common law is defensible as a matter of first principle. Insofar as customary norms create individual rights, "it is a general and indisputable rule that where there is a legal right, there is also a legal remedy by

76 *Jones & Milling*, above note 23 at para. 62, Lord Hoffman.

77 *Ibid.* at para. 23.

78 *Filártiga*, above note 67 at 890; *Sosa*, above note 49 at 57; International Law Association, Committee on International Human Rights Law and Practice, "Report on Civil Actions in the English Courts for Serious Human Rights Violations Abroad" (2001) 2 Eur. H.R.L. Rev. 129 at 159.

79 *Tel Oren*, above note 67.

80 *Sosa*, above note 49 at 739.

suit or action at law, whenever that right is invaded."[81] Historically, in this respect, the common law played an important supplemental role, providing remedies for violations of legal rights not covered by the jurisdiction of other courts. In the eighteenth century, "all possible injuries whatsoever, that did not fall within the exclusive cognizance of either the ecclesiastical, military, or maritime tribunals, are for that very reason, within the cognizance of the common law courts of justice; for it is a settled and invariable principle in the laws of England, that every right, when withheld, must have a remedy, and every injury its proper redress."[82] More recently, Lord Scarman expressed the principle in these terms:

> Unless statute has intervened to restrict the range of judge-made law, the common law enables the judges, when faced with a situation where a right recognised by law *is* not adequately protected, either to extend existing principles to cover the situation or to apply an existing remedy to redress the injustice. There is here no novelty; but merely the application of the principle "*ubi jus ibi remedium*."[83] [Emphasis in original.]

Arguably, Blackstone's reference to "all possible injuries whatsoever" includes twenty-first century violations of international human rights, which through incorporation, amount to violations of legal rights at common law. Insofar as no statute has intervened to curtail the powers of common law courts in this respect, their historical authority to adjudicate remains intact.

The Court in *Sosa* recognized *ATCA* "to underwrite litigation of a narrow set of common law actions derived from the law of nations."[84] In the eighteenth century, the Court noted, it was not uncommon for states to enact legislation reinforcing and clarifying the "brooding omnipresence" of the common law.[85] Significantly, the Court stated that no legislative grant of authority was required to empower courts to exercise jurisdiction over civil actions for violations of customary

81 Blackstone, above note 4, vol. 3 at 23.

82 *Ibid.* at 109.

83 *Sidaway v. Board of Governors of the Bethlem Royal Hospital and the Maudsley Hospital*, [1985] A.C. 871 at 884, Lord Scarman; *In Re: F. v. West Berkshire HA*, [1990] 2 A.C. 1 (H.L.).

84 *Sosa*, above note 49 at 722.

85 *Ibid.*

law and to provide remedies "already available at common law."[86] Indeed, pursuant to Article III§2 of the US constitution, federal courts have jurisdiction over "all Cases, in Law and Equity, arising under . . . the Laws of the United States." The "laws of the United States" include the law of nations as incorporated into the common law.[87] Moreover, the original terms of *ATCA* make plain that civil jurisdiction over violations of the law of nations existed at common law; it specified that the jurisdiction of the district courts over torts in violation of the law of nations was "concurrent with [that of] the courts of the several states."[88] As courts of law of general jurisdiction, state courts—and, arguably, UK and Canadian courts—may assert jurisdiction over *ATCA*-style claims as a matter of common law.[89]

Incorporation is conditioned by two important principles: (1) parliamentary supremacy and (2) the government control of foreign relations and policy. Accordingly, these principles ought to direct any judicial decision to derive civil causes of actions from customary international norms through the common law.

a) Incorporation and National Legislation

In the words of Lord Atkin, once judicially ascertained, customary law is treated as "incorporated into the domestic law, so far as it is not inconsistent with rules enacted by statutes."[90] In short, legislation supersedes incompatible customary law.[91] The subordination of custom to legislation underscores the presumptive aspect of incorporation. That is to say, custom is presumed to form part of the common law unless barred by the contrary will of the legislature, thus giving effect to the constitutionally mandated hierarchy of norms within the national

86 *Ibid.*

87 American Law Institute, *Restatement of the Law (3d) of Foreign Relations Law of the United States* (St. Paul, MN: American Law Institute, 1988) at § 111, Comment d and Reporter's note 4. [Restatement].

88 *Judiciary Act of 1789*, § 9, cl. 4. The concurrent jurisdiction with state courts is the joint product of a political compromise and of the distinct eighteenth century US preoccupation with the enforcement of international law in every part of the union. See Chapter 2, Section C(1).

89 See Chapter 3, Section E(4).

90 *Chung Chi Cheung*, above note 32 at 168.

91 A noteworthy exception exists in US law. As part of the "supreme law of the land" pursuant to art. IV § 2 of the Constitution customary international law supersedes inconsistent legislation of the several states. See *United States v. Belmont*, 301 U.S. 324 (1937); Restatement, above note 87 at § 111(1).

legal order and to the principle of parliamentary supremacy. Indeed, the legislative omnipotence of states includes the power to enact legislation that is contrary to international law.[92] In practice however, states seek to harmonize their laws with those of the international community, lest they "cease to be a part of the civilized world."[93] Accordingly, to strike the appropriate balance between state sovereignty and the imperatives of international communitarianism, national courts endeavour where possible, as a matter of statutory interpretation, to construe and apply legislation in conformity with international law. Marshall CJ expressed the rule in his first decision as Chief Justice: "the laws of the United States ought not, if it be avoidable, so to be construed as to infract the common principles and usages of nations."[94] Likewise, Cockburn CJ in *Keyn* said: "the true canon of construction is to assume that the legislature has not so enacted as to violate the rights of other nations."[95] In Canada also, "Parliament is not presumed to legislate in breach of a treaty or in any manner inconsistent with the comity of nations and the established rules of international law."[96]

National statutes enacted expressly to clarify or to give particular effect to customary norms raise important questions with regards to the subsequent incorporation of emerging customary norms. As stated above, according to classic doctrine, legislation such as the *Diplomatic Privileges Act, 1708*, and the various twentieth-century state immunity statutes are "not to be considered as introductive of any new rule, but merely as declaratory of the old fundamental constitutions of the kingdom."[97] This being so, how must courts treat the emergence of further customary law exceptions to state immunity given the presence of state immunity legislation? Can courts recognize and give effect to new customary law exceptions to state immunity not contained within the four corners of the legislation? It will be argued in Chapter 7 that courts may take cognizance of emerging customary norms that relate to matters on which Parliament has chosen to legislate insofar as the

92 *Hape*, above note 23 at para. 39; *Mortensen v. Peters* (1906), 8 F. (J.C.) 93 at 100; *R. v. Meiklebam* (1906), 11 O.L.R. 366 at 373 (H.C.J.).

93 Blackstone, above note 4 at 67.

94 *Talbot v. Seeman*, 5 U.S. 1 at 43 (1801); *Murray v. The Charming Betsy*, 6 U.S. 64 at 118 (1804).

95 *Keyn*, above note 24 at 210.

96 *Daniels v. White*, [1968] S.C.R. 517 at 541; *Hape*, above note 23 at §§ 53–54.

97 Blackstone, above note 4 at 67.

emerging customary norms are materially compatible with existing legislation.

b) Incorporation and the Executive's Power over Foreign Relations

Because transnational human rights proceedings tend to involve foreign states or their officials, they potentially bring the judiciary into uneasy proximity with the executive's management of foreign relations. Mindful of the government's exclusive power over foreign affairs and policy and of the limits of the judicial role, courts have developed various rules and prudential doctrines allowing them to decline jurisdiction they otherwise possess where it is appropriate or expedient to do so. These include comity, the political question doctrine, *forum non conveniens*, act of state, and state immunity. The operation of these doctrines in the context of transnational human rights litigation is discussed at length in other chapters,[98] but for the purposes of the present discussion, it is enough to comment on the manner in which they generally interact with the principle of incorporation.

The doctrines of justiciability do not bar the reception of customary norms as such, but they do condition the judicial authority to give effect to domestically received international law in certain matters. The *Sosa* Court noted that judicial recognition of actionable customary norms necessarily involves "an element of judgment about the practical consequences of making that cause of action available to litigants in the federal courts."[99] In particular, the Court referred to a possible "policy of case-specific deference" in which "serious weight" would be given "to the executive branch's view of the case's impact on foreign policy."[100] In this respect the political question doctrine and Act of State doctrine are particularly relevant. However, giving serious weight to the executive's assessment of the foreign relations implications of a particular case does not release the judiciary from its adjudicative responsibility in cases where clear questions of law arise and where manageable standards exist for their determination.[101]

---

98 See Chapters 5, 6, and 7.

99 *Sosa*, above note 49 at 732.

100 *Ibid.* at 733, n. 21.

101 *Kuwait Airways Corporation v. Iraqi Airways Co.*, [2002] 2 A.C. 883 (H.L.); See Chapter 5, Section B.

3) Customary Norms and *Stare Decisis*

Another implication of incorporation is the duty of courts to ascertain and apply the rule of international law that prevails at any given time. Simply stated, despite Lord Atkin's view to the contrary in *Chung Chi Cheung* (1939),[102] given the evolving nature of international law, judicial determinations concerning the existence of a particular customary rule are not subject to the doctrine of *stare decisis*. Accordingly, the Court of Appeal's holding in *Parlement Belge* (1880) that the doctrine of absolute immunity applied in English law did not prevent the same court in *Trendtex* (1977) from finding that the principle of restrictive immunity had since emerged at international law and was *ipso facto* incorporated into the common law.[103] As Lord Denning MR stated, "If this court today is satisfied that the rule of international law on a subject has changed from what it was 50 or 60 years ago, it can give effect to that change — and apply the change in our English law — without waiting for the House of Lords to do it."[104] Likewise, in *Filártiga*, Judge Kaufman said that "courts must interpret international law not as it was in 1789, but as it has evolved and exists among the nations of the world today."[105]

An important qualification is warranted. Lower courts are bound by the decisions of higher courts in all cases, including cases involving international norms. Specifically, lower courts are bound by the interpretations or applications of incorporated customary norms by higher courts. For instance, the Supreme Court of Canada's characterization of the employment of maintenance staff on military bases as an act *jure imperii* for state immunity purposes binds Canadian lower courts in all cases in which that issue arises.[106] The doctrine of *stare decisis* however does not apply to judicial findings that a new customary norm has crystallized at international law and is incorporated into the common law. *Stare decisis* does not apply in such circumstances because no binding precedent regarding the freshly emerged customary norm exists. Shaw LJ articulated the rule in clear terms:

---

102 *Chung Chi Cheung*, above note 32.
103 *Trendtex*, above note 23.
104 *Trendtex*, *ibid.* at 365–66.
105 *Filártiga*, above note 67 at 881.
106 *Re Canada Labour Code*, [1992] 2 S.C.R. 50.

> What is immutable is the principle of English law that the law of nations (not what *was* the law of nations) must be applied in the courts of England. The rule of *stare decisis* operates to preclude a court from overriding a decision which binds it in regard to a particular rule of (international) law, it does not prevent a court from applying a rule which did not exist when the earlier decision was made . . . [107]

Accordingly, one year after the Supreme Court of Canada's inconclusive judgment concerning the emergence of the restrictive principle of state immunity,[108] the Quebec Court of Appeal held that "it is open for this Court to reaffirm its belief in the existence in Canada of a doctrine of restrictive immunity."[109] Likewise, the Supreme Court ruling in *Sosa* that the prohibition against arbitrary detention was not a customary international norm of sufficient specificity to be actionable in US law[110] does not preclude a future court from determining arbitrary detention to be actionable should the international law on the matter evolve.

O'Keefe has argued that the non-application of *stare decisis* to judicial determinations of customary law implies that customary norms, once incorporated, "are not, strictly speaking, rules of common law" but that they enjoy rather "an independent existence, alongside common law, within the non-statutory law of England."[111] As evidence that incorporated customary norms are *like* common law without being completely assimilated to it, O'Keefe states that "no other part of the common law benefits from an exception to the rule of *stare decisis*."[112] Moreover, he continues,

> both Lord Denning MR and Shaw LJ studiously avoided all reference in *Trendtex* to "the common law," stating respectively that customary international law was part of "our English law" or was "applied in the courts of England." In this light . . . reference in the pre- and sometimes post-*Trendtex* cases to international law "being part of the

107 *Trendtex*, above note 23 at 388.

108 *Congo (République démocratique) v. Venne*, [1971] S.C.R. 997.

109 *Zodiak International Products Inc. v. Polish People's Republic* (1978), 81 D.L.R. (3d) 656 at 659 (Que. C.A.).

110 *Sosa*, above note 49 at 738.

111 O'Keefe, above note 29 at 307–8.

112 *Ibid.* at 308.

> common law" is better read . . . to mean "part of that body of English law not made by Parliament."[113]

However this may be, the absence of reference to the "common law" in the majority's decision in *Trendtex* establishes little. Moreover, it is arguably inaccurate to state that incorporated custom "benefits from an exception to the rule of *stare decsis*." In the interest of maintaining stability in the law, lower courts must follow binding precedent in all cases. The only limited sense in which *stare decisis* can be said to be inapplicable is with regards to the judicial notice of newly emerged customary norms. In such circumstance, *stare decisis* does not apply because, logically, there cannot be any judicial pronouncements in respect of customary norms that hitherto did not exist.

4) The Creative International Function of Common Law Courts

As a corollary to the three previous issues relating to the municipal judicial task, the incorporation of customary law underscores the creative, lawmaking function of national courts on the international plane. By ascertaining, interpreting, and applying incorporated customary norms, national courts participate in the ongoing formation and adaptation of customary international law, not only for their own state but also for the international community as a whole. National courts are powerful participants in the international legal order, shaping and directing the future path of the law, alongside the governments and legislatures of the states they serve. Westlake understood the international function of national courts to flow from the unity of customary law and the common law. The international law that is received into the common law, he wrote, is that "which at the time exists between States, without prejudice to the right and duty of the courts to assist in developing its acknowledged principles in the same manner in which they assist in developing the principles of the common law."[114] In no area of international law is the influence of national courts more apparent than the law of state immunity, which, until the twentieth century codifications, was largely developed in national

113 *Ibid.*

114 Westlake, above note 2 at 26.

courts and applied internationally as customary law. As will be seen in Chapter 7, the development of the restricted principle of state immunity occurred gradually over the course of a century of steady, though at times inconsistent, judicial practice.[115] "Domestic court decisions are a patchwork process and often conflict with each other, but from such stuff is customary international law made and modified."[116]

The international lawmaking function of national courts is also manifest in the bottom-up incorporation of the so-called "general principles of law recognized by civilized nations." According to Franck, national courts are "the principal progenitors of third-party international law"; they are "profoundly and quite properly involved in the process of international law-making, for international law is part of the law of all civilized states, just as, reciprocally, the 'general principles of law recognized by civilized States' has been incorporated, by Article 38 of the Statute of the World Court, in the international *corpus juris*."[117]

That national courts fulfil a prominent international role in developing the law of nations has long been understood. In 1795, Irdell J stated that, insofar as its jurisdiction was determined by the law of nations, a prize court is "in effect, a court of all the nations in the world, because all persons, in every part of the world, are concluded by its sentences."[118] No other legal scholar, except perhaps Falk,[119] has emphasized the international role of domestic courts more than Scelle. Though part of a broader monistic vision of international law, which will not be discussed here, Scelle's theory of *dédoublement fonctionnel* aptly describes the *de jure* (if not *de facto*) double-duty of national courts. For Scelle, *« le juge national, lorsqu'il rend un jugement dans une affaire entre nationaux et étrangers ou entre étrangers, cesse d'être un juge national pour devenir un juge international. »*[120]

---

115 See Chapter 7, Section C(1).

116 Richard B. Lillich, "The Proper Role of Domestic Courts in the International Legal Order" (1970) 11 Va. J. Int'l L. 9 at 32–33.

117 Thomas M. Franck, *The Structure of Impartiality: Toward the Organization of World Law* (New York: MacMillan, 1968) at 223.

118 *Penhallow v. Doane's Administrators*, 3 U.S. 54 at 91(1795).

119 See, generally, Richard A. Falk, *The Role of Domestic Courts in the International Legal Order* (Syracuse: Syracuse University Press, 1964).

120 Georges Scelle, *Précis de droit des gens* (Paris: Recueil Sirey, 1932) at 56; O'Keefe above note 29 at 335; Martii Koskenniemi, *The Gentle Civilizer of Nations* (Cambridge: Cambridge University Press, 2001) at 333.

As domestic courts are increasingly called upon to resolve transnational disputes of all kinds, commentators have observed a concomitant broadening of comparative judicial methodology and greater institutional convergence.[121] Slaughter calls this phenomenon "judicial globalization," that is, the "diverse and messy process of judicial interaction across, above and below borders, exchanging ideas and cooperating in cases involving national as much as international law."[122] Curial interaction is particularly visible in human rights and constitutional cases, as courts turn to each other to gain greater insight into the consequences of different solutions to common legal problems. Slaughter posits that courts

> . . . feel a particular common bond with one another in adjudicating human rights cases because such cases engage a core judicial function in many countries around the world. They ask courts to protect individuals against abuses of state power, requiring them to determine the appropriate level of protection in light of a complex matrix of historical, cultural, and political needs and expectations.[123]

Transnational human rights litigation judgments illustrate the heightened judicial willingness to refer not only to international norms but also to the decisions of other national courts.[124] While some eloquent voices on the US Supreme Court[125] fail to appreciate the relevance of the legal experience of other countries, particularly in constitutional cases, the predominant approach has shown itself amenable to the persuasive authority of foreign judgments. Any other posture would be astonishing, as Justice Breyer noted, "in a Nation that from its birth has given a 'decent respect to the opinions of mankind.'"[126]

121 H. Patrick Glenn, "Persuasive Authority" (1987) 32 McGill L.J. 261; Karen Knop, "Here and There: International Law in Domestic Courts" (2000) 32 N.Y.U. J. Int'l L. & Pol. 501 at 518–19.

122 Anne-Marie Slaughter, "Judicial Globalization" (2000) 40 Va. J. Int'l L. 1103 at 1104 [Slaughter 2000]. See also, generally, Anne-Marie Slaughter, "A Typology of Transjudicial Communication" (1994) 29 U. Rich. L. Rev. 99.

123 Slaughter 2000, *ibid.* at 1111.

124 See for example, the comparative approaches in *Bouzari* 2002 above note 46; *Presbyterian Church of Sudan v. Talisman Energy Inc.*, 244 F. Supp. 2d 289 (S.D.N.Y. 2003).

125 *Sosa*, above note 49 at 750, Scalia J. See also the dissenting opinions of Justice Scalia in *Thompson v. Oklahoma*, 487 U.S. 815 (1988) and *Roper v. Simmons*, 543 U.S. 551 (2005).

126 *Knight v. Florida*, 528 U.S. 990 at 997 (1999), citing the US Declaration of Independence. See also Harry Blackmun, "The Supreme Court and the Law of Nations:

Whether indirectly through their decisions or directly through face-to-face interactions and exchanges,[127] the world's courts are engaging in a dialogue. Significantly, this curial dialogue is occurring, as Slaughter suggested, not among national flag-bearing tribunals, but among courts in their capacity as adjudicative bodies of the international community charged with a common responsibility: that of resolving disputes and saying the law.[128] While inexorably linked to the globalization of markets, telecommunications, and travel, the phenomenon of judicial globalization also owes its vitality to the common legal heritage of all judiciaries, that is, the domestic incorporation of customary international law. Just as judicial globalization is the effect of many causes, it will likely prove to be the cause of many effects, including, most desirably, the effective adherence to and further development of legal norms intended to protect individuals by internationally minded judiciaries. Justice La Forest remarked: "In the field of human rights . . . our courts are assisting in developing general and coherent principles that apply in very significant portions of the globe. These principles are applied consistently, with an international vision and on the basis of international experience. Thus our courts — and many other national courts — are truly becoming international courts in many areas involving the rule of law."[129]

D. CONCLUSION

In the common law tradition, customary international law is incorporated into the law of the land, and judges may apply and administer its principles in appropriate cases. Thus pursuant to *ATCA*, US federal courts have jurisdiction in civil proceedings in respect of violations

Owing a decent respect to the Opinions of Mankind" (1994) 88 A.S.I.L. Proceedings 383 at 384.

127 Judicial colloquia and regional judicial associations are flourishing. See Slaughter 2000, above note 122 at 1120–23. Notably, see also *Charter of the Organization of Supreme Courts of the Americas* (OSCA), 26 October 1995, the mission of which is to serve "as a permanent link between the judicial systems of the Americas, and promoting international judicial cooperation in the hemisphere." The OSCA charter is printed in (1996) 2 International Judicial Observer 1 at 1–2. The Organisation of American States and Canada have formally registered their support for OSCA: AG/RES. 1407 (XXVI-O/96), 7 June 1996.

128 Slaughter 2000, above note 122 at 1114.

129 La Forest, above note 63 at 100.

of international law, which are made actionable through the common law. Whatever the case may be in respect of crimes, no feature of English and Canadian law appears to preclude the courts of those countries to derive actionable torts from customary international law. As the Supreme Court of Canada noted in *R. v. Hape* (2007), "absent an express derogation, the courts may look to prohibitive rules of customary international law to aid in the interpretation of Canadian law and the development of the common law."[130] Such a view is consistent with the creative function of common law courts, both at home and increasingly on the international plane.

130 *Hape*, above note 23 at para. 39.

CHAPTER FIVE

Extraterritorial Jurisdiction, Applicable Law, and Justiciability

"It is to the underlying reality of the international legal order, then, that we must turn if we are to structure a rational and workable system of private international law."

—Justice G.V. La Forest[1]

A. INTRODUCTION

In terms of the propriety of the jurisdiction in transnational human rights claims against private parties (as compared with ordinary jurisdiction over local or foreign torts), three problems are commonly raised. First, the wrongs in question — grave breaches of international human rights — will have been committed abroad by foreigners, so that the forum's jurisdiction to enforce human rights norms is called into question. Second, the content of the applicable law is reviewed: on what basis can a foreign forum apply international human rights norms against private parties and in disregard of the *lex loci*, which in terms of private international law rules would be the proper law of the tort, normally the law of the place where the tort was committed? Third, how are international human rights norms justiciable in a foreign forum, as contrasted perhaps with an international human rights committee or tribunal specifically mandated for that purpose? These three objections are considered together in this chapter on the basis that they share a common foundation — a denial that the human rights norms in question really constitute generally applicable international

1 *Tolofson v. Jensen*, [1994] 3 S.C.R. 1022 at para. 37 [*Tolofson*].

law, which, if they are to be meaningful, must supervene and prevail over inconsistent rules of domestic law — whether those rules relate to jurisdiction, justification, or justiciability.

The first section of this chapter (Section B) examines the question of judicial competence of the state in civil proceedings involving extraterritorial human rights breaches, both as a matter of international law and municipal law. Canadian and UK practice receives particular attention. Beyond broad principles, as will be seen, international law provides little guidance on the scope of national civil jurisdiction, with the result that every state enjoys a large measure of discretion in determining the extent of its own competence pursuant to its own rules of private international law. It will be argued that while territorial jurisdiction remains a sound basis for the exercise of judicial competence in most cases, it fails to engage with the particular problems raised by transnational human rights claims. In this connection, the contours of universal civil jurisdiction will be examined, a principle for which there is evidence of growing international approval. In addition to the question of whether civil jurisdiction can be asserted, transnational human rights litigation raises important problems with regards to the applicable law and justiciability. These issues will be addressed in Sections C and D, respectively.

B. EXTRATERRITORIAL JURISDICTION

1) At International Law

In the broadest terms, at international law, jurisdiction is understood as the authority of states to make and enforce law within their territory.[2] The legal competences of states are often coordinately associ-

2 Michael Akehurst, "Jurisdiction in International Law" (1972) 46 Brit. Y.B. Int'l L. 146 [Akehurst]; Derek W. Bowett, "Jurisdiction: Changing Patterns of Authority over Activities and Resources" (1982) 53 Brit. Y.B. Int'l L. 1 [Bowett]; Ian Brownlie, *Principles of Public International Law*, 6th ed. (Oxford: Oxford University Press, 2003) at 297 [Brownlie]; Michael Byers, *Custom, Power and the Power of Rules: International Relations and Customary International Law* (Cambridge: Cambridge University Press, 1999) at 53; Patrick Capps, Malcolm Evans, & Stratos Konstadinidis, eds., *Asserting Jurisdiction: International and European Legal Perspectives* (Oxford: Hart, 2003) at xix; Research in International Law Under the Auspices of the Harvard Law School, Part II, *Jurisdiction with Respect to Crime* (1935) 29 A.J.I.L. Supp. 435 [Harvard Research]; Vaughan Lowe, "Jurisdiction" in Malcolm D. Evans, ed., *International Law* (Oxford: Oxford University Press, 2003) at 336 [Lowe]; Lassa

ated with the three organs of power: the authority to prescribe (the legislative), the authority to enforce (the executive), and the authority to adjudicate (the judiciary). Jurisdiction is *prima facie* territorial.[3] It is the case however that states, from time to time, extend the application of their laws to persons, things, and events outside their territory. This section sets out in broad terms the principles of international law relevant to the extraterritorial adjudicative jurisdiction of states in civil proceedings.

The *Lotus Case* remains an important starting point. When a French steamer collided with a Turkish collier in the high seas resulting in the deaths of eight Turkish seamen, two French officers present on Turkish territory were arrested and convicted of manslaughter under Turkish criminal law. The French government protested, claiming that Turkey could not exercise criminal jurisdiction over a foreigner in relation to extraterritorial events on the sole basis that one of its nationals had been a victim of the crime. Before the Permanent Court of International Justice, France contended that states are prohibited from exercising extraterritorial jurisdiction unless authorized by a specific rule of international law. Turkey took the opposite view, arguing that states may freely exercise their jurisdiction unless expressly prohibited by international law. The Court agreed with Turkey, emphasizing that as a matter of principle states are sovereign and bound solely by the norms to which they consent and, accordingly, restrictions upon their jurisdiction should not be presumed.[4] In the Court's opinion, "far from laying down a general prohibition to the effect that States may not extend the application of their laws and the jurisdiction of their courts to persons, property and acts outside their territory, [international law] leaves them in this respect with a wide measure of discretion, which is only limited in certain cases by prohibitive rules."[5] First among the restrictions imposed by international law, the Court noted, is the prohibition of exercising power in the territory of another state without the latter's consent. A second restriction, not mentioned by the Court but which stands as a corollary of the first, is the doctrine of state

Francis Lawrence Oppenheim, *Oppenheim's International Law*, 9th ed. Robert Jennings & Arthur Watts, eds. (London: Longman, 1992) [Oppenheim] at 456.

3 Brownlie, *ibid.* at 297.

4 *The Case of the S.S. Lotus (France v. Turkey)* (1927), P.C.I.J. (Ser. A) No. 10 at 18 [*The Lotus*].

5 *Ibid.* at 19.

immunity from judicial process with regards to sovereign acts. On the whole, international law places few limits on the extraterritorial jurisdiction of states, and aside from these, "every State remains free to adopt the principles which it regards as best and most suitable."[6] This wide jurisdictional discretion of states at international law explains "the great variety of rules which they have been able to adopt without objections or complaints" in asserting jurisdiction over extraterritorial matters.[7] This, particularly, is the case in criminal proceedings. Though criminal law is presumptively territorial in scope and application, in practice, national legal systems extend their reach to crimes and persons outside the territory of the state, and do so on the basis of various rationales. The Court noted that the "territoriality of criminal law is . . . not an absolute principle of international law, and by no means coincides with territorial sovereignty."[8] Lauterpacht agreed: "Territoriality of jurisdiction is a rule of convenience . . . . It is not a requirement of justice or even a necessary postulate of the sovereignty of the State."[9]

The most exhaustive inquiry into the practice of states with regards to criminal jurisdiction remains the 1935 *Harvard Research on Jurisdiction With Respect to Crime* (Harvard Research). After analyzing numerous national criminal codes, the works of publicists and the decisions of national courts, the Harvard Research identified five permissive principles under which states assert criminal jurisdiction. The principles are well known and have become standard features of international law textbooks.[10] In summarizing the principles of criminal jurisdiction, one can do no better than to quote the Harvard Research itself.

---

6 *Ibid.*

7 *Ibid.*

8 *Ibid.* at 20; *R. v. Cook*, [1998] 2 S.C.R. 597 at 618. On the extraterritorial reach of Canadian constitutional and criminal law generally, see *R. v. Hape*, [2007] 2 S.C.R. 292 [*Hape*].

9 Hersch Lauterpacht, "Allegiance, Diplomatic Protection and Criminal Jurisdiction Over Aliens" (1945–47) 9 Cambridge L.J. 330 at 348, n. 61.

10 Akehurst, above note 2 at 152–69; Brownlie, above note 2, c. 15; Antonio Cassese, *International Criminal Law* (Oxford: Oxford University Press, 2003) c. 15 [Cassese]; Lowe, above note 2 at 336–43; Malcolm Shaw, *International Law* (Cambridge: Cambridge University Press, 2003) c. 12. See also Luc Reydams, *Universal Jurisdiction: International and Municipal Legal Perspectives* (Oxford: Oxford University Press, 2003) at 21–22 (identifies two further principles: "the flag principle" and "the representation principle") [Reydams].

> These five general principles are: first, the *territorial principle*, determining jurisdiction by reference to the place where the offence is committed; second, the *nationality principle*, determining jurisdiction by reference to the nationality or national character of the person committing the offence; third, the *protective principle*, determining jurisdiction by the national interest injured by the offence; fourth, the *universality principle*, determining jurisdiction by reference to the custody of the person committing the offence; and fifth, the *passive personality principle*, determining jurisdiction by reference to the nationality or national character of the person injured by the offence. Of these five principles, the first is everywhere regarded as of primary importance and of fundamental character. The second is universally accepted, though there are striking differences in the extent to which it is used in the different national systems. The third is claimed by most States, regarded with misgivings in a few, and generally ranked as the basis of an auxiliary competence . . . The fourth is widely though by no means universally accepted as the basis of an auxiliary competence, except for the offence of piracy, with respect to which it is the generally recognized principle of jurisdiction. The fifth, asserted in some form by a considerable number of States and contested by others, is admittedly auxiliary in character and is probably not essential for any State if the ends served are adequately provided for on other principles.[11] [Emphasis added.]

A few observations are warranted. First, these principles form part of international law *qua* "general principles of law recognized by civilized nations."[12] Second, the principles of criminal jurisdiction are generally permissive, not restrictive.[13] Each one justifies the assertion of jurisdiction over foreign nationals. They are not limits per se on the authority of states. It may be, as Brownlie supposed, that "each individual principle is only evidence of the reasonableness of the exercise of jurisdiction."[14] Third, certain principles overlap and may lead to concurrent jurisdiction. In *The Lotus*, for instance, both France and Turkey had jurisdiction under the nationality and passive personality

11 Harvard Research, above note 2 at 445. See also Akehurst, *ibid.* at 152–69; Brownlie, *ibid.* at 299–306.

12 Harvard Research, *ibid.* at 444–45.

13 *The Lotus*, above note 4 at 20.

14 Brownlie, above note 2 at 305.

principles respectively. For the time being, international law contains no rules to resolve situations of conflicting or concurrent jurisdiction; it does not give "pride of place to one legal ground of national jurisdiction (say, territoriality) over another such ground (say, passive nationality)."[15] Some commentators have called for a distillation of the five principles into a streamlined analysis modelled on national practice in civil proceedings under which jurisdiction hinges on the assessment of connecting factors between the claim, the forum, and on the balance of interest of the parties.[16]

The principles governing the extraterritorial civil jurisdiction at international law are not as determinate as in the criminal sphere. Other than the few treaties on the matter, of which the 1968 *Brussels Convention on Jurisdiction and Enforcement of Judgments in Civil and Commercial Matters*[17] is the most notable example, it is unclear whether other norms of international law determine the extraterritorial civil jurisdiction of national courts. Custom is a doubtful candidate. While noting the exception of state and consular immunity, Akehurst found it "hard to resist the conclusion that . . . customary international law imposes no limits on the jurisdiction of municipal courts in civil trials."[18] Courts often evoke international comity as the underlying basis for conflicts rule. Indeed, in *Spar Aerospace*, the Supreme Court of Canada referred to comity as "a useful guiding principle when applying rules of private international law."[19] However useful it may be, comity remains a non-binding expression of reciprocal expectations among sovereign states. In *Hilton v. Guyot*, the US Supreme Court defined comity as

> neither a matter of absolute obligation, on the one hand, nor of mere courtesy and good will, upon the other. But it is the recognition which one nation allows within its territory to the legislative, exec-

---

15 Cassese, above note 10 at 348.

16 Lotika Sarkar, "The Proper Law of Crime in International Law" (1962) 11 I.C.L.Q. 446 at 466–70; Florian Alexander Mann, "The Doctrine of Jurisdiction in International Law" (1964-I) 111 R.C.A.D.I. 1 at 43–51 [Mann].

17 European jurisdictional issues are governed by E.C., *Council Regulation (E.C.) No 44/2001, as of 22 December 2000 on jurisdiction and the recognition and enforcement of judgments in civil and commercial matters*, [2001] O. J. L 44/2001 [*Brussels Convention*] at paras. 19–23, which remains in force.

18 Akehurst, above note 2 at 177.

19 *Spar Aerospace Ltd. v. American Mobile Satellite Corp.*, [2002] 4 S.C.R. 205 at para. 17 [*Spar*]; See also *Hape*, above note 8 at paras. 47–52.

> utive or judicial acts of another nation, having due regard both to international duty and convenience, and to the rights of its own citizens or of other persons who are under the protection of its laws.[20]

Though not bereft of normative value, comity is not international law and in the context of civil jurisdiction, Akehurst argues that there is "a strong presumption" that the requirements of the former do not necessarily coincide with those of the latter.[21]

Nevertheless, international law is not indifferent to the extraterritorial exercise of civil jurisdiction. Insofar as the *Brussels Convention* can be taken as evidence of the general direction of international law in this area, there would appear to exist widespread consensus that extraterritorial civil jurisdiction could be asserted where there is a real and substantial connection between the forum and the claim.[22] This standard of civil jurisdiction is most likely a "general principle of law recognized by civilized nations."[23] In any event, it is difficult to understand why international law would treat civil and criminal exercises of extraterritorial jurisdiction differently when both amount in substance to the exercise of state power. Sir Franklin Berman argues that there exists a cardinal difference between civil and criminal extraterritorial jurisdiction in that the latter is concerned with the general public interest, while the former is by definition a "pursuit of the unilateral interests of the asserting State or of its nationals."[24] Admittedly, "ordinary" civil claims relating to trade or family law largely concern the immediate private interests of the parties involved. However, Berman's objection falters in the "extraordinary" context of transnational human rights litigation where the subject matter of the proceedings—violations of fundamental human rights and, often, of peremptory norms of international law—relates to the public interest of the international com-

---

20 *Hilton v. Guyot*, 159 U.S. 113 at 164 (1895) [*Hilton*]; Harold G. Maier, "Jurisdictional Rules in Customary International Law" in *Extraterritorial Jurisdiction in Theory and Practice* (The Hague: Kluwer Law International, 1996) at 71 [Maier].

21 Akehurst, above note 2 at 217.

22 Brownlie, above note 2 at 297; Lowe, above note 2 at 336. Of course, one could forcefully argue that a defendant's presence or residence in the forum could justify an assertion of civil jurisdiction with respect to extraterritorial wrongs. Consent would also clearly suffice.

23 Harvard Research, above note 2 at 444–45.

24 Frank Berman, "Jurisdiction: The State" in Patrick Capps *et al.*, eds., *Asserting Jurisdiction: International and European Legal Perspectives* (Oxford: Hart, 2003) at 13.

munity as a whole. The better view was taken by Mann and Brownlie: "there is in principle no great difference between the problems created by the assertion of civil and criminal jurisdiction over aliens."[25] Jessup would have agreed: "From the standpoint of considering transnational law there seems to be little reason for attempting to distinguish between civil and criminal cases in determining jurisdiction."[26]

It is conceivable that certain principles justifying the criminal jurisdiction of states could equally serve as grounds for the assertion of jurisdiction over foreign nationals in transnational human rights claims. Territoriality is the clearest case: a state is empowered to take jurisdiction over claims for death or personal injuries that occur on its territory. The authority of states in such cases is so well established that it is widely held to even override state immunity at international and national law.[27] The protective principle is often evoked as one of the rationales for the *Alien Tort Claims Act* (*ATCA*), in that the assertion of jurisdiction over violations of international law bolsters the national security interests of the US.[28] Likewise, as will be discussed below, there are cogent arguments for the recognition of a universality principle in relation to transnational human rights jurisdiction.[29]

A state's inappropriate treatment of legitimate claims involving foreign nationals might in certain circumstances amount to a denial of justice, which in turn could lead to state responsibility at international law.[30] It will be recalled that the historical US anxiety that

25 Brownlie, above note 2 at 298; Mann, above note 16 at 44–46; Reydams, above note 10 at 2–3. But see Akehurst, above note 2 at 170.

26 Philip C. Jessup, *Transnational Law* (New Haven: Yale University Press, 1956) at 64.

27 *United Nations Convention on Jurisdictional Immunities of States and Their Property*, GA Res. 59/38, UNGAOR, 59th Sess., UN Doc. A/RES/59/38 (2004) at art. 12 (not yet in force); *European Convention on State Immunity*, 16 May 1972, E.T.S. No. 74 at art. 11; *State Immunity Act 1978* (U.K.), 1978, c. 33, s. 5; *Foreign Sovereign Immunities Act of 1976*, 28 U.S.C. § 1605(5); *State Immunity Act*, R.S.C. 1985, c. S-18, s. 6. See also Hazel Fox QC, *The Law of State Immunity* (Oxford, Oxford University Press, 2002) at 309–22; *Letelier v. Chile*, 488 F. Supp. 665; *Schreiber v. Canada (A.G.)*, [2002] 3 S.C.R. 269 [*Schreiber*].

28 *Sosa v. Alvarez-Machain*, 542 U.S. 692 at 743–46 (2004) [*Sosa*]; See also William R. Casto, "The Federal Court's Protective Jurisdiction over Torts Committed in Violation of the Law of Nations" (1986) 18 Conn. L. Rev. 467; Anne-Marie Burley, "The Alien Tort Statute and the Judiciary Act of 1789: A Badge of Honor" (1989) 83 A.J.I.L. 461.

29 See Section B(3), below in this chapter.

30 Brownlie, above note 2 at 506–8; *Draft Articles on the Responsibility of States for Internationally Wrongful Acts*, UN GAOR, 56th Sess, Supp No 10, p. 43, UN Doc A/56/10 (2001), art. 4; James Crawford, *The International Law Commission's Articles on State*

foreigners be denied justice or a fair trial was a major impetus for the creation of the federal judiciary and of *ATCA*.[31] The public interest in guarding against denials of justice is expressed in the right to access justice, which is a fundamental tenet of many legal systems, including the Canadian and European human rights regime.[32] In *Al-Adsani* (2001), the European Court of Human Rights (ECtHR) emphasized that the right to access justice cannot easily be denied. In that case however the majority held that state immunity was an acceptable limitation at international law on the right to access justice, insofar as it pursued the legitimate aim of promoting "comity and good relations between States through the respect of another State's sovereignty."[33]

In short, as Mann and Bowett have argued, international law concerns itself with civil jurisdiction to the extent that "the civil jurisdiction of the State is an instrument of State policy, used as a means of exercising control over activities or resources in the interests of the State."[34] Accordingly, it is reasonable to suppose that litigation involving issues of public policy and international interests, such as transnational human rights litigation, would be subject to general principles of public international law. The manner in which international law conditions the extraterritorial civil jurisdiction of national courts raises larger considerations concerning the relationship between conflicts, rules, and public international law. Because national courts exercise the authority conferred unto them by the constitution of their states, the extent to which they may adjudicate international cases is a direct function of their constitutional empowerment on one hand and of the constitutional relationship between municipal and international law on the other. To borrow Judge Moore's image, in states like the US, UK, and Canada where the direct reception of customary international law is an organizing principle of the national legal system, the extraterritorial jurisdiction of municipal courts flows in

---

Responsibility: Introduction, Text and Commentaries (Cambridge: Cambridge University Press, 2002) at 96; Harvard Research, above note 2 at 179.

31 See Chapter 2, Section C(2)(a).

32 *Canadian Bill of Rights*, S.C. 1960, c. 44, s. 2(e); *Canadian Charter of Rights and Freedoms*, Part I of the *Constitution Act, 1982*, being Schedule B to the *Canada Act 1982* (U.K.), 1982, c. 11, ss. 7, 11, and 24; *Convention for the Protection of Human Rights and Fundamental Freedoms*, 4 November 1950, E.T.S. No. 5, 213 U.N.T.S. 221 (entered into force 3 September 1953), art. 6 [ECHR].

33 *Al-Adsani v. United Kingdom*, (2001) 34 E.H.R.R. 273 at para. 54.

34 Bowett, above note 2 at 557; Mann, above note 16.

part from the "majestic stream of the common law united with international law."[35] In such legal systems, the relationship between conflicts rules and public international law can be characterized as one of dynamic monism. Conflict rules must align with international legal principles, which in turn influence the formulation and evolution of conflict rules by national courts. As Mann put it:

> Conflict rules are a product of municipal law, which has to stand the test of the international doctrine of jurisdiction. In other words, it is the function of jurisdiction to define the international scope which the municipal legislator is entitled to give to his enactments. The conflict rule implements and gives effect to the requirements of public international law.[36]

In a similar vein, the Supreme Court of Canada has recognized that international principles of jurisdiction "may be adopted into the common law of Canada in the absence of conflicting legislation" and drawn upon in determining the scope of adjudicative jurisdiction of national courts in extraterritorial matters.[37]

In summary, as an aspect of sovereignty, states enjoy a large measure of discretion at international law to adopt rules and principles concerning the extension of their judicial jurisdiction over events, persons, and things outside their territory. However, international law, coupled with the persuasive pull of comity, conditions the exercise of that discretion by requiring the respect of certain broad principles such as sovereignty and territoriality. Exorbitant assertions of jurisdiction may lead to state responsibility at international law. Where justice cannot be obtained anywhere else, a state's refusal to exercise jurisdiction might also engage its responsibility. In short, the assertion of extraterritorial jurisdiction in civil proceedings is subject at international law to the general expectation that one state will not act unreasonably towards another.[38]

35 *The Lotus*, above note 4 at 75, Moore J.
36 Mann, above note 16 at 22.
37 *Hape*, above note 8 at para. 46.
38 *Spar*, above note 19 at para. 21; Maier, above note 20 at 72.

2) Civil Jurisdiction at Domestic Law

This section focuses on the US, the UK, and Canada, the only common law jurisdictions in which civil claims have been brought for extraterritorial human rights breaches. In the absence of *ATCA*-style legislation, courts have attempted to resolve jurisdictional issues on the basis of traditional rules of civil procedure and conflict of laws. In this section, it is argued that prevailing conflict of laws standards in the UK and in Canada, though not completely devoid of flexibility, inadequately address the specificity of transnational human rights claims in two important respects. First, the rules governing the assumption of jurisdiction are deeply rooted in the territoriality principle. Most transnational human rights claims, however, involve foreign parties and extraterritorial events with little or no link to the forum. Second, jurisdictional rules have hitherto been developed in the context of private claims and have proven unwieldy in the context of transnational human rights claims, which involve broad questions of public policy and human rights. In this connection, it is argued that there is evidence of growing international willingness to recognize a form of universal civil jurisdiction, which, without discarding the inherent prudence of the territoriality principle, would allow states to extend their civil jurisdiction over violations of well-defined and generally accepted norms of customary international law.[39]

a) Jurisdictional Rules Are Fundamentally Territorial

National courts in the UK and Canada have similar rules governing their civil jurisdiction in transnational matters, though there are differences in the details. In both countries, at common law, service of process defines the limits of personal jurisdiction.[40] Service is either effected on a defendant in the territory or abroad (*ex juris*). Service in the forum territory is generally straightforward and unexceptionable. In the case of the UK however it should be noted that the EC Regulation of 22 December 2000 on jurisdiction and the recognition and enforcement of judgments in civil and commercial matters and the

39 See Section B(3), below in this chapter.

40 Albert Venn Dicey, *et al.*, eds., *Dicey and Morris on the Conflict of Laws*, 13th ed. (London: Sweet & Maxwell, 2000) at 263 [Dicey & Morris]; Jean-Gabriel Castel, *Canadian Conflict of Laws*, 3rd ed. (Toronto: Butterworths, 1994) at 91 [Castel].

Brussels/Lugano regime have substantially modified traditional jurisdictional rules with regards to other contracting parties, generally EU and European Free Trade Association (EFTA) States. For instance, under the EC Regulation, jurisdiction is normally a function of domicile.[41] The traditional rules apply however with regards to all non-member states: service of process upon a defendant present in the UK or Canadian territory, even temporarily, is sufficient basis for jurisdiction "as of right," subject to the court's ability to dismiss proceedings in appropriate circumstances.[42] Accordingly, Norberto Peña-Irala[43] and Radovan Karadzić[44] (both served when travelling in the state of New York) could also have come under the personal jurisdiction of courts in London or Toronto.

Service outside the forum is more controversial since it is generally regarded as an invasion of the foreign state's sovereignty.[45] Accordingly, while UK and Canadian service *ex juris* rules differ in their operation, they both hinge on the demonstration of a genuine territorial connection between the foreign parties, the claim, and the forum.[46] In the UK, service *ex juris* is permitted on specific grounds or categories of cases set out at paragraph 3.1 of Practice Direction 6B (PD 6B), which supplements Part 6 of the current Civil Procedure Rules (CPR).[47] The circumstances there listed represent instances where it is thought to be reasonable for English courts to assert jurisdiction, provided the plaintiffs meet the sufficiency threshold specified at CPR Rule 6.37. In essence, in applying for permission to effectuate service outside the jurisdiction, claimants must show (1) that they have a good

41 *Brussels Convention*, above note 17 at arts. 2 & 3; Dicey & Morris, *ibid.* at 264–84.

42 *Ibid.* at art. 4. Transnational human rights claims brought so far in the UK have not involved Convention States. The following discussion will thus be restricted to the traditional rules as they would apply to non-Convention States.

43 *Filártiga v. Peña-Irala*, 630 F.2d 876 (2d Cir. 1980) [*Filártiga*].

44 *Kadić v. Karadzić*, 866 F. Supp. 734 (S.D.N.Y. 1994).

45 Anne C. McConville, "Taking Jurisdiction in Transnational Human Rights Tort Litigation: Universality Jurisdiction's Relationship to *Ex Juris* Service, *Forum Non Conveniens* and the Presumption of Territoriality," in Craig Scott, ed., *Torture as Tort: Comparative Perspectives on the Development of Transnational Human Rights Litigation* (Oxford: Hart Publishing, 2001) at 161 [McConville]; Genevieve Saumier, "Judicial Jurisdiction in International Cases: The Supreme Court's Unfinished Business" (1995) 18 Dalhousie L.J. 447 at 451.

46 McConville, *ibid.* at 160–65.

47 The 50th update of the Civil Procedure Rules (CPR) came into force on 1 October 2009.

arguable case falling within one of the enumerated grounds listed at paragraph 3.1 of PD 6B[48]; (2) that, on the merits, the case presents "real issue which it is reasonable for the court to try"[49]; and (3) that England and Wales "is the proper place in which to bring the claim."[50]

In transnational human rights claims where the wrongful acts occur wholly outside the forum, only one of the twenty grounds listed at paragraph 3.1 of PD 6B is likely to be of practical relevance, namely, "a claim . . . in tort where (a) the damage was sustained within the jurisdiction; or (b) the damage sustained resulted from an act committed within the jurisdiction."[51] Accordingly, a claimant who has been tortured in a foreign country and who continues to suffer the physical or mental effects of that torture upon his return to the UK can evoke PD 6B, paragraph 3.1(9)(a) in support of his application to serve process abroad. The continuing injuries of torture amount, at least for service *ex juris* purposes, to "damage . . . sustained within the jurisdiction."[52] In *Al-Adsani*, where the claimant sued the Government of Kuwait in relation to the torture he allegedly suffered in that country, the Court of Appeal allowed service *ex juris* and recognized that the continuing injury "should properly be regarded as a separate form of injury even if it is consequent upon the process which began . . . in Kuwait."[53] The court found that the plaintiff had established a good arguable case that Kuwait should not be afforded immunity in respect of acts of torture. Having thus satisfied the procedural requirements, service *ex juris* was permitted.[54] The action was ultimately barred by the *State Immunity Act, 1978*.

---

48 CPR, r. 6.37(1)(a).

49 CPR, r. 6.37(2). For a discussion of this factor under the former rules, see *Seaconsar Far East Ltd v. Bank Markazi Jomhouri Islami Iran*, [1994] 1 A.C. 438.

50 CPR , r. 6.37(3). For a discussion of this factor under the former rules, see *Spiliada Maritime Corp v. Cansulex Ltd*, [1987] A.C. 460 [*Spiliada*].

51 PD 6B, para. 3.1(9). For the sake of completeness, the grounds listed, para. 3.1(1) (where the defendant is domiciled in England) and para. 3.1(3)(b) (where the defendant is a necessary or proper party to existing proceedings), are also conceivably relevant, but unlikely to be capable of being invoked in the majority of cases. For a discussion of these grounds under the former rules, see International Law Association, Committee on International Human Rights Law and Practice, "Report on Civil Actions in the English Courts for Serious Human Rights Violations Abroad" (2001) 2 Eur. H.R.L. Rev. 129 at 142 [ILA Report].

52 PD 6B, para. 3.1(9).

53 *Al-Adsani v. Kuwait* (1995), 103 I.L.R. 420 at 469 (Q.B.).

54 The *Al-Adsani* case concerned Order 11, r. 1(1)(f) of the former Rules of the Supreme Court, the predecessor to the current CPR, r. 6.37.

The situation in Canada differs only slightly.[55] Under Ontario rules, plaintiffs are not required to obtain leave from the court before effectuating service *ex juris* if the subject matter of the claim falls within certain categories enumerated at Rule 17.02, which are similar to those listed at paragraph 3.1 of PD 6B in the UK rule. These categories of cases, though not conclusively determinative of the court's jurisdiction, "provide a rough guide to the kinds of cases in which persons outside Ontario will be regarded as subject to the jurisdiction of Ontario courts."[56] Much like in the UK, the listed categories of cases include proceedings for continuing injuries. Under Rule 17.02(h), service *ex juris* is permitted where the claim concerns "damage sustained in Ontario arising from a tort . . . wherever committed."[57] In *Saleh*, where a plaintiff sued the United Arab Emirates for torture, the Ontario court refused to validate an alternative method of service, and suggested that the plaintiff could have availed himself of Rule 17.02(h).[58] However that may be, as will be seen below, the grounds justifying service *ex juris* should not be conflated with the bases on which jurisdiction over extraterritorial defendants may be asserted.[59]

Once the foreign defendant has been served, one of several possible outcomes will usually follow. Where the foreign defendant chooses not to defend the claim, the plaintiff can move to have the defendant noted in default[60] and obtain judgment from the court.[61] Alternatively, the defendant may choose to either file a defence with the court,[62]

55 Since jurisdictional rules are largely similar among the common law provinces of the Canadian federation and Canadian transnational human rights practice has been limited to Ontario, the present discussion will accordingly be restricted to the caselaw and rules of that province. It is noted that the rules in Quebec are somewhat broader. Under the *Civil Code of Québec* (C.C.Q.), S.Q. 1991, c. 64, art. 3148(3) [C.C.Q.] the courts may assert jurisdiction if a "damage was suffered in Québec," without further need to ascertain the "real and substantial connection" between the claim and the province: *Spar*, above note 19.

56 *Muscutt v. Courcelles* (2002), 60 O.R. (3d) 20 at para. 51 (C.A.) [*Muscutt*]. In *Van Breda*, below note 75, the Court of Appeal for Ontario went further, holding that most of the categories listed under r. 17.02 can be seen as establishing presumptive jurisdiction.

57 *Rules of Civil Procedure*, R.R.O. 1990, Reg. 194, r. 17.02(h).

58 *Saleh v. United Arab Emirates* (2003), 15 C.C.L.T. (3d) 231 at para. 5 [*Saleh*].

59 See discussion below at note 91 and accompanying text.

60 UK CPR, r. 12.3; R.R.O. 1990, Reg. 194, r. 19.01(1).

61 UK CPR, r. 12.4; R.R.O. 1990, Reg. 194, r. 19.05(1).

62 UK CPR, r. 15.2; R.R.O. 1990, Reg. 194, r. 18.01.

or either move to set aside service[63] or to the stay the proceedings.[64] Whatever the scenario, the court usually comes to a determination of its own jurisdiction over the proceedings, which, both under Canadian and UK law, involves an assessment of the connection between the claim, the parties, and the forum. As stated above, UK courts take a preliminary view of their jurisdiction over transnational claims when authorizing or declining service *ex juris*. Under UK Rule 6.36 and paragraph 3.1 of PD 6B, the court will not give permission unless satisfied that England and Wales is the proper place in which to bring the claim. In practice however, in both the UK and Canada, the issue of the court's substantive jurisdiction and appropriateness as a forum is usually addressed after the defendant has been served in the context of a motion to set aside service or to stay the proceedings.[65]

In the UK, whether in the context of an application for leave to serve *ex juris* or a motion to stay proceedings, the rule in *Spiliada* applies.[66] In essence, the court will assert jurisdiction where there is a "real and substantial connection" between the proceedings and the forum. In *Connelly*, Lord Goff summarized the two-stage *Spiliada* test as follows:

> . . . the court will look first to see what factors there are which point in the direction of another forum, i.e. connecting factors which indicate that it is with the other forum that the action has its most real and substantial connection. This is the first stage. However even if the court concludes at that stage that the other forum is clearly more appropriate for the trial of the action, the court may nevertheless decline to grant the stay if persuaded . . . that justice requires that a stay should not be granted. This is the second stage.[67]

The *Spiliada* test will be discussed in greater detail in Chapter 6 in relation to stay of proceedings on the basis of *forum non conveniens*. For the present discussion on jurisdiction, it suffices to underscore the requirement at the first stage of the test of a "real and substantial connection" between the parties, proceedings, and the forum. The relevant connecting factors are fundamentally territorial in nature, and

63 UK CPR, r. 11(6)(b); R.R.O. 1990, Reg. 194, r. 17.06(1)(a).
64 UK CPR, r. 11(6)(d); R.R.O. 1990, Reg. 194, r. 17.06(1)(b).
65 ILA Report, above note 51 at 142.
66 *Spiliada*, above note 50.
67 *Connelly v. R.T.Z. Corporation Plc.*, [1998] A.C. 854 at 871–72 [*Connelly*].

include the convenience of the parties having regard to their place of domicile, the location of evidence and witnesses, and the place where the wrongful acts took place. Clearly, in the context of civil proceedings for extraterritorial human rights violations, the assessment of such factors, in the vast majority of cases, will lead to the conclusion that the foreign country is the most natural forum. The Human Rights Committee of the ILA British Branch made this observation in its 2001 report on transnational human rights litigation: in such cases, "the forum with which the action has its closest and most real connection is the forum in which the acts complained of . . . took place. The relevant witnesses will (usually) be there; relevant documents (if any) will be there; and the governing law will almost certainly (applying English choice of law rules) be the law of the foreign forum."[68]

Canadian courts have reached the same conclusion. Though initially applied to conflict cases among Canadian provinces, the *Spiliada* test has since been extended to international cases and permeates almost every Canadian rule of private international law. In Canada, the real and substantial connection test is applied in a variety of private international law contexts, notably with respect to jurisdiction *simpliciter*,[69] *forum non conveniens*,[70] choice of law,[71] and enforcement of inter-provincial[72] and international[73] judgments. Until recently, the controlling authority with regards to jurisdiction *simpliciter* had been the so-called *Muscutt Quintet*, a series of five judgments delivered by the Court of Appeal for Ontario in 2002 establishing the analytical framework and factors that govern the assumption of jurisdiction in inter-provincial and transnational tort claims.[74] The *Muscutt Quintet*

---

68 ILA Report, above note 51 at 146.

69 *Muscutt*, above note 56. For commentary on the Canadian approach to jurisdiction see, generally: Joost Blom QC & Elizabeth Edinger, *The Chimera of the Real and Substantial Connection Test* (2005) 38 U.B.C. L. Rev. 373; Cheryl D. Dusten & Stephen G.A. Pitel, *Lost in Transition: Answering the Questions Raised by the Supreme Court of Canada's New Approach to Jurisdiction* (2006) 85 Can. Bar Rev. 61; Tanya Monestier, *A Real and Substantial Mess: The Law of Jurisdiction in Canada* (2007) 33 Queen's L.J. 179.

70 *Amchem Products Inc. v. British Columbia (Workers' Compensation Board)*, [1993] 1 S.C.R. 897.

71 *Tolofson*, above note 1.

72 *Morguard Investments Ltd. v. De Savoye*, [1990] 3 S.C.R. 1077; *Hunt v. T&N plc*, [1993] 4 S.C.R. 289 [*Hunt*].

73 *Beals v. Saldanha*, [2003] 3 S.C.R. 416 [*Beals*].

74 The *Muscutt Quintet* includes *Muscutt*, above note 56; *Lemmex v. Sunflight Holidays Inc.* (2002), 60 O.R. (3d) 54 (C.A.); *Leufkens v. Alba Tours International Inc.* (2002), 60

analysis and the general principles on jurisdiction were recently reformulated by the Court of Appeal for Ontario in *Van Breda* (2010).[75] To better understand the developments introduced in *Van Breda* and their impact on jurisdictional determinations in transnational human rights proceedings, it is important to review the previous state of the law under the *Muscutt Quintet*.

In the leading decision, *Muscutt v. Courcelles*, Sharpe JA identified eight "factors emerging from the caselaw that are relevant in assessing whether a court should assume jurisdiction against an out-of-province defendant on the basis of damage sustained in Ontario as a result of a tort committed elsewhere." They are:

1) the connection between the forum and the plaintiff's claim;
2) the connection between the forum and the defendant;
3) unfairness to the defendant in assuming jurisdiction;
4) unfairness to the plaintiff in not assuming jurisdiction;
5) the involvement of other parties to the suit;
6) the court's willingness to recognize and enforce an extra-provincial judgement rendered on the same jurisdictional basis;
7) whether the case is provincial or international in nature; and
8) comity and the standards of jurisdiction prevailing elsewhere.[76]

Sharpe JA emphasized that no one factor is determinative. Rather, "all relevant factors should be considered and weighed together" in determining whether a real and substantial connection between the parties, the proceedings, and the forum exists.[77]

The *Muscutt* factors have been applied in two civil cases for extraterritorial torture, namely *Saleh* (2003) and *Bouzari* (2004). In *Saleh*, where a Canadian citizen sued the United Arab Emirates (UAE) in relation to his alleged detention and torture in that country, Chadwick J applied the *Muscutt* factors and found no real and substantial connection between the proceedings and Ontario. While the court acknowledged the unfairness to the plaintiff in not assuming jurisdiction given the latter's inability to sue (or even return to) the UAE, the extraterritorial

O.R. (3d) 84 (C.A.); *Sinclair v. Cracker Barrel Old Country Store Inc.* (2002), 60 O.R. (3d) 76 (C.A.); and *Gajraj v. DeBernardo* (2002), 60 O.R. (3d) 68 (C.A.).

75 *Van Breda v. Village Resorts* (2010), 98 O.R. (3d) 721 (C.A.) [*Van Breda*].

76 *Muscutt*, above note 56 at paras. 75–110.

77 *Ibid.* at para. 76.

nature of the claim and a thin evidentiary record ultimately weighed against the assertion of jurisdiction. The court stated: "The injuries suffered by the plaintiff occurred in [the UAE] and the majority of the damage suffered by the plaintiff occurred in the same location. The evidence with reference to his pain and suffering and loss of income in Canada is extremely sparse. As such, this court should not exercise jurisdiction."[78] The brief reasons in *Saleh* offer very little indication as to whether or to what extent the specific nature of transnational human rights claims formed part of the decision to decline jurisdiction. The court made no mention of peremptory norms, human rights, or international obligations. Rather, the court applied the eight *Muscutt* factors rather mechanically and concluded that it had no jurisdiction on the basis of the insufficiency of the evidentiary record and tenuous territorial connections between the events and Ontario.

By contrast, the Court of Appeal's reasons in *Bouzari* represent a thoughtful, though ultimately inconclusive, attempt at reconciling the "real and substantial connection" test with the particular nature of civil proceedings for extraterritorial torture. Goudge JA, writing for the court, struggled with the real and substantial connection test's unwieldiness in transnational human rights cases, recognizing that the straight application of the *Muscutt* factors "would probably yield the conclusion that there is no real and substantial connection to Ontario"[79] but found such a result "troubling."[80] Running through the relevant factors, Goudge JA stated:

> [33] Of particular importance is that at the time of the torture the appellant had absolutely no connection with Ontario . . . . While it is not suggested that the appellant came here merely to engage the jurisdiction of the Ontario court, he did not arrive until 1998, more than four years after the torture finally ended. In all, the appellant's connection to Ontario for the purposes of this test is very tenuous.
>
> [34] Moreover, the defendant Iran has no connection with Ontario beyond, presumably, the diplomatic. There is no suggestion that it is set up to easily defend a civil action in another state.

78 *Saleh*, above note 58 at para. 24.

79 *Bouzari et al. v. Islamic Republic of Iran* (2004), 71 O.R. (3d) 675 at para. 31 (C.A.) [*Bouzari*].

80 *Ibid.* at para. 36.

> [35] As well, there appears to be no broadly shared international practice among states to assume jurisdiction over civil actions in similar circumstances.
>
> [36] That said, there are several circumstances that make the presumptive conclusion of no jurisdiction troubling. First, the action is based on torture by a foreign state, which is a violation of both international human rights and peremptory norms of public international law. As the perpetrator, Iran has eliminated itself as a possible forum, although it otherwise would be the most logical jurisdiction. This would seem to diminish significantly the importance of any unfairness to the defendant due to its lack of connection to Ontario.
>
> [37] Second, if Ontario does not take jurisdiction, the appellant will be left without a place to sue. Given that the appellant is now connected to Ontario by his citizenship, the requirement of fairness that underpins the real and substantial connection test would seem to be of elevated importance if the alternative is that the appellant cannot bring this action anywhere.
>
> [38] Thus, I think that the application of the real and substantial connection test to the circumstances of this case is not easy. However, given the conclusion I have reached on the issue of state immunity, it is unnecessary to finally determine how the real and substantial connection test would apply here. That is best left for a case in which the issue must be resolved.[81]

The court went on to dismiss the action on the basis of the *State Immunity Act*.[82] Given the analytical priority of the issue of jurisdiction *simpliciter* over that of state immunity, as the ICJ noted in the *Arrest Warrant Case*, it was arguably improper to decline deciding the jurisdiction question,[83] though it is not uncommon for courts to resort to this adjudicative technique.[84]

---

81 *Ibid.* at paras. 33–38.

82 That aspect of the decision is discussed in Chapter 7.

83 *Case Concerning the Arrest Warrant of 11 April 2000 (Democratic Republic of Congo v. Belgium)*, [2002] I.C.J. Rep. 3 at para. 46 [*Arrest Warrant Case*].

84 See, for example, *Sinochem International Co. Ltd. v. Malaysia International Shipping Corp.*, 549 U.S. 422 (2007), where the action was dismissed on the basis of *forum non conveniens*, bypassing questions of subject matter and personal jurisdiction, when considerations of convenience, fairness, and judicial economy so warranted.

Significantly, Goudge JA emphasized the competing imperatives and problems of transnational human rights litigation. On the one hand, to be reasonable and legitimate, the extraterritorial civil jurisdiction of national courts must be rooted in some genuine connection between the parties, the claim, and the forum, or on an alternative jurisdictional ground, such as consent or necessity.[85] Bouzari's claim however involved foreign parties and extraterritorial events with no territorial link to Ontario other than his own presence in the jurisdiction and his ongoing physical and psychological suffering. On the other hand, as Goudge JA noted, the subject matter of the claim — torture — makes "the presumptive conclusion of no jurisdiction troubling."[86] It is troubling because torture violates fundamental human rights and peremptory norms of international law. Victims of torture are typically left without a forum in which to bring their claim, resulting in a denial of justice. In that case, Iran was both a place and a person. As the *loci delicti commissi*, it was the forum with the strongest connections to the claim. As the defendant, Iran had shown itself hostile to Bouzari and wholly unreceptive to his claim for redress. Not only had Iran not defended the lawsuit in Ontario, Iranian officials had allegedly made several death threats to Bouzari, warning him never to return to his native country. By contrast, while Ontario had very little connection with the proceedings and the parties, it was a forum in which Bouzari could reasonably expect a fair and impartial adjudication of his claim. Clearly, in cases like *Bouzari*, if territoriality is the test, jurisdiction must be declined and justice denied. In short, "transnational human rights torts litigation . . . does not easily fit into the framework of territorial jurisdiction."[87]

It is in this respect that *Van Breda* (2010) represents a significant development. *Van Breda* is the consolidated appeal from two separate tort claims by Canadian plaintiffs who were injured while on vacation at Cuban resorts. The court held that the *Muscutt* approach needed to be reformulated and streamlined in light of, among other factors, the growing salience of the Uniform Law Conference of Canada's model

---

These considerations of convenience and judicial economy will be addressed in Chapter 6.

85 Janet Walker, "*Muscutt* Misplaced: The Future of Forum of Necessity in Canada" (2009) 48 Can. Bus. L.J. 135 at 136 [Walker].

86 *Bouzari*, above note 79 at para. 36.

87 McConville, above note 45 at 165.

Court Jurisdiction and Proceedings Transfer Act (*CJPTA*),[88] and the generally negative assessment of the *Muscutt* approach by legal scholars and commentators.[89] Writing for a unanimous five-judge panel, Sharpe JA reformulated the eight-factor *Muscutt* analysis in order "to simplify the test and to provide for more clarity and ease in its application."[90]

The *Van Breda* test consists of two analytical steps. First, following the *CJPTA* model, the court held that a real and substantial connection with Ontario is presumed to exist if the case falls within the categories of cases listed at rule 17.02, with the specific exception of rules 17.02(h) ("damages sustained in Ontario") and 17.02(o) ("a necessary or proper party") which have generally not been recognized by Canadian courts as reliable indicators of a real and substantial connection.[91] If the presumption is made out, the defendant bears the burden of demonstrating the contrary position. Second, the relative strength of the presumptive connection is assessed in light of the "core" elements of the real and substantial connection test, namely, "the connection between Ontario and the plaintiff's claim and the defendant, respectively."[92] These are the first two factors identified in *Muscutt*. The remaining six *Muscutt* factors (unfairness to the defendant in taking jurisdiction; unfairness to the plaintiff in not taking jurisdiction; the involvement of other parties; the court's willingness to enforce a foreign judgment rendered on the same jurisdictional basis; whether the dispute is international or interprovincial; and comity and the standards of jurisdiction used

88 The Uniform Law Conference of Canada has developed a model *Court Jurisdiction and Proceedings Transfer Act* [*CJPTA*] intended to implement uniform statutory rules by which all Canadian courts establish jurisdiction over particular proceedings. The *CJPTA* has been adopted in Saskatchewan, the Yukon, Nova Scotia, and British Columbia. See, respectively, *Court Jurisdiction and Proceedings Transfer Act*, S.S. 1997, c. C-41.1; *Court Jurisdiction and Proceedings Transfer Act*, S.Y. 2000, c. 7; *Court Jurisdiction and Proceedings Transfer Act*, S.N.S. 2003, c. 2; *Court Jurisdiction and Proceedings Transfer Act*, S.B.C. 2003, c. 28. Other provinces, such as Alberta and Ontario, are still studying the issue.

89 *Van Breda*, above note 75 at paras. 51–55.

90 *Ibid.* at para. 83.

91 *Ibid.* at paras. 71–80. Section 10 of the *CJPTA* establishes a presumptive real and substantial connection if the case concerns one of the listed matters, most of which correspond to the codified categories of cases in which service *ex juris* is permitted. Note, however, that while the Ontario *Rules of Civil Procedure*, above note 57, permit service *ex juris* in cases where damages are sustained in Ontario (r. 17.02(h)) or if the defendant is a necessary or proper party (r. 17.02(o)), the *CJTPA* does not. See discussion above at notes 55–56 and accompanying text.

92 *Ibid.* at para. 109.

by other courts), are not to "be treated as independent factors having more or less equal weight when determining whether there is a real and substantial connection but as general legal principles that bear upon the analysis."[93]

It remains to be seen whether the *Van Breda* approach to jurisdiction will prove to be simpler and easier to apply, and some commentators are sceptical that *Van Breda* presents much of an improvement in this respect.[94] However this may be, the decision in *Van Breda* represents an important development for transnational human rights litigation not only because of its *ratio decidendi* but also because of its *obiter dicta*. Indeed, when discussing the various reasons that justified a reformulation of the *Muscutt* approach, the Court of Appeal for Ontario highlighted the emergence of the forum of necessity doctrine and its effect on the real and substantial connection criteria. Sharpe JA stated:

> [54] . . . [S]ince *Muscutt* was decided, the concept of "forum of necessity" or "forum of last resort" has emerged as a significant jurisdictional doctrine. This doctrine allows the forum to take jurisdiction in cases despite the absence of a real and substantial connection where there is no other forum in which the plaintiff could reasonably seek relief. "Forum of necessity" is recognized by Article 3136 of the Quebec *Civil Code*, incorporated in s. 6 of *CJPTA*, adopted by both the EU and the UK, and was hinted as a possible basis for jurisdiction by this court in *Bouzari v. Islamic Republic of Iran* 2004 CanLII 871 (ON C.A.), (2004), 71 O.R. (3d) 675 (C.A.), at paras. 36–38: see also Janet Walker, "*Muscutt* Misplaced: The Future of Forum of Necessity Jurisdiction in Canada" (2009) 48 C.B.L.J. 135.[95]

With specific reference to those paragraphs in *Bouzari* (2004) where it grappled with the real and substantial connection test's unsuitability in civil cases for extraterritorial torture, the Court of Appeal for Ontario explicitly recognized for the first time the residual discretion of Ontario courts to assert jurisdiction in cases where the ends of justice so require, even in the absence of territorial links. Clarifying the

---

93 *Ibid.*

94 See, for example, Stephen Pitel, "Reformulating a Real and Substantial Connection" (2010) 60 U.N.B.L.J. 177.

95 *Van Breda*, above note 75 at para. 54.

forum of necessity doctrine's relationship to the real and substantial connection test, Sharpe JA stated:

> [100] The post-*Muscutt* emergence of the forum of necessity doctrine has a direct bearing on this issue. The forum of necessity doctrine recognizes that there will be exceptional cases where, despite the absence of a real and substantial connection, the need to ensure access to justice will justify the assumption of jurisdiction. The forum of necessity doctrine does not redefine real and substantial connection to embrace "forum of last resort" cases; it operates as an exception to the real and substantial connection test. Where there is no other forum in which the plaintiff can reasonably seek relief, there is a residual discretion to assume jurisdiction. In my view, the overriding concern for access to justice that motivates the assumption of jurisdiction despite inadequate connection with the forum should be accommodated by explicit recognition of the forum of necessity exception rather than by distorting the real and substantial connection test.[96]

Van Breda's explicit recognition of the forum of necessity doctrine is a significant development that brings Ontario law in line with the law of other provinces, the EU, and the UK that have already recognized the doctrine.

A flexible approach to jurisdiction that takes into account and gives appropriate weight to the particular subject matter of the proceedings and that does not insist on direct territorial connections in cases where none could ever exist is surely a welcomed development. It is also in line with the guiding principles originally set out by the Supreme Court of Canada in *Hunt*, where La Forest J stated: "Whatever approach is used, the assumption of and the discretion not to exercise jurisdiction must ultimately be guided by the requirements of order and fairness, not a mechanical counting of contacts or connections."[97] Order and fairness require courts to take into account the subject matter of the proceedings, (i.e., torture and violations of well-established norms of international law) and the possibility of obtaining justice in the courts of a more territorially connected forum. In this respect, as

96 *Ibid.* at para. 100.

97 *Hunt* (1993), above note 72 at para. 59.

will be discussed below, the forum of necessity doctrine is also compatible with the emerging principle of universal civil jurisdiction.[98]

b) Conflict Rules Are Generally Based in Private Law

Another reason why traditional conflict rules fail to address the specificity of transnational human rights claims has to do with their private law character. Conflict rules have historically been developed in relation to private transborder disputes, such as trade, contracts, debts, child custody, and tort liability.[99] As the Supreme Court of Canada noted, the avowed purpose of conflict rules is "to facilitate the flow of wealth, skills and people across boundaries" by fostering juridical predictability and harmony among disparate legal regimes.[100] In Baxi's words: conflict rules seek to provide "a series of pragmatic answers to specific problems posed by transborder movement of capital and by human movement that occurs largely as some kind of by product of the structures of capital flow and resulting wealth allocation."[101]

Transnational human rights litigation, by contrast, refers to civil claims involving foreign parties and extraterritorial violations of international norms protecting individuals. The distinguishing feature of such claims is the particular mixture of public and private rights and duties that plaintiffs seek to enforce. By definition, international human rights—particularly those human rights that have achieved the status of peremptory norms of international law—embody the interests and concerns of the international community as a whole and constitute important components of world public order.[102] International human rights are formed in and derive from public international law, the law that governs the relations between states. In addition to the private rights guaranteed to individuals, public international law im-

98 See Section B(3), below in this chapter.

99 Dicey & Morris, above note 40; Castel, above note 40.

100 *Beals*, above note 73 at para. 21; Harold H. Koh "Transnational Public Law Litigation" (1991) 100 Yale L.J. 2347 at 2356.

101 Upendra Baxi, "Geographies of Injustice: Human Rights at the Altar of Convenience" in Craig Scott, ed., at 199 [Baxi].

102 Alexander Orakhelashvili, "State Immunity and International Public Order" (2002) 45 Ger. Y.I.L. 227 at 255 [Orakhelashvili 2002]; *Case Concerning Armed Activities on the Territory of the Congo (New Application: 2002) (Democratic Republic of the Congo v. Rwanda)*, [2006] I.C.J. Rep. 1, Separate Opinion of Judge (*ad hoc*) Dugard at para. 11 [*Armed Activities*]; *Barcelona Traction, Light & Power Co. (Second Phase) (Belgium v. Spain)*, [1970] I.C.J. Rep. 3 at paras. 33–34.

poses duties and obligations on states in furtherance of these individual rights. For instance, the international human right to be free from torture includes the concomitant and universal state obligation to refrain from torturing individuals. Whether framed in terms of individual entitlement or prohibited state behaviour, the right to be free from torture embodies the common and public interest of all nations and all peoples. Transnational human rights litigation is thus the process by which an individual seeks to enforce the private rights and concomitant state obligations created by public international law. In this way, transnational human rights litigation involves hybrid claims, incorporating both private and public rights and obligations, and as such, differs substantially from other forms of transborder disputes between private persons to which conflict rules traditionally apply.

According to Baxi, private international law has developed with a general indifference to human rights, focused as it has been on producing coherent and pragmatic solutions to complex transborder legal disputes. He characterizes the "epistemic insularity" of conflict rules in the following terms:

> Being *private law*, private international law must serve the overwhelming need to pursue uniformity, certainty and predictability (or "decisional harmony"). Being private *international* law, it is inappropriate to bring any other consideration than that of comity from the sphere of *public* international law, notably concerns about human rights or global justice. Being *law*, it is not amenable to the higher reaches of the discourse of jurisprudence, political theory or ethics. [103]

Overstated as such a characterization may seem, Baxi's essential point is taken, namely, that private international law often fails to make room in its tests and analyses for broad public considerations, such as human rights and policy, that arise from time to time in the course of private litigation.

Clearly, this is not always the case. Some private international law scholars have made valuable contributions.[104] Furthermore, national

---

103 Baxi, above note 101 at 197–98.

104 See for example, Friedrich K. Juenger, "Mass Disasters and the Conflict of Laws" (1989) U. Ill. L. Rev. 105; Lea Brilmayer, *Conflict of Laws: Foundations and Future Directions* (Boston: Little, Brown, 1991); Upendra Baxi, "Mass Torts, Multinational Enterprise Liability and Private International Law" (2000) 276 Rec. des Cours 305; Walker, above note 85.

courts, particularly those of Britain, have been known to leave the path of predictability and convenience in the interest of justice and public policy, as was notably done in the South African asbestos cases. In *Lubbe* (1998) and *Connelly* (2000), South African nationals sued UK corporations in relation to asbestos poisoning. Even though the foreign forum was clearly more appropriate having regard to the real and substantial connection test, it was held that justice required that UK courts assert jurisdiction given the unavailability of legal aid for the plaintiffs in South Africa. In those circumstances, the ends of justice and the interest of the parties were held to outweigh the inconvenience of the forum.[105] The long-held public policy rule in choice of law jurisprudence is also evidence of private international law's ability to countenance the normative content of human rights. More will be said on both of these issues further in the next chapter,[106] but the point is simply that private international law's epistemic insularity is not as complete as Baxi argues. In exceptional and appropriate circumstances, conflict rules are able to accommodate broader considerations of public policy and human rights, most clearly in the context of *forum non conveniens* and choice of law. It may be that such broad considerations might eventually come to bear with regards to the rules governing jurisdiction.

Given the hybrid nature of transnational human rights litigation, (i.e., civil claims incorporating both private and public law elements), traditional private international law rules should not be applied mechanically in such instances, as was done by the Ontario Superior Court in *Saleh* (2003). In that case, the court's perfunctory application of the *Muscutt* factors failed to address the particular public law dimensions of those proceedings. Admittedly, the decision in *Saleh* would likely be different now in light of the Court of Appeal's recent recognition of the forum of necessity doctrine in *Van Breda* (2010), which is premised on the unavailability of an alternative forum and the importance of avoiding denials of justice. Such an approach is not incompatible with the recognition of a broad, subject-matter-based jurisdictional principle, that is to say, a form of universal civil jurisdiction.

105 See the discussion of those cases in Chapter 7.

106 On *forum non conveniens*, see Chapter 6. On applicable law, see Section C of this chapter.

3) Towards Universal Civil Jurisdiction

The words "universal civil jurisdiction" weaved their way into legal literature after the *Filártiga* decision, as courts[107] and commentators[108] set out to describe the special *ATCA* jurisdictional grant using familiar language and concepts. While Judge Kaufman did not use the expression "universal civil jurisdiction" in his reasons for judgment, he did initiate the conceptual coalescence of two distinct and well-established jurisdictional doctrines, namely, transitory tort jurisdiction on one hand, and universal criminal jurisdiction over the so-called enemies of human kind (*hostes humani generis*) on the other. While the idea of universal civil jurisdiction does not enjoy widespread acceptance at international law, its constitutive elements remain largely unexceptionable.

Rejecting the respondent's argument that *ATCA* jurisdiction could not extend to extraterritorial events, Judge Kaufman observed that common law courts regularly adjudicate claims arising outside their territory, provided personal jurisdiction over the parties is established.[109] Thus, as Lord Mansfield put it in 1774,

> . . . if A becomes indebted to B, or commits a tort upon his person or upon his personal property in Paris, an action in either case may be maintained against A in England, if he is there found . . . . As to transitory actions, there is not a colour of doubt but that any action which is transitory may be laid in any county in England, though the matter arises beyond the seas.[110]

---

107 See, for example, *Sosa*, above note 28 at 772; *Xuncax v. Gramajo*, 886 F. Supp. 162 at 182 (D. Mass. 1995).

108 Jeffrey M. Blum & Ralph G. Steinhardt, "Federal Jurisdiction Over International Human Rights Claims: The *Alien Tort Claims Act* after *Filártiga v. Peña-Irala*" (1981) 22 Harv. Int'l L.J. 53 at 61 [Blum & Steinhardt]; *Restatement of the Law (3d) of Foreign Relations Law of the United States* (St. Paul, MN: American Law Institute, 1988) at § 404 cmt. b. [*Restatement*]; David J. Bederman, *et al.*, "Brief of Amici Curiae in Support of Respondents" (1997) 20 Hastings Int'l & Comp. L. Rev. 686 at 698; Beth Van Schaack, "In Defense of Civil Redress: The Domestic Enforcement of Human Rights Norms in the Context of the Proposed Hague Judgments Convention" (2001) 42 Harv. Int'l L.J. 141 at 194 [Van Schaack]; See also Kate Parlett "Universal Civil Jurisdiction for Torture" (2007) 4 Eur. H.R.L. Rev. 385; Donald Francis Donovan & Anthea Roberts, "The Emerging Recognition of Universal Civil Jurisdiction" (2006) 100 A.J.I.L. 142 [Donovan & Roberts].

109 *Filártiga*, above note 43 at 885.

110 *Mostyn v. Fabrigas* (1774), 1 Cowp. 161 quoted in *Filártiga*, *ibid.* at 885.

In England, and also later in Canada, jurisdiction over transitory torts was subject to what became known as the "double actionability rule" whereby an action could only be maintained for an extraterritorial tort if the wrong would have been actionable had it been committed in the forum and if it was also actionable in the place it was committed.[111] Whereas extradition of the wrongdoer would typically be the appropriate remedy in the criminal context, the adjudication of civil cases is also acceptable since it is recognized that states have a legitimate interest in the orderly resolution of disputes between persons in their territory.[112] Arguably, the forum's interest in the orderly resolution of disputes between parties within its boundaries is heightened in cases like *Filártiga* where the alleged wrong is a violation of international law, in addition to breaching the laws of the forum and foreign states. Indeed, transnational human rights cases engage the forum state's commitment to the international law of human rights and to the international community as a whole, in addition to its relations with the home state of the wrongdoer.

The other doctrine that supports a putative principle of universal civil jurisdiction is mentioned briefly, if somewhat grandiloquently, in the penultimate sentence of Judge Kaufman's reasons. He declared that "for purposes of civil liability, the torturer has become like the pirate and slave trader before him *hostis humani generis*, an enemy of all mankind."[113] This reference to the seventeenth century terminology of *hostis humani generis* is significant for at least two reasons. First, it is relevant to the spirit of *ATCA* as the doctrine was familiar to the drafters of the *Judiciary Act, 1789*, and thus sheds helpful light on the manner in which the statute should be read today. In *Sosa*, the Supreme Court

111 *Phillips v. Eyre* (1870), L.R. 6 Q.B. 1 [*Philips*]; *Boys v. Chaplin (sub. nom. Chaplin v. Boys)*, [1971] A.C. 356 (H.L.). In Canada, "double actionability" was adopted in *McLean v. Pettigrew*, [1945] S.C.R. 62 and was known as the "actionable and not justifiable" rule. In both countries, the rule pertained mostly to choice of law but also weighed heavily in the determination of jurisdiction *simpliciter*. See Blum & Steinhardt, above note 108 at 63; Christopher George John Morse, *Torts in Private International Law* (Amsterdam: North Holland, 1978). The rule has been abolished in the UK by s. 10 of the *Private International Law (Miscellaneous Provisions) Act 1995* (U.K.), 1995, c. 42 [*PIL Act*] and, as of 11 January 2009, by art. 4 of *Regulation (EC) No 864/2007 of the European Parliament and of the Council of 11 July 2007 on the law applicable to non-contractual obligations* [*Rome II*]. In Canada, the double actionability rule was abandoned in *Tolofson*, above note 1.

112 *Filártiga*, above note 43 at 885; Blum & Steinhardt, above note 108 at 63.

113 *Filártiga*, *ibid.* at 890.

found *ATCA* to apply only to those few norms of international law capable of being violated by individuals and that engage the common interests of all states. The Court upheld Judge Kaufman's assessment that the prohibition of torture had attained in the twentieth century a level of normative specificity and international acceptance equivalent to that of piracy, one of the paradigmatic violations of international law recognized in the eighteenth century. But quite apart from *ATCA* and the US experience, the doctrine of *hostis humani generis* underlies the principle of universal jurisdiction obligating all states to sanction individuals whose conduct threatens the security and interests of the international community as a whole.[114]

The origins of the doctrine are as old as the law of nations itself and appear to be historically inextricable from the offence of piracy.[115] As early as 1615, Coke CJ declared "*pirata hostis humani generis est.*"[116] In his charge to the admiralty sessions in 1668, Sir Leoline Jenkins defined pirates as "*hostis humani generis*, enemies, not of one nation, or of one sort of people only, but of all mankind. They are outlawed as I may say, by the laws of all nations; that is, out of the protection of all princes, and of all laws whatsoever. Everybody is commissioned, and is to be armed against them as rebels and traitors to subdue and root them out."[117] At a time when robbery and depredation on the high seas threatened international water-borne trade and traffic, universal competence to prosecute and punish pirates emerged as a necessary function of the international common interest. The universality principle however was not limited to piracy; it was understood to apply to all conduct that threatened the security and outraged the conscience of nations. Vattel counted poisoners, assassins, and professional larcenists among the enemies of humankind, which all states were duty bound to prosecute.

> *. . . si la justice de chaque État doit en général se borner à punir les crimes commis dans son territoire; il faut excepter de la règle ces scélérats, qui, par la qualité et la fréquence habituelle de leurs crimes, violent toute sûreté publique, et se déclarent les ennemis du Genre humain. Les empoisonneurs, les assassins, les incendiaires de profession peuvent être exterminés partout où ils on les saisit;*

114 Blum & Steinhardt, above note 108 at 61–62.

115 Harvard Research, above note 2 at 574; Lowe, above note 2 at 343.

116 *King v. Marsh* (1615), 3 Bulst. 27, 81 E.R. 23.

117 *United States v. Smith*, 18 U.S. 153 at 167 (1820), where the court quotes Jenkins; See also *In Re Piracy Jure Gentium*, [1934] A.C. 586 (P.C.).

> *car ils attaquent et outragent toutes les Nations, en foulant aux pieds les fondements de leur sûreté commune. C'est ainsi que les Pirates sont envoyés à la potence par les premiers entre les mains de qui ils tombent.*[118]

As Vattel noted, the principle of universal jurisdiction over «*les ennemis du Genre humain*» stood as a necessary exception to the rule of territoriality in order to protect the «*sûreté commune*» of all nations. At its 1931 Cambridge session, l'Institut de droit international adopted in its resolutions a principle of universal jurisdiction with regards to any offence against world public order, so called *delicta juris gentium*, which included piracy, slavery, the spreading of contagious disease, and the damaging of underwater communications cables.

> *Tout État a le droit de punir des actes commis à l'étranger par un étranger découvert sur son territoire lorsque ces actes constituent une infraction contre des intérêts généraux protégés par le droit international (tels que la piraterie, la traite des noirs, la traite des blanches, la propagation de maladies contagieuses, l'atteinte à des moyens de communication internationaux, canaux, câbles sous-marins, la falsification des monnaies, instruments de crédit, etc.), à condition que l'extradition de l'inculpé ne soit pas demandée ou que l'offre en soit refusée par l'État sur le territoire duquel le délit a été commis ou dont l'inculpé est ressortissant.*[119]

The Harvard Research noted that it is "the common interest and mutual convenience which gave rise to the [universality] principle that have conserved its vitality."[120]

Though it could be remarked that all forms of criminality engage to some extent the public interest of the international community, not all wrongs attract universal jurisdiction. As Lowe observes, there appears to be two "strands" of conduct that give rise to universal jurisdiction. The first consists of "heinous crimes, such as genocide, crimes against humanity and serious war crimes."[121] It is the particularly egregious and depraved nature of the acts that validate the exercise of universal

118 Emmerich de Vattel, *Le Droit des gens ou Principes de la loi naturelle* (Paris: Librairie de Guillaumin et Cie, 1863) Livre 1, Chapitre 19, § 233.

119 Institut de droit international, Résolutions de Cambridge, 1931 (A. Mercier Rapp): *Le conflit des lois pénales en matière de compétence*, art. 5, online: www.idi-iil.org/idiF/resolutionsF/1931_camb_04_fr.pdf.

120 Harvard Research, above note 2 at 566.

121 Lowe, above note 2 at 343; Brief of *Amicus Curiae* European Commission in *Sosa v. Alvarez-Machain*, 2004 WL 177036 at 15 [E.C. Brief in *Sosa*].

jurisdiction. The second strand includes serious wrongs for which no redress or legal sanction is likely to be available, owing to the particular circumstances surrounding their perpetration.[122] Piracy and aircraft hijacking are said to fall in this category because they are committed outside the territorial jurisdiction of all states and can potentially involve the nationals of any state. Systemic or social circumstances, such as wartime, civil unrest, and governmental corruption, may also conspire to make redress or justice impossible and justify the exercise of universal jurisdiction.[123] Aside from piracy and slavery, there is support at international law for universal jurisdiction with regards to torture,[124] genocide, war crimes and crimes against humanity.[125] Generally, universal jurisdiction appears to attach to crimes that have achieved the status of peremptory norms of international law (*jus cogens*). This comports with an understanding of peremptory norms as coextensive with and protective of world public order and of international security interests, the underlying rationale of universal jurisdiction.[126]

International law recognizes the authority of states to prosecute and punish foreigners in relation to certain serious extraterritorial wrongful acts. Arguably, the various rationales that form the basis of criminal universal jurisdiction produce equally credible and persuasive arguments in support of universal civil jurisdiction. While such a principle is not yet part of the mainstream, it has generated an increasing amount of commentary among courts, organizations, and scholars. The justifications put forth in support of universal jurisdiction appear to follow two distinct yet interrelated lines of arguments. The first line addresses the international legal plausibility of universal civil jurisdiction. For instance, the American Law Institute adopts the

---

122 Lowe, *ibid.*

123 *United States v. Yousef*, 327 F.3d 56 at 105 (2d Cir. 2003); Willard B. Cowles, "Universality of Jurisdiction Over War Crimes" (1945) 33 Cal. L. Rev. 177 at 194.

124 *Convention Against Torture and Other Cruel, Inhuman or Degrading Treatment or Punishment*, GA Res. 39/46, 39 U.N. GAOR Supp. No. 51 at 197, UN Doc. A/39/51 (1984), 1465 U.N.T.S. 85, arts. 4–5.

125 *Rome Statute of the International Criminal Court*, 17 July 1998, U.N. Doc. A/CONF.183/9, 2187 U.N.T.S. 90 [ICC Statute].

126 Menno T. Kamminga, "Report on the Exercise of Universal Jurisdiction in Respect of Gross Human Rights Offences" in Report of the 69th Congress of the International Law Association 403–31 (2000) [ILA Report]; *Armed Activities*, above note 102; Orakhelashvili 2002, above note 102 at 255; See also, generally, Alexander Orakhelashvili, *Peremptory Norms in International Law* (Oxford: Oxford University Press, 2006).

view, predicated on *The Lotus* case, that universal civil jurisdiction is permissible at international law insofar as it is not prohibited. "In general, jurisdiction on the basis of universal interests has been exercised in the form of criminal law, but international law does not preclude the application of non-criminal law on this basis, for example, by providing a remedy in tort or restitutions for victims of piracy."[127]

The second line of argument addresses the broad structural differences and commonalties between criminal punishment and civil redress. One such argument is put forth by Reydams for whom universal civil jurisdiction logically follows from universal criminal jurisdiction. Because civil jurisdiction is considered less intrusive, he argues, it ought to apply *mutatis mutandis* in the same manner as criminal jurisdiction. "The presumption is that if universal criminal jurisdiction is permissible under international law, universal civil jurisdiction is also permissible (*qui peut le plus peut le moins*, the greater includes the lesser)."[128] The distinguished editors of the ninth edition of *Oppenheim's International Law* cite *Filártiga*, a civil case, in support of the proposition that serious violations of human rights, such as torture, are subject to universal jurisdiction.[129]

In their concurring opinion in the *Arrest Warrant Case*, Judges Higgins, Kooijmans, and Buergenthal saw in the *ATCA* "the beginnings of a very broad form of extraterritorial jurisdiction."[130] The judges also noted however that the US model had "not attracted the approbation of States generally."[131] Indeed, states have taken varying and sometimes contradictory positions with regards to the exercise of *ATCA* jurisdiction.[132] However, in 2004, universal civil jurisdiction received the endorsement of the European Commission when it filed a brief with

127 *Restatement*, above note 108 at § 404 cmt. b.

128 Reydams, above note 10 at 2–3.

129 Oppenheim, above note 2 at 469–70.

130 *Arrest Warrant Case*, above note 83, Separate Concurring Opinion of Judges Higgins, Kooijmans, and Buergenthal at para 48.

131 *Ibid.*

132 Ecuador initially approved of the *ATCA* proceedings in *Aguinda v. Texaco Inc.*, 1994 U.S. Dist. LEXIS 4718 (S.D.N.Y. 1994) then later protested in *Jota v. Texaco*, 157 F.3d 153 (2d Cir. 1998) [*Jota*]. Similarly, South Africa protested against US civil jurisdiction in *In Re S. African Apartheid Litigation*, 238 F. Supp. 2d 1379 (S.D.N.Y. 2002) but supported broad-based, justice-oriented civil jurisdiction in *Connelly*, above note 67, and *Lubbe and Others and Cape plc and Related Appeals*, [2000] 1 W.L.R. 1545 (H.L.). See Chapter 8.

the US Supreme Court in the *Sosa* appeal. The Commission argued generally in support of universal civil jurisdiction over a limited set of wrongful acts, as long as it is exercised in a manner consistent with international law and only when the ends of justice so require. The Commission argued that, "to the extent recognized, [universal civil jurisdiction] should apply only to a narrow category of conduct and should be exercised only when the claimant would otherwise be subject to a denial of justice."[133]

European support for a cautious and justice-oriented principle of universal civil jurisdiction is not surprising given Europe's leading role in the ongoing work of the Hague Conference on Private International Law where universal civil jurisdiction remains on the agenda. In its dormant 2001 *Preliminary Draft Convention on Jurisdiction and Foreign Judgments in Civil and Commercial Matters*, the Conference explicitly recognized the right of states to assert universal civil jurisdiction over certain violations of international law. Draft Article 18(3) provides:

> **18(3.)** Nothing in this Article shall prevent a court in a Contracting State from exercising jurisdiction under national law in an action claiming damages in respect of conduct which constitutes —
>
> [a) genocide, a crime against humanity or a war crime;] [or]
>
> [b) a serious crime under international law, provided that this State has established its criminal jurisdiction over that crime in accordance with an international treaty to which it is a party and that the claim for civil compensatory damages for death or serious bodily injury arising from that crime.
>
> Sub-paragraph b) only applies if the party seeking relief is exposed to a risk of a denial of justice because proceedings in another State are not possible or cannot reasonably be required.]

The jurisdiction provided under sub-paragraph (b) is in line with the European Commission's submissions in *Sosa*, namely, that universal jurisdiction should be exercised in respect of violations of peremptory norms of international law where, in the circumstances, the claimant faces the prospect of being denied justice. It would appear that no such requirement is proposed with regards to genocide, crimes against humanity, and war crimes. The draft provision is evidence of

133 E.C. brief in *Sosa*, above note 121 at 26–27.

the growing international acceptance of some version of universal civil jurisdiction.

The availability of monetary damages in certain countries in the context of criminal prosecutions is suggestive of further support for universal civil jurisdiction. Indeed, in many civil law countries, victims are permitted to join criminal proceedings as a "*partie civile*" and obtain damages as part of the court's sentence.[134] In his concurrent opinion in *Sosa*, Justice Breyer explained the significance of such remedies in relation to universal civil jurisdiction.

> The fact this procedural consensus exists [viz. a consensus that "universal jurisdiction exists to prosecute a subset" of certain universally condemned behaviour which includes torture] suggests that recognition of universal jurisdiction in respect of a limited set of norms is consistent with principles of international comity. That is, allowing every nation's courts to adjudicate foreign conduct involving foreign parties in such cases will not significantly threaten the practical harmony that comity principles seek to protect. That consensus concerns criminal jurisdiction, but consensus as to universal criminal jurisdiction itself suggests that universal tort jurisdiction would be no more threatening. Cf. Restatement para. 404, Comment b. That is because the criminal courts of many nations combine civil and criminal proceedings, allowing those injured by criminal conduct to be represented and to recover damages in the criminal proceedings itself.[135]

The possibility of initiating civil proceedings for crimes of universal competence was also highlighted by the ICTY in *Furundzija*.[136] The fact that certain states allow under their laws the award of damages

---

134 Such civil actions are possible in Austria, Belgium, Denmark, Finland, France, Germany, Greece, Italy, Luxembourg, the Netherlands, Portugal, Spain, and Sweden. E.C. Brief in *Sosa*, *ibid.* at n. 48; Van Schaack, above note 108 at 143. Canadian courts can also award damages upon sentencing in certain circumstances: *Canadian Criminal Code*, R.S.C. 1985, c. C-48, s. 738.

135 *Sosa*, above note 28 at 762. Victims of crimes that attract universal jurisdiction may become civil parties in criminal proceedings in the courts of many countries, including Argentina, Austria, Belgium, Denmark, Finland, France, Germany, Greece, Ireland, Italy, Luxemburg, the Netherlands, Portugal, Senegal, Spain, and Sweden. See REDRESS, *Universal Jurisdiction in the European Union: Country Studies* (London: REDRESS Trust, 2004).

136 *Prosecutor v. Anto Furundzija*, IT-95-17/1-T, Judgment (10 December 1998) at para. 155 (International Criminal Tribunal for the Former Yugoslavia, Trial Chamber).

in relation to crimes, including crimes of universal competence, lends credence to the proposition that civil jurisdiction over such wrongful conduct does not require a material leap of faith. A criminal sentence that orders the offender to make restitution is not the same as an award for damages at the outcome of a civil trial, but this overlap of remedies reflects the broader point that "criminal punishment and civil liability operate with different intensity to vindicate important standards of conduct and deter future wrongdoing."[137]

Finally, it is possible to find some measure of support for universal civil jurisdiction in the framework of international criminal law, specifically, in the principle of complementarity on which the International Criminal Court (ICC) is based. Under the ICC statute, national courts have primary jurisdiction over international crimes.[138] The ICC has complementary jurisdiction and may only exercise it if national courts are unwilling or unable to carry out criminal investigations and prosecutions.[139] The subsidiary nature of the ICC's jurisdiction rests on two rationales. First, to avoid inundating the ICC with cases from all over the world, it was decided that states should have the first opportunity to prosecute international criminals, given that it is in fact their duty to do so.[140] Second, the ICC's complementary jurisdiction is respectful of each state's sovereignty. If a state is willing and able to conduct a proper and fair trial under one of the usual jurisdictional grounds (e.g., territoriality, nationality, or universality) the ICC should not usurp that state's jurisdiction in a given case. In short, complementarity is about deference to a particular state's power and duty to put its national laws and judicial system to the service of the international community by prosecuting and punishing acts that threaten world public order. Conceivably, the complementarity of national and international criminal jurisdiction might eventually come to bear in the civil sphere as well. The fact that the ICC may,

137 E.C. brief in *Sosa*, above note 121 at 22.

138 ICC Statute, above note 125, Preamble and art. 1.

139 Cassese, above note 10 at 348–61; Antonio Cassese *et al.*, eds., *The Rome Statute of the International Criminal Court: A Commentary* (Oxford: Oxford University Press, 2002) c. 18.1; Jann K. Kleffner, "The Impact of Complementarity on National Implementation of Substantive International Criminal Law" (2003) 1 J. Int'l Crim. Just. 86.

140 ICC Statute, above note 125, Preamble: "Recalling that it is the duty of every State to exercise its criminal jurisdiction over those responsible for international crime."

among other remedies, award damages upon sentencing[141] reflects an acknowledgment that the effects of international wrongs are felt both publicly and privately and require a correspondingly multidimensional response.

The public dimension of transnational human rights claims gives rise to a significant objection against universal civil jurisdiction. Arguably, because violations of peremptory norms of international law so fundamentally involve the interests of the international community, the legal responses to such violations should be initiated and controlled by the states themselves (as is the case with criminal prosecutions), not by private individuals seeking financial redress or personal vindication (as is often the case with civil actions). In deciding whether to prosecute or extradite a suspected war criminal, for instance, a state might take into consideration certain public policy factors, such as its own institutional capacity to hold the trial, or the greater interest of another state in the matter. It could be argued that this policy-based discretion of the executive is lost in civil actions where proceedings are commenced and controlled by private plaintiffs, without regard to the interests of the state, much less that of the international community.

It is true that transnational human rights claims raise important questions of public policy and comity, but these questions do not in themselves negate the possibility of universal civil jurisdiction. They do however counsel heightened judicial caution. In the context of transnational human rights proceedings, the policy-based discretion to assert or decline jurisdiction falls to the judiciary, rather than to the executive. And, insofar as the UK and Canadian experience can be taken as representative of curial dispositions generally, it is clear that broad considerations of public policy ought to weigh heavily in judicial determinations of jurisdiction and justiciability.[142] Moreover, in certain circumstances, public policy weighs heavily in favour of asserting jurisdiction. Just as a custodial forum might refuse to extradite an alleged offender towards a state where he is likely to be tortured,[143] public policy might require a state to exercise civil jurisdiction to avoid

141 *Ibid.*, art. 75.

142 See for example, *Al-Adsani v. Kuwait* (1996) 107 I.L.R. 536 (C.A.); *Bouzari*, above note 79.

143 *Soering v. United Kingdom*, (1989), E.C.H.R. (Series A No. 161), 11 E.H.R.R. 439; *Suresh v. Canada (M.C.I.)*, [2002] 1 S.C.R. 3.

a denial of justice where an adequate remedy could not reasonably be expected or required anywhere else.

In this light, universal civil jurisdiction appears to be compatible with the emerging jurisdictional doctrine of forum of necessity.[144] Similarly, the Québec Civil Code empowers courts of that province to act as "forum of necessity," that is, to assert jurisdiction where it appears that "proceedings cannot possibly be instituted outside Québec or where the institution of such proceedings outside Québec cannot reasonably be required."[145] LeBel JA (as he then was) noted that the provision was meant to guard against

> *certains problèmes d'accès à la justice, pour un plaideur qui se trouve dans le territoire québécois, lorsque le forum étranger normalement compétent lui est inaccessible pour des raisons exceptionnelles, comme une impossibilité en droit ou une impossibilité pratique, presqu'absolue. Ainsi, on peut penser à celles résultant de la rupture des relations diplomatiques ou commerciales avec un État étranger ou de la nécessité de la protection d'un réfugié politique, ou à l'existence d'un danger physique sérieux, si l'on entame un débat devant le tribunal étranger.*[146]

Following Quebec's lead, other common law Canadian provinces have also enacted forum of necessity legislation and Ontario now recognizes it as a matter of common law.[147] As Walker noted, forum of necessity jurisdiction "finds general support in art. 6 of the European Convention on Human Rights, which proscribes a denial of justice."[148] The spectre of a denial of justice, it will be recalled, provided a strong impetus for the creation of *ATCA* jurisdiction in 1789[149] and, as argued by the European Commission in *Sosa*, should properly stand as a *sine*

144 See above notes 94–98 and accompanying text.

145 C.C.Q., above note 55, art. 3136.

146 *Lamborghini (Canada) Inc. v. Automobili Lamborghini SPA*, [1997] R.J.Q. 58 at para. 44 (C.A.).

147 *Van Breda*, above note 75; For examples of forum of necessity legislation, see, for example, *Court Jurisdiction and Proceedings Transfer Act*, S.B.C. 2003, c. 28, s. 6; *Court Jurisdiction and Proceedings Transfer Act*, S.N.S. 2003 (2d Sess.), c. 2, s. 7; For general commentary on forum of necessity jurisdiction, see Walker, above note 85; Elizabeth Edinger, "New British Columbia Legislation: *The Court Jurisdiction and Proceedings Transfer Act*; *The Enforcement of Canadian Judgments and Decrees Act*" (2006) 39 U.B.C. L. Rev. 407.

148 Walker, above note 85; ECHR, above note 32, art. 6.

149 See Chapter 2, Section C(2)(a).

qua non to the exercise of universal civil jurisdiction if such a principle is to find general approval.

To summarize, traditional conflict of laws rules governing the assertion of jurisdiction in civil matters do not square easily with transnational human rights litigation, focused as they are on improbable territorial connections and limited private interests. Civil claims in respect of extraterritorial human rights violations and serious breaches of international law require a correspondingly broad view of jurisdiction that properly countenances the public interests of the international community as whole, in addition to the private interests of the litigants. In this connection, the forum of necessity doctrine will likely play an important role. Also, there is evidence of growing support for the recognition of a principle of universal civil jurisdiction, premised *mutatis mutandis* on the rationale of its criminal law counterpart, in situations where the claimant would otherwise face a denial of justice because adjudication of the claim could not be reasonably expected in the *loci delicti commissi*.

C. APPLICABLE LAW

Assuming that a Canadian or UK court asserts jurisdiction in a civil claim for an extraterritorial human rights violation such as torture, the next issue for the court to decide is usually the applicable law. In Britain, the choice of law analysis in tort actions is governed by Article 4 of *Rome II*.[150] As noted above, *Rome II* largely abolished the "double actionability" rule[151] and replaced it with a general rule favouring the *lex loci delicti commissi*.[152] Potentially, then, *Rome II* could have the effect of rendering moot the issue of whether customary norms are actionable in English common law since, as a general rule, courts are obliged to apply the law of the place where the wrong occurred. Virgo describes the implications of the general rule in the following terms:

> So if a claimant is tortured in Arcadia, Arcadian law will apply. If Arcadia recognises that torture is a tort or, at the very least, that there is some form of civil liability for torture, the victim's claim is

150 *Rome II*, above note 111.

151 See discussion above at note 111.

152 *Ibid*. s. 11.

likely to succeed. If, however Arcadia does not recognise civil liability, the application of that law by the English court will mean that the claim fails.[153]

The claim could also fail if the impugned acts are lawful in the foreign country. Admittedly, this would not be an issue in cases such as *Filártiga*, *Al-Adsani*, or *Bouzari*, since torture is outlawed in nearly every jurisdiction on the planet, including Paraguay, Kuwait, and Iran.[154] Alternatively, the application of the *lex loci delicti commissi* by English courts could be fatal to a plaintiff's claim where the foreign country has granted legal amnesties in relation to the impugned conduct. Plaintiffs may attempt to exclude such legalizing laws, but English courts have recognized retrospective legislation limiting civil liability in the past.[155]

Rome II provides for two exceptions to the general rule. First, under Article 4.3, the *lex loci deliciti commissi* may be displaced in favour of the law of another country deemed by the court to be "manifestly more closely connected" in light of the overall circumstances of the claim. But as the editors of Dicey & Morris point out, with reference to Article 4.3's predecessor — section 12(2) of the *PIL Act* — the burden of demonstrating that English law is substantially more appropriate than the *lex loci delicti commissi* is a heavy one. It must be shown that there is a "clear preponderance of factors declared relevant by s. 12(2) which point towards the law of the [forum]."[156] Where a plaintiff initiates a claim in England in relation to torture that occurred, for example, in China, the preponderance of factors are unlikely to weigh in favour of

153 Graham Virgo, "Characterisation, Choice of Law and Human Rights" in Craig Scott, ed., *Torture as Tort*, above note 45 at 338 [Virgo].

154 Iran has not signed the CAT, but torture is prohibited under art. 38 of its constitution.

155 See *Philips*, above note 111, where the Queen's Bench recognized the *Jamaican Act of Indemnity*, which absolved the defendant of the mass killings he ordered while in office as governor. See also John Terry, "Taking *Filártiga* on the Road: Why Courts outside the United States Should Accept Jurisdiction over Actions Involving Torture Committed Abroad" in Craig Scott, ed., *Torture as Tort*, above note 45 at 125; ILA Report, above note 51 at 161.

156 Dicey & Morris, above note 40 at paras. 35–102. Section 12(2) of the *PIL Act*, above note 111, states: "The factors that may be taken into account as connecting a tort or delict with a country for the purposes of this section include, in particular, factors relating to the parties, to any of the events which constitute the tort or delict in question or to any of the circumstances or consequences of those events."

England (or any other country for that matter) since the alleged torture remains linked to both the territory and government of China.[157] As Virgo noted, "[b]y its very nature the tort is likely to be closely connected with the country where the torture occurred, so this exception is unlikely to be of any use."[158]

The second exception to the general rule is codified at Article 26 of *Rome II*, which provides: "The application of a provision of the law of any country specified by this Regulation may be refused only if such application is manifestly incompatible with the public policy *(ordre public)* of the forum." Pursuant to the public policy rule, a court may refuse to apply the *lex loci delicti commissi* when the foreign law offends the public policy of the forum. Public policy is a broad concept in private international law, but it has consistently been upheld as "an escape route from the application of the relevant choice of law rule, or from recognition of a foreign judgment which would otherwise be entitled to it."[159]

In *Oppenheimer*, the House of Lords refused to recognize a German decree that stripped expatriated German Jews of their nationality. The Lords agreed that English law should not recognize a foreign law that results in a "grave infringement of human rights."[160] In *Kuwait Airways*, the human rights ground of the public policy rule was expanded to include violations of peremptory norms of international law. In that case, the House of Lords declined to recognize a confiscatory Iraqi decree passed in the wake of Iraq's illegal annexation of Kuwait. Lord Nicholls stated the public policy rule as follows:

> Exceptionally and rarely, a provision of foreign law will be disregarded when it would lead to a result wholly alien to fundamental requirements of justice as administered by an English court. A result of this character would not be acceptable to an English court. In the conventional phraseology, such a result would be contrary to public

---

157 ILA Report, above note 51 at 162.

158 Virgo, above note 153 at 338.

159 Peter Basil Carter, "Public Policy in English Private International Law" (1993) 42 I.C.L.Q. 1 at 1.

160 *Oppenheimer v. Cattermole*, [1976] A.C. 249 at 263 [*Oppenheimer*]; *Re Helbert Wagg & Co. Ltd.*, [1956] 1 Ch. 323 (German statute held to be confiscatory in nature and thus in violation of international law); *Laane & Balster v. Estonian Cargo & Passenger Steamship Line*, [1949] S.C.R. 530 [*Laane & Balster*] (Soviet expropriation law deemed contrary to Canadian public policy).

> policy. Then the court will decline to enforce or recognise the foreign decree to whatever extent is required in the circumstances.
>
> . . . the courts of this country must have a residual power, to be exercised exceptionally and with the greatest circumspection, to disregard a provision in the foreign law when to do otherwise would affront basic principles of justice and fairness which the courts seek to apply in the administration of justice in this country. Gross infringements of human rights are one instance, and an important instance, of such a provision.[161]

In his speech, Lord Steyn added, endorsing the judgment of the court below:

> It is true that the Court of Appeal broke new ground. It was the first decision to hold that the acts of a foreign state within its territory may be refused recognition because they are contrary to public international law. On the other hand, the Court of Appeal built on the *Oppenheimer* case which was permeated, as the Court of Appeal observed, by considerations of the public international law. In my view the Court of Appeal was right to extend the public policy exception beyond human rights violations to flagrant breaches of public international law.[162]

There is not likely to be a foreign law authorizing "gross infringements of human rights" or violations of peremptory norms of international law such as torture, but the *lex loci deliciti commissi* could conceivably absolve such wrongdoing or simply not recognize a civil remedy for victims. In such circumstances, Virgo argues, "if the foreign law does not recognise civil liability for serious violations of human rights, it should follow that the English court will, in the exercise of its discretion, not apply that foreign law."[163]

In Canada, there is no equivalent to *Rome II* but the *lex loci delicti commissi* rule is applied as matter of course since the Supreme Court's decision in *Tolofson* (1994), at least in interprovincial cases.[164] In international

161 *Kuwait Airways Corporation v. Iraqi Airways Co.*, [2002] 2 A.C. 883 at 1078 (H.L.) [*Kuwait Airways*].

162 *Ibid.* at 1102.

163 Virgo, above note 153 at 338.

164 Jennifer Orange, "Torture, Tort Choice of Law and *Tolofson*" in Craig Scott, ed., *Torture as Tort*, above note 45 at 292 [Orange].

tort matters, courts struggle to avoid injustices that might result from the rule's rigid application, as was done for instance in *Hanlan* (1997). In a case involving a car accident between two Ontario residents travelling in the state of Minnesota, the court (applying a rationale similar to that of Article 4.3 of *Rome II*) found that the rule would "work an injustice" in light of the overall factors connecting the parties and the claim to Ontario.[165] It is noted that the injustice the court sought to remedy in *Hanlan* was the unavailability in Minnesota law of a complete category of claim or cause of action available to the parties in Ontario, namely the claims of family members for damages pursuant to section 61 of the *Family Law Act* (*FLA*).[166] While this judgment is arguably at odds with *Tolofson*, "La Forest J did not make it clear how strictly the rule applies in international situations, and left open the possibility of 'rare' exceptions in international cases."[167] In *Wong* (2002), the Ontario Court of Appeal emphasized that *Tolofson* had established "a very narrow exception" to the *lex loci delicti commissi* rule and that the rule should prevail in most circumstances.[168] The Court of Appeal went on to note, however, that La Forest J had not articulated any criteria to discern the rare circumstances in which the exception would apply, and cited *Hanlan* as an appropriate example.[169] Therefore, in Ontario and in every other province where similar provisions exist,

165 *Hanlan v. Sernesky*, [1997] O.J. No. 3658 at para. 6 (Gen. Div.), aff'd (1998), 95 O.A.C. 297 (C.A.).

166 R.S.O. 1990, c. F.3, s. 61 provides that "[i]f a person is injured or killed by the fault or neglect of another under circumstances where the person is entitled to recover damages, or would have been entitled if not killed, the spouse, . . . children, grandchildren, parents, grandparents, brothers and sisters of the person are entitled to recover their pecuniary loss resulting from the injury or death from the person from whom the person injured or killed is entitled to recover or would have been entitled if not killed, and to maintain an action for the purpose in a court of competent jurisdiction."

167 Orange, above note 164 at 293. In the author's view, at 321, "La Forest J.'s reasoning in *Tolofson* more or less excludes the kinds of analysis set out in the United Kingdom's *PIL Act* as a method for selecting a law other than the *lex loci delicti*." There appears to be more flexibility in Quebec. Article 2809 of the C.C.Q., above note 55, "provides that Québec law is applied if the law of the country where the injurious act occurred is not pleaded or proven": *Bil'in (Village Council) v. Green Park International Inc.*, 2009 QCCS 4151 at para. 1186 [*Bil'in*].

168 *Wong v. Lee* (2002), 58 O.R. (3d) 398 at para. 12 (C.A.) [*Wong*].

169 *Ibid.* at para. 16. See also *Somers v. Fournier* (2002), 60 O.R. (3d) 225 (C.A.) where the Court of Appeal highlighted the exceptional nature of any derogation from the *lex loci delicti* rule.

it could be argued on the basis of *Hanlan* and *Wong* that the law of the forum should apply in cases where the *lex loci delicti* does not provide the plaintiffs' family members with a comparative cause of action as that under the *FLA*. As will be seen in Chapter 6, such juridical advantages are also relevant in the *forum non conveniens* analysis.

While *Tolofson* is an interprovincial tort case, the court addressed in *obiter* the issue of applicable law in international tort litigation. La Forest J begins his analysis by describing the principles that ought to direct the choice of law analysis in international cases.

> The underlying postulate of public international law is that generally each state has jurisdiction to make and apply law within its territorial limit. *Absent a breach of some overriding norm*, other states as a matter of "comity" will ordinarily respect such actions and are hesitant to interfere with what another state chooses to do within those limits. Moreover, to accommodate the movement of people, wealth and skills across state lines, a by-product of modern civilization, they will in great measure recognize the determination of legal issues in other states. And to promote the same values, they will open their national forums for the resolution of specific legal disputes arising in other jurisdictions consistent with the interests and internal values of the forum state. These are the realities that must be reflected and accommodated in private international law.[170]

He then goes on to hold that, while the *lex loci deliciti commissi* could be applied in most international cases, rare circumstances might warrant otherwise.

> However because a rigid rule on the international level could give rise to injustice, in certain circumstances, I am not averse to retaining a discretion in the court to apply our own law to deal with such circumstances. I can, however, imagine few cases where this would be necessary.[171]

La Forest J thus suggested the possibility of displacing the *lex loci delicti commissi* in international cases, without describing the "few cases" in which such a decision would be appropriate. It could be speculated, from his reference (without explanation) to a putative "breach of some

170 *Tolofson*, above note 1 at para. 36 [emphasis added].
171 *Ibid.* at para. 49.

overriding norm" and to shared "values," that violations of peremptory norms of international law may justify the displacement of foreign laws as was done in *Kuwait Airways*.[172]

Surprisingly, *Tolofson* made no mention of another Supreme Court of Canada decision in which the public policy rule was invoked as justification for refusing to recognize a foreign exproprietary decree. In *Laane & Baltser* (1949), the Court held that "it is now established that a common law jurisdiction will not enforce directly or indirectly the penal or the revenue laws of another state, to which Dicey in Rule 54, 5th Ed., adds, political law; and there is the general principle that no state will apply a law of another which offends against some fundamental morality or public policy."[173] Therefore, on the strength of *Laane & Balster*'s authority, and in light of the apparent willingness in *Tolofson* to recognize a judicial discretion to favour Canadian law in some circumstances, it is possible that the *lex loci delicti commissi* could be displaced by Canadian courts on public policy grounds, where the foreign law excuses an alleged human right abuses or violations of peremptory norms of public international law.

There is, however, another way of conceiving the choice of law analysis in transnational human rights cases. It is possible to argue that in cases such as *Bouzari* or *Al-Adsani*, the *lex loci delicti commissi* is irrelevant if and to the extent the cause of action is derived from international law itself, as opposed to from the *lex loci delicti commissi* or the *lex fori*.[174]

---

172 Orange, above note 164 at 301–6.

173 *Laane & Balster*, above note 160 at para. 50. See also C.C.Q., above note 55, art. 3081: "The provisions of the law of a foreign country do not apply if their application would be manifestly inconsistent with public order as understood in international relations." In *Bil'in*, above note 167 at para. 298, the Quebec court specified that art. 3081 operates only to bar the application of specific "provisions of law." It could not operate "prospectively" with respect to a presumed "legally unjustified refusal by the [foreign court] to apply" generally accepted international humanitarian norms.

174 See, for example, François Larocque, "The Tort of Torture" (2009) 17:3 Tort Law Review 158 which proposes the recognition of a new cause of action in tort for acts of torture as defined in international law. After discussing the normative particularities of torture as a hybrid public-private wrong, the possibility and desirability of expanding the classical categories of intentional torts to accommodate a new nominate tort of torture is discussed. Following the current taxonomy of Canadian tort law, it is suggested that torture could coherently be conceived as a distinct form of trespass against the person or, alternatively, as an especially violent form of misfeasance in public office. For an earlier articulation of a the similar proposal, see François Larocque, "Le délit transnational de la torture"

If one accepts, as did the US Supreme Court in *Sosa*, that customary international law may give rise to actionable rights, then customary international law is arguably the proper law, equally binding as it is on all states unless specifically and consistently objected to. Under this view, national law is the conduit through which existing international rights are applied and enforced, while, for its part, international law supplies the cause of action (as in *Filártiga*) and associated standards of liability (as in *Unocal*).[175] The law of the forum could be resorted to without impropriety for resolving ancillary procedural issues. As in the traditional choice of law approach, a foreign law that would excuse violations of peremptory norms or exclude recovery for such violations could be ignored on public policy grounds (as in *Kuwait Airways*).

D. JUSTICIABILITY

Quite apart from the issue of whether national courts have jurisdiction over a given transnational human right claim is the question of whether jurisdiction ought to or can be exercised in the particular circumstances of each case. Common law courts may decline jurisdiction they otherwise possess on the basis of various doctrines if, in their estimation, certain factors render the adjudication of the claim inappropriate or if the matter is better left for the courts of another country. Though used exceptionally and with discernment, the discretion to decline jurisdiction constitutes an important structural feature of common law legal systems allowing courts to manage their jurisprudence and resources by ensuring that only appropriate and meritorious claims are adjudicated. The most relevant justiciability doctrines in the context of the transnational human rights litigation are the doctrines of *forum non conveniens*, comity, the political question doctrine, Act of State, and the rule of state immunity.[176] *Forum non conveniens* and state immunity receive sustained attention in Chapters 6 and 7, respectively, since they frequently arise in transnational human rights cases. The remainder of this chapter can deal rather briefly with

---

in Sanda Rodgers, Rakhi Ruparelia, & Louise Bélanger-Hardy, eds., *Critical Torts* (Toronto: LexisNexis Canada, 2009) at 263–90.

175 See Chapter 2, Section D(5)(c).

176 Of course state immunity differs from the others in that it is not a prudential doctrine but rather, where it applies, a nondiscretionary rule of law.

the doctrines of comity, political question, and the Act of State, as they are typically only raised on a subsidiary basis in the caselaw.

1) Comity

Comity remains uncomfortably couched in vague conceptions of normativity, political goodwill, and morality.[177] Brownlie identifies no fewer than five incarnations of the concept: (1) comity as "the rules of politeness, convenience and goodwill observed by States in their mutual intercourse without being legally bound by them"; (2) comity as "a synonym for international law"; (3) comity as "equivalent to private international law"; (4) comity as "a policy basis for, and source of, particular rules of conflict of laws"; (5) comity as "the reason for and source of a rule of international law."[178] It would appear that English and Canadian courts are gradually moving away from the notion of "comity *qua* international law" in favour of the "comity as justification for rules" understanding, though this may be the result of changing judicial writing style rather than of revamped curial thinking.[179] It is accordingly difficult to assess what role comity plays in judicial determinations of jurisdiction, aside from serving as a general background principle against which established rules are interpreted and applied.[180]

Comity is no more determinate in the US, as the Supreme Court's treatment of the concept in *Hilton v. Guyot* (1895) reveals. In that case, concerning the enforcement of a French judgment, the Court enunciated its oft-quoted definition:

> Comity, in the legal sense, is neither a matter of absolute obligation, on the one hand, nor of mere courtesy and good will, upon the other. But it is the recognition which one nation allows within its territory to the legislative, executive or judicial acts of another nation, having due regard both to international duty and convenience, and to the rights of its own citizens or of other persons who are under the pro-

177 Hessel E. Yntema, "The Comity Doctrine" (1966) 65 Mich. L. Rev. 1 [Yntema].

178 Brownlie, above note 2 at 28.

179 UK: Compare *The Parlement Belge* [1879–90] 5 Prob. Div. 197 (1880) at 210 and 214; and *Jones v. Saudi Arabia*, [2004] EWCA Civ 1394 at para. 104 [*Jones*]. Canada: Compare *Dessaulles v. Republic of Poland*, [1944] S.C.R. 275 at 275; and *Schreiber*, above note 27 at para. 27.

180 John Greenwood Collier, *Conflict of Laws*, 3d ed. (Cambridge: Cambridge University Press, 2001) at 378–79.

> tection of its laws . . . . Comity is, and ever must be, uncertain; . . . it must necessarily depend on a variety of circumstances which cannot be reduced to any certain rule.[181]

Comity's indeterminacy however has not prevented jurists from invoking it, usually alongside *forum non conveniens*, as an additional basis for the dismissal of *ATCA* proceedings.[182] In this context, courts are asked to decline jurisdiction out of deference to the laws and interests of the foreign state, insofar as such deference can be reconciled with the laws and interests of the forum. As a threshold matter, US courts will only consider declining jurisdiction on the basis of comity where laws of the foreign state and the forum are in conflict, such as to make compliance with both laws impossible.[183] Such a conflict existed for instance in *Re Nazi Era Cases Against German Defendants Litigation* between the *ATCA* cause of action and the German *Foundation Law*, which prohibited victims of the Nazi regime from pursuing extraterritorial court actions.[184] In such cases, comity requires the forum to seek "a reasonable accommodation that reconciles the central concerns of both sets of laws."[185] Inversely, comity does not operate where declining jurisdiction would be inconsistent with the laws, policies, and interests of the forum. In this connection, executive statements of both the foreign and forum states weigh heavily in the judicial determination of what comity requires.[186] As Blackmun J noted, "it is the Executive that normally decides when a course of action is important enough to risk affronting a foreign nation or placing a strain on foreign commerce. It is the Executive, as well, that is best equipped to determine how to accommodate foreign interests along with our

181 *Hilton*, above note 20 at 163–64.

182 See for example, *Aquinda v. Texaco, Inc.*, 945 F. Supp. 625 (S.D.N.Y. 1996) (dismissing claim on basis of comity); overturned *Jota*, above note 132; *Iwanowa v. Ford Motor Co.*, 67 F. Supp. 2d 424 (D.N.J. 1999) [*Iwanowa*]; *Sarei v. Rio Tinto plc*, 221 F. Supp. 2d 1116 at 1202 (C.D. Cal. 2002) [*Sarei*]; *Wiwa v. Royal Dutch Petroleum*, No. 96 Civ. 8386, 2002 U.S. Dist. Lexis 3293 (S.D.N.Y. 2002) [*Wiwa*]; *Presbyterian Church of Sudan v. Talisman Energy Inc.*, 244 F. Supp. 2d 289 (S.D.N.Y. 2003) [*Talisman*].

183 *Sarei*, *ibid.* at 1202; *Société Nationale Industrielle Aerospatiale v. U.S. District Court*, 482 U.S. 522 at 555 (1987) [*Société Nationale*].

184 *In re: Nazi Era Cases Against German Defendants Litigation*, 129 F. Supp. 2d 370 (D.N.J. 2001) [*In re Nazi Era Cases*]. See also *Iwanowa*, above note 182 and *Sarei*, above note 182 for further examples of conflicting legislation.

185 *Société Nationale*, above note 183 at 555.

186 *Iwanowa*, above note 182 at 491.

own."[187] Accordingly, in *Sarei*, having taken judicial notice of the Papua New Guinean government's objections to the *ATCA* proceedings and of the US Department of State's opinion that the litigation would strain the peaceful relations between the two states, the court held that comity required the dismissal of the plaintiffs' environmental claims.[188] By contrast, in *Talisman*, where the US government officially characterized the atrocities in Sudan as genocide, the court was of the view that "any adjudication of private plaintiffs' rights . . . would certainly have far less impact than either of these government pronouncements" and that, accordingly, comity did not apply.[189]

By virtue of their subject matter, transnational human rights cases are not likely to trigger the operation of comity. Since Huber's articulation of the doctrine, comity as always entailed the deference of national courts in respect of competing foreign laws, policies, or interests, provided such deference would not prejudice the laws or interests of the forum.[190] Transnational human rights cases however typically do not involve foreign enactments or decisions to which courts could defer. Any legislation or order authorizing the violations of peremptory norms of international law would likely attract international disavowal, not deference. In *Talisman*, the defendant corporation moved to dismiss the claims against it on comity grounds, arguing that US courts should defer to Sudan's interests in the proceedings. The court flatly rejected this position, holding that "granting comity to allegedly genocidal acts violates the strong United States interest in addressing *jus cogens* violations through the ATCA."[191] In *Sarei*, Papua New Guinean plaintiffs sued a multinational corporation for environmental damage, war crimes, and crimes against humanity.[192] The State had enacted legislation prohibiting the filing of claims in foreign courts arising out of industrial development in Papua New Guinea. Recognizing Papua New Guinea's legislation, the court dismissed the plaintiffs' environmental claims on the basis of comity, but refused to rely on comity to dismiss the claims relating to crimes against humanity and war crimes. It stated: "The fact that the conduct

187 *Société Nationale*, above note 183 at 552.
188 *Sarei*, above note 182.
189 *Talisman*, above note 182 at 343.
190 Yntema, above note 177 at 26.
191 *Talisman*, above note 182 at 343; *Wiwa*, above note 182 at 103–4.
192 *Sarei*, above note 182.

in which defendants engaged is alleged to constitute war crimes and crimes against humanity argues strongly in favour of the retention of jurisdiction."[193] Moreover, the interests and policies embodied in *ATCA* are arguably aligned, or at the very least, not inconsistent with those of the international community. Such was Justice Breyer's assessment in *Sosa*. In his view, the assertion and retention of jurisdiction in relation to violations of peremptory norms of international law "is consistent with principles of comity. That is, allowing every nation's courts to adjudicate foreign conduct involving foreign parties in such cases will not significantly threaten the practical harmony that comity principles seek to protect."[194] In *R. v. Hape*, the Supreme Court of Canada recognized similar limits to the principle of comity in the context of transnational criminal investigations: "Comity means that when a state looks to another for help in criminal matters, it must respect the manner in which the other state chooses to provide the assistance within its borders. That deference ends where clear violations of international law and fundamental human rights begin."[195]

2) Political Question Doctrine

Under the political question doctrine, a court may refrain from deciding an inherently political issue in the course of proceedings otherwise falling within its jurisdiction. The doctrine is rooted in the division of powers and operates to prevent the judiciary from interfering in matters constitutionally mandated to either the executive or legislative branches. In the leading case on the issue, *Baker v. Carr* (1962), Justice Brennan enumerated the characteristics by which courts might identify non-justiciable political questions:

> [1] a textually demonstrable constitutional commitment of the issue to a coordinate political department; or [2] a lack of judicially discoverable and manageable standards for resolving it; or [3] the impossibility of deciding without an initial policy determination of a kind clearly for nonjudicial discretion; or [4] the impossibility of a court's undertaking independent resolution without expressing lack of the

---

193 *Ibid.* at 1107.

194 *Sosa*, above note 28 at 121.

195 *Hape*, above note 8 at para. 52.

> respect due coordinate branches of government; or [5] an unusual need for unquestioning adherence to a political decision already made; or [6] the potentiality of embarrassment from multifarious pronouncements by various departments on one question.[196]

In short, out of prudence and respect for the constitutional order, courts will refrain from assessing the substantive merits or wisdom of executive and legislative policies and actions, passing judgment instead solely on their legality and constitutionality. This restraint has been the cornerstone of US judicial review at least since the time of *Marbury v. Madison* (1803) where Marshall CJ stated: "The province of the court is, solely, to decide on the rights of individuals, not to enquire how the executive, or executive officers, perform duties in which they have a discretion. Questions, in their nature political, or which are, by the constitution and laws, submitted to the executive, can never be made in this court."[197] The political question doctrine will operate to prevent courts from adjudicating individual rights to the extent that such adjudication would cause the court to overstep its authority.[198]

Though US federal courts are often invited to refrain from adjudicating transnational human rights cases on this basis, the political question doctrine has not proven to be much of an impediment to claims, except in cases where the executive branch has adopted a clear policy of ensuring compensation through government-to-government negotiations. Following the factors identified in *Baker*, the *Kadić* court gave short shrift to the first three elements, noting that

> ... the decision in *Filártiga* established that universally recognized norms of international law provide judicially discoverable and manageable standards for adjudicating suits brought under the *Alien Tort Act*, which obviates any need to make initial policy decisions of the kind normally reserved for nonjudicial discretion. Moreover, the existence of judicially discoverable and manageable standards further undermines the claim that such suits relate to matters that are constitutionally committed to another branch.[199]

196 *Baker v. Carr*, 369 U.S. 186 at 217 (1962) [*Baker*].

197 *Marbury v. Madison*, 5 U.S. 137 at 163–64 (1803). For a critical analysis of the doctrine, see Louis Henkin, "Is There a 'Political Question' Doctrine?" (1976) 85 Yale L.J. 597.

198 *Alperin v. Vatican Bank*, 2005 U.S. App. LEXIS 14794 (9th Cir. 2005).

199 *Kadić v. Karadzić*, 70 F.3d 232 at 249 (2d Cir. 1995) [*Kadić*].

Because transnational human rights claims must ultimately be settled according to well-established common law standards of liability and because *ATCA* and the *TVPA* clearly express the US policy and interest in having such claims adjudicated in federal courts, the first three elements listed in *Baker* do not come into play.

Problems arise however when transnational human rights cases engage the final three *Baker* elements in circumstances where adjudication might interfere with or run counter to established government foreign policy. The Supreme Court cautioned against this danger in *Sosa*, advising federal courts to "give serious weight to the Executive Branch's view of the case's impact on foreign policy."[200] In *Kadić*, an *ATCA* case against Radovan Karadzić who was served with process while visiting the UN in New York, the court wrote to the Attorney General, asking whether the United States had any concerns about the proceedings. The Solicitor General and State Department replied, expressly disclaiming the application of the political question doctrine in the context of the litigation: "Although there might be instances in which federal courts are asked to issue rulings under the Alien Tort Statute or the Torture Victim Protection Act that might raise a political question, this is not one of them."[201] Clearly, executive statements about the potential political impact of transnational human rights cases on foreign relations change with the political winds[202] and do not bind the judiciary.[203] The Supreme Court has accordingly warned: "it is error to suppose that every case or controversy which touches foreign relations lies beyond judicial cognizance."[204] One striking example of this is *Linder v. Portocarrero* (1992), a diversity claim by the family of a US citizen who was tortured and killed while working in Nicaragua during the civil war between the Contras and Sandinistas. The Court of Appeal for the Eleventh Circuit dismissed the application of the political question doctrine in the circumstances of the case,

---

200 *Sosa*, above note 28 at 733.

201 *Kadić*, above note 199 at 250.

202 Compare, for instance, the positions taken by the executive branches in *Filártiga*, above note 43 and *Doe v. Unocal Corp.*, No. 00-56603 (9th Cir. 2002) [*Unocal*].

203 *Kadić*, above note 199 at 250; Michael Swan, "International Human Rights Tort Claims and the Experience of United States Courts: An Introduction to the US Case Law, Key Statutes and Doctrines" in Craig Scott, ed., *Torture as Tort*, above note 45 at 82 [Swan]; *In re Nazi Era Cases*, above note 184 at 382.

204 *Japan Whaling Association v. American Cetacean Society*, 478 U.S. 221 at 229–30 (1986); *Abebe-Jiri v. Negewo*, 72 F.3d 844 at 848 (11th Cir. 1996).

despite well-known US links with the conflict because "the complaint challenges neither the legitimacy of the United States foreign policy toward the contras, nor does it require the court to pronounce who was right and who was wrong in the Nicaraguan civil war. On the contrary, the complaint is narrowly focused on the lawfulness of the defendants' conduct in a single incident."[205] The politically charged nature of transnational human rights cases does not necessarily counsel against permitting proceedings to proceed. Such a determination must instead be made on an issue-by-issue basis. As Justice Brennan put it in *Baker v. Carr*, the doctrine "is one of political questions, not one of political cases."[206]

One particular issue that appears to lie beyond judicial cognizance is the justiciability of claims where an established policy of ensuring compensation through government initiatives exists. The long-standing US policy to facilitate compensation for victims of WW II through negotiated agreements with Germany is a good example.[207] Litigation in the federal courts of claims arising out of the Holocaust would significantly undermine the executive's commitment to settle compensation on the basis of government-to-government negotiations. Accordingly, in *Iwanowa*, an *ATCA* case for forced labour against a German subsidiary of the Ford Motor Company, the court declined jurisdiction on the basis of the political question doctrine, holding that "courts may not pass judgment upon the political negotiations of the executive branch and the international community. Such intrusion into the realm of foreign policy would undermine the executive branch's sole discretion in the field of international relations."[208] Similarly, in *Belk*, using Justice Brennan's language in *Baker*, the court upheld the government negotiated extinguishment of all claims arising from the Iran hostage crisis, stating:

> The determination of whether and upon what terms to settle the dispute with Iran over its holding of the hostages and obtain their release, necessarily was for the President to make in his foreign rela-

205 *Linder v. Portocarrero*, 963 F.2d 332 at 337 (11th Cir. 1992). See also *Committee of U.S. Citizens Living in Nicaragua v. Reagan*, 859 F.2d 929 (D.C. Cir. 1988).

206 *Baker*, above note 196 at 217.

207 *In re Nazi Era Cases*, above note 184.

208 *Iwanowa*, above note 182 at 487. In that case, several reparations treaties between Germany and Allied forces were held to apply.

> tions role. That determination was "of a kind clearly for nonjudicial discretion," and there are no "judicially discoverable and manageable standards" for reviewing such a Presidential decision. A judicial inquiry into whether the President could have extracted a more favorable settlement would seriously interfere with the President's ability to conduct foreign relations.[209]

The propriety and sufficiency of such agreements are generally beyond the purview of the national courts.

The Supreme Court of Canada refused to formulate a "political question" doctrine that would bar the adjudication of cases involving foreign affairs and national security in *Operation Dismantle v. Canada* (1985). In that case, a group of disarmament activists challenged the constitutionality of the government's decision to allow the US to test cruise missiles in Canadian territory. It was alleged that the Cabinet decision would increase in the risk of nuclear war, thereby causing their right to "life and security of the person" guaranteed under section 7 of the *Charter of Rights and Freedoms* to be violated. In dismissing the claim as speculative, the Court discussed the constitutional justiciability of Cabinet decisions, holding that "disputes of a political or foreign policy nature may be properly cognizable by the courts."[210] In declining to formulate a political question doctrine, the Court held that every time "[we are asked] to decide whether any particular act of the executive violates the rights of the citizens, then it is not only appropriate that we answer the question; it is our obligation under the *Charter* to do so."[211]

3) Act of State Doctrine

The Act of State doctrine is a "non-jurisdictional prudential doctrine based on the notion that 'the courts of one country will not sit in judgment on the acts of the government of another, done within its own territory.'"[212] As a threshold matter, the doctrine can only be raised in cases requiring the court to assess the validity of public acts

---

209 *Belk v. United States*, 858 F.2d 706 at 710 (1988).

210 *Operation Dismantle Inc. v. Canada*, [1985] 1 S.C.R. 441 at 459.

211 *Ibid.* at 472.

212 *Unocal*, above note 202 at 71, citing *Underhill v. Hernandez*, 168 U.S. 250 at 252 (1897) [*Underhill*].

of a foreign state within its own boundaries.[213] Like state immunity, the doctrine does not apply to conduct of private parties that cannot otherwise be attributed to a sovereign state. Nor does it apply to misconduct of foreign state officials in the forum state.[214] In *Banco Nacional de Cuba v. Sabbatino* (1964), the Supreme Court enunciated the modern three-pronged test to determine whether the Act of State doctrine should apply in a given case:

> [1] The greater the degree of codification or consensus concerning a particular area of international law, the more appropriate it is for the judiciary to render decisions regarding it. . . . [2] The less important the implications of an issue are for our foreign relations, the weaker the justification for exclusivity in the political branches. [3] The balance of relevant considerations may also be shifted if the government which perpetrated the challenged act of state is no longer in existence.[215]

In *Liu*, the Court of Appeal for the Ninth Circuit added a fourth factor, namely, "whether the foreign State was acting in the public interest."[216] Though the Ninth Circuit continues to apply this fourth factor,[217] it does not appear to have been adopted in other US judicial circuits. In any event, a "public interest" factor adds little to the scope of the Act of State doctrine and unnecessarily blurs the functional scopes of other doctrines such as comity and state immunity.

The applicability of the Act of State doctrine to transnational human rights litigation is doubtful on the basis of the first *Banco Nacional* factor alone, insofar as there is likely "great consensus" concerning such norms as torture, crimes against humanity, and genocide.[218] Indeed, the impropriety of retaining jurisdiction over acts that violate international law, the law of the forum, and the *lex loci delicti* is not easily demonstrated. In *Filártiga*, while not squarely faced with the issue, the Court of Appeal for the Second Circuit noted in passing: "we doubt whether action by a state official in violation of the Constitu-

213 *W.S. Kirkpatrick & Co. Inc. v. Environmental Tectonics Corporation*, 493 U.S. 400 at 406 (1990).

214 *Liu v. The Republic of China*, 892 F.2d 1419 at 1431–32 (9th Cir. 1989) [*Liu*].

215 *Banco Nacional de Cuba v. Sabbatino*, 376 U.S. 398 at 428 (1964) [*Banco Nacional*].

216 *Liu*, above note 214 at 1432; Swan, above note 203 at 79.

217 *Unocal*, above note 202 at 72 and 75.

218 *Talisman*, above note 182 at 345.

tion and laws of the Republic of Paraguay, and wholly unratified by that nation's government, could properly be characterized as an act of State."[219] On remand the district court ruled consonantly, stating with respect to the first *Banco Nacional* factor, that "where the principle of international law is as clear and universal as the Court of Appeal has found it to be, there is no reason to suppose that this court's assumption of jurisdiction would give justifiable offence to Paraguay."[220] The consensus means that courts can focus on the application of agreed principles to circumstances of fact "rather than on the sensitive task of establishing a principle not inconsistent with the national interest or with international justice."[221] The consensus regarding the conduct that is properly actionable under *ATCA* led the Kadić court to opine that "it would be a rare case in which the act of State doctrine precluded suit under section 1350."[222] As far as can be ascertained, at the time of writing, no US court has declined jurisdiction in transnational human rights proceedings on the basis of the Act of State doctrine.

The assessment of the second *Banco Nacional* factor — foreign relations implications — revisits the concerns addressed by the political question doctrine. Out of respect for the constitutionally mandated executive authority over foreign relations, courts must consider the effect the litigation might have on US foreign relations and policies. In Talisman, given the US government's characterization of the Sudanese conflict as a genocide, the court felt that "any criticism of Sudan that would arise as a result of the adjudication of this case would be a mere drop in the bucket" and could not reasonably be expected to further strain US–Sudan relations.[223] The final *Banco Nacional* factor directs courts to assess what changes in government might signify in the context of the litigation. The courts in *Bodner*,[224] *Bigio*,[225] and *Wiwa*[226] held that dissolution of the impugned regimes and the subsequent disavowal of the wrongful conduct by the current governments strongly tilted the balance in favour of retaining jurisdiction.

219 *Filártiga*, above note 43 at 889.
220 *Filártiga v. Peña-Irala*, 577 F. Supp. 860 at 862 (E.D.N.Y. 1984).
221 *Banco Nacional*, above note 215 at 428.
222 *Kadić*, above note 199 at 250.
223 *Talisman*, above note 182 at 346.
224 *Bodner v. Banque Paribas*, 114 F. Supp. 2d 117 at 130–31 (E.D.N.Y. 2000) (France).
225 *Bigio v. Coca-Cola Co.*, 239 F.3d 440 at 451 (2d Cir. 2001) (Egypt).
226 *Wiwa*, above note 182 at 91–95 (Nigeria).

The US Act of State doctrine, first enunciated by the Supreme Court in *Underhill* (1897), was derived from England.[227] Lord Wilberforce discussed the English principle in *Buttes Gas v. Hammer* (1980), calling it a "generally confused topic" in English law since the term "act of state" has been used "to cover situations which are quite distinct, and different in law."[228] Notwithstanding equivocal labels, His Lordship recognized that "there exists in English law a . . . general principle that the courts will not adjudicate upon the transactions of foreign sovereign states." Distinguishing the English rule from the US one, his Lordship continued: "Though I would prefer to avoid argument on terminology, it seems desirable to consider this principle . . . not as a variety of 'act of state' but one for judicial restraint or abstention."[229] Specifically, according to the English rule, courts should refrain from assessing the validity of foreign state acts or legislation where there is "no judicial or manageable standards by which to judge [the] issues" placing the court "in a judicial no-man's land."[230]

The rule has two important exceptions. First, in areas where Parliament has legislated, thus showing "a particular issue is to be justiciable in the English courts, there can be no place for the courts to apply this self-denying principle."[231] Arguably, the legislated definition of torture and other international crimes provides courts with the required "manageable standards" with which to resolve questions of law. Second, the restraint owed by English courts in respect of acts or

227 *Underhill*, above note 212, followed the House of Lords ruling in *Duke of Brunswick v. King of Hanover* (1844), 6 Beav. 1 (H.L.).

228 *Buttes Gas & Oil Co. v. Hammer*, [1981] 3 W.L.R. 787 at 803 (H.L.) [*Buttes Gas*], referring to the equivocal label describing both the justiciability doctrine at issue, and actions "by an officer of the Crown taken outside this country against foreigners otherwise than under colour of legal right." The confusion has led one commentator to suggest retiring the phrase "Act of State" from English law. See Martin Bühler, "The Emperor's New Clothes: Defabricating the Myth of 'Act of State' in Anglo-Canadian Law" in Craig Scott, ed., *Torture as Tort*, above note 45 at 370–71 [Bühler].

229 *Buttes Gas*, *ibid.* at 804.

230 *Ibid.* at 810; *Jones*, above note 179 at para. 10.

231 *R. v. Bow Street Metropolitan Stipendiary Magistrate, ex parte Pinochet (No.1)*, [2000] 1 A.C. 61 at 107 (H.L.). Of course, *Pinochet No. 1* was rendered a nullity and is not binding caselaw. However, the learned opinion of Lord Nicholls, with whom Lords Steyn and Hoffman agreed with regards to the inapplicability of the Act of State doctrine, carries much persuasive authority, given its consistency with Lord Wilberforce's ruling in *Buttes Gas*. See also Michael Byers "Decisions of British Courts During 1999" (1999) 70 Brit. Y.B. Int'l L. 276 at 294.

legislation of another state does not apply when such acts or legislation are repugnant to public policy or established principles of international law. Under this exception — perhaps more properly conceived as a rule of choice law than of justiciability — English courts have declined to give effect to a German decree stripping Jewish immigrants of their nationality and property[232] and to a post-invasion Iraqi decree unlawfully expropriating Kuwaiti aircrafts.[233] Since such acts of state violate the public policy of the forum and established principles of international law, national courts are entitled "to refuse to recognize [them] as law at all."[234] By the same rationale, it is likely, therefore, that the English "Act of State" doctrine would not operate in transnational human rights proceedings and that English courts would not abstain from assessing foreign conduct found on its face to violate public policy or established principles of international law, even if such acts occurred within the territory of a foreign state.[235] Mance LJ stated in *Jones* (2004):

> [W]hile the courts of one State should not lightly adjudicate upon the internal affairs of another State, there many circumstances, particularly in the context of human rights, when national courts do have to consider and form a view on the position in or conduct of foreign States. There are also further and different principles (the doctrine of act of State in particular) which require courts to refrain from adjudication in which no manageable standards exist to enable such adjudication . . . . But allegations of systematic torture are by themselves unlikely to raise such considerations.[236]

The same result would also likely follow in Canada. There is no Canadian equivalent to the US Act of State doctrine.[237] However, as in England, Canadian courts would likely decline to recognize foreign legislation that offends public policy or violates established principles of international law.[238]

---

232 *Oppenheimer*, above note 160 at 277–78.
233 *Kuwait Airways*, above note 161.
234 *Oppenheimer*, above note 160 at 278; Oppenheim, above note 2 at para. 113.
235 *Kuwait Airways*, above note 161.
236 *Jones*, above note 179 at para. 90, Mance LJ.
237 See, generally, Bühler, above note 228.
238 *Laane & Balster*, above note 160.

E. CONCLUSION

It would appear that no principle of international law or specific rule of UK or Canadian law directly bars the courts of those countries from exercising their civil jurisdiction in relation to extraterritorial human rights violations. To the contrary, on both planes the law is permissive. Additionally, there is evidence of growing international support for the recognition of some form of universal civil jurisdiction in proceedings involving violations of well-established norms of international law where there exists a material risk of denial of justice. Assuming such jurisdiction were asserted, existing choice of law rules would permit the courts of both countries to disregard the *lex loci delicti commissi* as a matter of public policy insofar as the impugned conduct could be said to contravene well-established rules of international law. Similar considerations would appear to counsel against the refusal to exercise jurisdiction on non-justiciability grounds.

CHAPTER SIX

Forum Non Conveniens

"[T]he court must exercise its jurisdiction unless there are very clear and weighty grounds for refusing to do so."

—Lord Kinear[1]

A. INTRODUCTION

A shared feature of common law systems,[2] the doctrine of *forum non conveniens* raises important questions and represents a significant opportunity for judicial restraint in the context of transnational human rights litigation. Pursuant to the doctrine, courts may exceptionally decline jurisdiction they otherwise possess if it is determined that another forum exists in which the action can be more appropriately adjudicated if the interests of the parties and the ends of justice so require. To quote Lord Kinear's classic statement of the rule in *Sim v. Robinow*: "the plea can never be sustained unless the court is satisfied that there is some other tribunal, having competent jurisdiction, in which the case may be tried more suitably for the interests of all the parties

1 *Sim v. Robinow* (1892), 19 R. 665 at 669 (Ct. Sess.) [*Sim*].

2 *Spiliada Maritime Corp v. Cansulex Ltd*, [1987] A.C. 460 at 474 (H.L.) [*Spiliada*]. The doctrine also forms part of the civil law of Quebec: see *Civil Code of Québec*, S.Q. 1991, c. 64, art. 3135 [C.C.Q.]; Paxton Blair, "The Doctrine of Forum Non Conveniens in Anglo-American Law" (1929) 29 Colum. L. Rev. 1; John Greenwood Collier, *Conflict of Laws*, 3d ed. (Cambridge: Cambridge University Press, 2001) at 84–94. See also *Spar Aerospace Ltd. v. American Mobile Ltd.*, [2002] 4 S.C.R. 205 [*Spar*].

and for the ends of justice."[3] Though UK, Canadian, and US courts differ in their appreciation of certain factors, all three jurisdictions apply a version of the doctrine predicated upon the requirement that actions be tried in the forum to which they are most genuinely connected. This chapter will first describe the doctrine in general terms as developed under UK, Canadian, and US law (Section B) before examining the manner of its application in civil proceedings for extraterritorial violations of international law (Section C). In this connection, *ATCA/TVPA* (Section C(1)) and non-*ATCA/TVPA* (Section C(2)) claims will be discussed separately.

B. THE DOCTRINE OF *FORUM NON CONVENIENS*

1) United Kingdom and Canada

The leading English case on *forum non conveniens* is *Spiliada Maritime Corp. v. Cansulex Ltd* (1987). Tracking closely the principle in *Sim v. Robinow*, the House of Lords articulated a two-step analysis that Lord Goff summarized in the following terms:

> the court will look first to see what factors there are which point in the direction of another forum, *i.e.* connecting factors which indicate that it is with the other forum that the action has its most real and substantial connection. This is the first stage. However, even if the court concludes at that stage that the other forum is clearly more appropriate for the trial of the action, the court may nevertheless decline to grant a stay if persuaded by the plaintiff, on whom the burden of proof then lies, that justice requires that a stay should not be granted. This is the second stage.[4]

The rule in *Spiliada* has been adopted in Canadian law in *Amchem* (1993).[5] In the first stage of the test, aimed at determining whether a competing forum is more genuinely connected to the claim, UK and Canadian

3 *Sim*, above note 1 at 668.

4 *Connelly v. R.T.Z. Corporation Plc.*, [1998] A.C. 854 at 871–72 (H.L.) [*Connelly*]; *Spiliada*, above note 2 at 476.

5 *Amchem Products Inc. v. British Columbia (Workers' Compensation Board)*, [1993] 1 S.C.R. 897 at 916–21 [*Amchem 1993*]. See also *Frymer v. Brettschneider* (1994), 19 O.R. (3d) 60 at para. 52 (C.A.); John Terry, "Taking *Filártiga* on the Road: Why Courts outside the United States Should Accept Jurisdiction over Actions Involving Torture Committed Abroad" in Craig Scott, ed., *Torture as Tort: Comparative Perspectives*

courts assess a series of factors including the residence of the parties, the location of evidence and witnesses, the location of assets, the applicable law, and the interest of the parties.[6] In the context of transnational human rights claims, as was noted in Chapter 5 with regards to jurisdiction *simpliciter*,[7] the first stage of the *Spiliada* analysis will almost always reveal the place where the human right violation occurred to be the most natural forum, focused as it is on territorial connections. The defendants, witnesses, and evidence will usually be in the foreign forum and the applicable law, following Anglo-Canadian choice of law rules, will usually be the *lex loci delicti commissi*, unless the foreign law is found to be repugnant to public policy or simply not presented to the court.

But the doctrine of *forum non conveniens* has a second step in which the findings of the first stage are weighed against the requirements of substantial justice. While the first stage of the *Spiliada* analysis seeks to identify whether a particular alternative forum is substantially connected to the proceedings, the second stage asks whether the ends of justice require the retention of jurisdiction, in spite of the alternative forum's greater connection to the claim, having regard to the alternative forum's practical availability. A forum's connection to a given claim says nothing about its availability to the claimant. A plaintiff may be effectively prevented from bringing his claim in the alternative forum for a range of reasons, including the inexistence of an impartial judiciary,[8] general civil unrest,[9] and the apprehension of danger due to death threats.[10] In such cases, a plaintiff is not required to risk life and limb to bring his claim in the alternative forum and the extraneous circumstances become material factors in the determination of what the ends of justice require. In *Connelly*, the unavailability of legal aid in the alternative forum in the context of a complex class action was an important factor in the denial of the stay of proceedings on the basis of

---

on the Development of Transnational Human Rights Litigation (Oxford: Hart, 2001) at 121–23.

6 *Spar*, above note 2 at para. 71.

7 See Chapter 5, notes 65–67 and accompanying text.

8 See, for example, *Presbyterian Church of Sudan v. Talisman Energy Inc.*, 244 F. Supp. 2d 289 (S.D.N.Y. 2003) [*Talisman*]; *The Abidin Daver*, [1984] A.C. 398 at 411 (H.L.).

9 See, for example, *Kadić v. Karadzić*, 70 F.3d 232 (2d Cir. 1995).

10 See, for example, *Bouzari v. Islamic Republic of Iran* (2004), 71 O.R. (3d) 675 (C.A.); *Oppenheimer v. Louis Rosenthal & Co.*, [1937] 1 All E.R. 23 (C.A.).

forum non conveniens. The House of Lords upheld the Court of Appeal's view that:

> [F]aced with a stark choice between one jurisdiction, albeit not the most appropriate in which there could in fact be a trial, and another jurisdiction, the most appropriate in which there never could, in my judgment, the interests of justice would tend to weigh, and weigh strongly, in favour of that forum in which the plaintiff could assert his rights.[11]

The ruling in *Connelly* is consistent with the essence of the *forum non conveniens* doctrine, which, despite its misleading Latin tag, as Lord Goff recalled in *Spiliada*, is a matter "not . . . of convenience, but of the suitability or appropriateness of the relevant jurisdiction."[12] In the final analysis, the more appropriate forum is the one in which substantial justice can be done, not the forum possessing the highest number of territorial connecting factors to the claim. But as the editors of Dicey & Morris point out, "the would-be claimant in the English court who wishes to resist a stay of proceedings on such grounds must assert it candidly and support the allegation with positive and cogent evidence."[13]

2) United States

In contrast to the English and Canadian version of the rule, the US doctrine of *forum non conveniens* holds the most convenient forum to be the most appropriate. The US doctrine is viewed as a housekeeping measure meant to allow courts to "resist impositions upon [their] jurisdiction even when jurisdiction is authorized" and to control a party's "temptation to resort to a strategy of forcing the trial at a most inconvenient place for an adversary, even at some inconvenience to himself."[14] Following the rule established in *Gulf Oil Corp. v. Gilbert*

11 *Connelly*, above note 4 at 866, quoting Sir Tom Bingham MR (as he then was) on appeal.

12 *Spiliada*, above note 2 at 476.

13 Albert Venn Dicey *et al.*, eds., *Dicey and Morrison on the Conflict of Laws*, 13th ed. (London: Sweet & Maxwell, 2000) at 398–99; International Law Association, Committee on International Human Rights Law and Practice, "Report on Civil Actions in the English Courts for Serious Human Rights Violations Abroad" (2001) 2 Eur. H.R.L. Rev. 129 at 148.

14 *Gulf Oil Corp. v. Gilbert*, 330 U.S. 501 at 507 (1947) [*Gulf Oil*].

(1947), US courts engage in a two-step analysis. First, courts must determine whether there exists an adequate alternative forum. Ordinarily, this requirement will be satisfied when the defendant is "amenable to process" in the other jurisdiction.[15] However, where the remedy offered by the other forum is clearly unsatisfactory or unavailable, the initial requirement is not satisfied and the stay must be declined. The practical unavailability of the foreign forum to the plaintiff due to unsafe conditions, civil unrest, or the absence of independent tribunals will typically cause the motion for dismissal to be denied.[16] In *Piper*, the Supreme Court stated that the doctrine should not operate "where the alternative forum does not permit litigation of the subject matter of the dispute."[17] The fact that no other jurisdiction outside the US offers a remedy similar to *ATCA* is usually taken into account at the first step of the *Gulf Oil* analysis.[18]

If an adequate alternative forum is found to exist, courts must then balance a series of factors involving the private interests of the parties and so-called public interest factors. Unless the defendant can show that the balance of interests tilt "strongly"[19] in favour of the foreign jurisdiction, the plea must be dismissed as "the plaintiffs' choice of forum should rarely be disturbed."[20] The relevant private interest of the parties relate to the cost and convenience of the litigation, such as

> . . . the relative ease of access to sources of proof; availability of compulsory process for attendance of unwilling, and the cost of obtaining attendance of willing, witnesses; possibility of view of premises, if view would be appropriate to the action; and all other practical problems that make trial of a case easy, expeditious and inexpensive.[21]

Contrary to what the label may suggest, the "public interest factors" at issue at this stage of the *forum non conveniens* analysis have traditionally not been aimed at ensuring the alignment of the litigation with

15 *Piper Aircraft Co. v. Reyno*, 454 U.S. 235 at 255 (1981) [*Piper Aircraft*].

16 *Rasoulzadeh v. Associated Press*, 574 F. Supp. 854 at 861 (S.D.N.Y 1983); *Cabiri v. Assasie-Gyimah*, 921 F. Supp. 1189 at 1199 (S.D.N.Y. 1996) [*Cabiri*].

17 *Piper Aircraft*, above note 15 at 255.

18 See below notes 30–38 and accompanying text.

19 *Wiwa v. Royal Dutch Petroleum Co.*, 226 F.3d 88 at 100 (2d Cir. 2000) [*Wiwa*].

20 *Gulf Oil*, above note 14 at 508.

21 *Ibid.*

the public policy or values of the US forum, but concern rather the administrative inconvenience or burden of the litigation on the US legal system. As will be seen below however, *ATCA* litigation appears to have caused courts to broaden their perspectives in this department. Traditional relevant "public interest factors" have included administrative difficulties associated with court congestion; the unfairness of imposing jury duty on a community with no relation to the litigation; the interest in having localized controversies decided at home; and avoiding difficult problems in conflict of laws and the application of foreign law.[22] Such considerations have been rejected in English law and are not commonly found in Canadian cases. The House of Lords stated in *Lubbe* that "judicial *amour propre*" forms no part of the *forum non conveniens* analysis: "the court cannot allege its own convenience, or the amount of its own business, or its distaste for trying actions which involve taking evidence in [a foreign language], as a ground for refusal."[23]

The United States Supreme Court recently further refined the *Gulf Oil* test, addressing the question of whether a court could resolve a plea of *forum non conveniens* before determining its own jurisdiction in the case. In *Gulf Oil*, the court had stated that "the doctrine of *forum non conveniens* can never apply if there is absence of jurisdiction."[24] In *Sinochem* (2007), the Court clarified that, at US law, there is "no mandatory sequencing of jurisdictional issues" and that, federal courts could "dispose of an action by a *forum non conveniens* dismissal, bypassing questions of subject-matter and personal jurisdiction, when considerations of convenience, fairness, and judicial economy so warrant."[25] The Court noted that such an inversion of jurisdictional questions would not be required in most cases:

> If . . . a court can readily determine that it lacks jurisdiction over the cause or the defendant, the proper course would be to dismiss on that ground. In the mine run of cases, jurisdiction "will involve no

22 *Gulf Oil*, above note 14 at 508–9; *Aguinda v. Texaco Inc.*, 303 F.3d 470 at 480 (2d Cir. 2002) [*Aguinda*].

23 *Lubbe v. Cape plc*, [2000] 4 All E.R. 268 at 282, Lord Bingham; and at 286, Lord Hope (H.L.) [*Lubbe*].

24 *Gulf Oil*, above note 14 at 504.

25 *Sinochem International Co. Ltd. v. Malaysia International Shipping Corp.*, 549 U.S. 422 at 431–32 (2007), Ginsberg J.

> arduous inquiry" and both judicial economy and the consideration ordinarily accorded the plaintiff's choice of forum "should impel the federal court to dispose of [those] issue[s] first." But where subject-matter or personal jurisdiction is difficult to determine, and *forum non conveniens* considerations weigh heavily in favor of dismissal, the court properly takes the less burdensome course.[26] [citations omitted]

By contrast to the US position, Canadian law apparently requires that jurisdiction be resolved prior to *forum non conveniens*.[27] In practice, however, where jurisdictional issues are particularly complex, it is not uncommon for courts to assume they possess jurisdiction and then address other dispositive doctrines, such as *forum non conveniens* or state immunity.[28]

C. *FORUM NON CONVENIENS* AND TRANSNATIONAL HUMAN RIGHTS LITIGATION

1) *ATCA* and *TVPA* Litigation

In the context of *ATCA* and *TVPA* litigation, the doctrine of *forum non conveniens* has mostly been invoked by defendant multinational corporations (MNCs) seeking to dismiss proceedings against them. Since the *Kadić* decision in 1995, which expanded the class of *ATCA* defendants to include non-state actors, a number of cases have been dismissed on the basis of *forum non conveniens*.[29] Generally, motions to dismiss fail at the first stage of the *Gulf Oil* analysis as a result of the difficulty of establishing the existence of adequate alternative forum. For the most part, courts remain doubtful that plaintiffs would be able to bring their claims — which often allege complicit involvement of government officials — in the state where the human right violations are said

---

26 *Ibid.* at para. 27.

27 See, for example, *Unifund Assurance Co. v. Insurance Corp. of British Columbia*, [2003] 2 S.C.R. 63 at para. 122, where Bastarache J commented: "I think the first issue presented to the applications judge was that of jurisdiction *simpliciter*, and that in any event he was required to deal with it before addressing the question of *forum [non] conveniens*."

28 See, for example, *Bouzari v. Islamic Republic of Iran*, [2002] O.J. No. 1624 at paras. 16–19 (S.C.J.) [*Bouzari* 2002].

29 See, for example, *Aguinda*, above note 22; *Flores et al. v. Southern Peru Copper Corp.*, 253 F. Supp. 2d 510 (S.D.N.Y. 2002); and *Abdullahi v. Pfizer Inc.*, 2003 U.S. App. LEXIS 20704 (2d Cir. 2003).

to have occurred.[30] Notwithstanding the improbability of obtaining a legal remedy of any kind, courts are slow to dismiss proceedings in favour of a foreign jurisdiction in which plaintiffs "would be put in harm's way."[31] In *Talisman*, accepting evidence concerning particular discriminatory features of the Sudanese legal system and recognizing the likely danger for plaintiffs of returning home, the court opined that "it would be perverse, to say the least, to require plaintiffs to bring this suit in the courts of the very nation that has allegedly been conducting genocidal activities to try to eliminate them." It arrived at the "self-evident" conclusion that "plaintiffs would be unable to obtain justice in Sudan and might well expose themselves to great danger in trying to do so."[32] Similarly in *Wiwa*, the court accepted that "victims cannot sue in the place where the torture occurred. Indeed, in many instances, the victim would be endangered merely by returning to that place."[33] Even in cases where an adequate alternative forum was found to exist, the balance of private and public interests has generally tilted in favour of the US forum. Important factors have included the relative means of the parties[34] and the uncertain availability of contingency fee agreements in the foreign forum.[35]

Corporations based in developed nations other than the US have not had much success in attempting to have *ATCA* claims dismissed in favour of their home jurisdiction. In *Talisman*, while the court "assumed" that plaintiffs could obtain a fair and adequate adjudication of their claim in Canadian courts, it held that certain aspects of the substantive law of Canada make it an inadequate forum. First, noting Canada's adherence to the *lex loci delicti* rule, the court stated rather oddly that it was "difficult to see how a Canadian court applying *Shari'a* law would be a great improvement over a Sudanese court applying *Shari'a* law."[36] Second, the court expressed concerns about the absence in Canada of an *ATCA*-style cause of action for international wrongs, thus requiring plaintiffs to frame their claims of genocide as violations of Canadian

30 *Cabiri*, above note 16 at 1198–99; *Sarei v. Rio Tinto plc*, 221 F. Supp. 2d 1116 at 1174 (C.D. Cal. 2002).

31 *Ibid.*

32 *Talisman*, above note 8 at 336.

33 *Wiwa*, above note 19 at 106.

34 *Talisman*, above note 8 at 341.

35 *Wiwa*, above note 19 at 107.

36 *Talisman*, above note 8 at 337.

tort law. In the court's view, available tort actions did not "reflect the gravity of the alleged offences, and in particular, the universally-condemned nature of these acts .... Such crimes are more than the sum of their parts. Genocide may quantitatively be the same as a large number of murders, but it is qualitatively different."[37] Notwithstanding these concerns, because the plaintiffs did not challenge *Talisman*'s assertion that Canada would be an adequate alternative forum, the court assumed that Canadian courts could provide adequate redress.

Even when another adequate forum can be shown to exist, as in *Talisman* and *Wiwa*, corporate defendants have rarely managed thus far to convince US courts that the balance of private and public interests tilt "strongly" in favour of the foreign jurisdiction. The wealth, mobility, and multi-jurisdictional presence of the corporate defendants were important considerations in the *Wiwa* court's dismissal of Royal Dutch-Shell's *forum non conveniens* motion. The court was satisfied that

> litigation in New York City would not represent any great inconvenience to the defendants. The defendants control a vast, wealthy, and far-flung business empire, which operates in most parts of the globe. They have a physical presence in the forum state, have access to enormous resources, face little or no language barrier, have litigated in this country on previous occasions, have a four-decade long relationship with one of the nation's leading law firms, and are the parent companies of one of America's largest corporations, which has a very significant presence in New York. New York City, furthermore, where the trial would be held, is a major world capital which offers central location, easy access, and extensive facilities of all kinds.[38]

The abundant resources of the corporate defendants stood in stark contrast to the substantially more modest means of the plaintiffs. In this connection courts weigh the availability of competent *pro bono* counsel in the US as an additional factor militating in favour of the plaintiffs' forum of choice.[39]

Another often cited factor is the general US policy and public interest — expressed by *ATCA*, and confirmed by the enactment of the

---

37 *Ibid.* at 337–38.

38 *Wiwa*, above note 19 at 99.

39 *Talisman*, above note 8 at 341; *Wiwa*, *ibid.* at 108.

TVPA—in upholding international law and vindicating grave violations of human rights. As the court in *Wiwa* noted, *ATCA* and *TVPA* express a clear US policy

> that torture committed under color of law of a foreign nation in violation of international law is "our business," as such conduct not only violates the standards of international law but also as a consequence violates our domestic law . . . . If in cases of torture in violation of international law our courts exercise their jurisdiction conferred by the 1789 Act only for as long as it takes to dismiss the case for *forum non conveniens*, we will have done little to enforce the standards of the law of nations.
>
> This is not to suggest that the TVPA has nullified, or even significantly diminished, the doctrine of *forum non conveniens*. The statute has, however, communicated a policy that such suits should not be facilely dismissed on the assumption that the ostensibly foreign controversy is not our business. The TVPA in our view expresses a policy favoring our courts' exercise of the jurisdiction conferred by the ATCA in cases of torture unless the defendant has fully met the burden of showing that the [*Gulf Oil*] factors "tilt strongly in favor of trial in the foreign forum." [40]

In this sense, *ATCA* and *TVPA* litigation appears to have caused federal courts to broaden their understanding of "public interest" considerations at the second stage of the *forum non conveniens* analysis and to weigh the burden of proceedings on the judiciary against the US interest in the adjudication of civil claims relating to violations of well-established norms of international law.

In *Aguinda*, the court was satisfied that Ecuador could provide an adequate alternative forum. In the court's opinion, nothing in the substantive law of Ecuador precluded plaintiffs from obtaining redress for personal injuries caused by industrial pollution. The record showed in fact that other plaintiffs had recovered judgments against the other named defendants (TexPet and PetroEcuador) for claims arising out of the same facts alleged in the *ATCA* proceedings.[41] The court was also satisfied that the balance of private and public interests tilted strongly towards the Ecuadorian forum. Factors considered included the location

---

40 *Wiwa*, *ibid.* at 105–6; *Talisman*, *ibid.* at 339–40.

41 *Aguinda*, above note 22 at 477–78.

in Ecuador of the parties, polluted sites, medical records, and other evidence; the difficulty of translating in New York several different indigenous dialects; the advantages gained of joining the State of Ecuador as defendant in terms of the equitable relief sought; the unfairness of imposing jury duty on a community with no relation to the litigation; and Ecuador's interest in having localized controversies decided at home.[42] The US policy in providing a forum for the adjudication of international tort claims did not alter the balance of factors militating for the Ecuadorian forum. The claim was accordingly dismissed. So far then, while providing courts with an opportunity for restraint in appropriate cases, such as *Aguinda*, the doctrine of *forum non conveniens* has not proven to be an insurmountable barrier for plaintiffs in the context of *ATCA* and *TVPA* litigation.

2) Home State Litigation

As an alternative to *ATCA* and *TVPA* claims, foreign plaintiffs have in some cases initiated civil proceedings against corporate defendants in their home state, that is, in the jurisdiction where the parent corporation of a multinational group is domiciled. Home state litigation differs from *ATCA* and *TVPA* actions in two important respects. First, while *ATCA* provides an explicit grant of jurisdiction for violations of international law, home state litigation is rooted in domestic tort categories of responsibility, such as negligence and vicarious liability and general company law. Second, while *ATCA* and *TVPA* cases hinge at the preliminary stages on whether courts have jurisdiction over the particular foreign defendants and the general claim, home state litigation turns more on the question of whether jurisdiction ought to be declined. It is indeed unexceptionable that national courts have jurisdiction over corporations or persons domiciled in the forum, even with respect to violations of international law committed abroad. In *Bil'in* for instance, a case brought against a Canadian corporation with reference to alleged *Geneva Convention* war crimes committed in Occupied Palestinian Territories, the court held that "[k]nowingly favouring a breach of a High Contracting Party's undertakings pursuant to an international instrument or knowingly assisting a state in the perpetration of a war

42 *Ibid.* at 479.

crime are both civil faults" under Quebec law.[43] Whether jurisdiction ought to be declined in favour of the foreign country where the tort occurred however is a different matter altogether. In this connection, the doctrine of *forum non conveniens* has proven to be a determinative factor in home state litigation against corporate defendants. Notable instances include the UK "asbestos cases," the *Cambior* and *Bil'in* cases in Canada, and the *United Carbide* litigation in the US.

a) UK Asbestos Litigation

Connelly v. RTZ Corporation plc involved a UK national who developed throat cancer caused by exposure to ore dust while working in an opencast uranium mine in Namibia owned by Rossing Uranium Ltd., a subsidiary of the UK-based RTZ Corporation. In 1994, Connelly commenced a tort action in English courts against the parent company, alleging that the RTZ negligently failed to provide a safe working environment. RTZ's motion to stay the proceedings was granted on the basis of *forum non conveniens*, the motion judge being of the view that Namibia was the most convenient forum. One factor however pointed to the suitability of the UK forum, namely the availability of financial support for the plaintiffs in England and its unavailability in Namibia. However, section 31(1)(b) of the *Legal Aid Act 1988* prevented the accessibility of legal aid from affecting the exercise of any discretion of the court. Thus statutorily prevented from taking into account the availability of UK legal aid in his assessment of the interests of the litigants for the purposes of the *forum non conveniens* analysis, the motion judge accordingly concluded that Namibia was the most proper forum in the circumstances of the case.

The Court of Appeal reversed that decision in light of an intervening contingency fee agreement between the plaintiff and his lawyers. The *Legal Aid Act 1988* being no longer an obstacle, the court queried whether the UK emerged as a better forum than Namibia for the adjudication of the case. Applying the rule in *Spiliada*, Lord Bingham MR stated:

> [F]aced with a stark choice between one jurisdiction, albeit not the most appropriate in which there could in fact be a trial, and another

---

43 *Bil'in (Village Council) v. Green Park International Inc.*, 2009 QCCS 4151 at para. 205 [*Bil'in*]. Civil fault in Quebec law is determined pursuant to C.C.Q., above note 2, art. 1457.

> jurisdiction, the most appropriate in which there never could, in my judgment, the interests of justice would tend to weigh, and weigh strongly, in favour of that forum in which the plaintiff could assert his rights.[44]

He found his weighty consideration of the requirements of justice to be supported by the right to access justice, as codified at Articles 6 and 14 of the ECtHR and ICCPR respectively. "Whether or not those provisions are strictly applicable (they are, of course, no part of our domestic law) it seems to me right to bear the international obligations of the United Kingdom in mind when the court is invited to make an order which would have the practical effect of preventing a plaintiff pursuing his rights anywhere."[45]

The House of Lords confirmed. Lord Goff for the majority took the view that the *Legal Aid Act 1988* could not, on proper construction, be understood to curtail the broad principles of justice involved in a motion to stay on the ground of *forum non conveniens*. The majority further held that, except in rare circumstances, the availability of a particular juridical advantage in one jurisdiction such as legal aid should not in itself justify the refusal to stay a claim that is more closely connected to another jurisdiction. They opined however that the circumstances of the present case demanded a different result. Given the highly complex evidence likely to be adduced at trial, the consequent need for experienced counsel, the plaintiff's lack of financial means, the unavailability of legal aid in Namibia, and its accessibility in the UK, the majority was satisfied that for substantial justice to be done, the stay should be denied.[46] Lord Hoffman dissented in strong terms, stating that the majority ruling meant that

> the action of a rich plaintiff will be stayed while the action of a poor plaintiff in respect of precisely the same transaction will not. It means that the more speculative and difficult the action, the more likely it is to be allowed to proceed in this country with the support of public funds. Such distinctions will do the law no credit.[47]

44 *Connelly v. R.T.Z. Corporation Plc.*, *Times Law Report* (12 July1996) at para. 30 (C.A.).

45 *Ibid.* at para. 33.

46 *Connelly*, above note 4 at 874.

47 *Ibid.* at 876.

His Lordship further objected that RTZ's presence in the UK and the court's personal jurisdiction over the corporation should not come to bear in a *forum non conveniens* analysis, the purpose of which, he insisted, is to determine whether such jurisdiction should be declined. In his view:

> If the presence of the defendants, as parent company and local subsidiary of a multinational, can enable them to be sued here, any multinational with its parent company in England will be liable to be sued here in respect of its activities anywhere in the world.[48]

Another significant case is that of *Lubbe v. Cape plc* wherein several South African plaintiffs sued Cape plc, an English corporation, in relation to asbestos disease contracted in South Africa. The plaintiffs were exposed to asbestos in the course of their employment with a subsidiary of Cape plc. The plaintiffs alleged that the parent corporation breached the duty of care it owed its employees in failing to implement safe working conditions, all while knowing the health dangers linked to asbestos. The writs were issued in 1997 and, in 1998, the defendant moved to stay the proceedings on the grounds of *forum non conveniens*. The High Court granted the stay and, applying the *Spiliada* principles, held that South Africa was the most appropriate forum. The Court of Appeal reversed, holding that the first judge had failed to take certain factors into consideration, including the unavailability of legal aid in South Africa. By this time, further proceedings had been initiated against Cape plc in relation to its asbestos operations in South Africa, bringing the total of plaintiffs to over 3,000 individuals, all of whom were included in a group action. In 1999, the High Court granted the defendant's motion to stay the group action, holding that South Africa was the most appropriate forum in accordance with *Spiliada* principles and in light of certain "public interest" factors, namely the cost and burden of the litigation on UK courts. The Court of Appeal confirmed.

In 2000, the House of Lords unanimously reversed the previous decisions for reasons similar to those invoked in *Connelly*. In Lord Bingham's leading judgment, the funding issue was decisive. In the absence of convincing evidence that legal aid could be made available

48 *Ibid.*

in South Africa to fund what would likely be protracted and expensive proceedings, he concluded:

> If these proceedings were stayed in favour of the more appropriate forum in South Africa the probability is that the plaintiffs would have no means of obtaining the professional representation and the expert evidence which would be essential if these claims were to be justly decided. This would amount to a denial of justice. In the special and unusual circumstances of these proceedings, lack of the means, in South Africa, to prosecute these claims to a conclusion provides a compelling ground, at the second stage of the *Spiliada* test, for refusing to stay the proceedings here.[49]

In his concurrence, Lord Hope addressed the lower courts' consideration of "public interest" factors in granting the stay. After a searching review of seminal Scottish cases on *forum non conveniens*, he held:

> However tempting it may be to give effect to concerns about the expense and inconvenience to the administration of justice of litigating actions such as these in this country on the one hand or in South Africa on the other, the argument must be resolved upon an examination of their effect upon the interests of the parties who are before the Court and securing the ends of justice in their case. I would hold that considerations of policy which cannot be dealt with in this way should be left out of account in the application to the case of the *Spiliada* principles.[50]

The English approach to *forum non conveniens* in *Connelly* and *Lubbe* has been described by one commentator as "refreshingly liberal."[51] There is indeed an element of novelty in refusing to stay an action on the basis of the unavailability of legal aid in a clearly more appropriate forum. However, it can also be said that introducing an equality of arms requirement in the second stage of the *Spiliada* test to ensure that substantial justice be done is entirely consistent with the century-

---

49 *Lubbe*, above note 23 at 279.

50 *Ibid.* at 287.

51 Michael Byers, "English Courts and Serious Human Rights Violations Abroad: A Preliminary Assessment" in Menno T. Kamminga & Saman Zia-Zarifi, eds., *Liability of Multinational Corporations under International Law* (The Hague, Kluwer Law International, 2000) at 246.

old, justice-rooted, essence of *forum non conveniens*,[52] and that, in this sense, the rulings in *Connelly* and *Lubbe* represent consistent and natural outcomes given the particular facts of those proceedings. The need to ensure that litigants be afforded a reasonable opportunity to present their case is felt particularly strongly in transnational human rights litigation against multinational corporations in which plaintiffs often have little or no financial resources. This is typically not a problem in commercial litigation where parties usually have sufficient means to hire competent counsel and where contracts determine the jurisdiction in which disputes are to be resolved. In such circumstances, litigants are not likely to suffer a denial of justice. Transnational human rights proceedings however are a different proposition. As Meeran observes, "a foreign personal injury victim bringing an action in England is likely to be in an 'all or nothing situation.' . . . Forum shopping is certainly not the objective of foreign personal injury claimants who choose to sue in England."[53] Indeed, while obtaining damages remains the ultimate goal, foreign plaintiffs suing corporations in their home state seek to overcome the impediments to redress and justice in the host state, such as fear of local persecution, corruption, delays, and lack of funding. Though perhaps a bit cynical, Meeran's point is taken: "The plain truth of the matter is that claimants want to sue in England because they cannot get justice overseas and [multinational corporations] want to stay the claims for precisely the same reason."[54] Accordingly, where jurisdiction over a defendant is properly asserted in its forum of domicile and plaintiffs satisfy the court that justice could not be done in another otherwise appropriate forum, the presumption in favour of the plaintiffs' choice of forum should not be disturbed. When unequally armed parties litigate, the law must level the playing field by ensuring that the ends of convenience defer to the dictates of justice. Arguably, this is not a "refreshingly liberal" direction; it is the proper application of an old doctrine to the new juridical phenomenon.

52 The "ends of justice" being a decisive factor in the *forum non conveniens* analysis since Lord Kinnear's judgment in *Sim*, above note 1.

53 Richard Meeran, "Liability of Multinational Corporations: A Critical Stage in the UK" in Menno T. Kamminga & Saman Zia-Zarifi, eds., *Liability of Multinational Corporations under International Law*, above note 51 at 254–55 [Meeran].

54 *Ibid*. at 261.

b) The Canadian Cases

Recherches Internationales Québec v. Cambior Inc is the first of two cases to have been brought in Canada against corporations in relation to alleged extraterritorial human rights breaches. A class action was filed in 1997 in Montreal by 23,000 Guyanese nationals against Canadian-based Cambior Inc. after a tailings dam ruptured at the site of a gold mine operated by a subsidiary corporation, Omai Gold Mines Ltd. (Omai), spilling billions of litres of cyanide and other pollutants into Guyana's Essequibo River. In a motion to dismiss the class proceedings, Cambior argued that the Superior Court of Quebec did not have jurisdiction over the claim or, alternatively, that the court should decline its jurisdiction on the basis of *forum non conveniens*, pursuant to Article 3135 of the Quebec Civil Code.

Justice Maughan asserted jurisdiction over the claim pursuant to Article 3148 of the Quebec Civil Code, which provides:

> **3148.** In personal actions of a patrimonial nature, a Quebec authority has jurisdiction where,
>
> 1° the defendant has his domicile or his residence in Quebec;
>
> . . .
>
> 3° a fault was committed in Quebec, damage was suffered in Quebec, an injurious act occurred in Quebec or one of the obligations arising from a contract was to be performed in Quebec

The court found it had jurisdiction under two heads. First, Cambior was domiciled in Montreal, and thus fell squarely under the terms of subsection 3148(1). Second, taking the plaintiffs' factual allegations as averred, Maughan J accepted that if Cambior was the directing mind of Omai, any decisions regarding the construction and operation of the Guyanese gold mine would have been made by the parent corporation, thus amounting to a "fault committed in Quebec" under subsection 3148(3) of the Quebec Civil Code.

Turning to *forum non conveniens*, the court followed the principles set out in *Amchem* (1993)[55] and held that, in the circumstances, there was no real and substantial connection between the claim and the province of Quebec, other than the domicile of the defendant. On the other hand, the events underlying the action, the plaintiffs, the evidence,

55 *Amchem 1993*, above note 5.

and the witnesses were all in Guyana, which the court accordingly held to be the most natural forum. Furthermore, in the court's view, no exceptional factor militated against the stay of the proceedings. While the court acknowledged that a dismissal would entail the loss of a particular juridical advantage — Quebec's class action procedure — it was satisfied that other, albeit less effective, legal avenues were open to the plaintiffs in Guyana and that no denial of justice would arise if the action were heard in that country. On this point, the court entertained contradictory evidence from various experts on the integrity of the Guyanese legal system. Ultimately, the court held that the plaintiffs "failed to bring forward any conclusive and objective evidence to substantiate [their] belief that Guyana is an inadequate forum due to the many deficiencies which plague its system of justice."[56] The court accordingly dismissed the claim.

The Quebec Superior Court also dismissed the claim in *Bil'in (Village Council) v. Green Park International Inc.*[57] on the basis of *forum non conveniens*. That case concerned the development of Israeli settlements in the West Bank by a Canadian-registered corporation on land said to belong to the plaintiffs, namely the Palestinian village of Bil'in and Ahmed Yassin. The plaintiffs alleged that the defendants' participation in the construction and marketing of residential properties on Palestinian land amounted to war crimes insofar as these activities furthered Israel's policy of transferring its population onto occupied territories, in violation of Article 49(6) of the *Fourth Geneva Convention*[58] and Article 8(2)(b)(viii) of the Statute of the International Criminal Court.[59] To the

---

56 *Recherches Internationales Québec v. Cambior* Inc., [1998] Q.J. No. 2554 at para. 98 (Sup. Ct.); Jeffrey A. Talpis & Shelley L. Kath, "The Exceptional as Commonplace in Quebec *Forum Non Conveniens* Law: *Cambior*, a Case in Point" (2000), 34 Revue Juridique Themis 761 [Talpis & Kath].

57 *Bil'in*, above note 43. The appeal on the merits had not been heard at the time of writing (January 2010), but the Quebec Court of Appeal dismissed the defendant's motion to dismiss the appeal without a hearing in December 2009: [2009] Q.J. No. 15847 (C.A.).

58 *Geneva Convention relative to the Protection of Civilian Persons in Time of War (Fourth Geneva Convention)*, 12 August 1949, 75 U.N.T.S. 288 (entered into force on 21 October 1950). Art. 49(6) reads in part as follows: "The Occupying Power shall not . . . transfer parts of its own civilian population into the territory it occupies."

59 *Rome Statute of the International Criminal Court*, 17 July 1998, U.N. Doc. A/CONF.183/9, 2187 U.N.T.S. 90 [ICC Statute]. Art. 8(2)(b)(viii), which defines the term "war crimes" at international law, reads in part as follows: "8(2.) Other serious violations of the laws and customs applicable in international armed conflict, within

extent both the corporate and personal defendants were domiciled in Quebec, the court readily acknowledged its jurisdiction over the matter and parties and recognized for the first time in Canadian law that war crimes are, theoretically at least, actionable civil wrongs:

> [175] A war crime is an indictable offence. As such, it is an imperative rule of conduct that implicitly circumscribes an elementary norm of prudence, the violation of which constitutes a civil fault pursuant to art. 1457 C.C.Q.
>
> [176] In theory, a person would therefore commit a civil fault pursuant to art. 1457 C.C.Q. by knowingly participating in a foreign country in the unlawful transfer by an occupying power of a portion of its own civilian population into the territory it occupies, in violation of an international instrument which the occupying power has ratified. Such a person would thus be knowingly assisting the occupying power in the violation of the latter's obligations and would also become a party to a war crime, thereby violating an elementary norm of prudence.[60]

The principal remaining issue to be determined therefore was whether "the judicial authorities of Israel are so clearly in a better position to decide the Action that pursuant to art. 3135 C.C.Q. the Court should exceptionally exercise its discretion to decline jurisdiction in their favour."[61]

Relying on the authority of *Spar*,[62] the court listed the relevant factors to be considered in motions to dismiss on *forum non conveniens*, namely,

> 1—The parties' residence, that of witnesses and experts; 2—The location of the material evidence; 3—The place where the contract was negotiated and executed; 4—The existence of proceedings pending between the parties in another jurisdiction; 5—The location of the defendant's assets; 6—The applicable law; 7—The advantages conferred upon the plaintiff by its choice of forum, if any; 8—The interest

---

the established framework of international law, namely, any of the following acts: . . . (viii) The transfer, directly or indirectly, by the Occupying Power of parts of its own civilian population into the territory it occupies."

60 *Bil'in*, above note 43 at paras. 175–76.

61 *Ibid.* at para. 208.

62 *Spar*, above note 2.

> of justice; 9—The interest of the parties; and 10—The need to have the judgment recognized in another jurisdiction.[63]

Cullen J ran quickly through the first five factors, concluding that they all clearly pointed towards Israel as the most appropriate forum, and concentrated the bulk of his analysis on the issue of the applicable law. On this point, the plaintiffs argued, pursuant to article 3081 of the C.C.Q., that the *lex loci delicti commissi*—that is, the law applied to the West Bank by Israel's High Court of Justice (HCJ)—should be disregarded for being "manifestly inconsistent with public order as understood in international relations"[64] insofar as the HCJ has shown itself unwilling in the past to review the legality of Israeli settlements under international humanitarian law. Therefore, according to the plaintiffs, the applicable law factor clearly favoured the Quebec forum.

The plaintiffs filed expert evidence in support of their position that Israeli courts refuse, as a matter of judicial policy, to determine the application of the *Fourth Geneva Convention* to the settlement of Palestinian occupied territories. The evidence of the defendants also substantiated the view that Israeli courts treat the settlement of the West Bank essentially as an unjusticiable political question and systematically decline to adjudicate allegations of war crimes out of deference to the executive branch. Both parties submitted a number of cases, some dating back to the 1970s, in which the HCJ considered the application of international humanitarian law to the Israeli settlement of occupied Palestinian territories.[65] Apparently disregarding both the plaintiffs' and defendants' positions, Cullen J took a different view of the evidence and concluded that the HCJ

> has not applied Article 49(6) of the *Fourth Geneva Convention*, not because of its unwillingness to adjudicate on its alleged violation by rea-

63 *Bil'in*, above note 43 at para. 211.

64 C.C.Q. above note 2, art. 3081: "3081. The provisions of the law of a foreign country do not apply if their application would be manifestly inconsistent with public order as understood in international relations."

65 *Khelou* v. *Government of Israel* (1973), 27 (2) PD 169; *Ayub* v. *Minister of Defense* (1978), 33 (2) PD 113; *Dweikat* v. *Government of Israel* (1979), 34 (1) PD 1; *Bargil* v. *Government of Israel* (1991), 47 (4) PD 210; *Iyad* v. *Commander of IDF Forces* (1998), Law 55 (1) PD 913; *Maraabe v. Israeli Prime Minister* (2005), Takdin-Alyon (3) 3333, HCJ 7957/04; and *"Nirit" Village Community Settlement v. Minister of Defense* (2005), Takdin-Alyon (1) 2122, HCJ 10024/04.

> son of the political significance of the matter, but either because it was unnecessary to do so or because the HCJ considered that it was not customary international law . . . and that it had not been incorporated into the domestic law of Israel through appropriate legislation.

The court accordingly held that this state of affairs did not offend public order as understood under article 3081 of the C.C.Q. and the fact that Canada had incorporated the *Geneva Conventions* in its domestic law[66] did nothing to alter this conclusion.

What is more, the court gave little weight to the plaintiffs' juridical advantage of avoiding the necessity of convincing Israeli judges that Article 49 of the *Fourth Geneva Convention* had since attainted the status of customary international law and was therefore binding upon Israel. In short, despite the presumptive jurisdiction over the domiciled defendants, Cullen J ultimately found the action to be

> one of those exceptional situations where the Superior Court is compelled to decline jurisdiction on the basis of *forum non conveniens*, as the Plaintiffs have selected a forum having little connection with the Action in order to inappropriately gain a juridical advantage over the Defendants and where the relevant connecting factors, considered as a whole, clearly point to the HCJ as the logical forum and the authority in a better position to decide.[67]

As in *Cambior*, the Quebec court in *Bil'in* dismissed the plaintiffs' legitimate choice of forum, a result that appears to stand at odds with the well-established principle of Canadian law that "the plaintiff's choice of forum should only be declined exceptionally."[68] There are other problems with the *Bil'in* decision. First, it was arguably improper for the judge to disregard the expert evidence submitted by the parties as to the state of Israeli law and to substitute his own interpretation of the HCJ's amenability to deciding whether Article 49 of the Fourth Geneva Convention is now part of customary international law. It is indeed well established that foreign law is a question of fact to be

---

66 *Geneva Conventions Act*, R.S.C. 1985, c. G-3. See also *Crimes against Humanity and War Crimes Act*, S.C. 2000, c. 24.

67 *Bil'in* above note 43 at para. 335.

68 Spar, above note 2 at para. 79, citing Jeffrey A. Talpis & Jean-Gabriel Castel, "Interpreting the Rules of Private International Law" in Private International Law, *Reform of the Civil Code*, vol. 5B (Montréal: Barreau du Québec, 1993) at 55.

proven by the parties, usually by way of expert evidence.[69] It is also acknowledged that, in the face of conflicting evidence as to the state of foreign law, Canadian courts are free to examine the cases and form an independent view.[70] In *Bil'in*, however, there was arguably no genuine conflict between the expert testimonies; both agreed that the HCJ would not likely assess the legality of Israeli settlements in the West Bank under the *Fourth Geneva Convention*. The reason for the judicial abstention is immaterial and it may be that Cullen J went too far in his efforts to provide one. Had the court accepted either party's evidence on this question, it would likely have had arrived at a different conclusion with respect to the applicable law.

A second surprising aspect of the *Bil'in* decision is that the court included in its reasoning the administrative inconvenience of encumbering the Quebec rolls with a trial that it considered insufficiently connected to the forum, thus, in the court's view, causing potential unfairness to other domestic proceedings or more appropriately connected cases. As mentioned above, though not uncommon in the US, it is unusual for Canadian and English courts to take such considerations into account as part of the *forum non conveniens* analysis.[71] Talpis and Kath observe that "[s]ince there are few private international law cases in Quebec relative to domestic cases, it cannot be convincingly argued that international litigation results in the delay of domestic trials."[72] The same can be said *a fortiori* of transnational human rights cases, which are still quite exceptional in Canada. The fact that Cullen J held the administrative inconvenience posed by such proceedings to be a relevant factor under the "interests of justice" prong of the *forum non conveniens* analysis is therefore puzzling. What is more irksome still is the court's apparent failure to consider the egregiousness of the alleged wrongs (i.e., war crimes) and the unfairness to the plaintiffs of declining otherwise lawful jurisdiction in favour of a forum that is not likely to adjudicate their claim. Canada's interest in preventing a denial of justice and in providing redress with respect to alleged violations of

69 See, generally, Jean-Gabriel Castel, "The Proof of Foreign Law" (1972) 22 U.T.L.J. 33 at 39 [Castel, *Proof*]; Gibran van Ert, "The Admissibility of International Legal Evidence" (2005) 84 Can. Bar Rev. 31 at 37 [van Ert, *Evidence*].

70 Castel, *Proof*, *ibid.* at 39–40.

71 Above notes 22–23 and accompanying text.

72 Talpis & Kath, above note 56 at para. 131.

peremptory norms of international law should have been included in the court's reasoning.

A similar omission occurred in *Bouzari v. Islamic Republic of Iran*,[73] where the plaintiff sued Iran for the torture he suffered in that country. While the case was ultimately barred by state immunity, the court had also considered dismissing the claim on the basis of *forum non conveniens*. Swinton J accepted the plaintiff's evidence regarding the death threats he had received and recognized that, "clearly, he cannot bring such an action in Iran."[74] After acknowledging that the plaintiff could never sue in Iran, Swinton J went on to state that, even if the court had jurisdiction, Mr. Bouzari's claim would likely be dismissed in Ontario on the basis of *forum non conveniens* since "the events occurred in Iran; Iranian law would apply; and there was no link to Canada at the time of these events."[75] While clearly obiter and rendered moot in any event by its ruling on state immunity, the court's comments on *forum non conveniens* are nevertheless disturbing as they disclose no attempt to address the plaintiff's potential denial of justice and the overarching issue of fairness in cases like *Bouzari*. It is hoped that such important considerations that underpin the doctrine of *forum non conveniens* will not be neglected in future Canadian cases.

c) The US Union Carbide Litigation

Re Union Carbide Corporation Gas Plant Disaster at Bhopal is an important US non-*ATCA* transnational human rights case. In December 1984, toxic gases leaked from a chemical plant owned and operated by an Indian subsidiary of New York–based Union Carbide, and blew over the densely populated city of Bhopal, instantly killing over 2,000 people, injuring over 200,000 more.[76] In 1985, the 145 lawsuits launched against Union Carbide in US federal courts were consolidated in the southern district of New York. That same year, India enacted legislation providing the Government of India with exclusive right to represent Indian plaintiffs in connection with the tragedy. In 1986, Union Carbide moved to dismiss the lawsuits on the basis of *forum non conveniens*.

73 *Bouzari 2002*, above note 28.

74 *Ibid.* at para.17.

75 *Ibid.*

76 *Re Union Carbide Corp. Gas Plant Disaster at Bhopal, India in December 1984*, 634 F. Supp. 842 at 844 (S.D.N.Y. 1986) [*Re Union Carbide*].

Despite the government of India's position that its judiciary was ill equipped to handle the size and complexity of the Bhopal litigation, the district court found that India was an adequate forum. Applying the rule in *Gulf Oil*, the court considered both private and public interest factors and held that the balance of convenience tilted strongly in favour of India. The reasons cited included the presence in India of nearly all the plaintiffs, witnesses, and evidence; the administrative burden on the US judicial system; the excessive cost of the litigation for US taxpayers; and India's strong regulatory interest. With regards to India's claims that its fledgling legal system had not yet attained maturity after decolonization and could not properly adjudicate the Bhopal lawsuits, the court begged to differ:

> In the Court's view, to retain the litigation in this forum, as plaintiffs request, would be yet another example of imperialism, another situation in which an established sovereign inflicted its rules, its standards and values on a developing nation. This Court declines to play such a role. The Union of India is a world power in 1986, and its courts have the proven capacity to mete out fair and equal justice. To deprive the Indian judiciary of this opportunity to stand tall before the world and to pass judgment on behalf of its own people would be to revive a history of subservience and subjugation from which India has emerged. India and its people can and must vindicate their claims before the independent and legitimate judiciary created there since the Independence of 1947.[77]

The consolidated claims were accordingly dismissed. In 1989, Union Carbide and the Government of India settled the litigation, extinguishing all civil claims against the corporation with regards to the 1984 disaster. The settlement barred the plaintiffs' subsequent *ATCA* claim.[78]

So it is that national judicial practice differs with regards to the weight and importance each jurisdiction ascribes to the so-called "public interest" factors in the context of the *forum non conveniens* analysis. Since *Gulf Oil*, US courts weigh the interest of the litigants against those of the forum itself when determining the appropriateness of retaining jurisdiction. Such public interest factors include "adminis-

---

77 *Ibid.* at 867.

78 *Bano v. Union Carbide Corp.*, 273 F.3d 120 at 129 (2d Cir. 2001).

trative difficulties associated with court congestion; the unfairness of imposing jury duty on a community with no relation to the litigation; the interest in having localized controversies decided at home; and avoiding difficult problems in conflict of laws and the application of foreign law."[79] Along with these factors, the court in *Re Union Carbide* also considered the financial burden the litigation would impose on New York taxpayers, and the strain on jurors who would be required to "endure continual translations." The court even extended its concern to the jurors' families, employers, and communities and worried about the effect the litigation would likely have on them.[80] UK courts by contrast exclude all questions of administrative difficulties and burden on the judicial system when applying the *Spiliada* test. In Lord Hope's words: "the principles on which the doctrine of *forum non conveniens* rest leave no room for considerations of public interest or public policy which cannot be related to the private interests of any of the parties or the ends of justice."[81] While it is difficult to discern what bearing the inconvenience of jurors or the burden on forum taxpayers might have on the interests of parties and the ends of justice, it is ultimately up to each state to formulate the criteria by which it determines whether jurisdiction should be declined in a particular case.

Finally, it is unclear whether official declarations from foreign states concerning the propriety of litigation have any effect in the *forum non conveniens* analysis. For instance, in *Jota*, the court took notice of the position of an Ecuadorian legislator that the lawsuit "in a federal court of NY against the Texaco Company, will bring to those affected the possibility of finding just treatment," but nevertheless granted the stay.[82] Likewise, in *Re Union Carbide*, India argued that its courts were not equipped to handle the Bhopal litigation and supported jurisdiction in the US. But the court disagreed with India's poor assessment of its own judiciary and dismissed the claim.[83] For its part, South Africa has taken varying positions in different cases. In *Lubbe*, the government of South Africa supported the plaintiffs in their quest to sue in the UK. It stated before the House of Lords: "South Africa sees no

79 *Aguinda*, above note 22 at 480; *Gulf Oil*, above note 14 at 508–9.
80 *Re Union Carbide*, above note 76 at 862.
81 *Lubbe*, above note 23 at 286.
82 *Jota v. Texaco*, 157 F.3d 153 at 158 (2d Cir. 1998).
83 *Re Union Carbide*, above note 76 at 867.

South African public interest which arise from alleged acts of an English company under the law of the old South Africa."[84] The Lords' judgment however does not reveal to what extent, if any, South Africa's position influenced the decision to deny the stay. In the US however, in the context of the *Apartheid Litigation*, South Africa took a different view of lawsuits against various MNCs, claiming that the litigation interfered with the efforts of the Truth and Reconciliation Commission, which "deliberately avoided a 'victors' justice' approach to the crimes of apartheid and chose instead one based on confession and absolution, informed by the principles of reconciliation, reconstruction, reparation and goodwill."[85] In this particular instance, the US Department of State agreed, which prompted the US Supreme Court in *Sosa* to comment "there is a strong argument that federal courts should give serious weight to the Executive Branch's view of the case's impact on foreign policy."[86] While the Supreme Court was not addressing the particular issue of *forum non conveniens*, it is likely that, given the particular US practice of considering "public interest" factors in applying the doctrine, foreign state declarations endorsed by the US Executive Branch would weigh heavily in the balance of interests.

D. CONCLUSION

The US cases brought under *ATCA* and *TVPA* reveal the plea of *forum non conveniens* to be a readily surmountable procedural obstacle for plaintiffs. Federal courts have largely been reluctant to stay proceedings in favour of the countries where the alleged wrongs occur, either because of the inability of plaintiffs of returning there or because of the perception that no adequate alternative remedy could be obtained in those jurisdictions. Significantly, federal courts appear to view *ATCA* and the *TVPA* as implements of a wider US policy of facilitating the adjudication civil claims for violations of well-established norms of

84 Statement of Case on Behalf of the Republic of South Africa (26 May 2000), in *Lubbe*, above note 23; see Halina Ward, "Securing Transnational Corporate Accountability through National Courts: Implications and Policy Options" (2001) 24 Hastings Int'l & Comp. L. Rev. 451 at 460.

85 Declaration of Penuell Mpapa, Minister of Justice and Constitutional Development, Republic of South Africa, cited in *Sosa v. Alvarez-Machain*, 542 U.S. 692 at 733 (2004).

86 *Ibid.*

international law. By contrast, the doctrine of *forum non conveniens* remains an important opportunity for judicial restraint in home state proceedings. In such cases, the *Spiliada/Gulf Oil* analysis applies in the usual way, but courts ought avoid parochial approaches to foreign processes — as in *Cambior* and *Re Union Carbide*. The English asbestos cases show that territorial connections do not always outweigh the requirements of justice. Contrarily to US practice, the burden of the litigation on the forum and other so-called public interest factors are excluded from the UK *forum non conveniens* analysis. The Canadian position on this point is in flux, as reflected most recently by *Bil'in*.

CHAPTER SEVEN

State Immunity

"If contracts, why not torture?"

—H. Koh[1]

A. INTRODUCTION

State immunity is a doctrine of international law aimed at regulating the adjudicative and enforcement jurisdiction of municipal courts in proceedings involving foreign states or their representatives. Grounded in the principle of sovereign equality, the doctrine generally operates to limit the ability of national courts to sit in judgment on foreign government actions. Though once supposed absolute, state immunity is now widely accepted as being restrictive, or relative, and as only applicable to "sovereign" or "public" acts of state. Courts and commentators have spent the last fifty years delineating a workable scope for the restrictive doctrine of state immunity. More recently, the growing salience of human rights, the effect of peremptory norms, and the development of international criminal law since WW II have intensified the debate regarding the proper extent of state immunity. For the last twenty years, the rise of transnational human rights litigation has prompted a further re-evaluation of the doctrine of state immunity as individuals bring civil claims in domestic courts against foreign states and their officials for

1 Harold Hongju Koh, "Transnational Public Law Litigation" (1991) 100 Yale L.J. 2347 at 2365.

human rights violations committed abroad. This chapter examines the evolving law of state immunity, particularly as developed in the UK, US, and Canada, and discusses the doctrine's effect on the jurisdiction of national courts in transnational human rights proceedings.

B. JURISDICTION AND IMMUNITY

In its most general sense, jurisdiction "relates to the power of a State to affect the rights of a person . . . by legislative, executive or judicial means."[2] In its narrower judicial meaning, jurisdiction refers to the power of a court over particular claims (jurisdiction *ratione materiae*) and particular parties (jurisdiction *ratione personae*) within particular geographical limits (jurisdiction *ratione loci*), as well as the authority to make determinations of law and of fact in the course of its proceedings. By contrast, the doctrine of state immunity is a procedural plea that "prevents the subjection of an independent State to proceedings in another country relating to a dispute about its exercise of governmental power."[3] In a manner similar to the doctrine of *forum non conveniens*, state immunity asks whether jurisdiction ought to be declined once it has been properly asserted.[4] As stated by the majority in the *Arrest Warrant* case, "it is only where a State has jurisdiction under international law in relation to a particular matter that there can be any question of immunities in regard of the exercise of that jurisdiction."[5] The ICJ further noted in the *Cumaraswamy case* that national courts are under "an obligation to deal with the question of immunity from legal process as a preliminary issue to be decided expeditiously *ex limine litis*."[6]

2 *Case Concerning the Arrest Warrant of 11 April 2000 (Democratic Republic of Congo v. Belgium)*, [2002] I.C.J. Rep. 3, Separate Opinion of Judge Koroma at para. 5 [*Arrest Warrant Case*].

3 Hazel Fox, *The Law of State Immunity* (Oxford: Oxford University Press, 2002) at 11 [Fox].

4 *Gulf Oil Corp. v. Gilbert*, 330 U.S. 501 at 504 and 506–7 (1947) [*Gulf Oil*]. But see *Sinochem International Co. Ltd. v. Malaysia International Shipping Corp.*, 549 U.S. 422 (2007) in which the US Supreme Court refined its position in *Gulf Oil*, noting that courts have the discretion to respond to a plea of *forum non conveniens* before resolving issues of personal or subject-matter jurisdiction. *Sinochem* shows that comparisons between the doctrines of state immunity and *forum non conveniens* cannot be taken too far given the discretion involved in the latter's application.

5 *Arrest Warrant Case*, Judgment, above note 2 at para. 46.

6 *Difference Relating to Immunity from Legal Process of a Special Rapporteur of the Commission on Human Rights*, Advisory Opinion, [1999] I.C.J. Rep. 62 at para. 67 (the *Cumaraswamy* case).

C. A BRIEF HISTORY OF STATE IMMUNITY

1) From Absolute to Restrictive Immunity

Until the 1970s, common law courts generally adhered to the notion that states, being equal in sovereignty and dignity, could never without their consent be subjected to the judicial process of other states, a principle expressed by the maxim *par in parem non habet imperium*.[7] The absolute theory of State immunity appears to be linked to the historical immunities enjoyed by monarchs and their representatives.[8] While the personal sovereign enjoyed immunity on the basis of his independence and dignity, ambassadors were granted a functional immunity predicated upon the freedom necessarily required to perform their duties. "*Ils sont la parole du prince qui les envoie, et cette parole doit être libre. Aucun obstacle ne doit les empêcher d'agir*," explained Montesquieu.[9] While in power or on duty, sovereigns and diplomats were deemed inviolable and immune. As Sir Ian Sinclair speculated, this inviolability of the personal sovereign may have been transposed to the nation state during the seventeenth and eighteenth centuries, "when more and more, the monarch came to personify the State. Louis XIV is alleged to have declared: "*L'État, c'est moi.*"[10] The language used to describe the common attributes — sovereignty, dignity, and independence — which previously had solely been associated with the personal sovereign, also signals this equation of the state with the monarch. By the end of the nineteenth century, sovereignty, dignity, and independence, the hallmarks of Westphalian Statehood, came to be seen as the foundational principles of absolute state immunity.[11]

---

7 *The Cristina*, [1938] A.C. 485 at 490 (H.L.); *I Congreso del Partido*, [1983] 1 A.C. 244 at 262 (H.L.) [*Congreso*].

8 Fox, above note 3 at 101–3; Sir Ian Sinclair, "The Law of Sovereign Immunity: Recent Developments" 167 Rec. des Cours 113 at 198 (1980 II) [Sinclair]; Hersch Lauterpacht, "The Problem of Jurisdictional Immunities of Foreign States" (1951) 28 Brit. Y.B. Int'l L. 220 at 228 [Lauterpacht].

9 Montesquieu, *De l'esprit des lois*, vol. 2 (1748; reprint, Victor Goldschmidt, ed., Paris: GF-Flammarion, 1979) at 199. This functional immunity is expressed by the maxim: "*Non datur actio adversus legatum, ne ab officio suscepto legationis avocetur, ne impediatur legatio.*"

10 Sinclair, above note 8 at 198; *Schreiber v. Canada (Attorney General)*, [2002] 3 S.C.R. 269 at para. 13 [*Schreiber*].

11 Fox, above note 3 at 24–25.

The restrictive doctrine's triumph in the twentieth century involves nearly 200 years of judicial history that has been described by others.[12] It is unnecessary to revisit every phase of the history of state immunity to understand the implications of the restrictive doctrine in the context of transnational human rights litigation. A broad sketch of the law's evolution will suffice for this purpose. According to Trooboff, the gradual shift to the restrictive doctrine of immunity can be attributed to five factors: (1) the growing accountability of governments before their own courts; (2) the increase of international trade; (3) the questionable rationale of defending immunity in relation to commercial activity; (4) a growing state practice of waiving immunity in the course of business; and (5) the unfairness to private parties of shielding states from court process.[13] Responding to these concerns, early nineteenth century courts in the US and UK attempted to distinguish between private and public acts of state, upholding immunity only with regards to the latter. In 1824, Marshall CJ held that "when a government becomes a partner in any trading company, it divests itself, so far as concerns the transactions of that company, of its sovereign character and takes that of a private citizen."[14] Early cases in the UK also reveal the pale outline of the restrictive theory with courts distinguishing between the private and public character of state acts. In 1851, the immunity of a foreign sovereign was upheld with regards to actions performed "in his public capacity."[15] Similarly, in 1873, Phillimore J found immunity inapplicable in proceedings against the property of a sovereign used in trade, though his decision was reversed on appeal.[16]

Despite this apparent early willingness to restrict state immunity to public acts and property, the absolute theory gripped the common

12 Fox, *ibid.*; Sompong Sucharitkul, "Immunities of Foreign States before National Authorities" 149 Rec. des Cours 89 (1976-I) [Sucharitkul]; Peter D. Trooboff, "Foreign State Immunity: Emerging Consensus on Principles" 200 Rec. des Cours 235 (1986-V) [Trooboff]; Sinclair, above note 8; Isabelle Pingel-Lenuzza, *Les immunités des Etats en droit international* (Bruxelles: Éditions Bruylant, 1998); *The Philippine Admiral*, [1977] A.C. 373 at 391–401 (P.C.) [*The Philippine Admiral*].

13 Trooboff, *ibid.* at 266–67.

14 *Bank of the United States v. Planters' Bank of Georgia*, 22 U.S. 904 at 907 (1824). This is not a foreign state immunity case. Marshall CJ made the public/private distinction in ruling that the State of Georgia's participation in a corporation did not exempt that corporation from being sued in US courts. Georgia's sovereign privileges and prerogatives did not extend to the corporation.

15 *De Haber v. Queen of Portugal* (1851), 17 Q.B. 171 at 206.

16 *The Charkieh* (1873), L.R. 4 (Adm. & Ecc.) 59.

law for nearly a century after having been definitively established in the case of the *Parlement Belge* (1880), and later reaffirmed by Lord Atkin in *The Cristina* (1938). The *Parlement Belge* is the "first clear formulation of a rule of State immunity in English law" and was treated for over fifty years "as authority . . . for an absolute doctrine of immunity."[17] The Court of Appeal's ruling on "the exemption of every sovereign from the jurisdiction of every court"[18] relied largely on Marshall CJ's decision in *The Schooner Exchange v. McFaddon* (1812). However, as many commentators have observed, the ratio of *The Schooner Exchange* concerned not the absolute immunity of states but rather their unlimited territorial jurisdiction.[19] Far from formulating an absolute rule, Marshall CJ's decision heralded the restrictive theory of immunity insofar as it distinguished between private and public "pursuits."[20] This being so, it is tempting to suppose that absolute immunity might have resulted from a historic misunderstanding. Indeed, as Trooboff put it, "with the benefits of later developments, we can see today that some of the earlier cases were probably read to stand for propositions that, on analysis, their authors did not necessarily intend."[21] However that may be, the absolute doctrine was adopted, formed part of the common law, and was followed as a matter of *stare decisis* for nearly a century. On the other hand, the doctrine was never literally absolute. Despite their adherence to a strict principle of immunity, courts nevertheless developed certain exceptions under which immunity was denied.[22] Therefore, given its uncertain origins and uneven application by national courts, it is doubtful whether the absolute doctrine of state immunity ever formed part of

---

17 Fox, above note 3 at 104.

18 *The Parlement Belge*, [1979–90] 5 Prob. Div. 197 at 207 (1880) [*The Parlement Belge*].

19 Gamal Badr, *State Immunity: An Analytical and Prognostic View* (The Hague: Martinus Nijhoff, 1984) at 11–14; Lauterpacht, above note 8 at 229; Sinclair, above note 8 at 122; Trooboff, above note 12 at 256.

20 *The Schooner Exchange v. McFaddon*, 11 U.S. 116 at 144 (1812) [*The Schooner Exchange*]. Marshall CJ held that the immunity of warships should not extend to "merchant vessels [that] enter for the purposes of trade" for such vessels "are not employed by [a foreign sovereign], nor are they engaged in national pursuits."

21 Trooboff, above note 12 at 257.

22 As summarized by Finlayson JA in *Jaffe v. Miller* (1993), 13 O.R. (3d) 745 at 752 (C.A.) [*Jaffe*], at common law there was no immunity in respect of (1) land situated in the host state, (2) trust funds or moneys lodged for the payment of creditors, (3) debts incurred for service of property in the host state, and (4) commercial transactions entered into with a trader in the host state.

customary international law.[23] Indeed, the restrictive doctrine was consistently employed in civil law jurisdictions as early as the 1880s, notably by Italy and Belgium.[24]

In the UK, the absolute doctrine of immunity gradually lost ground after the 1950s, partly due to the influence of Lord Denning.[25] It was he, with the concurrence of Shaw LJ, who finally adopted the restrictive doctrine in 1977 in *Trendtex* (1977), though the Privy Council had already adopted the restrictive rule with regards to actions *in rem* in *The Philippine Admiral* (1977).[26] Finally, drawing on the provisions of the *European Convention on State Immunity* (ECSI),[27] the UK adopted the *State Immunity Act, 1978* (UK *SIA*).[28]

In the US, courts upheld the immunity of foreign states following a mixed application of absolute immunity and "suggestions" from the executive branch.[29] In 1952, with the so-called "Tate Letter," the Department of State announced its adoption of the restrictive theory of state immunity.[30] The policy of direct intervention of the government in judicial proceedings involving foreign states continued until the enactment of the *Foreign Sovereign Immunities Act* (*FSIA*) in 1976, which

23 "Historically, in accordance with customary international law, foreign States were granted absolute immunity from proceedings in the courts of other States": *Bouzari et al. v. Islamic Republic of Iran*, [2002] O.J. No. 1624 at para. 18 (S.C.J.) [*Bouzari 2002*]. Contrast with Lauterpacht, above note 8 at 221: "insofar as the actual practice of States can be said to be evidence of customary international law, there is no doubt that the principle of absolute immunity forms no part of international custom."

24 See *Guttieres v. Elmilik* (1886), 1886-I Foro. It. 913 and *S.A. des chemins de fer Liégeois-Luxembourgeois v. l'État Néerlandais*, 11 June 1903, Pasicrisie Belge, both cited in Fox, above note 3 at 119–20.

25 In 1952, the Privy Council did "not consider that there had been finally established in England any absolute rule": *Sultan of Johore v. Abubakar Tunku Aris Brendahar*, [1952] A.C. 318 at 343 (H.L.); *Rahimtoola v. Nizam of Hyderabad*, [1958] A.C. 379 (H.L.) (where Lord Denning objected to the absolute theory) [*Rahimtoola*]; *Thai-Europe Tapioca Service Ltd. v. Government of Pakistan*, [1975] 1 W.L.R. 1485 (C.A.) (where Lord Denning MR recognized a commercial exception to state immunity but held it was inapplicable to the facts of the case) [*Thai-Europe*].

26 *The Philippine Admiral*, above note 12.

27 *European Convention on State Immunity*, 16 May 1972, E.T.S. No. 074 [ECSI]; Fox, above note 3 at 133.

28 *State Immunity Act 1978* (U.K.), 1978, c. 33 [UK *SIA*].

29 *Ex parte Republic of Peru*, 318 U.S. 578 (1943); Fox, above note 3 at 183–85.

30 *Changing Policy Concerning the Granting of Sovereign Immunity to Foreign Governments*, Letter to US Acting Attorney-General (19 May 1952), (1952) 26 US Department of State Bulletin 984 at 985.

codified the restrictive theory and left its application to the courts.[31] The US government still influences judicial determinations of immunities by unilaterally designating so-called "State sponsors of terrorism," who are denied immunity in proceedings relating to terrorism, torture, and extrajudicial killings.[32]

For its part, Canada adhered to the absolute rule until the enactment of the *SIA* in 1982, though lower courts were not insensitive to the rise of the restrictive doctrine in other jurisdictions. In *Dessaulles* (1944), Taschereau J stated:

> *Il ne fait pas de doute qu'un état souverain ne peut être poursuivi devant les tribunaux étrangers. Ce principe est fondé sur l'indépendance et la dignité des états, et la courtoisie internationale l'a toujours respecté. La jurisprudence l'a aussi adopté comme étant la loi domestique de tous les pays civilisés.*[33]

In *Congo v. Venne*, a Canadian architect sued the Congo for unpaid fees regarding the design of its pavilion for the 1967 World Fair in Montreal. Both the Quebec Queen's Bench and the Court of Appeal applied the restrictive doctrine and denied the immunity plea.[34] A majority of the Supreme Court reversed those judgments without deciding whether the restrictive theory formed part of Canadian law. The majority held that the hiring of an architect to design a national pavilion in the context of Expo 67 was a sovereign act that could not be impugned in Canada, "even if the so-called doctrine of restrictive sovereign immunity had been adopted in our courts."[35] Laskin and Hall JJ, dissenting, stated that the absolute doctrine of state immunity was "spent."[36] In light of the inconclusive judgment in *Venne*, Quebec courts remained unwavering; in the following year the Québec Court of Appeal said that "it is open for this Court to reaffirm its belief in the existence in Canada of a doctrine of restrictive immunity."[37] Ontario courts also

31 *Foreign Sovereign Immunities Act of 1976*, 28 U.S.C. § 1330 [*FSIA*].

32 See discussion below at notes 57–67 and accompanying text.

33 *Dessaulles v. Republic of Poland*, [1944] S.C.R. 275 at para. 1.

34 *Republic of Congo v. Venne*, [1968] R.P. 6. (Sup. Ct.), aff'd [1969] B.R. 818 (C.A.). Later that year, the Court of Appeal confirmed its *Venne* ruling in *Penthouse Studios v. Republic of Venezuela* (1969), 8 D.L.R. (3d) 686 (Que. C.A.).

35 *Republic of Congo v.Venne*, [1971] S.C.R. 997 at 1003 [*Venne*].

36 *Ibid.* at 1025.

37 *Zodiak International Products Inc. v. Polish People's Republic* (1978), 81 D.L.R. (3d) 656 at 659 (Que. C.A.).

came to accept the restrictive theory as part of the common law.[38] Before the Supreme Court of Canada could have another say in the matter, Parliament codified the restrictive theory of immunity in 1982 with the enactment the *State Immunity Act*.

2) The Codification of State Immunity

Until the late twentieth century, there were no general international instruments on state immunity save for the very narrow 1926 *Brussels Convention for the Unification of Certain Rules Relating to the Immunity of State Owned Vessels*.[39] The ECSI was the first international attempt to codify the restrictive principle of state immunity. It remains widely unpopular among European countries, having been ratified by only eight states since coming into force in 1976.[40] Fox surmises that the ECSI's unpopularity is due, among other factors, to its complexity and optional regime for the execution of judgments.[41]

The International Law Commission (ILC) began its work on jurisdictional immunities in 1977 at the request of the UN General Assembly.[42] Twenty-seven years later, in 2004, the General Assembly adopted the *United Nations Convention on the Jurisdictional Immunities of States and their Property* (UNCSI) and opened it for signature.[43] Pursuant to Article 30, the UNCSI will come into force on the thirtieth day following the deposit of the thirtieth instrument of ratification.[44]

---

38 See *Smith v. Canadian Javelin Ltd.* (1976), 12 O.R. (2d) 244 (H.C.J.) (accepted the rule of "qualified immunity" developed in *Thai-Europe*, above note 25, but it did not apply to the facts of the case); *Corriveau v. Republic of Cuba* (1979), 26 O.R. (2d) 674 (H.C.J.) (refused to apply absolute doctrine as the "law is evolving on the subject"); *Khan v. Fredson Travel Inc. (No. 2)* (1982), 36 O.R. (2d) 17 (H.C.J.) (held that the absolute "doctrine had been abandoned in commercial matters in Ontario").

39 *International Convention for the Unification of Certain Rules Relating to the Immunity of State Owned Vessels*, 10 April 1926, 176 L.N.T.S. 199 (1926); Fox, above note 3 at 85–86.

40 ECSI, above note 27. As of January 2010, the ECSI has been ratified or acceded to by Austria, Belgium, Cyprus, Germany, Luxemburg, Netherlands, Switzerland, and the United Kingdom.

41 Fox, above note 3 at 94.

42 UN General Assembly Resolutions, 32nd session, A/RES/32/151 (19 December 1977).

43 *United Nations Convention on the Jurisdictional Immunities of States and their Property*, 2 December 2004, A/RES/59/38 [UNCSI].

44 The signature round for the UNCSI closed on 17 January 2007. At the time of writing, twenty-eight states have signed and seven have ratified the UNCCI, namely Austria, Iran, Lebanon, Norway, Portugal, Romania, and Sweden.

In the absence of positive international law on the matter, many countries of the Anglo-American legal world had adopted legislation codifying the doctrine of restrictive immunity,[45] while other countries continued to develop the rule as a matter of common law.[46] Ironically, courts in many civil law countries—which traditionally favour legislation over judge-made law—apply the restrictive theory of immunity without the benefit of legislation with reference to customary international law.[47] The discussion in the present chapter is restricted to the US *Foreign Sovereign Immunities Act* of 1976,[48] the UK *State Immunity Act* of 1978,[49] and the Canadian *State Immunity Act* of 1982 (*SIA*)[50] since they are the only immunity statutes to have been interpreted in the context of transnational human rights litigation.

In their basic structure and operation, the *FSIA*, UK *SIA*, and Canadian *SIA* resemble the ECSI. They proceed by first establishing the immunity of foreign states, and then go on to enumerate certain exceptions to immunity, such as waiver,[51] commercial activity,[52] local torts,[53] and certain maritime issues.[54] In short, other than in cases of waiver, the grant or denial of state immunity under the restrictive theory hinges upon the subject matter of the proceedings rather than on the identity of the defendant as a state. As Lord Millet explained in both *Pinochet (No. 3)* and *Lampen-Wolfe* (2000), state immunity is a subject-matter immunity.[55] Similarly, the US Supreme Court stated that the *FSIA* "must be applied by the district courts in every action against a foreign sovereign, since subject-matter jurisdiction in any such action depends on the existence of one of the specified exceptions to foreign sovereign immunity."[56]

---

45 For example, Australia, Canada, Malaysia, Pakistan, the United Kingdom, and the United States.

46 For example, Kenya, Ireland, New Zealand, Nigeria, and Zimbabwe.

47 Fox, above note 3 at 118.

48 *FSIA*, above note 31 at §§ 1602–11.

49 UK *SIA*, above note 28.

50 *State Immunity Act*, R.S.C. 1985, c. S-18 [*SIA*].

51 ECSI, above note 27, art. 2; *FSIA*, above note 31, § 1605(a)(1); UK *SIA*, above note 28, s. 2; *SIA*, above note 50, s. 4.

52 ESCI, *ibid.*, art. 7; *FSIA*, *ibid.*, § 1605(a)(2); UK *SIA*, *ibid.*, s. 3; *SIA*, *ibid.*, s. 5.

53 ECSI, *ibid.*, art. 11; *FSIA*, *ibid.*, § 1605(a)(5); UK *SIA*, *ibid.*, s. 5; *SIA*, *ibid.*, s. 6.

54 FSIA, *ibid.*, § 1605(b); UK *SIA*, *ibid.*, s. 11; *SIA*, *ibid.*, s. 7.

55 *R. v. Bow Street Metropolitan Stipendiary Magistrate, ex parte Pinochet (No. 3)*, [2000] 1 A.C. 147 at 269 (H.L.) [*Pinochet III*]; *Holland v. Lampen-Wolfe*, [2000] 1 W.L.R. 1573 at 1583 (H.L.) [*Lampen-Wolfe*].

56 *Verlinden BV v. Central Bank of Nigeria*, 461 U.S. 480 at 493 (1983).

So far, all transnational human rights claims against states have failed outside the US, mainly because no other national statute provides for the denial of immunity in proceedings for extraterritorial human rights violations. In addition to the traditional exceptions contained in the UK and Canadian statutes, the *FSIA* provides for the denial of immunity in proceedings for certain violations of international law, including human rights violations. After the rehabilitation of *ATCA* in *Filártiga*, plaintiffs and lawyers attempted to make use of the statute in lawsuits against states for violations of international law. In *Amerada Hess* (1988), a Liberian corporation sued Argentina in US courts after its military aircrafts bombed a private oil tanker in the South Atlantic during the war of the Falkland Islands. The unprovoked bombing, the plaintiffs alleged, amounted to a tort "committed in violation of the law of nations" that triggered *ATCA* jurisdiction.[57] The Supreme Court held that *ATCA* did not apply to the proceedings and that the *FSIA* was the sole basis for obtaining jurisdiction against a foreign state.[58] The court further noted that unless a plaintiff's claim falls within the exceptions contained within the four corners of the *FSIA*, state immunity applies and the action is barred.

Responding to pressure from the families of victims and survivors of the Pan Am Flight 103 bombing, the US Congress amended the *FSIA* in 1996 by creating a new exception to state immunity for serious human rights violations. The *Antiterrorism and Effective Death Penalty Act*,[59] codified as part of the *FSIA* at 28 U.S.C. § 1605(a)(7), allows (1) US citizens; (2) to bring a claim for compensatory and punitive damages;[60] (3) against certain designated foreign states;[61] (4) for death or personal

57 *Alien Tort Claim Act*, 28 U.S.C. § 1350.

58 *Argentine Republic v. Amerada Hess Shipping Corp.*, 488 U.S. 428 at 434 (1989) [*Amerada Hess*].

59 *Antiterrorism and Effective Death Penalty Act*, Pub. L. 104-132, § 221, 221 Stat. 1214, 24 April 1996.

60 Originally, the amendment only permitted the recovery of compensatory damages. Five months after its enactment however, Congress returned with the *Omnibus Consolidated Appropriations Act, 1997*, Pub. L. 104-208, Title V § 589, 110 Stat. 3009, 30 September 1996, which authorized the award of punitive damages.

61 The designation is made pursuant to § 6(j) of the *Export Administration Act of 1979*, 50 U.S.C. App. 2405(j) and § 620A of the *Foreign Assistance Act of 1961*, 22 U.S.C. 2371. At the time of writing, Cuba, Iran, Sudan, and Syria are designated state sponsors of terrorism for *FSIA* purposes. Iraq, Libya, and North Korea had also been designated at one point. Iraq was removed from the list in 2003 by Presidential Determination (69 Fed. Reg. 18,810 (9 April 2004)), and its designation

injury arising from an act of torture, extrajudicial killing, aircraft sabotage, hostage taking, or for supporting such activities; (5) provided the plaintiff afforded the foreign state with a reasonable opportunity to resolve the matter through arbitration.

Though § 1605(a)(7) is often referred to as the "Flatow Amendment" in memory of the deceased student in *Flatow v. Islamic Republic of Iran* (1998),[62] the first judicial application of the *FSIA* torture and terrorism exception is *Alejandre v. Cuba* (1997).[63] In *Alejandre*, plaintiffs sued the government of Cuba after fighter jets shot down two civilian planes in international airspace, killing four people. The plaintiffs were awarded $49.9 million in compensatory damages and $137.7 million in punitive damages. In *Flatow*, parents of a student killed in a suicide bombing in Israel sued Iran for financially supporting the terrorist group responsible for the attack, the Palestine Islamic Jihad. The Flatow family was awarded $22.5 million in compensatory damages and $225 million in punitive damages.[64] In both cases however—indeed, as in most transnational human rights cases[65]—the plaintiffs could not collect on their judgments since most foreign state assets located in the US are consular or diplomatic in nature and thus protected under international law.[66] To overcome this difficulty, Congress returned with further amendments to the *FSIA*, controversially allowing plaintiffs to access frozen assets and certain diplomatic property to satisfy judgments obtained under § 1605(a)(7).[67]

---

was officially rescinded later that year (69 Fed. Reg. 61,702 (20 October 2004)). Libya's designation was rescinded by Presidential Determination dated 12 May 2006 (71 Fed. Reg. 31,907 (1 June 2006)), in keeping with the Bush administration's policy of restoring diplomatic relations with that country. President G.W. Bush also authorized the rescission of North Korea's designation as a state sponsor of terrorism in 2008 (73 Fed. Reg. 37,351 (26 June 2008)), which was effectuated by the Secretary of State later that year (73 Fed. Reg. 63,570 (11 October 2008)), as part of an understanding providing for the dismantlement of North Korean plutonium processing plants and international inspections.

62 *Flatow v. Islamic Republic of Iran*, 999 F. Supp. 1 (D.C.C. 1998) [*Flatow*].

63 *Alejandre v. Republic of Cuba*, 996 F. Supp. 1239 (S.D. Fla. 1997) [*Alejandre*].

64 See also *Cicippio v. Islamic Republic of Iran*, 18 F. Supp. 2d 62 (D.C.C. 1998), decided shortly after *Flatow* in which three men were awarded $65 million after having been kidnapped and held hostage by Hezbollah in Beirut.

65 Richard B. Lillich, "Damages for Gross Violations of International Human Rights Awarded by U.S. Courts" (1993) 15 Hum. Rts. Q. 207.

66 Most notably under the *Vienna Convention on Diplomatic Relations* (18 April 1961), 500 U.N.T.S. 95, to which the United States became a party on 13 December 1972.

67 *Omnibus Consolidated and Emergency Supplemental Appropriations Act, 1998*, Pub. L. 105–277, § 117, 112 Stat. 2681, 21 October 1998 (Permits the attachment of frozen

As a matter of international law, it is irrelevant whether terrorism or torture is committed in Iran, Israel, or Ireland. These crimes are outlawed wherever they occur. Under United States law however, the *locus* of the offence and nationality of the offender are determinative of legal consequences. Clearly, the unhappy distinction the *FSIA* creates between friendly states and state sponsors of terrorism is reflective of policy, not principle. While it is undoubtedly, as Lord Denning MR noted, the prerogative of every sovereign state to formulate its own rules — "[e]ach country delimits for itself the bounds of sovereign immunity. Each creates for itself the exceptions from it" — such legislation should be enacted "in terms which are consonant with justice rather than adverse to it."[68] The US model is unprincipled and generally understood to be inconsistent with fundamental tenets of public international law.[69]

There is increasing pressure in Canada to amend the *SIA* to include human rights exceptions in light of several cases in which Canadians have been tortured or killed abroad. Since 2002, Houshang Bouzari of Toronto sued Iran for torture,[70] Jamil Sarif Saleh of Ottawa sued the United Arab Emirates for torture,[71] Maher Arar of Ottawa sued Syria for

---

and diplomatic assets of foreign states to satisfy judgments under § 1605(7).); *Victims of Trafficking and Violence Protection Act, 2000*, Pub. L. 106-386, § 2002, 114 Stat. 1464, 28 October 2000. (Permits specified successful § 1605 claimants against Cuba and Iran to be paid the compensatory portion of their awards out of frozen assets.) For analysis of the *FSIA* amendments see Allison Taylor, "Another Front in the War on Terrorism? Problems with Recent Changes to the *Foreign Sovereign Immunities Act*" (2003) 45 Ariz. L. Rev. 533; W. Michael Reisman & Monica Hakimi, "Illusion and Reality in the Compensation of Victims of International Terrorism" (2003) 54 Ala. L. Rev. 561.

68 *Trendtex Trading Coporation v. Central Bank of Nigeria*, [1977] 2 W.L.R. 356 at 364 (C.A.) [*Trendtex*].

69 Ronald Bettauer, "Germany Sues Italy at the International Court of Justice on Foreign Sovereign Immunity — Legal Underpinnings and Implications for U.S. Law" (2009) 13:22 *ASIL Insights* 1 at 5: "Fox sees the U.S. legislation as 'partisan' and not a satisfactory precedent for other states to adopt. Gattini calls the U.S. approach 'of dubious value' because of its 'unilateral nature and political overtones.' Bankas called subsection (a)(7) and the pre-2008 amendments to it 'draconian in many respects and therefore may be vigorously contested by defendant states.' Professor van Alabeek says that 'the terrorist state exception to the FSIA causes the United States to violate its obligations under international law.'" [References omitted.]

70 *Bouzari 2002*, above note 23 and *Bouzari et al. v. Islamic Republic of Iran* (2004), 71 O.R. (3d) 675 (C.A.) [*Bouzari 2004*].

71 *Saleh v. United Arab Emirates* (2003), 15 C.C.L.T. (3d) 231. (Ont. S.C.J.) [*Saleh*].

torture,[72] William Sampson of Vancouver joined a lawsuit in England against Saudi Arabia for torture,[73] a Montreal family is suing Iran and Iranian officials following the torture and killing of Zahra Kazemi,[74] and Kunlun Zhang and other Falun Gong practitioners based in Toronto are suing former Chinese state officials for torture.[75] Furthermore, in response to the *Bouzari* litigation, the Committee against Torture recommended in 2005 that Canada make provisions in its law to allow civil actions against states for torture.[76] These developments have prompted advocates to propose draft legislation that would deny immunity in civil proceedings for certain violations of peremptory norms of international law, including torture, war crimes, crimes against humanity, and genocide. The key provision of one of the proposed amendments reads as follows:

> 8.1 (1) Subject to subsection (2), a foreign state is not immune from the jurisdiction of a court in any proceedings that relate to genocide, a crime against humanity, a war crime or torture.
>
> (2) Subsection (1) shall apply only after all domestic remedies have been invoked and exhausted in the matter, in conformity with the generally recognized principles of international law.[77]

---

72 *Arar v. Syrian Arab Republic*, [2005] 28 C.R. (6th) 187 (Ont. S.C.J.). See also online: www.cbc.ca/news/background/arar/ [Arar].

73 *Mitchell v. Al-Dali*, No. HQ04X00431, *sub. nom Jones v. Saudi Arabia*, [2004] EWCA Civ 1394 [*Jones 2004*]; See online: www.cbc.ca/news/background/sampson.

74 *Kazemi Estate v. Islamic Republic of Iran*, No. 500-17-031760-062 (Que. Sup. Ct.). The motion to dismiss on the basis of state immunity was heard on 2–8 December 2009. The Superior Court of Quebec's decision was still on reserve at the time of printing. See online: www.cbc.ca/news/background/kazemi [*Kazemi*].

75 *Zhang v. Zemin*, No. 04-CV-278915CM2 (Ont. S.C.J.). The defendants have been noted in default. On a motion brought under rule 21 (determination of an issue of law before trial) of the Ontario *Rules of Civil Procedure*, Pollak J declined to determine whether, as a matter of law, the defendants were entitled to immunity for torture, holding that "the trial judge will be in a better position to decide this legal issue having had the benefit of the evidence that will have to be adduced at trial." *Zhang v. Zemin* (30 March 2010), No. 04-CV-278915CM2 (Ont. S.C.J.), Pollak J. Justice Pollak's refusal to determine the question of immunity as a preliminary matter is at odds with the settled practice of Ontario courts to address immunity issues under rule 21 before sending the case to trial on the merits.

76 Below note 121 and accompanying text.

77 Bill C-483: *An Act to amend the State Immunity Act (genocide, crimes against humanity, war crimes or torture)*, first reading on 26 November 2009. Bill C-483 was tabled by the Hon. Irwin Cotler, with broad support from members of government and the opposition.

In June 2009, the Minister of Public Safety introduced another bill aimed at amending the *SIA*, which would create an exception to state immunity with respect to terrorist activities.[78] Bill C-35, entitled *An Act to Deter Terrorism, and to Amend the State Immunity Act*, is not the first draft legislation to be introduced in the Canadian Parliament proposing the creation of a terrorism exception for the *SIA*,[79] but it is the first such proposal to emanate from the government. The salient paragraphs of Bill C-35's preamble read as follows:

> Whereas Canadians and people everywhere are entitled to live their lives in peace, freedom and security; . . .
>
> Whereas acts of terrorism threaten Canada's political institutions, the stability of the economy and the general welfare of the nation; . . .
>
> Whereas United Nations Security Council Resolution 1373 (2001) reaffirms that acts of international terrorism constitute a threat to international peace and security, and reaffirms the need to combat by all means, in accordance with the Charter of the United Nations, threats to international peace and security caused by acts of terrorism;
>
> Whereas Canada ratified the 1999 International Convention for the Suppression of the Financing of Terrorism on February 15, 2002;
>
> . . .
>
> Whereas certain states that support terrorism should not benefit from state immunity in this regard;

78 Bill C-35: *An Act to Deter Terrorism, and to Amend the State Immunity Act*, first reading on 2 May 2009 [Bill C-35]; second reading on 30 October 2009.

79 Previous private member initiatives include Bill C-394: *An Act to Amend the State Immunity Act and the Criminal Code (terrorist activity)*, first reading on 17 May 2005. An identical bill, *sub nom.* Bill S-35 was introduced in the Senate on 18 May 2005. Both bills lapsed when the 38th Parliament dissolved in November 2005, but they were reintroduced in both houses without substantive modification in the opening weeks of the thirty-ninth Parliament as Bill C-272 (first reading on 10 May 2006) and Bill S-218 (first reading on 15 June 2006, second reading and debates on 22 and 27 June 2006). Oddly, another private member's bill nearly identical to C-272 was introduced in June 2006 in the House of Commons as Bill C-346: *An Act to Amend the State Immunity Act and the Criminal Code (terrorist activity)* (first reading on 22 June 2006). For a discussion of the these bills and the broader proposal of removing immunity with respect to terrorist activities, see François Larocque "Civil Remedies for Terrorism and State Immunity" in Nicole LaViolette & Craig Forcese, eds., *The Human Rights of Anti-Terrorism* (Toronto: Irwin Law, 2008) at 425–57.

> And whereas Parliament considers that it is in the public interest to enable plaintiffs to bring lawsuits against terrorists and their supporters, which will have the effect of impairing the functioning of terrorist groups in order to deter and prevent acts of terrorism against Canada and Canadians . . .

The preamble makes clear that the Canadian government considers terrorism to be a threat to world and Canadian public order, unassailably noting that attacks against civilian populations violate the right of all human beings to live in peace, freedom, and security. The third and fourth paragraphs quoted above refer to specific international legal instruments, thus linking the proposed legislation with existing international efforts to combat terrorism.[80] While previous incarnations of this legislation explicitly stated that terrorism was prohibited by peremptory norms of international law,[81] the preamble of Bill C-35 arguably suggests as much. Finally, as a corollary of the international public interest in prohibiting terrorism, the last preambular paragraph explicitly links the right of victims to seek redress for their injuries to the deterrent effect the law is meant to have on terrorists and those who support them.

The most objectionable part of the government's draft legislation is the manner in which it proposes to administer the removal of immunity, namely, by following the US example of designating certain states that would not be immune from civil process in Canadian courts. As noted in the preamble, Bill C-35 operates on the premise that "*certain* states that support terrorism should not benefit from state immun-

---

80 The explicit reference to Canada's ratification of the *International Convention for the Suppression of the Financing of Terrorism* (GA Res. 109, U.N. GAOR, 54th Sess., Supp. No. 49, U.N. Doc A/54/49 (Vol. 1) (1991)) on 15 February 2002 could arguably signal that Bill C-35 implements some of the obligations contained in that Convention, such as art. 5, which provides in part "5. Each State Party, in accordance with its domestic legal principles, shall take the necessary measures to enable a legal entity located in its territory or organized under its laws to be held liable when a person responsible for the management or control of that legal entity has, in that capacity, committed an offence set forth in art. 2. Such liability may be criminal, civil or administrative." For a discussion of what is required to implement specific treaty obligations, see Hugh Kindred, "The Use and Abuse of International Legal Sources by Canadian Courts: Searching for a Principled Approach" in Oonagh Fitzgerald, ed., *The Globalized Rule of Law: Relationships between International and Domestic Law* (Toronto: Irwin Law, 2006) at 10–17.

81 Such as Bill S-218, *ibid.*, and Bill C-408, below note 84.

ity" (emphasis added). The draft legislation creates a cause of action for victims of terrorism (section 4) and then goes on to amend the *SIA* by adding a new section 6.1, which reads as follows:

> 6.1 (1) A foreign state that is set out on the list referred to in subsection (2) is not immune from the jurisdiction of a court in proceedings against it for its support of terrorism on or after January 1, 1985.
>
> (2) The Governor in Council may, by order, establish a list on which the Governor in Council may set out the name of a foreign state if, on the recommendation of the Minister of Foreign Affairs made after consulting with the Minister of Public Safety and Emergency Preparedness, the Governor in Council is satisfied that there are reasonable grounds to believe that the foreign state supported or supports terrorism.[82]

The selective removal of immunity for states that appear on a list drawn up by the executive would be as unprincipled in Canada as it is in the United States.[83] Such executive designations have the effect of politicizing the judicial process, and runs counter to the purpose and rationale of the *SIA* insofar as that enactment implements the subject-matter assessment required by the doctrine of restrictive immunity. Assessments of whether an impugned state act is an *actus jure imperii* are exclusively for the courts to make, not the executive branch. Another though only marginally less political counter-proposition to Bill-35 was tabled shortly after the government bill, which would only deny the immunity of those states with which Canada has not signed an extradition treaty.[84] The theory that underpins this proposal is that Canada's extradition partners are presumed to respect the rule of law, and connected claims could thus be brought in their courts in appropriate circumstances rather than in Canada.

Similar legislative efforts have also been made in the UK in respect of torture. In 2008, Lord Archer of Sandwell's *Torture (Damages) Bill* successfully passed all three readings in the House of Lords[85] and had

---

82 Bill C-35, above note 78, s. 4.

83 See discussion above at notes 59–69 and accompanying text.

84 Bill C-408: *An Act to Amend the State Immunity Act and the Criminal Code (deterring terrorism by providing a civil right of action against perpetrators and sponsors of terrorism)* (first reading on 4 May 2009). The bill was sponsored by the Hon. Irwin Cotler.

85 *Torture (Damages) Bill* [HL] 2008 (House of Lords: first reading on 5 February 2008, second reading on 16 May 2008, third reading on 11 November 2008).

a First Reading in the House of Commons before lapsing at the end of the parliamentary year.[86] It was reintroduced again in the House of Lords in 2009[87] and most recently in the House of Commons in January 2010.[88] The 2009 incarnation of the legislation proposes a cause of action (section 1); a six-year limitations period (section 2); a definition of torture (section 4); establishes the laws of England and Wales as the applicable law (section 5); and, more relevantly to the present discussion, amends to the UK *SIA* (section 3) by adding the following:

> 5A (1) A State is not immune in respect of proceedings instituted against it under the *Torture (Damages) Act 2009*.[89]

As a private member's initiative, the UK bill stands very little chance of being enacted, but it nevertheless evinces a certain measure of willingness to make certain violations of international law actionable in domestic courts and to amend domestic state immunity rules accordingly.

As will be seen below, international law contains no human rights exception to the rule of state immunity, but here too there is evidence that international thinking is in a state of flux. As the House of Lords noted in *Jones* (2006) the ILC working group debated the inclusion of a human rights exception to the UNCSI in 1999.[90] The fact that no consensus was reached during the drafting of the convention is surely significant, but the debate inversely reveals that a number of judges, scholars, and governments support the recognition of a human rights exception to state immunity. In this connection, Norway's understanding filed upon ratification of the UNCSI in March 2006 is illuminating: "Norway understands that the Convention is without prejudice to any future international development in the protection of human rights."[91] Sweden filed an identical declaration when it ratified the UNCSI in December 2009.[92]

---

86 *Torture (Damages) Bill* 2008 (House of Commons, first reading on 18 November 2008).

87 *Torture (Damages) Bill* [HL] 2009 (House of Lords: first reading on 14 January 2009).

88 *Torture (Damages) Bill* 2010 (House of Commons: first reading on 6 January 2010).

89 The 2009 bill is available online: www.redress.org/downloads/torture-bill/tdb24Jan09.pdf.

90 *Jones v. Saudi Arabia* (2006), [2007] 1 A.C. 270 at para. 26 (H.L.) [*Jones 2006*].

91 Declaration of Norway upon ratification of the 2004 *United Nations Convention on Jurisdictional Immunities of States and their Property*, C.N.280.2006.TREATIES-2 (27 March 2006).

92 Declaration of Sweden upon ratification of the 2004 *United Nations Convention on Jurisdictional Immunities of States and their Property*, C.N.912.2009.TREATIES-1

D. STATE IMMUNITY AND TRANSNATIONAL HUMAN RIGHTS LITIGATION

This section discusses the manner in which the established exceptions to state immunity have been applied in US, UK, and Canadian transnational human rights cases involving foreign states. In addition to the codified commercial activity and local torts exceptions, plaintiffs have sought to have courts deny state immunity on the basis of emerging international law. Each will be discussed in turn.

1) Commercial Activity

Not only is commercial activity the oldest exception to state immunity, it embodies the essence of the restrictive doctrine by distinguishing between public and private acts of states, denying immunity with regards to the latter. As states increased their trading activity in the nineteenth century, behaving more like private corporations than public entities, it became common ground among the courts of trading nations that states should not be able to escape liability by merely invoking their sovereign independence and dignity, a view vividly expressed in 1879 by Phillimore J in *The Charkieh*:

> No principle of international law, and no decided case, and no dictum of jurists of which I am aware, has gone so far as to authorize a sovereign prince to assume the character of a trader, when it is for his benefit; and when he incurs an obligation to a private subject to throw off, if I may so speak, his disguise, and appear as a sovereign, claiming for his own benefit, and to the injury of a private person, for the first time, all the attributes of his character.[93]

The commercial activity exception was thus developed in part to prevent denials of justice to private parties injured in their business dealings with sovereign states. Moreover, it was acknowledged that no affront to the dignity and independence of foreign states could result from their involvement in legal proceedings concerning non-sovereign activities in which they had voluntarily engaged.[94] Indeed, as Lord

---

(24 December 2009).

93 *The Charkieh*, above note 16 at 99–100; *Thai-Europe*, above note 25 at 1491.

94 *Rahimtoola*, above note 25 at 422; *Trendtex*, above note 68 at 386.

Denning pithily observed, "[i]t is more in keeping with the dignity of a foreign sovereign to submit himself to the rule of law than to claim to be above it."[95]

Distinguishing between sovereign and non-sovereign state acts is not free of difficulties, as has been notably shown by Lauterpacht[96] and Crawford.[97] Insofar as the distinction is reflective of the separation of public and private law at the municipal level, courts have arrived at disparate conclusions as to what constitutes *acta jure imperii* and what does not, because the respective limits of public and private spheres vary from one jurisdiction to another, and from one period to the next. As was observed by the concurring judges in the *Arrest Warrant Case*, the category of *acta jure imperii* "is not fixed in stone" and is "subject to changing interpretation which varies with time reflecting the changing priorities of society."[98] To give one example, the purchase of army boots by a foreign government was held to be a sovereign act in France and a commercial act in Italy.[99] Also, depending on whether courts focus on the nature and/or the purpose of the impugned state activity, different characterizations may result. In Canada, "the proper approach to characterizing State activity is to view it in its entire context. This approach requires an examination predominantly of the nature of the activity, but its purpose can also be relevant."[100] By contrast, US courts characterize state acts exclusively by reference to their "nature," without regard to their "purpose," as required by § 1603(d) of the *FSIA*.

In *Bouzari*, the plaintiff, an Iranian oil and gas broker, alleged that he was abducted, held, and tortured by police officers because he refused to bribe a state official in connection to an oil-drilling venture. The question arose as to whether the commercial activity exception applied to the facts of the claim. Both the motions judge and the Court

95 *Rahimtoola*, *ibid.* at 418.

96 Lauterpacht, above note 8 at 222–26.

97 James Crawford, "International Law and Foreign Sovereigns: Distinguishing Immune Transactions" (1983) 54 Brit. Y.B. Int'l L. 75 [Crawford].

98 *Arrest Warrant Case*, Joint Separate Opinion of Judges Higgins, Koojimans, and Burgenthal, above note 2 at para. 72.

99 See *Cassaux v. Spain* (1849), S. 1849-I 81 and *Trutta v. Governo Rumeno* (1926), 3 Annual Digest 192, in *Sinclair*, above note 8 at 211.

100 *Re Canada Labour Code*, [1992] 2 S.C.R. 50 at 70.

of Appeal held that the impugned acts were not of a "commercial character" within the meaning of the *SIA*. Swinton J stated:

> Here, the activity or conduct that gives rise to the litigation was imprisonment by agents of the foreign State and acts of torture performed by them in a State prison. Even if the motive behind these acts was to obtain funds from Mr. Bouzari by way of ransom or to remove him from the South Pars project, the acts were those of State officials, and the funds paid were deposited to bank accounts of the State.
>
> In my view, regardless of the State's ultimate purpose, the exercise of police, law enforcement, and security powers are inherently exercises of governmental authority and sovereignty.[101]

Swinton J relied on the US Supreme Court decision in *Saudi Arabia v. Nelson* as authority for this last proposition. In that case, a plaintiff sought damages against Saudi Arabia for wrongful imprisonment, battery, and torture inflicted by police officers as retaliation against the plaintiff for reporting safety defects in his work place, a public hospital. A majority of the US Supreme Court held that the "conduct boils down to abuse of the power of its police by the Saudi government," upholding the latter's immunity on the basis that "a foreign State's exercise of the power of its police has long been understood for the purposes of the restrictive theory as particularly sovereign in nature."[102]

Mindful as she was of the differing Canadian and US approaches,[103] Swinton J's characterization of the impugned state acts appears inconsistent with the Canadian test and more in line with the US criterion, as she held the impugned acts to be inherently *jure imperii* "regardless of the State's ultimate purpose."[104] Swinton J held that, even if one assumed the conduct to be financially motivated and related to the oil-drilling project, the fact that "the acts were those of State officials, and the funds paid were deposited to bank accounts of the State" effectively brought them within the realm of *acta jure imperii*. Arguably, the court's analysis discloses an undue focus on the identity of the actors as state functionaries and offers little assessment of the Acts themselves or of the context in which they arose. As mentioned above,

101 *Bouzari 2002*, above note 23 at paras. 27–28.
102 *Saudi Arabia v. Nelson*, 507 U.S. 349 at 361 (1993) [*Nelson*].
103 *Bouzari 2002*, above note 23 at para. 29.
104 *Ibid.* at para. 28.

the distinguishing feature of the restrictive theory of immunity is precisely the relative unimportance it places on state participation in a given activity, the emphasis having shifted rather to the activity itself. It cannot be the case that the mere involvement of police officers in a given activity results, without more, in the classification of that activity as *jure imperii*.

Nevertheless, it cannot be said that the proceedings in *Bouzari* or *Nelson* related to a commercial activity. Both claims were for torture, and not, as the commercial activity exception requires, for breach of contract or default of commercial obligations. As noted by La Forest J, "it is not enough that the proceedings merely 'touch on' or 'incidentally affect'" a commercial activity. A "more substantial connection is needed" between the substance of the proceedings and impugned acts.[105] As neither the *Bouzari* nor *Nelson* claims were premised on the commercial relationship between the plaintiffs and the states they sued, the commercial activity exception to state immunity could not apply.

The peremptory prohibition of torture under international law does not alter the assessment of its non-commercial character. To the contrary, the decision to torture and to violate international law remains a governmental act. In *Letelier v. Chile*, the court stated that "a decision calculated to result in injury or death to a particular individual . . . made for whatever reason, would be one most assuredly involving policy judgment."[106] In that case however, immunity was ultimately denied since the impugned events occurred on US soil and it was held that, despite the governmental nature of political assassinations, "there is no discretion to commit, or to have one's officers or agents commit, an illegal act."[107] That result is to be contrasted with the one in *Jaffe* (1993) where the Ontario Court of Appeal held that the illegal and malicious conduct of state functionaries acting in the scope of their duties did not deprive them of the protection of the *SIA*. While it may be that the unlawfulness of a governmental act might give rise to a new exception to state immunity (as will be discussed below), illegality does not alter the character of an act once it has been classified as *jure imperii* or *gestionis* for the purposes of the statutory commercial activity exception. As Crawford noted, if a "transaction can fairly be

105 *Re Canada Labour Code*, above note 100 at 79.

106 *Letelier v. Chile*, 488 F. Supp. 665 at 673 (D.D.C. 1980) [*Letelier*].

107 *Ibid.*

classified as a 'commercial transaction' . . . then the transaction will not lose that character or classification because extraneous facts or aspects surrounding the individual transaction suggest or would attract a different classification."[108] If an exception to state immunity is to emerge in relation to unlawful acts, it should do so on its own merits and for its own reasons, and not by artificially shoe-horning illegal governmental conduct in the commercial activity exception.

2) Local Torts

The local torts exception was previously unavailable at common law prior to its inclusion in the various national statutes on jurisdictional immunities.[109] Though the exception is generally thought to have first appeared in the ECSI (Article 11), Fox notes that the Institut de droit international proposed an exception for delictual or quasi-delictual acts committed within the forum state in its 1891 Hamburg Resolutions.[110] In more recent times, the exception was applied to claims for personal injuries resulting from the negligent use of motor vehicles by foreign officials in the host state, though it was eventually widened to apply to all non-commercial torts committed by foreign state officials in the forum territory.[111] Endorsed by the ILC, the purpose of the tort exception is to allow injured parties to access justice and recover their losses in cases where the foreign state is bound to make reparation under the law of the forum. The exception generally covers insurable risks, as well as intentional, indeed criminal, misconduct occurring in the forum state.[112] The US, UK, and Canadian formulations of the exception all require a territorial connection between the tort and the forum state.[113]

---

108 Crawford, above note 97 at 96.

109 *Bouzari 2002*, above note 23 at para. 31.

110 Fox, above note 3 at 309. See Institut de droit international, Resolutions, 1891 Hamburg Sessions, Rapps. John Westlake, Ludwig von Bar, and Adolphe Hartmann, *Projet de règlement international sur la compétence des tribunaux dans les procès contre les Etats, souverains ou chefs d'Etat étrangers*, art. 4(6), which provides «*4. Les seules actions recevables contre un Etat étranger sont . . . (6) Les actions en dommages-intérêts nées d'un délit ou d'un quasi-délit, commis sur le territoire.*»

111 Fox, *ibid.*

112 *Draft Articles on Jurisdictional Immunities of States and Their Property and Commentary*, ILC Reports, 43rd session, 1991, A/46/10(Supp. 10) at 44–46.

113 UK *SIA*, above note 28, s. 5; *FSIA*, above note 31, s. 1605(a)(5); *SIA*, above note 50, s. 6.

In *Bouzari*, where the torture alleged occurred in Iran, the local tort exception was held not to apply, even if the lingering effects of the tort are felt in Canada.[114] This territorial restriction exceeds the ties typically required by Canadian rules for service *ex juris* where it is sufficient for the damage to be continued in the forum province. For example, as noted in Chapter 5, the Ontario *Rules of Civil Procedure* permit the service of originating process in proceedings "in respect of damage sustained in Ontario arising from a tort . . . wherever committed."[115] Thus, the local tort exception to state immunity can be viewed as striking a balance between the principles of territorial jurisdiction and state independence, allowing the forum state to exercise unimpeded authority over persons (including other states), things, and events within its territory, without going so far as permitting it to sit in judgment of extraterritorial state conduct.

Significantly, the tort exception applies regardless of the nature of the impugned act of state, be it *jure gestionis* or *jure imperii*. This was confirmed by the Supreme Court of Canada in *Schreiber* (2002), where a Canadian citizen sued Germany for personal injuries suffered in the course of his arrest and detention in Canada. The plaintiff was arrested and detained by Canadian officers at the behest of Germany, under the terms of a bilateral extradition treaty. The plaintiff alleged having suffered mental distress, denial of liberty, and damage to his reputation, all of which were held not to be "personal injuries" within the meaning of section 6 as they did not result from a bodily or physical injury. The United States intervened in the proceedings, urging the Supreme Court to read the Canadian local torts exception as applying solely to non-governmental acts.[116] However, on a plain reading of the relevant provision and relying on international authorities, the Court held "that the 'death or personal injury' restriction to immunity is applicable to both *jure imperii* and *jure gestionis* acts."[117]

In other words, the local torts exception hinges solely on territoriality, and not on the character of the impugned state act, and thus represents another, alternative rationale for the removal of immunity

114 *Bouzari 2002*, above note 23 at paras. 32–34.

115 R.R.O. 1990, Reg. 194, r. 17.02(h).

116 It is observed that the position advocated by the US State Department in *Schreiber* has not been accepted by US courts. See particularly *Letelier*, above note 106.

117 *Schreiber*, above note 10 at para. 36.

under the restrictive doctrine. Here, it is the *situs* of the state act that is determinative of its justiciability, not its sovereign or non-sovereign character. In this sense, the tort exception represents a further restriction on state immunity and is consistent with the principle noted in *The Schooner Exchange* that "the jurisdiction of a nation within its own territory is necessarily exclusive and absolute."[118]

Moreover, the exception is consistent with the imperatives of redress, that is, insofar as there exists a principled basis for doing so, the law commands that wrongs be righted and that justice be done.[119] To exclude the tortious governmental conduct of foreign states from the jurisdiction of national courts, when authority over such cases can otherwise be asserted, would seriously compromise the forum state's ability to do justice in its own territory. This is perhaps what the Supreme Court of Canada had in mind when, in refusing to apply a *jure imperii/gestionis* distinction to the tort exception, it stated:

> [T]he interpretation advanced by the United States would deprive the victims of the worst breaches of basic rights of any possibility of redress in national courts. Given the recent trends in the development of international humanitarian law enlarging this possibility in cases of international crime, . . . such a result would jeopardize at least in Canada a potentially important progress in the protection of the rights of the person. [120]

Given the local tort exception's reliance on the territoriality principle, it is unclear what convincing basis can be asserted in defence of a judicial extension of its ambit to include extraterritorial torts in absence of legislative action. It is thus likely to remain of limited application in transnational human rights litigation.

3) International Law

Finally, plaintiffs have argued that international law requires the denial of immunity in civil proceedings for violations of peremptory

---

118 *The Schooner Exchange*, above note 20 at 136–37.

119 As stated by Bingham MR, "that wrongs be remedied" is the rule of public policy "which has first claim on the loyalty of the law": *X (minors) v. Bedfordshire County Council*, [1995] 2 A.C. 633 at 663 (C.A.).

120 *Schreiber*, above note 10 at para. 37.

norms such as torture and that the various national immunity statutes should be construed accordingly. This line of argument runs along two alternate paths. First, in the US, UK, and Canada, Congress and Parliament are "not presumed to legislate in breach of a treaty or in any manner inconsistent with the comity of nations and the established rules of international law."[121] Relying on this interpretative presumption, plaintiffs have argued that the *Convention Against Torture* (CAT) obligates state parties to provide victims of torture with civil redress. Accordingly, when courts interpret state immunity legislation as barring civil claims, they *ipso facto* cause states to violate their treaty obligations. Second, plaintiffs have argued that the peremptory status of the torture prohibition itself requires the availability of a civil remedy and the denial of immunity for states that torture. As will be seen below, these arguments have not been successful in Canadian and English courts, but they have gained some traction in the Italian courts.

a) The *Convention Against Torture*[122]

Under the CAT, state parties (including the US, UK, and Canada) agreed to prohibit torture under their criminal law (Article 4) and to prosecute or extradite all torturers present in their territory (Article 5) regardless of where the torture occurred. Article 14 of the CAT obligates a state party to "ensure in its legal system that the victim of an act of torture obtains redress and has an enforceable right to fair and adequate compensation," without indicating, however, whether such a remedy is to be made available with regards to extraterritorial torture. One possible interpretation is that the absence of territorial language in Article 14 indicates that the provision has no geographical constraints and is applicable to torture wherever committed. The opposite view was taken by the courts in *Bouzari* and *Jones*, namely, that Article 14 is "not designed to require . . . [State B] to provide redress in its civil legal system for acts of torture committed in State A."[123] As for state practice, the court in *Bouzari* noted that "both at the time the treaty was signed and since, . . . no State interprets Article 14 to require it to

121 *Daniels v. White*, [1968] S.C.R. 517 at 541; Gibran van Ert, *Using International Law in Canadian Courts*, 2d ed. (Toronto: Irwin Law, 2008) c. 5 [van Ert].

122 *Convention Against Torture and other Cruel, Inhumane and Degrading Treatment and Punishment*, GA Res. 39/46, 39 U.N. GAOR Supp. No. 51 at 197, UN Doc. A/39/51 (1984), 1465 U.N.T.S. 85, entered into force on 26 June 1987 [CAT].

123 *Jones 2004*, above note 73 at para. 21.

take civil jurisdiction over a foreign State for acts committed outside the forum State."[124]

Reasonable people can disagree as to the meaning of Article 14. Unfortunately, the surrounding treaty provisions do very little to clarify its scope: its position among other articles containing territorial restrictions can suggest both that it too should apply solely to torture committed within the jurisdiction of a party state or, alternatively, that the drafters deliberately omitted geographical language to encapsulate torture wherever committed. Following a purposive interpretation as directed by Article 31 of the *Vienna Convention on the Law of Treaties*, this second possibility appears to resonate with the aim of the CAT, as expressed in the preamble, "to make more effective the struggle against torture . . . throughout the world." However, proponents of this interpretation eventually face the task of justifying why the putative grant of universal civil jurisdiction was not formulated in a manner resembling the grant of universal criminal jurisdiction under Article 5. The enigma deepens when one considers the drafting history of Article 14, which reveals that, at one point, following a Netherlands proposal, it contained the words "committed in any territory under its jurisdiction." While the decision to include the phrase is documented, its ultimate exclusion remains inexplicable, except perhaps, as surmised by Andrew Byrnes, as the result of a mistaken omission.[125]

Byrnes further points to an uncontested "understanding" entered by the United States "that Article 14 requires a State party to provide a private right of action for damages only for acts of torture committed in territory under the jurisdiction of that State party."[126] Internal Canadian practice however may be evidence of a possible wider construction of Article 14. In 1988, with the enactment of the *Torture Prohibition Act* (*TPA*) the Yukon legislature explicitly created a civil cause of action for torture. After recognizing in its preamble that Canada is a party to

---

124 *Bouzari 2002*, above note 23 at para. 50.

125 Andrew Byrnes "Civil Remedies for Torture Committed Abroad: An Obligation Under the Convention Against Torture?" in Craig Scott, ed., *Torture as Tort: Comparative Perspectives on the Development of Transnational Human Rights Litigation* (Oxford: Hart, 2001) at 542–49 [Byrnes]. On the drafting history of art. 14, see Manfred Nowak & Elizabeth McArthur, *The United Nations Convention Against Torture: A Commentary* (Oxford: Oxford University Press, 2008) at 452–61 [Nowak & McArthur].

126 Byrnes, *ibid.* at 546.

the CAT, the *Yukon Act* provides that "every public official, and every person acting at the instigation of or with the consent or acquiescence of a public official, who inflicts torture on any other person commits a tort and is liable and renders his or her employer liable to pay damages to the victim of the torture."[127] Section 5 of the Act defines "public official" as "any person in the public service of the Yukon (a) who is authorized to do or enforce the doing of any act or thing or to exercise any power, or (b) upon whom any duty is imposed by or under any act." While it is clear that the Act only imputes the civil liability of Yukon public officials who commit torture, it does not place any territorial restrictions on the torture itself. Under the Act, it is thus possible to sue the Yukon for torture committed by its officials, whether in Whitehorse, Washington, or Wellington. As such, it cannot be said that the Yukon legislation is inconsistent with Article 14 of the CAT, which, if nothing else, underscores that provision's ambiguity.

Professor Greenwood (as he then was) noted in 2002 that the CAT monitoring body—the Committee against Torture—had not disapproved of the US "understanding" or otherwise clarified the scope of Article 14.[128] This is not entirely accurate. In a 2000 report on its compliance with CAT obligations, and with specific reference to Article 14(2)[129] and to the US *Torture Victims Protection Act* (*TVPA*),[130] the Committee against Torture praised the United States for its "broad legal recourse to compensation for victims of torture, whether or not such torture occurred in the United States of America."[131] Without going so far as stating that Article 14 mandated remedies for extraterritorial torture, the Committee's approval of the *TVPA* in specific reference to Article 14 is arguably supportive of this interpretation. In any event, whatever weight the US executive "understanding" of Article 14 might have had upon ratification of the CAT in 1990, it was almost certainly superseded by the statements of both houses of Congress when they enacted the *TVPA*. In their 1991 reports accompanying the *TVPA* bill, both the House of Representatives and the Senate explicitly noted that

---

127 *Torture Prohibition Act*, S.Y. 1988 c. 26, s. 1. [*YTPA*].

128 *Bouzari 2002*, above note 23 at para. 51.

129 Article 14(2) provides that "[n]othing in this article shall affect any right of the victim or other persons to compensation which may exist under national law."

130 See Chapter 3.

131 Conclusions and Recommendations of the Committee against Torture: United States of America, UN Doc. A/55/44 (2000) at § 178(b).

the *TVPA* was primarily intended to implement the Article 14 obligation to provide civil jurisdiction over torture. The congressional reports explicitly refer to *Filártiga v. Peña-Irala*,[132] a landmark case on civil redress for extraterritorial torture, and to the general "no safe haven" policy the *TVPA* implements with respect to foreign officials who commit torture. For example, in its report, the Senate Committee on the Judiciary stated that "this legislation will carry out the intent of the CAT . . . . This legislation will do precisely that—by making sure that torturers and death squads will no longer have a safe haven in the United States."[133] Also, US courts have consistently characterized the *TVPA* as an implementation of the CAT obligation under Article 14 to provide a private remedy for torture,[134] and accordingly routinely assert civil jurisdiction over acts of torture committed outside the United States by foreign officials.[135]

Further clarification regarding the territorial and substantive scope of Article 14 came in 2005 as the Committee against Torture considered Canada's periodic report. After hearing testimony concerning, among other issues, the dismissal of the *Bouzari* case, the Committee against Torture expressed concern at "the absence [in Canada] of effective measures to provide civil compensation to victims of torture *in all cases*" and recommended that Canada "review its position under article 14 of the Convention to ensure the provision of compensation through its civil jurisdiction to *all victims of torture*."[136] These observations and recommendations from the Committee support a broader

---

132 *Filártiga v. Peña-Irala*, 630 F.2d 876 (2d Cir 1980).

133 Senate Committee on the Judiciary, Report on the *Torture Victim Protection Act of 1991* to accompany s. 313, as amended, S. Rep. No. 249, 102d Cong., 1st Sess. (1991). See also Committee on Foreign Affairs and on the Judiciary, House of Representatives, Report to accompany HR 2092, H.R. Rep. No. 367, 102d Cong., 1st Sess., pt. 1 (1991). Both congressional reports are reprinted in Beth Stephens *et al.*, *International Human Rights Litigation in U.S. Courts*, 2d ed. (The Hague: Brill, 2008) App. E at 561 and 568 [Stephens].

134 *Flores v. Southern Peru Copper Corp.*, 414 F.3d 233 at 247, n. 20 (2d Cir. 2002); *Price v. Socialist People's Libyan Arab Jamahiriya*, 294 F.3d 82 at 92 (D.C. Cir. 2002). See also Stephens, *ibid.* at 77–79.

135 As noted in Stephens, *ibid.* at 281: "Until the mid-1990s, international human rights litigation in U.S. courts focused primarily on lawsuits against foreign government officials sued for violations committed outside the United States."

136 Conclusions and recommendations of the Committee against Torture: Canada, UN CAT, 34th Sess., UN Doc. CAT/C/CR/34/CAN (2005) at §§ 4(g) and 5(f) [emphasis added].

interpretation of Article 14, but arguably still leave room for doubt. As Nowak and McArthur point out, the Committee could have ended all speculation by, "for instance, ending its expression of concern with the words 'wherever or by whomever committed.'"[137]

Since 2005 the Committee against Torture has made similar comments and recommendations to other state parties to the CAT.[138] In 2006, the Committee recommended that the Republic of Korea "ensure in its legal system . . . that *all victims* obtain redress and have an enforceable right to fair and adequate compensation."[139] Similarly, in 2007, the Committee recommended that Japan "should take all necessary measure[s] to ensure that *all victims* of acts of torture or ill-treatment can exercise fully their right to redress, including compensation and rehabilitation."[140] Most recently, in 2009, the Committee urged New Zealand to "consider withdrawing its reservation to article 14 of the Convention and ensure the provision of fair and adequate compensation through its civil jurisdiction to *all victims of torture*."[141] These repeated references to "all victims" of torture ostensibly include persons who were tortured abroad.

In *Jones* (2006), the House of Lords gave short shrift to the Committee's recommendations to Canada. Lord Bingham noted that the Committee was "not an exclusively legal and not an adjudicative body" and that "whatever its value in influencing the trend of international thinking, the legal authority of this recommendation is slight."[142] Lord Hoffman was more severe in his appraisal of the Committee's work. He stated: "Quite why Canada was singled out for this treatment is unclear, but as interpretation of article 14 or a statement of

137 Nowak & McArthur, above note 125 at 493.

138 See List of issues (Benin), UN Doc. CAT/C/BEN/Q/2 (2007) at para. 20 and List of issues (Ukraine), UN Doc. CAT/C/UKR/Q/5/Rev.1 (2007) at para. 30 where the Committee asked Benin and Ukraine to clarify whether existing compensation mechanisms were available to non-nationals as required by art. 14.

139 Conclusions and recommendations of the Committee against Torture: Republic of Korea, UN CAT, 36th Sess., UN Doc. CAT/C/KOR/CO/2 (2006) at para. 8(a) [emphasis added].

140 Conclusions and recommendations of the Committee against Torture: Japan, UN CAT, 38th Sess., UN Doc. CAT/C/JPN/CO/1 (2007) at para. 23 [emphasis added].

141 Conclusions and recommendations of the Committee against Torture: New Zealand, UN CAT, 42nd Sess., UN Doc CAT/C/NZL/CO/5 (2009) at para. 14 [emphasis added].

142 *Jones 2006*, above note 90 at para. 23, Lord Bingham.

international law, I regard it as having no value."[143] These are baffling pronouncements.[144]

While reports and recommendations from treaty-monitoring bodies are not binding, they are nevertheless persuasive authority that international courts properly refer to in framing treaty obligations.[145] Canadian courts regularly consult and apply the interpretations proffered by treaty-monitoring bodies. For instance, in *Suresh* (2002), the Supreme Court of Canada relied on a 2000 report from the Committee against Torture to support its reading of the CAT in that case.[146] Other such examples abound in Canadian law,[147] illustrating that Canadian courts are receptive to the authoritative interpretations advanced by treaty-monitoring bodies. Justice La Forest described the Canadian judicial approach to treaty monitoring bodies in these terms: "[W]e do not confine ourselves to polite references to the international agreements themselves, but examine with care the interpretations given to them by international institutions."[148]

Some commentators argue that, through their reports and recommendations, treaty-monitoring bodies have a measurable impact on the development of international law as a whole. According to van Ert,

> the reports, statements and recommendations of treaty-monitoring bodies serve principally to ensure compliance with their respective instruments. They also serve, however, to elucidate and develop the content of the international obligations they enforce. In this sense, the treaty-monitoring bodies may not only apply international law but also develop it.[149]

---

143 *Ibid.* at para. 57, Lord Hoffman.

144 Nowak & McArthur, above note 125 at 500.

145 *Legal Consequences of the Construction of a Wall in the Occupied Palestinian Territory*, Advisory Opinion, [2004] I.C.J. Rep. 136 at paras. 109–12 (relying on the views of two treaty-monitoring bodies for the geographic scope of their respective treaties).

146 *Suresh v. Canada (M.C.I.)*, [2002] 1 S.C.R. 3 at para. 73.

147 See, for example, *Li v. Canada (M.C.I.)*, [2005] F.C.J. No. 1 at paras. 20–24 (C.A.); *Li v. Canada (M.C.I.)*, [2003] F.C.J. No. 1934 at paras. 34–35 (Fed. Ct.); *Bouaouni v. Canada (M.C.I.)*, [2003] F.C.J. No. 1540 at paras. 34–40 (Fed. Ct.); *Thamotharampillai v. Canada (M.C.I.)*, [2001] F.C.J. No. 599 at paras. 24–30 (Fed. Ct.); *Gosselin v. Quebec (P.G.)*, [1999] J.Q. no 1365 at paras. 342–47 (C.A.).

148 Gérard V. La Forest, "The Expanding Role of the Supreme Court of Canada in International Law Issues" (1996) 34 Can. Y.B. Int'l L. 89 at 98.

149 van Ert, above note 121 at 38.

Of course the power to recommend and the ultimate weight of the recommendations very much depend on the mandate of the monitoring body as defined in the treaty itself. By the terms of the CAT, all 146 state parties are obligated to report to the Committee against Torture, which is composed of "experts of . . . recognized competence in the field of human rights" (Article 17). The CAT empowers the Committee to make "such comments or suggestions on the report as it considers appropriate" (Article 19). The House of Lords in *Jones* (2006) was improperly dismissive of the Committee against Torture's paramount role in interpreting the CAT and effectively devalued the international legal framework of the convention with which the United Kingdom agreed to comply. As demonstrated above, the House of Lords' dismissal of the Committee against Torture's recommendations is not in line with Canadian practice and policy.

The text of Article 14 is capable of bearing both a restrictive and a broad interpretation. According to Nowak & McArthur, the prevailing view is that "State parties are not yet legally required by Article 14(1) to ensure universal civil jurisdiction before their domestic courts. However this provision may be interpreted differently in the near future."[150] Indeed, human rights treaties, much like constitutions, are properly regarded as living instruments[151] and should be interpreted generously, with a view of progressively fulfilling their primary object and purpose. The object and purpose of the CAT is "to make more effective the struggle against torture . . . throughout the world."[152] Courts should therefore prefer interpretations of Article 14 that further that fundamental goal. As indicated above, the practice of the Committee against Torture since 2005 supports the perspective that Article 14 applies to both local and extraterritorial torture.

150 Nowak & McArthur, above note 125 at 502.

151 The House of Lords stated with reference to the Geneva Conventions: "It is clear that the signatory states intended that the Convention should afford continuing protection for refugees in the changing circumstances of the present and future world. In our view *the Convention has to be regarded as a living instrument: just as, by the Strasbourg jurisprudence, the European Convention on Human Rights is so regarded*": *R. v. Secretary of State for the Home Department, Ex Parte Adan*, [2000] UKHL 67 at para. 18, citing with approval Laws LJ's decision at the Court of Appeal, [1999] 3 W.L.R. 1274 at 1296 (C.A.) [emphasis added]. See also Shaheed Fatima, *Using International Law in Domestic Courts* (Oxford: Hart, 2005) at 100.

152 CAT, above note 122, Preamble.

b) Peremptory Norms

It has also been argued that the peremptory prohibition of torture includes a concomitant state obligation to provide victims with a remedy and that state immunity statutes should be interpreted accordingly.[153] The argument is one of normative hierarchy: *jus cogens* rules are said to "trump" incompatible international norms, such as state immunity, which can be waived by states or overridden by the exceptions developed under the restrictive theory. By contrast, as was stated in *Furundzija*, peremptory norms

> . . . cannot be derogated from by States through international treaties or local or special customs or even general customary rules not endowed with the same normative force. Clearly, the *jus cogens* nature of the prohibition against torture articulates the notion that the prohibition has now become one of the most fundamental standards of the international community.[154]

Article 53 of the *Vienna Convention on the Law of Treaties* defines *jus cogens* as "a norm accepted and recognized by the international community of States as a whole as a norm from which no derogation is permitted and which can be modified only by a subsequent norm of general international law having the same character."[155] In *Bouzari* (2002), following the majority's decision in *Al-Adsani* (2002), the court held that there is no "general State practice which provides an exception from State immunity for acts of torture committed outside the forum State" and that "there is no conflict between the [*SIA*] as written, with its limited exceptions, and customary international law."[156] The courts in *Bouzari* (2004) and *Jones* (2004) and (2006) agreed.

Not only was there no conflict in the *Bouzari* court's view among the peremptory prohibition of torture and state immunity, the court further opined that "there is an ongoing rule of customary international law providing immunity for acts of torture committed outside

153 See *Siderman de Blake v. Republic of Argentina*, 965 F.2d 699 (9th Cir. 1992) [*Siderman*]; *Princz v. Federal Republic of Germany*, 26 F.3d 1166 (D.C. Cir. 1994) [*Princz*]; *Bouzari 2002*, above note 23; *Al-Adsani 2001*, below note 162; *Jones 2004*, above note 73; *Bouzari 2004*, above note 70.

154 *Prosecutor v. Anto Furundzija*, IT-95-17/1-T, Trial Judgment (10 December 1998) at paras. 153–54 (International Criminal Tribunal for the Former Yugoslavia).

155 *Vienna Convention on the Law of Treaties*, 23 May 1969, 1155 U.N.T.S. 331, art. 53.

156 *Bouzari 2002*, above note 23 at para. 73.

the forum State."[157] There are serious reasons to doubt the accuracy of this proposition. While judicial decisions are evidence of state practice for the purposes of finding custom, it is highly unlikely that the few judgments in civil proceedings for extraterritorial torture against foreign states have resulted in the crystallization of a customary norm upholding state immunity in such cases. At the time it was decided *Bouzari*, after *Al-Adsani*, was the second case of its kind in the Commonwealth. Even in the United States, where transnational human rights litigation began, there have only been a handful of cases in which damages were sought against foreign states for extraterritorial torture. Moreover, each of these decisions ultimately turned on judicial precedent and on the particularities of the forum's own immunity legislation, not on a general interpretation of customary international law. Most notably, in the US, judicial development in the area of *jus cogens* and state immunity was arrested by the Supreme Court's decision in *Amerada Hess* where the *FSIA* was held to be "the sole basis for obtaining jurisdiction over a foreign State," with the result that "immunity is granted in those cases involving alleged violations of international law that do not come within one of the FSIA's exceptions."[158] In *Siderman*, the court stated that, "as a matter of international law, the [*jus cogens*] argument carries much force." The court continued, "unfortunately we do not write on a clean slate . . . . We must interpret the FSIA through the prism of *Amerada Hess*."[159] Accordingly, the jurisprudential progeny of the US Supreme Court's restrictive interpretation of the *FSIA* in *Amerada Hess* does not afford much guidance in determining what effect, if any, the violations of *jus cogens* norms should have on the law of state immunity elsewhere.

The decisions of the ICJ in the *Arrest Warrant Case* and of the European Court of Human Rights (ECtHR) in *Al-Adsani* are no doubt instructive as concerning the interplay of immunity and *jus cogens* but

157 *Ibid*. at para. 63.

158 *Amerada Hess*, above note 58 at 434–36.

159 *Siderman*, above note 153 at 718. Also bound by *Amerada Hess* were the decisions in *Sampson v. Federal Republic of Germany*, 250 F.3d 1145 (7th Cir. 2001) (Germany immune for mass murder of plaintiff's family and detention in Nazi concentration camp); *Smith v. Socialist People's Libyan Arab Jamahiriya*, 101 F.3d 239 (2d Cir. 1996) (Libya immune in relation to the bombing of Pam Am 103 over Lockerbie); *Princz*, above note 153 (Germany immune in connection to slave labour in Nazi concentration camps); and *Nelson*, above note 102 (Saudi Arabia immune in a claim for torture by police officers).

remain ultimately inconclusive as to the requirements of customary law. In the *Arrest Warrant Case*, the ICJ upheld the immunity of foreign ministers (not the state) from criminal (not civil) proceedings, in relation to war crimes and crimes against humanity. The majority held the immunity of incumbent ministers to be absolute on the functional basis that ministers ought to be able to perform their duties without impediments (*ne impediatur legatio*), a rationale quite different from that of state immunity (*par in parem not habet imperium*).[160] Surprisingly, the majority sidestepped the issue of *jus cogens* and normative hierarchy (the words "jus cogens" do not appear in the judgment, save in a quotation of Lord Millet from *Pinochet*), referring instead only to "serious crimes." By contrast, the dissenting opinions of Judge Al-Khasawneh and Judge *ad hoc* van der Wyngaert take into account the tension between immunity and *jus cogens*, holding that the latter should prevail in case of conflict insofar as they are reflective of the common and vital interests of the international community.[161]

In *Al-Adsani*, a Kuwaiti national sued the State of Kuwait in British courts for the torture he suffered in that country. The High Court held that the applicant's claim did not fall within the exceptions of the UK *SIA*. The Court of Appeal agreed that none of the exceptions to immunity applied and that no new exception could be created. The House of Lords denied leave to appeal. At the ECtHR, Al-Adsani argued that the UK had effectively denied his rights under the *European Convention on Human Rights* (ECHR) to be free from torture (Article 3) and to access justice (Article 6). The ECtHR unanimously held that the UK had not caused or contributed to the torture of Al-Adsani in Kuwait, thus dismissing the Article 3 claim. The court then queried whether, by upholding Kuwait's immunity, the UK had deprived Al-Adsani of his right to bring a civil claim and seek redress under Article 6, an issue that eventually split the court 9:8. Though the majority recognized the peremptory status of the torture prohibition, it declined to give effect to that characterization in terms of normative hierarchy. Acknowledging that the *jus cogens* nature of the torture prohibition entailed the removal of immunity of individuals in criminal trials, the majority observed that no such rule had emerged with regards to

160 *Arrest Warrant Case*, Judgment, above note 2 at paras. 53–58.
161 *Ibid.*, Dissenting Opinion of Judge Al-Khasawneh at para. 7.

immunity of states in the context of civil proceedings.[162] Eight judges strongly disagreed with the majority's distinction between criminal and civil proceedings in deciding how peremptory norms should be applied with regards to state immunity.[163]

The majority's decision in *Al-Adsani* begs more questions than it answers. If one accepts, as did the ECtHR, that peremptory norms enjoy "a higher rank in the international hierarchy than treaty law and even 'ordinary' customary rules"[164] on what basis can this normative anteriority be disregarded in relation to state immunity? One answer to this question was offered by Fox, and endorsed by Lord Bingham in *Jones* (2006):

> State immunity is a procedural rule going to the jurisdiction of a national court. It does not go to substantive law; it does not contradict a prohibition contained in a *jus cogens* norm but merely diverts any breach of it to a different method of settlement. Arguably, then, there is no substantive content in the procedural plea of State immunity upon which a *jus cogens* mandate can bite.[165]

Fox's analysis is problematic for a few reasons. First, there is no "different method of settlement" for the torture victim who has died from her injuries (such as Zahra Kazemi)[166] or for survivors who cannot reasonably be expected to return to the country where they were tortured to seek redress (such as Houshang Bouzari or Maher Arar).[167] Where alternative compensation schemes exist, they often remain inaccessible to substantial classes of victims.[168] Indeed, the plaintiffs in *Princz*[169] and the recent Italian cases[170] "had attempted to adjudicate their dispute in Germany but were refused access to the courts because they did not

---

162 *Al-Adsani v. United Kingdom* (2001), 34 E.H.R.R. 273 at para. 66 [*Al-Adsani 2001*].

163 *Ibid.* See the dissenting opinions of Judges Rozakis and Calflisch, joined by Judges Wildhaber, Costa, Cabral Barreto, and Vajić. Judges Ferrari Bravo and Loucaides each issued separate dissenting reasons along similar lines.

164 *Al-Adsani 2001*, *ibid.* at para. 60.

165 Fox, above note 3 at 525. See also *Jones 2006*, above note 90 at para. 24, Lord Bingham.

166 *Kazemi*, above note 74.

167 *Bouzari 2004* and *Arar*, above notes 70 and 72, respectively.

168 Lorna McGregor, "Torture and State Immunity: Deflecting Impunity, Distorting Sovereignty" (2008) 18 E.J.I.L. 903 at 906 [McGregor].

169 *Princz*, above note 153.

170 See below notes 210–15 and accompanying text.

fall within the precise terms of national legislation on compensation for crimes committed during World War II."[171] As those cases illustrate, the application of state immunity does not redirect the claims to an alternative forum, but rather manages to ensure the impunity of the wrongdoers and to deny survivors the fair and equitable compensation to which they are entitled.[172]

Secondly, as Orakhelashvili correctly pointed out, "international law knows of no straightforward distinction between 'substantive' and 'procedural' norms. All international norms derive from the agreement of states or acceptance by the international community as a whole, and there are neither established criteria nor a recognized agency to split them into such categories." [173] A norm forms part of *jus cogens* or it does not. Once the international community recognizes the peremptory character of a given norm — as it has done with respect to the torture prohibition — all other norms of international law must be interpreted and applied consistently with that characterization. National courts should strive to avoid inconsistencies by giving full effect to the peremptoriness of the international norms they apply in the domestic legal order, irrespective of the substantive or procedural nature of that effect, subject only to specific and contrary direction from Parliament. As the Supreme Court of Canada stated in *R. v. Hape*, "Parliamentary sovereignty dictates that a legislature may violate international law, but that it must do so expressly. Absent an express derogation, the courts may look to prohibitive rules of customary international law to aid in the interpretation of Canadian law and the development of the common law." [174] In other words, it is the entire body of domestic law — be it substantive or procedural, statutory or common law — that must be interpreted and developed consistently with international law.[175]

---

171 McGregor, above note 168 at 906.

172 *Basic Principles and Guidelines on the Right to a Remedy and Reparation for Victims of Gross Violations of International Human Rights Law and Serious Violations of International Humanitarian Law*, GA Res. 60/147, UNGAOR, 60th Sess., UN doc. A/RES/60/147 (2006).

173 Alexander Orakhelashvili, "State Immunity and the Hierarchy of Norms: Why the House of Lords Got It Wrong" (2007) 18:5 E.J.I.L 955 at 968 [Orakhelashvili].

174 *R. v. Hape*, [2007] 2 S.C.R. 292 at para. 39.

175 See Chapter 4.

Another related question is the apparent inconsistency in the law of state immunity with respect to criminal and civil proceedings. The House of Lords held in *Jones* (2006) and *Pinochet III* that the universal criminal jurisdiction over torture "implies" the removal of immunity *ratione materiea* in criminal matters, but not in civil proceedings,[176] presumably because the concept of universal civil jurisdiction was not understood at the time as being firmly established at international law.[177] Accordingly, if such a notion were to become part of general international law, it too, "by necessary implication" would cause the removal of immunity *ratione materiae* in civil proceedings.[178] But in *Jones* (2006) Lord Bingham went on to state "the distinction between criminal proceedings (which were the subject of universal jurisdiction under the Torture Convention) and civil proceedings (which were not) was fundamental to [the *Pinochet III*] decision. This is not a distinction which can be wished away."[179] With respect, Lord Bingham's account of *Pinochet III* is incomplete. While the universal criminal jurisdiction mandated under the CAT was unquestionably central to the denial of immunity in that case, some of the lords also shored up their conclusion on the basis of the overriding effect of peremptory norms with respect to conflicting immunities.[180] It is thus unclear why peremptory norms could not have the same overriding effect in civil proceedings.

Factitious distinctions between procedure and substance, or between criminal and civil proceedings, fail to address the superiority of peremptory norms and the determinative effect their higher rank is meant to produce. As properly noted by the dissenting judges in *Al-Adsani* (2001), such distinctions are not

> . . . consonant with the very essence of the operation of the *jus cogens* rules. It is not the nature of the proceedings which determines the effects that a *jus cogens* rule has upon another rule of international law, but the character of the rule as a peremptory norm and its interaction with a hierarchically lower rule. The prohibition of torture,

176 *Jones 2006*, above note 90 at para. 89, Lord Hoffman; *Pinochet III*, above note 55 at 205, Lord Browne-Wilkinson; and at 264, Lord Hutton.

177 See Chapter 5, Section B(3); Donald Francis Donovan & Anthea Roberts, "The Emerging Recognition of Universal Civil Jurisdiction" (2006) 100 A.J.I.L. 142.

178 *Jones 2006*, above note 90 at para. 71, Lord Hoffman.

179 *Ibid.* at para. 32, Lord Bingham.

180 See, for example, *Pinochet III*, above note 55 at 247, Lord Hutton; at 278, Lord Millet; and at 289, Lord Phillips.

> being a rule of *jus cogens*, acts in the international sphere and deprives the rule of sovereign immunity of all its legal effects in that sphere. *The criminal or civil nature of the domestic proceedings is immaterial.* The jurisdictional bar is lifted by the very interaction of the international rules involved [be they substantive or procedural], and the national judge cannot admit a plea of immunity.[181]

As will be seen below, this reasoning has recently found traction in the Italian courts in civil proceedings against Germany for war crimes and crimes against humanity.[182]

E. A RESIDUAL COMMON LAW OF STATE IMMUNITY

Whereas courts in the US and Canada have characterized their respective immunity statutes as exhaustive codifications of immunity law, the House of Lords has taken a wider view of the UK *SIA*. In *Amerada Hess* (1989), the US Supreme Court, held the *FSIA* to be "the sole basis for obtaining jurisdiction over a foreign State," with the result that "immunity is granted in those cases involving alleged violations of international law that do not come within one of the FSIA's exceptions."[183] The Court of Appeal for Ontario took a similar position in *Bouzari* (2004).[184] By contrast, in *Lampen-Wolfe* (2000), Lord Hope explained that

> immunity which is accorded by English law to foreign States in civil proceedings is the subject of two separate regimes. The first is that laid down by Part I of the State Immunity Act 1978 . . . . The second regime is that under the common law. It applies to all cases that fall outside the scope of Part I of the Act."[185]

---

181 *Al-Adsani 2001*, above note 162, Joint Dissenting Opinion of Judges Rozakis and Calflisch, to which Judges Wildhaber, Costa, Cabral Barreto, and Vajić subscribed, at para. 4. Dissenting Judges Ferrari Bravo and Loucaides also rejected the criminal-civil distinction for analogous reasons.

182 See below notes 210–15 and accompanying text.

183 *Amerada Hess*, above note 58 at 434–36.

184 *Bouzari 2004*, above note 70 at paras. 56–59.

185 *Lampen-Wolfe*, above note 55 at 1575–76. Section 16(2) of the UK *SIA* provides for the Act's own inapplicability in claims involving visiting forces. In *Lampen-Wolfe*, a claim involving an allegedly defamatory performance report produced by a US military education services officer, s. 16(2) was held to result in the *SIA* inapplicability and the immunity issues was resolved under the common law.

In so stating, the House of Lords effectively rejected the view taken by the Court of Appeal in *Al-Adsani* (1996) that the UK *SIA* is a "comprehensive code."[186] The common law applies to "all cases" not explicitly covered in Part 1 of the UK *SIA*. Under the common law analysis, as concisely summarized by Lord Millet, "the question is whether, in accordance with the law laid down in *I Congreso* . . . the act complained of was *jure imperii* or *jure gestionis*. This must be judged against the background of the whole context in which the claim is made."[187] Fox agrees "the Act has not replaced the common law in its entirety . . . . [T]he common law of State immunity continues to apply to proceedings relating to a foreign State which are excluded from the Act."[188]

The existence in England of a common law regime of state immunity operating in tandem with the *SIA* affords some measure of flexibility and responsiveness to changing customary law. Indeed, as shown in Chapter 4, customary norms are immediately incorporated into the common law. Accordingly, if international practice eventually gave rise to further exceptions to state immunity, these would arguably be valid in the UK by virtue of the common law. The UK *SIA* applies exclusively to the exceptions codified therein and does not preclude the application by English courts of further exceptions forged by state practice and received in the common law. Of course, it is not suggested that the common law should be used to circumvent the written exceptions contained in the UK *SIA*, such as commercial activity or local torts. Rather, it is contended that the common law may act as a conduit for the reception of new or emerging customary exceptions consistent with but not already contained within the four corners of the immunity legislation, such as violations of international law.[189] Arguably, it is open to courts, pursuant to their inherent jurisdiction to modify the common law, to develop new exceptions to state immunity, which in their view reflect emerging international law.[190]

---

186 *Al-Adsani v. Kuwait* (1996), 107 I.L.R. 536 at 538–47 (C.A.).

187 *Lampen-Wolfe*, above note 55 at 1585.

188 Fox, above note 3 at 136

189 By analogy, see *R. v. Amato*, [1982] 2 S.C.R. 418 at 443, where Estey J noted that the "common law would be allowed to develop defences not inconsistent with the provisions of the *Criminal Code*."

190 For an earlier version of this argument, see François Larocque, "*Bouzari v. Iran*: Testing the Limits of State Immunity in Canadian Courts" (2003) 41 Can. Y.B. Int'l L. 343. See also François Larocque, "La *Loi sur l'immunité des états* canadienne et la torture" (2010) 55 McGill L.J. 81 in which it is argued that the Court of Ap-

However as the UK experience shows, there is little or no curial appetite for the recognition of further exceptions to state immunity at common law. The Court of Appeal in *Jones* (2004) attempted to carve out a new exception in proceedings against state officials for torture. Noting that "the [UK *SIA*] makes no express reference to the position of individual officials of the State,"[191] the Court of Appeal went to great lengths to distinguish binding precedent and to conclude that Saudi Arabia had no "absolute right to claim immunity in respect of civil claims against its officials for systematic torture."[192] While the Court of Appeal's judgment discloses a certain measure of willingness to further develop the common law of state immunity, such developments cannot occur in a vacuum. In *Jones* (2006), the House of Lords overturned the decision below, reaffirming the rule in *Propend* (1997) that the UK *SIA* affords "individual employees or officers of a foreign state 'protection under the same cloak as protecting the state itself.'"[193]

F. *DE LEGE FERENDA*: RECONCILING *JUS COGENS* AND *ACTA JURE IMPERII*

Let us disregard the *SIA* for the sake of discussion. Assuming a court may properly assert jurisdiction over a transnational human rights claim, on what basis should immunity be upheld or denied? At first glance, following the principles of *I Congreso*, the problem presents itself as whether the impugned conduct can be characterized as an *actus jure imperii*. Under the view espoused by Lord Hoffman in *Jones* (2006), given the definitional requirement of the CAT that torture be "inflicted by or at the instigation of or with the consent or acquiescence of a public official or other person in an official capacity,"[194] torture will always be an *actus jure imperii*, and thus always entitled to immunity. Such circular reasoning fails to distinguish between acts performed by public officials and the legal character of those acts, that is, whether they represent the lawful exercise of sovereign authority. The better view was taken in *Jones* (2004) by Mance LJ:

---

peal for Ontario erred in characterizing the Canadian *SIA* as exhaustive enactment of state immunity.

191 *Jones 2004*, above note 73 at para. 31.

192 *Ibid.* at para. 96.

193 *Jones 2006* above note 90 at para. 68, Lord Hoffman, citing *Propend Finance Pty Ltd v Sing* (1997), 111 I.L.R 611 at 669 (E.W.C.A.).

194 CAT, above note 122, art. 1; See *Jones 2006*, above note 90 at para. 83, Lord Hoffman.

> [T]he requirement that the pain or suffering be inflicted by a public official does no more in my view than identify the author and the public context in which the author must be acting. It does not lend to the acts of torture themselves any official or governmental character or nature, or mean that it can in any way be regarded as an official function to inflict, or that an official can be regarded as representing the state in inflicting, such pain or suffering.[195]

As Judges Higgins, Koojimans, and Burgenthal stated in the *Arrest Warrant* case, the notion of *acta jure imperii* is continually evolving, "reflecting the changing priorities of society."[196] In this connection, given the growing salience of peremptory norms and human rights, it seems, intuitively at least, that the peremptory illegality of torture should somehow be factored into its characterization as a sovereign or non-sovereign act, or at the very least, in the ultimate grant or denial of immunity. This has not been the case in Canada, where, in *Jaffe* (1993), illegality did not result in the loss of immunity under *SIA*.[197] Moreover, as noted above, the *Bouzari* courts held that violations of peremptory prohibitions are equally inconsequential in the determination of immunities under the *SIA*. In *Jones* (2004), the UK Court of Appeal expressly declined to follow the rule in *Jaffe* in proceedings against state officials for torture,[198] but this result was overturned by the House of Lords. In his speech, Lord Hoffman expressly rejected "the argument that torture or some other contravention of a *jus cogens* cannot attract immunity *ratione materiae* because it cannot be an official act."[199]

However, grossly unlawful state conduct does not attract immunity everywhere and in every circumstance. As noted above, a 1996 amendment to the *FSIA* has removed the immunity of certain designated states in lawsuits initiated by US nationals for sovereign acts which are repugnant to the United States and the international community, including torture, extra-judicial killing, aircraft sabotage, and

195 *Jones 2004*, above note 73 at para. 71, Mance LJ.

196 *Arrest Warrant Case*, Joint Separate Opinion of Judges Higgins, Koojimans, and Burgenthal, above note 2 at para. 72.

197 *Jaffe*, above note 22 at 760: "The illegal and malicious nature of the acts alleged do not of themselves move the actions outside the scope of the official duties of the responding defendants." It should be noted however that *Jaffe* did not concern violations of peremptory norms.

198 *Jones 2004*, above note 73 at para. 126.

199 *Jones 2006*, above note 90 at para. 85.

hostage taking. The distinction created by the *FSIA* between torture in Cuba and torture in, say, Canada, is clearly discriminatory, but it is noteworthy that the US reserves these extreme measures only for acts of extreme international illegality, as would also the proposed amendments to the Canadian and UK *SIA*.[200]

Aside from the exceptional framework of the *FSIA* under US law, Greece and Italy are the only two countries whose courts have ruled that state immunity did not apply to violations of peremptory norms. In *Prefecture of Viotia v. Germany* (1997), a claim arising from the Nazi massacre in the village of Distomo during WW II, the court of first instance at Leivadia held that Germany had implicitly waived its immunity by committing acts that clearly contravened peremptory norms of international law.[201] It is noted that the implied waiver argument had been considered and dismissed in US courts, on the theory that waiver ultimately hinges upon some indication, either explicit or implicit, of the foreign state's amenability to suit.[202] In 2000, on appeal, the Hellenic Supreme Court (Areios Pagos) affirmed the decision below, holding that Germany's violations of *jus cogens* amounted to "an abuse of sovereign power" and therefore did not attract immunity.[203] That decision was reversed in 2002 by a 6:5 majority of the Greek Special Supreme Court (Anotato Eidiko Dikasterio), holding that "international law at its present stage of development still vests foreign States with immunity when sued for acts which took place in the territory of the forum and in which its armed forces were implicated," without further discussing peremptory norms.[204]

---

200 Above notes 70–89 and accompanying text.

201 *Prefecture of Voiotia v. Federal Republic of Germany*, Case No. 137/1997, Court of First Instance of Leivadia, Greece, 30 October 1997. A summary and comment of the decision is available at (1998) 92 A.J.I.L. 765.

202 Fox, above note 3 at 269; *Siderman*, above note 153; *Princz*, above note 153. See also Adam C. Belsky *et al.*, "Implied Waiver under the *FSIA*: A Proposed Exception to Immunity for Violations of Peremptory Norms of International Law" (1989) 77 Cal. L. Rev. 365 (the article that first articulated the implied waiver argument).

203 *Prefecture of Voiotia v. Federal Republic of Germany*, Case No. 11/2000, Areios Pagos (Helenic Supreme Court), 4 May 2000. A summary and commentary of the decision is available at (2001) 95 A.J.I.L. 198.

204 Andrea Gattini "To What Extent Are State Immunity and Non-Justiciability Major Hurdles to Individuals' Claims for War Damages?" (2003) 1 Journal of International Criminal Justice 343 at 356; *Federal Republic of Germany v. Margellos*, No. 6/2002, Special Supreme Court, 17 September 2002, I.L.D.C. 87 (GR 2002).

The Italian cases also involved allegations of war crimes against Germany. Contrary to the Greek decisions however, the Italian courts denied immunity, not on the basis of implied waiver, but on the more straightforward logic of normative hierarchy. The leading case is *Ferrini v. Germany* (2004), where the plaintiff sued Germany in relation to forced deportation and slave labour during World War II.[205] In holding that the right to civil redress for violations of peremptory norms trumps the hierarchically lower rule of state immunity, the Italian Supreme Court stated that peremptory norms "stand at the apex of the international legal system, taking precedence over all other norms, whether of conventional or customary nature"[206] and that their violation "threaten[s] humanity as a whole and undermine[s] the very foundations of international coexistence."[207] The Court further noted the corresponding obligation of every state to abstain from recognizing as lawful such violations of peremptory norms.[208] The Court went on to state that the

> recognition of immunity from jurisdiction for States that are responsible for such offences is in blatant contrast with the normative framework outlined above, since this recognition obstructs rather than protects such values, the protection of which is rather to be considered . . . essential for the entire international community, so that in the most serious cases it should justify mandatory forms of response. Moreover, there can be no doubt that this antinomy must be resolved by giving precedence to the higher-ranking norms.[209]

In *Jones* (2006), the House of Lords doubted that the *Ferrini* decision could be "treated as an accurate statement of international law as generally understood" and that, in any event, "one swallow does not make a rule of international law."[210] Be that as it may, *Ferrini* was not the

205 *Ferrini v. Germany*, No. 5044/2004 (11 March 2004), ILDC 19 (IT 2004) [*Ferrini*].

206 *Ferrini*, *ibid.* at para. 9.

207 *Ibid.*

208 *Ibid.* On this point, the court referred to art. 41 of the ILC Draft Articles on State Responsibility. See James Crawford, *The International Law Commission's Articles on State Responsibility: Introduction, Text and Commentaries* (Cambridge: Cambridge University Press, 2002) at 249–51.

209 *Ferrini*, above note 205 at para. 9.1 (Book of Authorities, Tab 62).

210 *Jones*, above note 90 at para. 22, Lord Bingham. But see Elina Steinerte & Rebecca M.M. Wallace, "Case Note: *Jones v. Ministry of Interior of the Kingdom of Saudi Arabia*" (2006) 100 A.J.I.L. 901 at 905–6 for a criticism of the House of Lords' dismissive treatment of the Italian and Greek authorities.

last word on the matter. The Italian Supreme Court reiterated[211] or followed[212] its ruling in *Ferrini* in fifteen other cases since 2004. In *Mantelli* (2008), the Court explicitly registered its awareness that the *Ferrini* jurisprudence was contributing to the emergence of a new customary exception to state immunity for violations of hierarchically superior norms, an exception the Court considered already inherent ("*già insita*") to the international legal system.[213] Germany is challenging the *Ferrini* jurisprudence and instituted proceedings against Italy before the International Court of Justice.[214]

In light of the diverging practice of Anglo-American (i.e., US, UK, and Canada) and European (i.e., Greek and Italian) national courts on the interaction of *jus cogens* and state immunity, an important question remains as to what role the peremptory illegality of certain wrongful acts (such as torture) should play in characterizing state conduct for immunity purposes. In proposing an answer to that question, it is helpful to refer to some theory of the state and of the power it wields, as well as to some theory of international law as a whole, and both will be normative, not merely descriptive. Under the view that states are the ultimate embodiment of social power, including the power to make and break laws, torture — that is, extraordinary state-directed violence against an individual — can be conceived as the sovereign act *par excellence*. Under

---

211 The court affirmed *Ferrini* in *obiter dicta* in *Borri v. Argentina*, No 11225 (27 May 2005), I.L.D.C. 296 (IT 2005) and *Lozano v. Italy*, No 31171/2008 (24 July 2008), I.L.D.C. 1085 (IT 2008), stating that a new customary exception to state immunity was emerging in relation to violations of peremptory norms.

212 *Germany v. Mantelli and others*, No 14201/2008 (29 May 2008), I.L.D.C. 1037 (IT 2008) [*Mantelli*]. The ruling in *Mantelli*, which applied *Ferrini*, was followed in eleven other decisions issued on 29 May 2008: No 14202/2008, No 14203/2008, No 14204/2008, No 14205/2008, No 14206/2008, No 14207/2008, No 14208/2008, No 14209/2008, No 14210/2008, No 14211/2008, and No 14212/2008. Finally, the *Ferrini* rule was applied in the *Milde* case of 2009, a war crimes prosecution against a German soldier in which the victims sought civil redress from Germany: Corte suprema di cassazione, sez. I penale, No. 1072/2008 (21 October 2008), registered 13 January 2009, (Milde) in 92 Rivista di diritto internazionale (2009) 618*ff*.; affirming the decision of the Corte militare d'appello, No. 72/2007 (18 December 2007), registered 25 January 2008. See Annalisa Ciampi "The Italian Court of Cassation Asserts Civil Jurisdiction over Germany in a Criminal Case Relating to the Second World War" (2009) 7 Journal of International Criminal Justice 597.

213 *Mantelli*, *ibid*. at para. 11.

214 *Case Concerning Jurisdictional Immunities (Germany v. Italy)*, General List No. 143, proceedings instituted on 23 December 2008. The case was still in its preliminary stages at the time of writing .

this worldview, described by Marshall CJ in *The Schooner Exchange*, the planet is inhabited by equal and independent sovereigns, owing nothing to each other but that which they politely concede.[215] However, through constant and deliberate practice, in their mutual interest and for that of their members, states have outlawed torture, imbuing that prohibition with the full force of their combined sovereignties, elevating it amongst those rules that govern the formation of all others. Arguably, in so restricting their respective sovereignties, states have permanently excluded torture from the panoply of possible policies that they may pursue, *ipso facto* gaining in protection what they have lost in prerogative. In other words, the sovereign discretion to torture has been reallocated to the empowerment of its peremptory prohibition. Thus, every time and everywhere torture is ordered, it is never an exercise of social power but simply the utterance of words, just words, not law, mere *flatus vocis*, not *acta jure imperii*. Following this conception of things, the *jus cogens* illegality of torture becomes a decisive component of the contextual characterization of state acts resulting in its *ab initio* removal from the ambit of immunity.

The public policy of the forum should also inform the characterization of state acts under the restrictive theory insofar as such policy is consistent with peremptory norms of international law. This approach was taken by the New Zealand Court of Appeal in developing a common law iniquity exception to state immunity. In that case, officials from the Cook Islands refused to answer questions and produce documents in the course of a public enquiry into tax evasion, invoking state immunity. The court held that notwithstanding the sovereign nature of the impugned acts (i.e., the issuance of tax certificates), public policy required that immunity be denied. Richardson J defined the public policy exception as follows: "Where the conduct of the foreign State is in question, refusal of a claim to sovereign immunity could be justified only where the impugned activity, if established, breaches a fundamental principle of justice or some deep-rooted tradition of the forum State."[216] Though he characterized the issuance of tax certificates a commercial activity and would have denied immunity on that basis, Cooke P recognized the relevance of public policy in the determination of immunities.

215 *The Schooner Exchange*, above note 20.

216 *Controller & Auditor General v. Sir Ronald Davison*, [1996] 2 N.Z.L.R. 278 at 305–6 (C.A.).

> Faced with a serious issue of illegality or iniquity, a court cannot fall back on a bland answer that this sort of thing is beyond its scope . . . . A warning seems appropriate that older doctrines such as sovereign immunity, privilege against self-incrimination and the like, will not necessarily be apt when dealing with this sophisticated phenomenon [tax havens]. The public policy or interest of the country of the forum may properly require a different approach and in my view does so in this case.[217]

While Cooke P was careful to confine the public policy exception to the issue of tax evasion, he recognized

> that the law may gradually but steadily develop, perhaps first excepting from sovereign immunity atrocities or the use of weapons of mass destruction, perhaps ultimately going on to except acts of war not authorized by the United Nations. But this is to peer optimistically into the future . . .[218]

Both Richardson J and Cooke P agreed that the relevance of public policy to the characterization of state acts stems from the general view that it cannot be an exercise of sovereign authority to disregard fundamental principles of international and municipal law. Such an analysis may eventually lead to the re-characterization of violations of peremptory norms of international law for state immunity purposes.

G. STATE OFFICIALS

This chapter did not distinguish between the immunity of the state and the immunity of state officials because in Canada and the United Kingdom, despite the silence of the *SIA* and UK *SIA* on this point, courts have generally held that "when acting in pursuit of their duties, officials or employees of foreign states enjoy the benefits of sovereign immunity."[219] The rationale for the Canadian and UK approach was succinctly stated by Lord Bingham in *Jones* (2006): "a state can only act through servants and agents; their official acts are the acts of the state; and the state's immunity in respect of them is fundamental to the

217 *Ibid.* at 287.

218 *Ibid.* at 290.

219 *Jaffe*, above note 22 at 759; *Propend Finance Pty Ltd v. Sing* (1997), 111 I.L.R. 611 at 669 (E.W.C.A.).

principle of state immunity."[220] Until recently, the US cases were divided on this point, with some courts favouring a positivist approach to the *FSIA* (i.e., the exclusion of state officials from the statutory definition of the "foreign state" implies their non-immunity)[221] and others adopting the Canadian and UK approach of cloaking foreign officials with the immunity afforded to their home state under the *FSIA*.[222]

In *Samantar v. Yusuf*,[223] a lawsuit by Somali plaintiffs against the former prime minister of Somalia under *ATCA* and the *TVPA* for torture and extrajudicial killings, the United States Supreme Court had to decide whether the the *FSIA* protected the defendant from lawsuits for actions taken in his official capacity. A unanimous court held that it did not, holding that, as a matter of statutory interpretation, nothing in the text, legislative history, or purpose of the *FSIA* justified the construction of the words "foreign state" to include individual officials acting on the state's behalf.[224] As a result of the decision in *Samantar*, it is now settled law in the US that the justiciability of claims against foreign state officials is to be determined at common law, and not under the *FSIA*. The Supreme Court did not decide whether, on the merits, Samantar would be entitled to immunity at common law in a civil suit for torture and extrajudicial killing—this issue will be decided by the courts below on remand.

Of course, the decision in *Samantar* is not binding on Canadian and UK courts, but it is persuasive authority for the proposition that codifying statutes should be read narrowly, in a manner that preserves rather than supersedes pre-existing common law. As noted above,[225] common law immunities are capable of organic growth in light of emerging customary international norms and state practice. Accordingly, the US Supreme Court must be taken to have understood that, by directing this issue to be resolved at common law, it accepted the possibility that state officials could be held liable for their wrongful conduct even while their state would be immune under the *FSIA*. In other words, there is no necessary requirement of symmetry between

---

220 *Jones 2006*, above note 90 at para. 30.

221 For example, *Philippines (Republic) v. Marcos*, 665 F. Supp. 793 at 797 (N.D. Cal. 1987).

222 For example, *Kline v. Kaneko*, 685 F. Supp. 386 at 389 (S.D.N.Y. 1988); *Chuidian v. Philippine Nat'l Bank*, 912 F.2d 1095 (9th Cir. 1990).

223 *Samantar v. Yousuf*, 2010 U.S. LEXIS 4378, 130 S. Ct. 2278 (10 June 2010) [*Samantar*].

224 *Ibid.* at 2289 and 2292–93.

225 See notes 183–90 and accompanying text.

the scope of the immunity afforded by statute to the state and the immunity of state officials at common law. This insight is relevant in the Canadian context where, in matters such as the ongoing *Kazemi* litigation, claims have been brought against both the state and certain named officials.

H. CONCLUSION

Aside from the limited terms of the *FSIA* and possible amendments to the Canadian and UK *SIA*, national statutes on state immunity do not require the removal of immunity in civil claims for grave violations of human rights. The US model is unprincipled and should not be duplicated. Moreover, aside from the *Ferrini* line of cases, international and national courts have taken the view that general international law does not, as of yet, command the denial of state immunity in civil proceedings for violations of peremptory norms, though judicial opinions on this matter appear to be shifting as evinced by the slim majorities in *Al-Adsani* (2002) and *Prefecture of Viotia* (2002). Change is also heralded by the Committee against Torture's 2005 interpretation of Article 14 of the CAT, and Norway's and Sweden's statements upon ratification of the UNCSI. For the moment however, state immunity remains an absolute bar to transnational human rights litigation. In short, transnational human rights litigation is still awaiting, as it were, its *Trendtex* moment, where Lord Denning MR first acknowledged the restrictive theory of immunity to be part of the common law. The denial of immunity in civil proceedings for violations of well-established international norms protecting the human person, should it be pursued, will also require a bold first step by a legislature or by a court of law. But as the law currently stands, state immunity remains an absolute bar to transnational human rights proceedings.

part three

Synthesis

CHAPTER EIGHT

A Theory and Assessment of Transnational Human Rights Litigation

"While this unilateral exercise of the function of guardian of international values has been much commented on, it has not attracted the approbation of States generally."

—Judges Higgins, Kooijmans, and Buergenthal[1]

A. INTRODUCTION

This final chapter seeks to achieve two things. First, Section B sets out a theoretical framework, modelled on the analogy of translation, by which the particular adjudicative mode that is engaged by US transnational human rights litigation can be described and situated within a wider judicial tradition. More specifically, it will be argued that *Filártiga*-type cases engage national judiciaries in a form of supervisory role—which will be termed "transnational judicial review"—that is rooted in the historical function of common law courts as declarers of the law, expounders of the constitution, and righters of wrongs. Under this view of transnational human rights litigation, national courts assume the function of a decentralized international judiciary in matters involving the common interests and values of humanity. Second, using this chapter's epigraph as a starting point, Section C examines the perceived problems and advantages of transnational human rights litigation as exemplified by the US experience under *ATCA* and the *TVPA*.

1 *Case Concerning the Arrest Warrant of 11 April 2000 (Democratic Republic of Congo v. Belgium)*, [2002] I.C.J. Rep. 3 at para. 48, concurring opinion of Judges Higgins, Kooijmans, and Buergenthal [*Arrest Warrant Case*].

As will be seen, there are significant problems with the US model. It will nevertheless be argued that there exists a range of cases in which *ATCA*-type jurisdiction may be constructively asserted to complement existing international legal enforcement mechanisms.

B. TRANSNATIONAL HUMAN RIGHTS LITIGATION'S PARTICULAR MODE OF ADJUDICATION

1) Questions of Translation

The use of metaphor in international legal writing is sometimes helpful.[2] In discussing the desirability and portability of US-style transnational human rights litigation, Craig Scott and Beth Stephens have both made use of the metaphor of "translation" to describe the challenges involved. Scott's enquiry focuses on vertical normative translation, asking: "Can [an international] human rights norm . . . be translated into a civil cause of action within a domestic legal system?"[3] One of the central issues for Scott is that of translating the "message" of human rights accountability expressed at international law (the language of origin) into an enforceable paradigm at national law (the target language). For her part, Stephens asks "why there have been no *Filártiga* lawsuits in other countries."[4] Developing the metaphor in another direction, she argues that one should not seek to produce a literal translation ("exact duplicates") of *Filártiga* but rather to recognize that the "message" of human rights accountability can be rendered in other legal systems through procedures appropriate to each country. The Second Circuit understood its decision in *Filártiga* to be "a small but important step in the fulfilment of the ageless dream to free all people from brutal violence."[5] But perhaps more accurately, it can be stated that *Filártiga* was a small but novel step on the well-trodden path

2 Stephen Toope, "The Uses of Metaphor: International Law and the Supreme Court of Canada" (2001) 80 Can. Bar Rev. 534; Philip Allott, "Language, Method and the Nature of International Law" (1971) 45 Brit. Y.B. Int'l L. 79.

3 Craig Scott ed., *Torture as Tort: Comparative Perspectives on the Development of Transnational Human Rights Litigation* (Oxford: Hart, 2001) at 45.

4 Beth Stephens, "Translating *Filártiga*: A Comparative and International Law Analysis of Domestic Remedies for International Human Rights Violations" (2002) 27 Yale J. Int'l L. 1 at 3 [Stephens].

5 *Filártiga v. Peña-Irala*, 630 F.2d 876 at 890 (2d Cir. 1980) [*Filártiga*].

of US civil litigation. Other nations need not follow this path. Other means — such as official inquiries, administrative legal measures, or criminal prosecutions — may be more suited to other legal cultures.[6]

With its established tradition of public interest litigation, contingency fee agreements, flexible jurisdictional rules, provisions for class actions and default judgments, the US offers litigants a highly specialized framework in which to make and defend civil claims.[7] The UK and Canada also possess many of the same pro-claimant features that facilitate transnational human rights claims in the US. Indeed, the existence of legal aid and *pro bono* legal counsel in the UK were determinative factors in the retention of jurisdiction in the *Connelly* and *Cape* cases.[8] Similarly, in *Bouzari*, public interest groups intervened in support of the plaintiff against the Islamic Republic of Iran, which was noted in default for not defending the claim in Canada.[9] Though not to the same extent as the US legal system, Canada and the UK are no strangers to public and private litigation and it would appear that the most significant obstacle to transnational human rights claims in those countries is the absence of *ATCA*-style legislation authorizing jurisdiction and lingering judicial uneasiness with the relative novelty of the cases.[10] This state of affairs is not likely to last. For one thing, as noted in Chapter 7, there is currently draft legislation under consideration in the UK and Canadian Parliaments aimed at creating civil causes of action for extraterritorial torture and terrorism, respectively.[11] While some are private members' bills that stand little chance of becoming law, the Canadian proposal with respect to terrorism is a government bill, which means it should enjoy the required legislative support to be enacted. Time will tell. Taken together, they evince an increasing

---

6 Stephens, above note 4 at 25.

7 *Ibid.* at 16.

8 See Chapter 6, Section C(2).

9 For example, in *Bouzari v. Islamic Republic of Iran* (2004), 71 O.R. (3d) 675 (C.A.), Amnesty International and Canadian Lawyers for International Human Rights both intervened for the plaintiff.

10 Anne C. McConville, "Taking Jurisdiction in Transnational Human Rights Tort Litigation: Universality Jurisdiction's Relationship to *Ex Juris* Service, *Forum Non Conveniens* and the Presumption of Territoriality," in Scott, ed., *Torture as Tort*, above note 3 at 157; International Law Association, Committee on International Human Rights Law and Practice, "Report on Civil Actions in the English Courts for Serious Human Rights Violations Abroad" (2001) 2 Eur. H.R.L. Rev. 129.

11 See Chapter 7, notes 70–89 and accompanying text.

measure of interest in making certain violations of international law actionable in domestic courts. Arguably, as a matter of civil procedure and substantive law, both the UK and Canada are capable of appropriately translating *Filártiga* within their respective "legal languages," thereby enhancing the principle of international human rights accountability without transgressing international law limitations on the exercise of jurisdiction.

Translation is about movement, that is, the transferring or rendering of something from one form to another. However, this is precisely where the translation metaphor becomes more constraining than liberating. The translation of torture into tort is not, as the metaphor suggests, a unidirectional conveyance of an international message into a domestic medium. Transnational law—the interpretative space between international law and municipal law—is a two-way street. Scott recognizes that "translation has its limitations as a metaphor because it risks conjuring up the image of a one-way rendering of an original into its mirror in another language . . . and thus obscuring the fact that the 'torture as tort' issue involves two-way normative traffic, a conversation between two originals neither of which can be understood entirely within the existing language of the other."[12] The better view, as Scott suggests, is to conceive transnational human rights litigation as a dynamic "process of mutual translation" whereby public international norms are given private domestic expression without losing their *public* or *international* character. In turn, the litigated outcome and rule of decision modulate the transnational matrix through which international norms are interpreted for the future.

As was explored in Chapter 4, one of the common law modes of normative translation is incorporation, that is, the direct reception of evolving customary norms into the law of the land and the constant fine-tuning of custom through the common law. Using a metaphor of his own, Lord Denning MR expressed the dynamism of the process as follows: "I would use of international law the words which Galileo used of the earth: 'But it does move.' International law does change: and the courts have applied the changes without the aid of any Act of Parliament."[13] In a classic Denning flourish, the cosmic allegory is

12 Scott, ed., *Torture as Tort*, above note 3 at 61.

13 *Trendtex Trading Coporation v. Central Bank of Nigeria*, [1977] 2 W.L.R. 356 at 365 (C.A.) [*Trendtex*].

quickly followed by its plain practical implications: customary international law remains an ever-changing part of the common law and is applied as such by national courts, subject to contrary legislation and to issues of justiciability. In this sense, common law courts have long acted as bilingual interpreters, charged with the responsibility of moderating the on-going conversation between municipal and international law, while obligated to remain mindful of their function and responsibility in each sphere. As national institutions, courts interpret statutes and creatively administer the common law in accordance with their respective constitutions. In a wider sense, as courts of law, national courts interpret and apply incorporated customary international norms and so participate in the ongoing formation and adaptation of customary international law, not only for their own jurisdictions, but also for the international community as a whole.

National courts have long been aware of the global implications of domestic adjudication and of their creative international legal function. However, with the notable exception of state immunity and international criminal law, the international activity of municipal courts has traditionally been restricted to private law adjudications, including commercial transactions, torts, and family law. By contrast, transnational human rights claims require courts to ascertain and apply a mixture of public and private principles to matters that did not arise at the domestic level in earlier times. Indeed, the notion of human rights as legal limits on the exercise of public power possessed little weight before the end of WW II.[14] Until that time, the judicially determined limits on domestic government action were largely restricted to administrative law standards of due process and reasonableness. However, the twentieth century "legalization" of human rights—that is, the enactment of obligatory norms protecting the individual—has recast and expanded the public law function of courts within the national legal order beyond the traditional common law curial guardianship of fundamental rights.[15] Likewise, the crystallization of customary human rights norms at international law has potent implications for the public law functions of national courts within the transnational legal order.

14 Martii Koskenniemi, *The Gentle Civilizer of Nations* (Cambridge: Cambridge University Press, 2001) at 388–99.

15 Mark Elliott, *The Constitutional Foundations of Judicial Review* (Oxford: Hart, 2001) at 229–37.

Scott asks whether "the historical role of judges in forging non-statute-based private law should continue into the transnational realm."[16] The answer, I argue, is yes. But *Filártiga* poses a prior question: whether national courts can and should, in appropriate cases, scrutinize the legality of state action in light of international human rights norms. As it will be argued in the following section, this question too must be answered in the affirmative.

2) Transnational Judicial Review

In the context of the present discussion, transnational judicial review refers to the supervisory, law-declaring function of national courts in the transnational legal order.[17] More specifically, it designates the legitimate authority of courts to evaluate the lawfulness of forum and foreign state conduct in the course of adjudicating transnational human rights claims. Insofar as such claims have both a private and a public dimension, transnational judicial review concerns the latter aspect in that it involves the assessment by competent judicial authorities of the legality of state action in light of prevailing and applicable customary norms protecting the human person. The appraisal of whether a state has acted within the internationally lawful limits of power forms an essential ingredient of the adjudication of transnational human rights claims. In short, transnational judicial review is a rules-based judicial appraisal of state action beyond borders, which is concomitantly entwined with the determination of the rights of litigants.

At the outset, transnational judicial review must be distinguished from the supervisory jurisdiction of municipal courts in respect of

---

16 Scott, ed., *Torture as Tort*, above note 3 at 57.

17 Professor Cappelletti first coined the expression "transnational judicial review" in describing the role of national courts within the European Community in light of the decision in *Amministrazione delle Finanze dello Stato v. Simmenthal SpA (II)*, E.C.J. no. 106/77, [1978] E.C.R. 629, [1978] 3 C.M.L.R. 263 [*Simmenthal*]: Mauro Cappelletti, *The Judicial Process in Comparative Perspective* (New York: Oxford University Press, 1989) at 167. In *Simmenthal*, after affirming the primacy of Community law, the European Court of Justice stated that national courts had the responsibility of verifying the compliance of national rules with those of the EC. See also, generally, Karen J. Alter, *Establishing the Supremacy of European Law: The Making of an International Rule of Law in Europe* (Oxford: Oxford University Press, 2001); Tamara Capeta, *The Judiciary of the European Union: National Courts as European Courts* (Zagreb: Institut za Medunarodne Odnose, 2002).

administrative authority. Transnational judicial review does not concern itself with the question of whether a public or private body has acted within the scope of its delegated powers. Nor does transnational judicial review involve the assessment of whether otherwise properly delegated authority was exercised unreasonably or in a manner inconsistent with principles of natural justice. Transnational judicial review is not internationalized administrative law. Rather, transnational judicial review can be more properly likened to constitutional adjudication insofar as both entail the assessment of state action against superior or controlling norms. Of course, transnational judicial review and constitutional adjudication differ considerably in their outcomes. Whereas constitutional adjudication may lead to such far-reaching judicial remedies as the striking down of repugnant legislation, transnational judicial review may result in the finding that state conduct violates established rules of international law and the award of damages.

In *Sosa*, the Supreme Court noted that civil actions under *ATCA* involved an assessment of whether alleged wrongdoing exceeds the internationally defined legal limits of state action. The Court stated:

> It is one thing for American courts to enforce constitutional limits on our own State and Federal Governments' power, but quite another to consider suits under rules that would go so far as to claim a limit on the power of foreign governments over their own citizens, and to hold that a foreign government or its agent has transgressed those limits. Yet modern international law is very much concerned with just such questions, and apt to stimulate calls for vindicating private interests in § 1350 cases.[18]

Because customary human rights norms—particularly those norms that are *jus cogens*—represent limits on state action, and because these norms are actionable at common law, courts must necessarily assess the international legality of state conduct in the course of adjudicat-

---

18 *Sosa v. Alvarez-Machain*, 542 U.S. 692 at 727 (2004) [*Sosa*]. See also *Filártiga*, above note 5 at 884–85 where the Second Circuit held that the dictum in *Dreyfus v. Von Finck*, 534 F.2d 24 (2d Cir. 1976) to the effect that "'violations of international law do not occur when the aggrieved parties are nationals of the acting state,' is clearly out of tune with the current usage and practice of international law. The treaties and accords cited above, as well as the express foreign policy of our own government, all make it clear that international law confers fundamental rights upon all people vis-à-vis their own governments."

ing transnational human rights claims. For instance, in the course of *ATCA* proceedings for extraterritorial torture, federal courts cannot evade the task of determining whether the alleged state misconduct amounts to a breach of the internationally defined prohibition of torture. Transnational judicial review is inextricable from the legal determination of the rights and liabilities of the litigants because state participation is by definition a necessary component of the transnational "tort" of torture.[19]

The court in *Filártiga* understood the historical international legal context in which its decision arose. Writing for the court Judge Kaufman stated:

> In the twentieth century the international community has come to recognize the common danger posed by the flagrant disregard of basic human rights and particularly the right to be free of torture. Spurred first by the Great War, and then the Second, civilized nations have banded together to prescribe acceptable norms of international behaviour. From the ashes of the Second World War arose the United Nations Organization, amid hopes that an era of peace and cooperation had at last begun. Though many of these aspirations have remained elusive goals, that circumstance cannot diminish the true progress that has been made. In the modern age, humanitarian and practical considerations have combined to lead the nations of the world to recognize that respect for fundamental human rights is in their individual and collective interest.[20]

As the *Sosa* Court noted, these are questions with which "modern international law is very much concerned."[21] It is because human rights have been made into law that they are actionable under *ATCA*. It is because human rights norms represent established legal limits on the power of states that US federal courts engage in transnational judicial review. Whether a state or its officials have exceeded the accepted limits on public power by violating customary human rights norms is

19 *Convention Against Torture or other Cruel, Inhumane and Degrading Treatment and Punishment*, GA Res. 39/46, 39 U.N. GAOR Supp. No. 51 at 197, UN Doc. A/39/51 (1984), 1465 U.N.T.S 85, entered into force on 26 June 1987, art. 1.

20 *Filártiga*, above note 5 at 890.

21 *Sosa*, above note 18 at 728.

fundamentally a question of law that US courts must answer in adjudicating transnational human rights claims under § 1350.

The Second Circuit in *Filártiga* introduced the transnational judicial review paradigm as a necessary component of the judicial function it had to perform in that particular case. In order to determine the rights of the Filártiga family under *ATCA*, the court had to ascertain whether torture constituted "a tort . . . in violation of the law of nations"[22] and decide whether Norberto Peña-Irala had violated that law when he tortured and killed Joelito Filártiga. While the particular context of the claim was novel and the judgment correspondingly innovative, the adjudicative mode was anything but new. In holding that "for purposes of civil liability, the torturer has become like the pirate and slave trader before him *hostis humani generis*," the Second Circuit exercised the inherent law-declaring authority of courts in the classic common law tradition. Though nowhere mentioned in the judgment, *Marbury v. Madison*[23] could properly have been cited as an authority for *Filártiga*.

3) Higher Law and Judicial Duty

It would be difficult to overstate the importance of the United States Supreme Court's decision in *Marbury v. Madison* both within the US legal system and elsewhere. A comprehensive analysis of the many dimensions of *Marbury* is unnecessary for present purposes.[24] The simple

22 *Filártiga*, above note 5 at 880–81.

23 *Marbury v. Madison*, 5 U.S. 137 (1803) [*Marbury*].

24 The various 2003 symposia commemorating *Marbury v. Madison*'s bicentennial produced many insightful articles on the significance and wider legacy of Marshall CJ's classic decision. The better collections are 89 Va. L. Rev. Issue 6; 36 Geo. Wash. Int'l L. Rev. Issue 3; 72 Geo. Wash. L. Rev. Issues 1 & 2; and Volume 148 Proc. Amer. Phil. Soc'y Number 1. On the domestic significance of *Marbury*, see Louise Weinberg, "Our *Marbury*" (2003) 89 Va. L. Rev. 1235 [Weinberg]; G. Edward White, "The Constitutional Journey of *Marbury v. Madison*" (2003) 89 Va. L. Rev. 1463; Noah Feldman, "The Voidness of Repugnant Statutes: Another Look at the Meaning of *Marbury*" (2004) 148 Proc. Amer. Phil. Soc'y 27 [Feldman]. On its international impacts, see James Crawford, "*Marbury v. Madison* at the International Level" (2004) 36 Geo. Wash. Int'l L. Rev. 505 [Crawford]; Louis Henkin, "John Marshall Globalized" (2004) 148 Proc. Amer. Phil. Soc'y 53 [Henkin]; Jean Leclair, "Judicial Review in Canadian Constitutional Law: A Brief Overview" (2004) 36 Geo. Wash. Int'l L. Rev. 543; Michael J. Matheson, "ICJ Review of Security Council Decisions" (2004) 36 Geo. Wash. Int'l L. Rev. 615; Markus G. Puder, "Supremacy of the Law and Judicial Review in the European Union: Celebrating *Marbury v. Madison* with *Costa v. Enel*" (2004) 36 Geo. Wash. Int'l L. Rev. 567; and

argument made here regarding the nature of the judicial task in the context of transnational human rights litigation requires no more than a broad grasp of *Marbury*'s principles to understand how they translate to *Filártiga*.

The narrative of *Marbury v. Madison* begins with the 1800 election in which the Republicans swept to power, taking control of the political branches of government, leaving the judiciary in the hands of Federalist-appointed judges. The newly elected President Jefferson complained in a letter: "The principal [Federalist leaders] have retreated into the judiciary as a stronghold, the tenure of which renders it difficult to dislodge them."[25] Though to "dislodge" his political adversaries he certainly tried. Jefferson's campaign to purge the Federalist judiciary was conducted on many fronts: the Republican-led Congress impeached several nominees and dismissed all the federal circuit judges by repealing the statute that created the circuit court.[26] To ensure that these measures would not be immediately challenged, Congress closed down the United Sates Supreme Court for the entire year of 1802.[27] Moreover, upon taking office, Jefferson refused to recognize a number of former President Adam's last-minute judicial appointments, personally ordering that the commissions not be delivered.[28] Among these figured the commission of one William Marbury as justice of the peace for the District of Columbia.

Marbury and three other would-be justices of the peace applied to the US Supreme Court for a *mandamus* compelling the Secretary of State (James Madison) to deliver the commissions. The tense partisan context of the day and Jefferson's war on the judiciary, some commentators argue, placed the anaemic Supreme Court in an awkward position.[29] A decision directing Madison to deliver the commissions

---

Luc V. Tremblay, "*Marbury v. Madison* and Canadian Constitutionalism: Rhetoric and Practice" (2004) 36 Geo. Wash. Int'l L. Rev. 515.

25 Thomas Jefferson to Joel Barlow, 14 March 1801 in Andrew A. Lipscomb, ed., *The Writings of Thomas Jefferson*, vol. 10 (Washington, DC: The Thomas Jefferson Memorial Association, 1903) at 123.

26 *Judiciary Act of 1802*, 2 Stat. 132 (8 March 1802), repealing *Judiciary Act of 1801*, 2 Stat. 89 (13 February 1801).

27 Weinberg, above note 24 at 1237; Louis H. Pollak, "*Marbury v. Madison*: What did John Marshall Decide and Why?" (2004) 148 Proc. Amer. Phil. Soc'y 7 [Pollak].

28 Joseph J. Ellis, *Founding Brothers: The Revolutionary Generation* (London: Faber & Faber, 2002) at 208; Pollak, *ibid.* at 4–5.

29 Weinberg, above note 24 at 1238–39; Pollak, *ibid.* at 8–9.

would likely be ignored by the Jefferson administration, further marring the Court's prestige. If it declined to issue the writ of *mandamus*, the Court would appear weaker still. The solution: a carefully crafted decision by Marshall CJ at once holding that the Court lacked jurisdiction to provide the remedy sought in the instant proceedings while affirming the more "transcendent power" of the judiciary to declare the law and interpret the constitution.[30]

Marshall CJ set out his reasons following a three-pronged analysis. "1st. Has the applicant a right to the commission he demands? 2dly. If he has a right, and that right has been violated, do the laws of his country afford him a remedy? 3dly. If they do afford him a remedy, is it a mandamus issuing from this court?"[31] Regarding the first two questions, the Court held that the applicants possessed vested rights in their respective judicial appointments and that the government's failure to deliver the commissions amounted to a wrong that US law would remedy by way of *mandamus*. The *ratio decidendi* of *Marbury v. Madison* however lies in the answer to the third question, namely, that the Supreme Court had no power to issue a *mandamus*, such an order being an exercise of original jurisdiction not mandated by the constitution.[32] Indeed, the applicants relied on § 13 of the *Judiciary Act 1789*, the fourth clause of which purported to empower the Supreme Court to issue writs of *mandamus*. This congressional grant of authority, the Court ruled, could not be reconciled with that part of Article III, § 2 of the constitution that limited the Supreme Court's original jurisdiction to "cases affecting ambassadors, other public ministers and consuls, and those in which a state shall be a party." But, in order to reach the disposition of the case — that § 13 of the *Judiciary Act* was unconstitutional and that the Court had no jurisdiction in the proceedings — Marshall CJ first had to affirm two crucial principles, namely, that the constitution was supreme law and that courts possessed the authority to declare what the law requires. It was a deft ruling given the climate following the 1800 election: Marshall CJ scaled back the jurisdiction of the Court in the case at hand by anchoring it for the future in pre-constitutional notions of higher law and judicial duty.

30 Edward S. Corwin, "*Marbury v. Madison* and the Doctrine of Judicial Review" (1914) 12 Mich. L. Rev. 538 at 543 [Corwin 1914].

31 *Marbury*, above note 23 at 154.

32 *Ibid.* at 176.

There is, as Corwin observed, a pedagogical tone to Marshall's reasons, almost as if he were "lecturing the President"—who was not a delegate at the constitutional convention of 1787—as to the true status of the constitution and the responsibility of the judiciary.[33]

> Certainly all those who have framed written constitutions contemplate them as forming the fundamental and paramount law of the nation, and consequently the theory of every such government must be, that an act of the legislature, repugnant to the constitution, is void.[34]

As "fundamental" law, the constitution establishes and binds all three branches of government, directing the will of the legislature, controlling the actions of the executive, and guiding the judgment of the judiciary. As "paramount" law, the constitution must prevail over conflicting ordinary statutes and regulations. But more fundamentally, and this is the crux of Marshall's decision, as "law," the constitution must be interpreted exclusively by the judicial department.

> *It is emphatically the province and duty of the judicial department to say what the law is.* Those who apply the rule to particular cases, must of necessity expound and interpret that rule. If two laws conflict with each other, the courts must decide on the operation of each.
>
> So if a law be in opposition to the constitution; if both the law and the constitution apply to a particular case, so that the court must either decide that case conformably to the law, disregarding the constitution; or conformably to the constitution, disregarding the law; the court must determine which of these conflicting rules governs the case. *This is of the very essence of judicial duty.*[35]

Those two principles—the hierarchy of laws and the duty of the judiciary to authoritatively declare the law—lie at the heart of Marshall's judgment.

Mabury v. Madison is a landmark decision concerning the US constitution. But it is easy to lose sight of the general assumptions about law and judicial duty that informed the Court's decision, assumptions

33 Corwin 1914, above note 30 at 543. Jefferson was in France at the time of the Constitutional convention. Marshall, for his part, was not a delegate in Philadelphia but he was a member of the Virginia House of Delegates that lobbied for the ratification of the federal constitution.

34 *Marbury*, above note 23 at 177.

35 *Ibid.* at 177–78 [emphasis added].

that predate *Marbury* and the US constitution. As the Chief Justice suggested in the above-quoted passage, the Framers fully expected the constitution to become the supreme law of the land to be expounded and applied by a learned and independent judiciary. Publius (Hamilton) made this clear in *The Federalist* No. 78:

> The interpretation of the law is the proper and peculiar province of the courts. A constitution is, in fact, and must be regarded by the judges, as a fundamental law. It therefore belongs to them to ascertain its meaning, as well as the meaning of any particular act proceeding from the legislative body. If there should happen to be an irreconcilable variance between the two, that which has the superior obligation and validity ought, of course, to be preferred; or, in other words, the Constitution ought to be preferred to the statute, the intention of the people to the intention of their agents.[36]

For the framers, the hierarchical structure of laws and the limitation of state power under the constitution provided the basis for judicial review.

The great innovation of the American colonies and later of the United States — Marshall CJ insisted on this point[37] — was the adoption of written constitutions as embodiments of the fundamental law. However, the notion that state power was subject to unwritten "higher law" predates US independence and indeed the discovery of the Americas. "This idea reaches back far beyond *Magna Carta*; it furnishes the basis of Parliament's argument against the pretensions of the Stuarts, and Locke's justification of the Glorious Revolution of 1688."[38] Historically the notion of (written and unwritten) higher law

---

36 Alexander Hamilton, James Madison, & John Jay, *The Federalist Papers* (New York: J. and M. Lean, 1788; reprint, Oxford: Oxford University Press, 2008), No. 78 (Hamilton) at 381–82.

37 *Marbury*, above note 23 at 178. Marshall CJ refers to written constitutions as "the greatest improvement on political institutions."

38 Edward S. Corwin, "The Establishment of Judicial Review" (1911) 9 Mich. L. Rev. 102 at 104 [Corwin 1911]; David M. Beatty, *The Ultimate Rule of Law* (Oxford: Oxford University Press, 2004) at 2–3; See also, generally, Edward S. Corwin, "The Establishment of Judicial Review (II)" (1911) 9 Mich. L. Rev. 283; Edward S. Corwin, "The 'Higher Law' Background of American Constitutional Law" (1928) 42 Harv. L. Rev. 149 [Corwin 1928]; H. Patrick Glenn, "Persuasive Authority" (1987) 32 McGill L.J. 262; and Philip Hamburger, "Law and Judicial Duty" (2003) 72 Geo. Wash. L. Rev. 1 [Hamburger].

has been founded on changing grounds such as divine will, natural law, "right reason," and, comparatively more recently, popular will.[39] In the Anglo-American tradition, commentators have detected lines of legal thinking running between Marshall's understanding of the constitution as higher law in Marbury and Coke's conception of the common law in *Dr Bonham's Case* (1610).[40] In both cases the constitution and the common law (or rather, the rule of right reason contained therein) embody superior norms that override repugnant legislation. But the similarities are more than merely thematic. For Feldman, the language uniting the two judgments is "no coincidence."[41] Lord Coke declared that "when an act of parliament is against common right and reason, or repugnant, or impossible to be performed, the common law will controul [*sic*] it and adjudge such act to be void."[42] Two centuries later, Marshall CJ echoed, "an act of the legislature, repugnant to the constitution, is void." Of course, eighteenth century jurists were familiar with the *cause célèbre* of Dr. Bonham and it may be that Marshall was attempting to varnish his judgment with Coke's authority by tracking his language. In any event, the legal concepts of voidness and repugnancy "swim in a sea of continuity"[43] that cannot be separated from some conception of higher law and, at least in the common law tradition, from the declaratory duty of courts in respect of that law.

Perhaps more relevant to the present argument linking *Marbury v. Madison* to *Filártiga v. Peña-Irala*, it can be argued that courts have a duty to determine the law in all cases properly brought before them, including cases involving foreign parties and international law. As Koh correctly observed, "nothing in *Marbury* had limited this law-declaring function to cases involving domestic law. To the contrary, within a year after writing *Marbury*, Chief Justice John Marshall ruled that 'an act of Congress ought never to be construed to violate the law of nations if any other possible construction remains.'"[44] Indeed, the inter-

39 Corwin 1928, *ibid.* at 152; *Marbury*, above note 23 at 176.

40 See, generally, Feldman, above note 24; Hamburger, above note 38; Corwin 1911, above note 38.

41 Feldman, *ibid.* at 31.

42 *Dr Bonham's Case* (1610), 8 Co. Rep. 107a (C.P.).

43 Feldman, above note 24 at 31.

44 Harold Hongju Koh, "Transnational Public Law Litigation" (1991) 100 Yale L.J. 2347 at 2356 [Koh], citing Marshall CJ in *Murray v. Schooner Charming Betsy*, 6 U.S. 64 at 118 (1804).

national law-declaring duty of domestic courts has been an important feature of common law jurisdictions since at least the eighteenth century by virtue of the principle of incorporation.[45] Since the law of nations forms part of the common law, it too must be ascertained and declared. The Supreme Court affirmed that duty in clear terms in *Hilton v. Guyot* (1895). Writing for the Court, Justice Gray began his judgment by stating the principle of incorporation and the duty of the judiciary to declare and administer international law.

> International law, in its widest and most comprehensive sense — including not only questions of right between nations, governed by what has been appropriately called the law of nations; but also questions arising under what is usually called private international law, or the conflict of laws, and concerning the rights of persons within the territory and dominion of one nation, by reason of acts, private or public, done within the dominions of another nation — is part of our law, and must be ascertained and administered by the courts of justice, as often as such questions are presented in litigation between man and man, duly submitted to their determination.

In language reminiscent of Marshall's famous ruling in *Marbury v. Madison*, Justice Gray added:

> The most certain guide, no doubt, for the decision of such questions is a treaty or a statute of this country. But when, as is the case here, there is no written law upon the subject, *the duty still rests upon the judicial tribunals of ascertaining and declaring what the law is*, whenever it becomes necessary to do so in order to determine the rights of parties to suits regularly brought before them. In doing this, the courts must obtain such aid as they can from judicial decisions, from the works of jurists and commentators, and from the acts and usages of civilized nations.[46]

Though noting the advantages of written rules, the absence of codification in no way diminishes the law-declaring function of courts. Indeed the absence of written law may be thought to enhance the need for courts to authoritatively declare what the law is. Five years later, Justice Gray repeated these principles almost verbatim in *The Paquete*

45 See Chapter 5.

46 *Hilton v. Guyot*, 159 U.S. 113 at 163 (1895) [emphasis added].

Habana (1900),[47] the precedent that Judge Kaufman cited as authority in *Filártiga* in determining whether torture amounted in 1980 to a "tort . . . committed in violation of the law of nations."[48]

Simply put, the declaratory judicial duty that Coke CJ defended in respect of the common law, that Marshall CJ applied with regards to the US constitution, and that Gray J affirmed in respect of international law, was followed by Judge Kaufman in *Filártiga* in the novel context of transnational human rights litigation. In order to determine the rights of the litigants in that case, the court had to declare whether the prohibition of torture had become a binding rule of international law. Though *ATCA* required the court to make this determination, no special grant of authority was needed. Such an assessment of the facts and declaration of the law inheres to the judicial function, "unless validly and specifically excluded."[49]

Filártiga resembles *Marbury* not just in respect of their common paradigm of judicial duty but also with regards to the operation of higher law. In *Marbury*, the Supreme Court exercised its inherent jurisdiction to interpret the US constitution and to declare that the First Congress had overstepped its authority in enacting § 13 of the *Judiciary Act 1789*. In *Filártiga*, the Court of Appeal for Second Circuit exercised its jurisdiction to ascertain the current state of international law and determine whether Norberto Peña-Irala had acted in violation of that law. In that case, the operative higher law was the international law of human rights. The court declared that the prohibition of torture had crystallized into a rule of customary international law with the effect of limiting the discretion of states and state officials in their treatment of individuals. Interestingly, and perhaps counterintuitively, the peremptory character of the prohibition of torture does not enhance or otherwise modify the jurisdiction of the court to declare and interpret international law. For national courts, that duty exists regardless of the character of the law at issue.[50] That being said, the peremptory

47 *The Paquete Habana*, 175 U.S. 677 at 700 (1900).

48 *Filártiga*, above note 5 at 880–81.

49 Crawford, above note 24 at 508.

50 In this respect the inherent jurisdiction of national courts differs significantly from that of the consent-based jurisdiction of the ICJ. In the *Armed Activities Case*, the ICJ stated at para. 64: "the fact that a dispute relates to compliance with a norm having such a character [*jus cogens*], which is assuredly the case with regard to the prohibition of genocide, cannot of itself provide a basis for the jurisdiction

character of norms may be relevant once the court begins the task of elucidating the content of the law for the purposes of determining the rights of the parties. Indeed according to Orakhelashvili, the invalidating effect of *jus cogens* becomes an important element in considering the manner in which the peremptory prohibition of torture interacts with the other norms (e.g., state immunity) and prudential doctrines (e.g., political question, act of state, and *forum non conveniens*) that might require the court to decline jurisdiction it otherwise possesses.[51]

Koh once called *Filártiga* transnational law's *Brown v. Board of Education*.[52] It is better described as the *Marbury v. Madison* of transnational human rights litigation insofar as it builds upon Marshall's paradigms of declarative judicial duty and higher law. Judge Kaufman's decision is every bit as bold and innovative as Chief Justice Marshall's, but ultimately *Filártiga* remains part of *Marbury's* wider international legacy. This legacy is visible in Europe where the ECtHR has declared the *European Convention of Human Rights* to be a "'constitutional instrument of European public order in the field of human rights' and has successfully established itself as the exclusive interpreter of the Convention's provisions."[53] Henkin has observed:

> One can detect some influence of *Marbury* . . . in the birth and spread of international courts and tribunals, and in the increase of 'universal jurisdiction' by national courts to try and punish selected offenses (even by foreign persons, including high officials, as in the case of Pinochet of Chile).[54]

Crawford's assessment is consonant:

---

of the Court to entertain that dispute. Under the Court's Statute that jurisdiction is always based on the consent of the parties." *Case Concerning Armed Activities (Democratic Republic of Congo v. Rwanda)*, [2006] I.C.J. Rep. 126 at para. 64. See also *Case Concerning East Timor (Australia v. Portugal)*, [1995] I.C.J. Rep. 90 at para. 29.

51 Alexander Orakhelashvili, "State Immunity and International Public Order" (2002) 45 German Y.B. Int'l L. 227 at 255–66; See also, generally, Alexander Orakhelashvili, *Peremptory Norms in International Law*, (Oxford: Oxford University Press, 2006) c. 23.

52 Koh, above note 44 at 2366.

53 Anne-Marie Slaughter, "Judicial Globalization" (2000) 40 Va. J. Int'l L. 1103 at 1109, quoting *Chrysostomos v. Turkey* (1991), App. No. 15299/89, 68 Eur. Comm'n H.R. D.R. 216 at 242.

54 Henkin, above note 24 at 9.

The international legal system is in the process of making links between declarations, jurisdiction and remedies, thereby more broadly affirming the declaratory tradition. This is why, in my opinion, "judicial review" in the declaratory mode is not merely useful but inevitable.[55]

C. ASSESSMENT OF TRANSNATIONAL HUMAN RIGHTS LITIGATION

In their concurring opinion in the *Arrrest Warrant Case* (2002), Judges Higgins, Kooijmans, and Buergenthal commented briefly on "the broad form of extraterritorial jurisdiction" granted under *ATCA*. They noted: "While this unilateral exercise of the function of guardian of international values has been much commented on, it has not attracted the approbation of States generally."[56] It is certainly the case that US transnational human rights litigation has generated a considerable amount of commentary, but the concurring judges' dictum to the effect that "it has not attracted the approbation of States generally" should be qualified. Aside from the opposition of the so-called "State sponsors of terrorism" involved in actions brought under the *FSIA*, there have been no general state protests or condemnation of the judicially developed *Filártiga* doctrine. Rather, states have taken varying and sometimes contradictory positions with regards to the exercise of transnational civil jurisdiction in specific cases.

To give a few examples, India fully supported US litigation following the disaster in Bhopal in *Re Union Carbide* (1986).[57] It was the Philippines that sued former president Marcos in US courts in 1986.[58] Ecuador initially approved of the *ATCA* proceedings in *Aguinda* (1993)[59] then later protested in *Jota* (1998).[60] South Africa protested against US civil jurisdiction in *Re South African Apartheid Litigation* (2002) but supported broad-based, justice-oriented civil jurisdiction in *Connelly* (1998)

55 Crawford, above note 24 at 514.

56 *Arrest Warrant Case*, above note 1, concurring opinion of Judges Higgins, Kooijmans, & Buergenthal, at para. 48.

57 *Re Union Carbide Corp. Gas Plant Disaster at Bhopal, India in December 1984*, 634 F. Supp. 842 (S.D.N.Y. 1986).

58 *Republic of the Philippines v. Marcos*, 818 F.2d 1473 (9th Cir. 1987); *Republic of the Philippines v. Marcos*, 806 F.2d 344 (2d Cir. 1986).

59 *Aguinda v. Texaco Inc.*, 1994 U.S. Dist. LEXIS 4718 (S.D.N.Y. 1994).

60 *Jota v. Texaco*, 157 F.3d 153 (2d Cir. 1998).

and *Lubbe* (2000). In *Sarei* (2006), the governor of Papua New Guinea urged the US government "to support the Prime Minister's position to permit the case [against Rio Tinto plc] to proceed in the courts of America."[61] Moreover, as noted above, while no other state has enacted *ATCA*-style legislation, at the time of writing both the UK and Canadian Parliaments are studying draft legislation to grant a civil remedy and deny immunity in lawsuits for extraterritorial torture and terrorism, respectively.[62] Finally, as was discussed in Chapter 5, there is evidence of increasing state support for some notion of universal civil jurisdiction. While this variegated state practice, taken as a whole, does not amount to general approbation, it also falls short of stark opposition.

There are many ways to be skeptical about US-style transnational human rights litigation, some more reasonable than others. Of course, it is no longer possible to sustain, as Oppenheim did in 1905, that international law is "unable to confer directly rights and duties upon individuals."[63] But one may question whether grave violations of human rights give rise to enforceable claims to a remedy at international law.[64] In any event, transnational human rights litigation is the quest for a remedy under domestic law. Some deny the principle of incorporation.[65] Others question the binding character of customary international law, including human rights norms.[66] These arguments falter on many levels and most of them are addressed elsewhere in this study. On balance, the majority of authorities and states recognize that fundamental principles of human rights form part of customary inter-

61 *Sarei v. Rio Tinto plc*, 456 F.3d 1069 at 1076–77 (9th Cir. 2006).

62 Above notes 11 and 12 and accompanying text.

63 Lassa Oppenheim, *International Law: A Treatise* (London: Longman, Green, & Co., 1905) at 200.

64 See, for example, Christian Tomuschat, "Reparation for Victims of Grave Human Rights Violations" (2002) 10 Tul. J. Int'l & Comp. L. 157 at 182. But see Basic Principles and Guidelines on the Right to a Remedy and Reparation for Victims of Gross Violations of International Human Rights Law and Serious Violations of International Humanitarian Law, GA/RES/60/147, Annex , para. 18, U.N. Doc. A/Res/60/147 (2005).

65 See, for example, Curtis A. Bradley & Jack L. Goldsmith, "The Current Illegitimacy of International Human Rights Litigation" (1997) 66 Fordham L. Rev. 319; Scalia J's dissent in *Sosa*, above note 18. See, generally, Chapter 4.

66 See, for example, Samuel Estreicher, "Rethinking the Binding Effect of Customary International Law" (2003) 44 Va. J. Int'l L. 5; But see Rosalyn Higgins, *Problems and Process: International Law and How We Use It* (Oxford: Clarendon Press, 1994) at 210.

national law.[67] As has been argued in Chapters 4 through 7, states may choose to give effect to these rights through their national courts. The international law on this matter is permissive, subject to applicable rules of jurisdiction, justiciability, and immunity. Whether they ought to do so following the US model, however, is another question.

1) Problems with US-style Transnational Human Rights Litigation

a) International Law Problems

The most significant problem with the US model of transnational human rights litigation is its questionable compliance with international norms governing extraterritorial jurisdiction and state immunity. Simply put, unbridled litigation under *ATCA* may cause the US to breach the very body of law that the statute was originally intended to enforce. As we have seen, international law imposes few limitations on the adjudicative jurisdiction of national courts, but it generally requires some substantial connection (territorial or otherwise) between claims and the forum in which they are brought. For its part, the principle underlying *ATCA*'s "very broad form of extraterritorial jurisdiction"[68] is something akin to universal civil jurisdiction. While there is some evidence of growing acceptance of the notion of civil redress for wrongs that attract universal criminal jurisdiction,[69] it is by no means widespread, and US unilateralism in this respect remains controversial.

More controversial still are the so-called *Flatow* amendments under the *FSIA* that selectively remove the immunity of certain states designated by the executive (so-called "state sponsors of terrorism") in proceedings where US nationals sue in relation to acts of torture, extrajudicial killing, aircraft sabotage, hostage taking, or for supporting such activities. These parts of the *FSIA* contravene the customary and conventional principles of state immunity, namely, that sovereign states forebear from impeaching one another in each other's

---

67 Ian Brownlie, *Principles of Public International Law*, 6th ed. (Oxford: Oxford University Press, 2003) at 537.

68 *Arrest Warrant Case*, above note 1, concurrent opinion of Judges Higgins, Kooijmans, & Buergenthal at para. 48.

69 *Sosa*, above note 18 at 762. See Chapter 5, Section B(3).

courts, unless the subject matter of the claim falls within certain recognized exceptions to the general rule.[70] The *FSIA*'s denial of immunity in respect of the enumerated acts is dubious enough — as of yet, there is no generally accepted exception at international law for torture, extrajudicial killing, and terrorism — but the discriminatory manner of its denial is even more problematic. With reference to the US model, Fox observed that "the extension of the domestic jurisdiction of one State over another without the latter's consent can look dangerously like some form of hegemony or imperialism."[71]

b) Political Problems

Another way to cast the desirability of transnational human rights litigation into doubt is to highlight the political aspects of human rights. Klabbers has argued, for instance, that

> . . . because human rights go to the heart of a political community, foreign courts run the heightened risk of misreading the political map of the originating State or, where they read the map correctly, they may be torn between attempts to do justice to the individual plaintiffs and the desire to avoid causing major embarrassment in the relations between their own States and the relevant foreign State.[72]

This objection unhappily relies on anachronistic paradigms of cultural relativism and Westphalian sovereignty to conclude that human rights are simply too political to be adjudicated. "Insisting on judicialised individual rights," Klabbers laments, "tragically results in the defeat of our best, perhaps only way to combat evil: through the hard-won decisions and evolving consensus of political processes."[73] This surely overstates the matter. Transnational human rights litigation does not entail the death of the political process, or its subordination. To the contrary, US, UK, and Canadian public interest litigation may spur the political branches into action and lead to creative responses to social

---

70 See, generally, Chapter 7.

71 Hazel Fox, "Approaches of Domestic Courts to the Assertion of International Jurisdiction" in Patrick Capps, Malcolm Evans, & Stratos Konstadinidis, eds., *Asserting Jurisdiction: International and European Legal Perspectives* (Oxford: Hart, 2003) at 187.

72 Jan Klabbers, "Doing the Right Thing? Foreign Tort Law and Human Rights," in Scott, ed., *Torture as Tort*, above note 3 at 562 [Klabbers].

73 *Ibid.* at 564.

problems.[74] In these countries, both at common law and under their respective constitutions, individual rights are matters of law, not politics. Rights have been legalized and constitutionally entrenched precisely so to raise them above the often turbulent and changing political plane.[75]

c) Foreign Relations Problems

The human-rights-are-too-political objection also touches on the perceived negative foreign relations ramifications of transnational human rights litigation. Just as the judicial department should not second-guess the wisdom of the decisions of the political branches of government, *a fortiori* courts should refrain from sitting in judgment of the legitimate sovereign acts of foreign states, or else risk overstepping their authority and embarrassing the executive's management of foreign affairs. This line of argument, which relies on the rationales underpinning state immunity and the Act of State doctrines, also ultimately fails to convince. The reasons for judicial restraint with regards to foreign state conduct — respect for territorial sovereignty, comity, reasonable expectations, and good relations — are arguably not enhanced by the fact that the cases at issue involve human right violations. To the contrary, those reasons lose much of their strength when the impugned conduct is alleged to involve breaches of legal norms embodying the common interest of the international community. Of course, the international community has an interest in peaceful and principled relations. In this connection, the majority's opinion in *Al-Adsani* that upholding state immunity in civil claims for extraterritorial torture "pursues the legitimate aim of complying with international law to promote comity and good relations between States through the respect of another State's sovereignty" is apposite.[76] However sound this objective, it is unclear why civil proceedings in respect of violations of well-established customary international norms protecting individuals should fall within the category of cases that ought not be adjudicated. States may reasonably expect that lawful and sovereign acts performed within their territory will not be subjected to the scrutiny

---

74 Koh, above note 44.

75 *Marbury*, above note 23 at 176–77; *Reference re Motor Vehicle Act (British Columbia)*, [1985] 2 S.C.R. 486 at para. 16. See also Weinberg, above note 24 at 1240–41; Judge Edward D. Re, "The Universal Declaration of Human Rights: Effective Remedies and the Domestic Courts" (2003) 33 Cal. W. Int'l L.J. 137 at 168.

76 *Al-Adsani v. United Kingdom*, [2001] 34 E.H.R.R. 273 at para. 54.

of foreign courts and gauged by "idiosyncratic legal rules."[77] Inversely, states surely cannot expect other nations to disregard actions that violate customary norms of international law. Arguably, by declining to give effect and consequence to violations of the most fundamental norms of international law, states undermine the very order that collectively sustains them. Or, as Justice White put it in Sabbatino, "to refuse inquiry into the question of whether norms of the international community have been contravened by the act of state under review would seem to deny the existence or purport of such norms, a view that seems inconsistent with the role of international law in ordering the relations between nations."[78]

According to Bradley, the "foreign relations costs" of transnational human rights litigation include the potential hindering of cooperative efforts in such areas as trade, environmental protection, and combating terrorism.[79] Such ramifications are clearly not negligible, though they are, as Bradley states, "admittedly difficult to measure."[80] Another more readily quantifiable cost, Bradley argues, is the possibility of retaliatory litigation in foreign states. As an example of this prospect, Bradley cites the 2000 motion by the Iranian Majlis authorizing "victims of US interference" to sue the US in Iranian courts, characterizing the move as a "measure of reciprocity."[81] But as Stephens has noted, in that particular instance, Iran was responding to the enactment of certain *FSIA* amendments by the US Congress permitting the freezing of Iranian assets to ensure payment of awards under the *Flatow* provisions.[82] *FSIA* amendments permitting lawsuits against certain designated "state sponsors of terrorism" for certain violations of international law are plainly discriminatory and it is unclear whether Iran's withdrawal of US immunity in response to the *Flatow* provisions amounts to a legitimate countermeasure. But Bradley's wider point is a fair one: if the *Filártiga* model is replicated elsewhere, the US government and its officials might one day face civil proceedings in other

77 *Filártiga*, above note 5 at 881.

78 *Banco Nacional de Cuba v. Sabbatino*, 376 U.S. 398 at 457 (1964) [*Sabbatino*].

79 Curtis A. Bradley, "The Cost of International Human Rights Litigation" (2001) 2 Chi. J. Int'l L. 457 at 460–61 [Bradley 2001].

80 *Ibid.*

81 *Ibid.* at 461, n. 15.

82 Beth Stephens, "Taking Pride in International Human Rights Litigation" (2001) 2 Chi. J. Int'l L. 485 at 490–91; See also Chapter 7.

countries for alleged human rights violations. Given the US disavowal of the International Criminal Court (ICC) and its reaction to the Belgian universal jurisdiction law, it is not difficult to imagine how it would react to putative civil actions for breaches of human rights norms in other jurisdictions. In response, it could be argued that as a state prepares to open its courts to victims of human rights abuses anywhere in the world, it should also be prepared, as matter of a fair play, to submit itself and its officials to foreign jurisdictions.

d) Democratic Problems

Bradley also objects to the undemocratic aspects of transnational human rights litigation. First, he notes that the private parties and human rights advocates who bring *ATCA* claims do so without the incentive and responsibility of weighing the foreign relations costs of initiating potentially vexatious litigation.[83] Second, in his view it cannot be a desirable state of affairs to have unelected, unaccountable federal judges discovering customary law and applying it in civil proceedings for extraterritorial human rights violations without explicit authorization from Congress.[84] The court in *Sosa* acknowledged that it had "no congressional mandate to seek out and define new and debatable violations of the law of nations."[85] However, as noted in Chapter 3, Congress has never sought to repeal or restrict *ATCA*. To the contrary, it has broadened the scope of transnational human rights litigation by enacting the *TVPA* in 1992 and various amendments to the *FSIA*. On the other hand, one should be careful not to read too much into these enactments: the *TVPA* is restricted to specific subject matter (torture and extrajudicial killing) and the *FSIA* permits recovery in limited circumstances against very few designated states. Arguably, the *Sosa* court's conclusion that federal courts may recognize new internationally derived torts at common law in the absence of unambiguous legislative authorization is anachronistic and at odds with prevailing positivistic paradigms and some conceptions of the modern judicial function.[86]

83 Bradley, above note 79 at 460.
84 *Ibid.* at 465–67.
85 *Sosa*, above note 18 at 728.
86 *Ibid.* at 744, Scalia J dissenting.

e) Evidentiary Problems

There are at least two types of evidentiary problems in *ATCA* cases. First, plaintiffs have the burden of adducing evidence in support of the facts they allege, which usually involves finding material, documents, and witnesses in foreign countries, often times in remote or troubled locations. As the court in *Talisman* noted, "the challenges of gathering the admissible evidence required to support plaintiffs' case in a desperately poor, distant country engulfed in civil war are significant."[87] Because of the logistical difficulties and financial costs this task entails, plaintiffs are often unable to build a sufficiently credible record to go to trial. In 2006, after four years of procedural jousting between the parties, the district court for the Southern District of New York finally dismissed the claims against Talisman because the plaintiffs' had failed to gather enough admissible evidence supporting their allegations that the corporation or its subsidiary had aided and abetted the Sudanese government in committing acts of genocide, war crimes, crimes against humanity, and torture.

The second type of evidentiary problem that arises in *ATCA* litigation flows from § 1350's "law of nations" requirement. In *Sosa*, the US Supreme Court established a high threshold for the recognition of new causes of action derived from customary international law, namely, actionable norms must be found to possess at least as much "definite content and acceptance among civilized nations than the historical paradigms familiar when § 1350 was enacted."[88] This in turn requires parties and judges to consult a wide range of international sources and materials with a view of not merely affirming or denying the existence of a particular customary norm, but also of establishing the extent of that norm's specificity. As some commentators have noted,

> [t]he Court made clear that this test for the domestic enforcement of CIL [customary international law] under the ATS is more demanding than the test for whether a CIL norm is internationally binding according to traditional standards for CIL. It made clear, in other words, that the CIL violations congress made actionable in ATS cases are a subset of all customary violations.[89]

---

87 *Presbyterian Church of Sudan v. Talisman Energy Inc.*, 453 F. Supp. 2d 633 at 639 (S.D.N.Y. 2006), aff'd 582 F.3d 244 (2d Cir. 2009).

88 *Sosa*, above note 18 at 732.

89 Curtis A. Bradley, Jack L. Goldsmith, & David H. Moore, "*Sosa*, Customary Inter-

The challenges ordinarily involved in proving customary international law in domestic proceedings have been well documented.[90] Arguably, the evidentiary standard now required for *ATCA* purposes compound those difficulties for both bench and bar.

f) Enforcement Problems

While some *ATCA* plaintiffs have managed to obtain favourable judgments, they have seldom been able to enforce them or to collect the damages awarded.[91] Though theoretically feasible, foreign recognition of *ATCA* awards is also fraught with procedural and political difficulties.[92] Likewise, litigants under the *FSIA* exceptions have generally not been able to secure the multi-million-dollar awards obtained from juries and judges. Those awards that have been enforced through congressional action freeing up blocked assets of so-called "state sponsors of terrorism" (despite consistent executive opposition) have produced mixed results. The compensation of victims of terrorism who have brought suit under the terrorist state exception to the *FSIA* seems likely to continue in an *ad hoc* fashion, with substantial benefit for some and little or none for others.[93] For their part, *ATCA* advocates and plaintiffs argue that financial compensation is not always the ultimate goal and that litigation offers human rights victims other meaningful forms of reparation, such as denunciation and vindication. Stephens insists on this point:

---

national Law and the Continuing Relevance of *Erie*" (2007) 120 Harv. L. Rev. 869 at 897.

90 Anne Warner La Forest, "Evidence and International and Comparative Law" in Oonagh Fitzgerald, ed., *The Globalized Rule of Law: Relationships Between International and Domestic Law* (Toronto: Irwin Law, 2006) at 380–88; Hon. Justice Louis LeBel & Gloria Chao, "The Rise of International Law in Canadian Constitutional Litigation: Fugue or Fusion? Recent Developments and Challenges in Internalizing International Law. " (2002) 16 Sup. Ct. L. Rev. (2d) 23 at 61. See also Gibran van Ert, "The Admissibility of International Legal Evidence" (2005) 84 Can. Bar Rev. 31.

91 International Law Association, Committee on International Human Rights Law and Practice, "Report on Civil Actions in the English Courts for Serious Human Rights Violations Abroad" [2001] 2 Eur. H.R.L. Rev. 129 at 130, n.5; Caroline Davidson, "Tort au Canadien: A Proposal for Canadian Tort Legislation on Gross Violations of International Human Rights and Humanitarian Law" (2005) 38 Vand. J. Transnat'l L. 1403 at 1441 [Davidson].

92 Edward A. Amley, Jr., "Sue and Be Recognized: Collecting § 1350 Judgments Abroad" (1998) 107 Yale L.J. 2177 at 2209–10.

93 Jennifer K. Elsea, *Suits against Terrorist States by Victims of Terrorism* (Washington DC: Congressional Research Service, 2008).

> Just as important, plaintiffs in these cases are often concerned about more than money. They take tremendous personal satisfaction from filing a lawsuit, forcing the defendant to answer in court or to leave the United States, and creating an official record of the human rights abuses inflicted on them or their families.[94]

However beneficial these outcomes may be for victims of human rights abuses, there are arguably speedier and less costly ways of obtaining them than filing a lawsuit in a court of law. In the absence of effective enforcement of the judgments obtained, one may reasonably question whether transnational human rights proceedings are a worthwhile endeavour.

2) Arguments in Support of Transnational Human Rights Litigation

a) The Complementarity of Criminal and Civil Redress

In addition to pursuing compensatory goals, civil litigation serves several other functions. For instance, tort actions have a distributive effect.[95] Indeed, once the injured person has been made whole by the award of damages against the responsible party, it is assumed that the latter will in turn transfer the cost of his responsibility to the wider community, for example, by increasing prices (in case of manufacturer) or taxes (where a government body is sued). Another important function of civil actions is deterrence, that is, the discouraging of further repetitions of the injurious behaviour through legal sanctions. It is thought that the award of damages achieves both specific and general deterrence by not only causing the wrongdoer to avoid a recurrence of the injury, but also by putting others on notice with regards to the consequences that await them if they too engage in the harmful con-

94 Beth Stephens *et al.*, *International Human Rights Litigation in U.S. Courts*, 2d ed. (Leiden: Martinus Nijhoff Publishers, 2008) at xxiv.

95 The "distributive justice" function of civil actions is to be distinguished from the paradigm of "corrective justice." It seeks to compensate the injured party not by virtue of the injurer's fault, but rather on the basis of the membership of the parties to the community. On corrective and distributive justice generally, see Aristotle, *The Nichomachean Ethics*, Book 5 (Trans. David Ross) (Oxford: Oxford University Press, 1998). See also Ernest Weinrib, "Aristotle's Forms of Justice" (1989) 2 Ratio Juris 211.

duct.[96] Also, tort law "can be used to apply pressure upon those who wield political, economic or intellectual power; in short, it empowers the injured."[97] The adverse publicity of a lawsuit is believed to be a powerful weapon against powerful tortfeasors, spurring them to act more responsibly lest they suffer a loss of prestige or esteem in the court of public opinion. Finally, tort law serves a psychological function. Much like criminal law, civil actions bring a substantial measure of relief and vindication to injured parties by providing them with a forum in which to air their grievances and, if they are successful, obtain some official recognition of the wrong they have suffered.[98] In a similar vein, tort actions can help to assuage an injured party's thirst for revenge or to "get even" with the tortfeasor, thus promoting peaceful dispute settlements.

Criminal law, for its part, is more concerned with punishing the offender, deterring future crimes, and where possible, rehabilitating the offender and facilitating his or her eventual reintegration into society. Together, criminal law and tort law collaborate by responding to both public and private interests of the community and the individual, respectively, and by fostering acceptable, safe standards of social behaviour and responsibility. It is more by virtue of their methods and operations than of their goals and functions that criminal prosecutions and civil litigation differ from one another. Civil actions, for instance, are instigated by the plaintiff at his own cost. By contrast, it is the government that controls and funds criminal prosecutions. The evidentiary standards are also different: while civil liability is established on the balance of probabilities, criminal culpability must be proven beyond all reasonable doubt. Finally, while criminal law potentially results in the punishment of the offender through fines or imprisonment, tort law seeks to make the victim whole by way of financial compensation. But even here there is overlap between these two forms of corrective justice. For instance, the award of punitive damages in tort is avowedly aimed at punishing and deterring particularly egregious conduct. Similarly, in criminal trials, a judge upon sentencing may order the

96 Allen M. Linden, *Canadian Tort Law*, 7th ed. (Toronto: Butterworths, 2001) at 8.

97 *Ibid.* at 22. See also Allen M. Linden, "Tort Law as Ombudsman" (1973) 51 Can. Bar Rev. 155.

98 Linden, *Canadian Tort Law*, *ibid.* at 16.

offender to make restitution.[99] In short, at the national level, criminal law and tort law work hand in hand towards consonant goals of corrective justice, employing their own methods and standards, each one enhancing the other's functions and effects.

b) Transnational Complementarity

The complementariness of criminal punishment and civil redress at the domestic level may come to bear at the international level. In this connection, the development of international criminal law and the establishment of the ICC is an important event. International criminal law is aimed at deterring and punishing individuals who commit acts that are contrary to international law, violations that are held to be the concern of all nations and peoples: for example, torture, genocide, war crimes, and crimes against humanity. In this sense, international criminal law, much like its domestic counterpart, is protective of the public interest, that is, the international public interest. The elevation of human rights among the organizing principles of international society after WW II helped crystallize the notion—intuitively felt and expressed at least since the time of the Stoics—that the members of the human family are linked by bonds that transcend nationality and geography.[100] Contemporary international society strives to advance with the hard lessons learned from recent history in mind, notably that "the recognition of the inherent dignity and of the equal and inalienable rights of all members of the human family is the foundation of freedom, justice and peace in the world." These opening words of the *Universal Declaration of Human Rights* are not mere grandiloquent cosmopolitan sentimentalism; they express an axiom of the United Nations and of the nascent international criminal law. The enforcement of international law, specifically of the prohibitions that go to the heart and health of all nations is an indication that international society is at long last beginning to conceive of itself as a society and to behave like a society does, that is, by fulfilling its own interest in the fulfilling of the interests of its members.[101] It may be that by

99 See, for example, *Canadian Criminal Code*, R.S.C. 1985 c. C-46, s. 738; *Rome Statute of the International Criminal Court*, 17 July 2008, U.N. Doc. A/CONF.183/9, 2187 U.N.T.S. 90, art. 75(2) [ICC Statute].

100 Davidson, above note 91 at 1428.

101 See, generally, Philip Allott, *Eunomia: New Order for a New World*, (Oxford: Oxford University Press, 1990); Philip Allott, *The Health of Nations: Society and Law Beyond*

purporting to enforce those norms of international law that are said to be the concern of all states and all peoples, transnational human rights litigation, like international criminal law, may contribute in protecting the public interest.

Concerns about a chilling effect of transnational human rights litigation on the international legal order, serious as they may be, remain largely speculative. It is unclear why the prospect of adjudication of civil claims in one country for atrocities committed in another would be less appropriate than criminal prosecutions for the same offences. If properly administered by prudent judiciaries, transnational human rights litigation may meaningfully complement existing international criminal legal mechanisms. Arguably, given the public and private interests they embody, international human rights require a correspondingly layered enforcement. The new era of international criminal justice under the aegis of the ICC promises to alleviate important lacunae of the previous enforcement models by making provision to address the private interests of the victims of international crime. By borrowing certain features of civil proceedings, such as ensuring participation of victims in the criminal process[102] and allowing for the compensation,[103] the ICC represents an ambitious experiment which, perhaps, will yield a fuller, more complete form of justice for victims of international crime. It might be argued that the victim-friendly provisions of the ICC make transnational human rights litigation redundant and, given the pyrrhic victories it produces in the US, other nations would do well not to pursue this model of law enforcement. Clearly, as noted above, in the absence of meaningful enforcement of the awards obtained, transnational human rights litigation remains a questionable exercise to say the least.

The basic proposition is that transnational human rights litigation and international criminal law, in their ends and functions, are complementary means of law enforcement. As remarkable an achievement as the ICC might be, it is by no means a panacea, and while its victim-friendly provisions hold some promise, important jurisdictional gaps remain, which might readily be filled by civil proceedings in domestic courts. First, *ratione personae*, the jurisdiction of national courts over

---

the State (Cambridge: Cambridge University Press, 2002).

102 ICC Statute, above note 99, art. 68(3).

103 *Ibid.*, art. 75(2).

non-state actors, including individuals and corporations, not to mention their limited jurisdiction over sovereign states, complement the narrow, membership and consent-based jurisdiction of the ICC over natural persons. Second, *ratione materiae*, the putative jurisdiction of national courts over violations of customary law and implemented treaties complements the ICC's jurisdiction over the four core crimes, which, by definition, are limited to situations of widespread and systemic patterns of criminality. Transnational human rights litigation appears particularly well suited for isolated violations of international law, such as in the *Filártiga* and *Bouzari* cases.

Other restrictive aspects inherent to the criminal process might be alleviated by the possibility of pursuing a civil remedy in national courts. First, as matter of accessibility, transnational civil proceedings are initiated by the plaintiff without the need, like at the ICC, for the case to be referred to the court by a member state, the Prosecutor, or the Security Council. The procedure of the ICC might seem too onerous for victims of international crime and may dissuade them from seeking justice. In this respect, the self-directed civil procedure of domestic courts appears to be a far more approachable and speedy option. Finally, the lighter evidentiary standard of civil proceedings seems better suited to situations like the *Bouzari* case, where sufficient evidence of an isolated occurrence of torture might be difficult to gather in order to secure a criminal conviction. On these fronts at least, transnational human rights litigation appears to be an effective complement to the criminal prosecutions by the ICC. By excelling where the other falters and by doing what the other cannot, both international criminal law and transnational human rights litigation can collaborate in putting an end to impunity by ensuring a broad spectrum of avenues for the enforcement of international law.

D. CONCLUSION: WHAT POSSIBILITY FOR THE UK AND CANADA?

Significant as they may be, the specific shortcomings of the US model of transnational human rights litigation do not lead to the conclusion that the notion of civil redress for violations of international norms protecting the human person is without merit. The US experience should inform the debate in other countries on what states can and should do to advance the fight against impunity and the right of victims to a remedy, but it clearly should not be replicated wholesale. If the UK and Canada ultimately choose to make their courts available to victims of extraterritorial human rights violations, it ought to be in a manner that is consistent with their respective constitutions and the principles of international law. It is submitted that the adjudicative model outlined above is aligned with the historical function of Anglo-American courts. Moreover, there arguably exists a range of circumstances in which civil jurisdiction may constructively be asserted over extraterritorial violations of well-established international human rights norms, for instance, in cases where a real and substantial connection exists between the claim and the forum, where no problems of immunity exist, and where the failure to take cognizance of the claim would result in a denial of justice. Such was the case for instance in the *Unocal* litigation.

Another question is whether Canadian and UK courts may, in theory at least, entertain transnational human rights claims without the benefit of special legislation. As noted above, the Canadian and British Parliaments are both currently studying draft legislation aimed at establishing a cause of action for international terrorism and torture, respectively, and denying state immunity in respect of these acts.[104] It is interesting to note that these proposals are not open-ended equivalents of *ATCA* in which jurisdiction is granted in respect of any "tort . . . in violation of the law of nations." Rather, they contemplate narrow grants of subject-matter jurisdiction over specific breaches of international law, in manner that more resembles the *TVPA*. Such explicit legislative boundaries on the jurisdiction of courts to apply international norms is consistent with contemporary positivistic conceptions of Canadian and British law, but they also raise the question of whether Canadian or British versions of the *TVPA* are even required in principle. The US Supreme Court in *Sosa* found *ATCA* to provide federal district courts with jurisdiction to recognize internationally derived causes of action already available at common law.[105] Such a jurisdictional grant is required for the district courts because, in the US, federal adjudicative authority is prescribed exclusively by statute.

104 Above note 11.

105 *Sosa*, above note 18 at 730.

By contrast, unless otherwise restrained by Parliament, Canadian and English courts possess general jurisdiction over all civil and criminal controversies, much like US state courts. In other words, no special legislative grant of authority is required for these courts to administer claims at common law. Moreover, as far as can be ascertained, it appears that no feature of either legal system makes the common law of either jurisdiction less amenable than US common law to the recognition of internationally derived causes of action. In short, Canadian and UK courts participate in the same declaratory judicial tradition that links *Marbury* to *Filártiga*; they too ascertain and apply international norms as a matter of course in appropriate cases. Thus the Privy Council declared that the restrictive rule of immunity operated in English actions *in rem*, despite the absence of legislation on the matter.[106] Similarly, prior to its codification by Parliament, the Court of Appeal held that the customary international exception to state immunity in relation to commercial transaction formed part of English law.[107]

The point of the foregoing is not to argue that Canadian and UK courts would not benefit from an appropriately defined legislated grant of authority to entertain transnational human rights claims — they clearly would. The potential political problems that *Filártiga*-type cases pose call for appropriate attention from the political branches. The point, rather, is to argue that even if Parliament fails to enact an *ATCA*-style jurisdictional grant or a *TVPA*-style cause of action, UK and Canadian courts may still be able to adjudicate certain transnational human rights claims on the basis of their general civil jurisdiction and normal rules of justiciability.

It is useful to recall Justice White's "unassailable propositions," namely, "that our courts are obliged to determine controversies on their merits, in accordance with the applicable law; and that part of the law . . . courts are bound to administer is international law."[108] If the resolution of a given case requires the determination of whether a foreign state or one of its officials has acted in violation of established norms of international law, national courts should not shy away from that responsibility. In transnational human rights cases where plaintiffs frequently stand no chance of obtaining justice in their own country,

106 *The Philippine Admiral*, [1977] A.C. 373 (P.C.).

107 *Trendtex*, above note 13.

108 *Sabbatino*, above note 78 at 450–51.

foreign courts often stand as the only viable opportunity for victims of taking wrongdoers to task. An important common thread running through the US, UK, and Canadian transnational human rights cases is the perceived judicial duty to prevent justice being denied to plaintiffs who cannot reasonably expect a fair adjudication of their claim in the *loci delicti commissi* or in an international tribunal. For example, one of the important historical motivations for *ATCA* is believed to be the duty to enforce international law and prevent denials of justice.[109] Moreover, in its intervention in *Sosa*, the European Commission emphasized the need to prevent denial of justice as an essential rationale for universal civil jurisdiction.[110] Likewise, in *Bouzari*, Goudge JA was uncomfortable with the *prima facie* conclusion that the court lacked jurisdiction given the implausibility of an alternative remedy in Iran or elsewhere.[111] Also, in *Connelly* and in *Cape*, the prospect of justice being denied on account of the doubtful adequacy of the legal representation available in South Africa was a determinative element in the retention of jurisdiction in the UK. In short, where possible, denials of justice are to be avoided, including in transnational human rights cases. Though good foreign relations are important and legitimate considerations unto themselves, they should not override the importance the international community collectively places on the legal norms protecting the human person, nor do they override, to borrow Bingham MR's oft-quoted words, "the rule of public policy which has first claim on the loyalty of the law: that wrongs should be remedied."[112] Fundamental fairness to the parties as well as the global interest in the enforcement of human rights call for adjudication whenever a national court is properly seized of a case.

Transnational human rights litigation is not judicial heroism. The suggestion that national courts have a duty to enforce international law of human rights through their criminal and civil jurisdiction does not rely on naive assumptions about the power of national courts. As Kuum put it, "it is not necessary to stylize national courts as Herculean institutions able to resist strong-willed national politics under all

---

109 Chapter 2.

110 Chapter 5.

111 *Ibid.*

112 *X. (minors) v. Bedfordshire County Council*, [1995] 2 A.C. 633 at 663 (H.L.).

circumstances."[113] Courts may not always declare, as Lord Mansfield is reported to have in *Somersett*: "*fiat justitia, ruat cœlum*, let justice be done whatever be the consequence."[114] Rather more modestly, the assumption is merely that "courts, as comparatively independent institutions, have a possible role to play in placing a thumb on the scales in favour of the international rule of law."[115]

Transnational human rights litigation is a desirable development, but like the ICC, it too is clearly no panacea. It cannot replace multilateral responses to international crime and injustice, but it can supplement and enhance those efforts. Other nations with other legal cultures need not adopt the model of US-style litigation (they clearly should not replicate that model's objectionable features) but Anglo-American courts cannot close their doors to the most vulnerable members of the international family without fettering their inherent discretion or abdicating four centuries of legal tradition. "Why," asks Koh, "shouldn't [Anglo-]American courts stick to deciding domestic cases and controversies, staying out of foreign policy, and avoiding judgment on the conduct of foreign sovereigns? The answer: they have traditionally done more; they are institutionally capable of doing more; and their traditional performance demonstrates that they are not only constitutionally authorized, but uniquely positioned, to play a more constructive role in the international legal process."[116] Through the careful and authoritative resolution of transnational human rights claims, Anglo-American courts carry on their historical function as declarers of the law and righters of wrongs. For over half a century, the international community has imbued its highest aspirations with the force of law. Unless specifically and validly excluded, the jurisdiction of common law courts to apply that law remains legitimate.

---

113 Mattias Kuum, "International Law in National Courts: The International Rule of Law and the Limits of the Internationalist Model" (2003) 44 Va. J. Int'l L. 19 at 24 [Kuum].

114 *Somersett v. Stewart* (1772), Lofft 1, 98 E.R. 499 at 509 (K.B.).

115 Kuum, above note 113 at 24. See also Institut de droit International, Resolutions, 1993 Milan Session (B. Conforti Rapp.) *The Activities of National Courts and the International Relations of their States.*

116 Koh, above note 44 at 2396.

POSTSCRIPT

Corporate Civil Liability under *ATCA*

"For those who believe the Filártiga-Sosa *line represents a meaningful advance in the protection of human rights, the majority's decision here marks a very bad day."*

—Judge Leval[1]

During the final phases of this book's production, the Court of Appeals for the Second Circuit handed down a decision too important to be left out. *Kiobel v. Royal Dutch Petroleum* is a class action by Nigerian plaintiffs against the Royal Dutch Petroleum Company and the Shell Transport and Trading Company in which it is alleged that the defendant corporations, acting through a Nigerian subsidiary, aided and abetted Nigeria's abusive suppression of environmental protests against development in the Ogoni region of the Niger Delta. The Court of Appeals for the Second Circuit granted the defendants' motion to dismiss for failing to state an actionable claim, holding somewhat surprisingly that *ATCA* does not apply to corporate defendants because "corporate liability is not a discernable—much less universally recognized—norm of customary international law."[2] The decision is surprising and significant for several reasons. First, as a decision emanating from the same court that first rehabilitated the 200-year-old *ATCA* in *Filártiga* (1982) and then later expanded its application to non-state actors in *Kadić* (1995), it is likely to have a significant impact on the

1 *Kiobel v Royal Dutch Petroleum*, 2010 U.S. App. LEXIS 19382 at 116 (2d Cir. 2010) [*Kiobel*].

2 *Ibid.* at 1.

development of transnational human rights litigation in the US.[3] Barring any legislative or judicial intervention, it certainly signals the end of *ATCA* litigation against corporations in the Second Circuit.[4] Second, in a forceful and lengthy concurring opinion, Judge Leval emphatically rejected Judge Cabranes's majority holding that corporations cannot be sued under *ATCA*.[5] Judge Leval's disagreement underscores the ongoing controversy, discussed elsewhere in this book, regarding the position of juridical persons under international law in general and under *ATCA* in particular.[6] Third, after more than thirteen years of *ATCA* corporate litigation,[7] and several multi-million-dollar settlements,[8] it is somewhat surprising that courts waited so long to address the fundamental question of whether corporations are legally capable of breaching the norms that *ATCA* seeks to enforce. One would have thought that this question could and should have been settled long ago.

Due to editorial time constraints, the modest aim of this postscript is to summarize the court's reasons for judgment, cursorily provide my preliminary analysis of certain problematic aspects, and, to the extent it is helpful, refer the reader to relevant portions of this book.

It will be recalled that *ATCA* provides federal courts with jurisdiction over "any civil action by an alien for a tort only, committed in violation of the law of nations or a treaty of the United States."[9] In *Kiobel*, the main question was whether the court had jurisdiction under *ATCA* to adjudicate a claim against a corporation. In answering that question, the court proceeded in two steps:

3 The 2d Circuit decision in *Kiobel* has already been followed twice in the 7th Circuit. See *Viera et al. v. Eli Lilly & Co.*, 2010 U.S. Dist. LEXIS 103761 (S.D. Ind. 2010); and *Flomo et al. v. Firestone Natural Rubber Co.*, 2010 U.S. Dist. LEXIS 10806 (S.D. Ind. 2010).

4 The plaintiffs submitted a petition for rehearing *en banc* on 14 October 2010.

5 *Kiobel* above note 1 at 113–265.

6 See Chapter 2, Section D(5)(b), notes 229–62 and accompanying text for a discussion of the existing debate concerning the legal personality and subjectivity of corporations at international law. See also Chapter 2, Section D(4), notes 191–98 and accompanying text, for a discussion of the district court's decision in *Kiobel* on the post-*Sosa* standards under *ATCA*.

7 As Judge Cabranes noted, "[t]he first ATS case brought against a corporate defendant appears to have been *Doe v. Unocal Corp.*, 963 F. Supp. 880 (C.D. Cal. 1997), aff'd in part and rev'd in part, 395 F.3d 932 (9th Cir. 2002)." See *Kiobel*, above note 1 at 5, n. 5.

8 See Chapter 2, Section D(5)(b), note 131.

9 28 U.S.C. § 1350. See Chapter 2, Section C(1), notes 29–33 and accompanying text.

> First, we consider which body of law governs the question—international law or domestic law—and conclude that international law governs. Second, we consider what the sources of international law reveal with respect to whether corporations can be subject to liability for violations of customary international law. We conclude that those sources lead inescapably to the conclusion that the customary international law of human rights has not to date recognized liability for corporations that violate its norms.[10]

With respect to the first part of its inquiry, the court zeroed in on a footnote in *Sosa v. Alvarez-Machain*,[11] noting that

> the Supreme Court instructed the lower federal courts to consider "whether *international law* extends the scope of liability for a violation of a given norm to the perpetrator being sued, if the defendant is a private actor such as a corporation or individual" *Sosa*, 542 U.S. at 732 n. 20 (emphasis added).[12]

Notwithstanding the questionable methodology of relying on a footnote containing a single-sentence *obiter dictum* to ground the majority's approach, it is clear that the Supreme Court in *Sosa* was not deciding or even discussing the question of corporate liability, but rather defining the standard of specificity required to make a violation of international law actionable under federal common law. In any event, the Supreme Court in *Sosa* advised federal courts to "consider" the state of international law, not to limit their inquiry to this body of law. Indeed, *ATCA* claims are governed by a blend of US and international norms: while international law prohibits certain wrongful acts, federal common law supplies the cause of action.[13] Moreover, federal courts resolve a variety of ancillary issues in *ATCA* proceedings, such as statutes of limitations,[14] exhaustion of local remedies,[15] and standards of complicity,[16] by referring to a variety of legal norms, such as state and federal legislation, federal case law, and the jurisprudence

---

10 *Kiobel*, above note 1 at 33.
11 542 U.S. 692 (2004) [*Sosa*].
12 *Kiobel*, above note 1 at 33.
13 See Chapter 2, Section D(4).
14 See Chapter 2, Section D(6)(b).
15 See Chapter 2, Section D(6)(c).
16 See Chapter 2, Section D(5)(c).

of *ad hoc* international tribunals. In short, *ATCA* litigation is transnational law,[17] and is best approached as such. As was explained by the International Commission of Jurists: "[*ATCA*] requires that the 'tort be committed in violation of international law, not that international law itself recognize a right to sue or define the scope of liability' and that 'the cause of action under the Statute is a creature of the common law, not the law of nations *per se*.'"[18]

After deciding to limit its inquiry to international law, the majority then decided to narrow its view even further in the second part of its analysis by focusing exclusively on customary international law: "Having concluded that international law controls our inquiry, we next consider what the sources of international law reveal with respect to the existence of a norm of corporate liability under customary international law."[19] The majority appears to proceed on the premise that liability under *ATCA* is only determined by customary international law and that a survey of the various sources of international law would reveal what customary international law requires. While the court properly identified the various sources of international law set out in Article 38 of the *Statute of the International Court of Justice*,[20] it goes on to address only treaties and doctrinal writing, finding them to be inconclusive on the question of whether customary international law recognizes some concept of corporate liability.

The bulk of the majority's decision is spent discussing the historical and ongoing work of international criminal tribunals. The majority concludes that since Nuremberg, "no international tribunal of which we are aware has *ever* held a corporation liable for a violation of the law of nations."[21] Though there are reasons to doubt this conclusion,[22] it is

17 See Chapter 1, Section A.

18 International Commission of Jurists, *Corporate Complicity and Legal Accountability*, vol. 3 (Civil Remedies) (Geneva: International Commission of Jurists, 2008) at 57 [ICJ Report].

19 *Kiobel*, above note 1 at 52.

20 *Ibid*. at 55–56.

21 *Ibid*. at 57 [*emphasis added*].

22 See Chapter 6, Section C(2)(b), notes 59–60 and accompanying text discussing the holding in *Bil'in (Village Council) v. Green Park International Inc*., 2009 QCCS 4151 that the Quebec Superior Court had jurisdiction over corporate defendants in a civil action for war crimes. See also *Kiobel v. Royal Dutch Petroleum*, above note 1 (Brief of *Amici curiae* Nuremberg Scholars in support of Plaintiffs-Appellants/Appellants-Cross Appellee's Petition for Rehearing and for Rehearing en banc, filed 15 October 2010) at 10–13 (arguing that International Occupation Author-

unclear why the court would look to the experience of international *criminal* tribunals to determine whether a norm of corporate *civil* liability exists at international law. For instance, the majority referred to a French proposal to include corporations as part of the jurisdiction of the International Criminal Court (ICC). This proposal was rejected, the court explains, because "criminal liability of corporations is still rejected in many national legal orders and thus would pose challenges for the ICC's principle of 'complementarity.'"[23] From this, the majority concludes that the "history of the *Rome Statute* . . . confirms the absence of any generally recognized principle or consensus among States concerning corporate liability for violations of customary international law."[24] In my view, this argument cuts the other way. To the extent that *ATCA* is concerned with civil (not criminal) liability, the international community's failure to reach a consensus on the issue of corporate criminal culpability during the *Rome Statute* negotiations proves little.

What is relevant, however, is the fact that every nation on the planet recognizes some form of civil liability for juristic persons and corporations who act in contravention of established norms.[25] The International Court of Justice (ICJ) has directed, with respect to the legal personality of corporations, "to not only take cognizance of municipal law, but also to refer to it."[26] However, contrary to ICJ's teachings, the majority's reasons conspicuously fail to consider "general principles of law recognized by civilized nations," one of the widely recognized sources of international law enumerated at Article 38 of the *Statute of the International Court of Justice*,[27] as the operative basis for a potential

---

ity had found the Farben corporation civilly liable for violations of international law, ordering punitive reparations as a consequence).

23 *Kiobel*, above note 1 at 71–72.

24 *Ibid.* at 72.

25 See Chapter 2, Section D(5)(b), note 244 and accompanying text.

26 *Barcelona Traction, Light & Power Co. (Second Phase) (Belgium v. Spain)*, [1970] I.C.J. Rep. 3 at §50.

27 As the International Commission of Jurists noted, the phrase "law of nations" in *ATCA* "could be legitimately interpreted as encompassing international laws contained in, or derived from, international treaties, customary international law, or general principles of law recognised by civilised nations. These are denoted as accepted sources of international law in the *Statute of the International Court of Justice*, Article 38." See ICJ Report, above note 18 at 56, n. 136. See also Ian Brownlie, *Principles of Public International Law*, 6th ed. (Oxford: Oxford University Press, 2003) at 15–18; Bin Cheng, *General Principles of Law as Applied by International Courts and Tribunals* (1953, repr. Cambridge: Cambridge University Press, 2006).

rule of corporate civil liability. The majority puzzlingly characterizes general principles of law as a "secondary" source of international law and confines its comments of their relevance to a single footnote, dismissing them as being an interesting exercise in comparative law.[28]

The majority concludes its analysis by contextualizing the implications of its finding that *ATCA* does not apply to corporations:

> Acknowledging the absence of corporate liability under customary international law is not a matter of conferring "immunity" on corporations. It is, instead, a recognition that the States of the world, in their relations with one another, have determined that moral and legal responsibility for heinous crimes should rest on the individual whose conduct makes him or her "*hostis humani generis*, an enemy of all mankind." Nothing in this opinion limits or forecloses suits under the ATS against a corporation's employees, managers, officers, directors, or any other person who commits, or purposefully aids and abets, violations of international law. Moreover, nothing in this opinion limits or forecloses corporate liability under any body of law *other than the ATS* — including the domestic statutes of other States — and nothing in this opinion limits or forecloses Congress from amending the ATS to bring corporate defendants within our jurisdiction. Corporate liability, however, is simply not "accepted by the civilized world and defined with a specificity comparable to the features of the 18th-century paradigms" recognized as providing a basis for suit under the law prescribed by the ATS, customary international law.

It is difficult to agree with the majority's assertion that its finding of no corporate liability under *ATCA* does not confer immunity to multinational corporations who directly or indirectly take part in violations of well-established norms of international law. In barring civil actions against juristic persons under *ATCA*, the majority's holding effectively deprives foreign plaintiffs of one of the only meaningful avenues for redress and allows corporations to profit from their proximity to human rights abuses by shielding their assets from execution through creative structuring. While legal action against corporate officers and directors may still be pursued, such claims impose a heavier eviden-

28 *Kiobel* above note 1 at 84, n. 43.

tiary burden on plaintiffs who must establish personal knowledge and involvement of the individual defendants.[29]

On its bare terms, *ATCA* does not limit the jurisdiction of federal courts to a specific class of defendants. Courts have nevertheless excluded foreign states[30] and incumbent head of states[31] from *ATCA*'s jurisdictional reach. But other than these special exceptions, *ATCA* has been successfully invoked in proceedings against a variety of defendants, including individuals acting under the colour of law, non-state organizations, and multinational corporations.[32] While it purported to settle an unresolved question lurking in its jurisprudence, the majority decision in *Kiobel* arguably marks the beginning of a new era of judicial debate on the scope of *ATCA* and the policy of holding corporations liable for violations of international norms protecting the human person.

---

29 For an overview of the challenges involved in gathering evidence in *ATCA* claims, see Beth Stephens *et al.*, *International Human Rights Litigation in U.S. Courts*, 2d ed. (Leiden: Martinus Nijhoff, 2008) c. 19.

30 *Argentine Republic v. Amerada Hess Shipping Corp.*, 488 U.S. 428 at 434 (1989).

31 *Lafontant v. Aristide*, 844 F. Supp. 128 (E.D.N.Y. 1994).

32 See Chapter 2, Section D(5), notes 204 and 206 and accompanying text.

Bibliography

ACEVES, W.J., "Affirming the Law of Nations in US Courts" (2002) 49 Fed. Law. 33

———, "Liberalism and International Legal Scholarship: The *Pinochet* Case and the Move toward a Universal System of Transnational Law Litigation" (2000) 41 Harv. Int'l L.J. 129

ADAIR, E.R., *The Extraterritoriality of Ambassadors in the Sixteenth and Seventeenth Centuries* (London: Longmans, Green, 1929)

AKEHURST, M., "Jurisdiction in International Law" (1972) 46 Brit. Y.B. Int'l L. 146

ALLOTT, P., "Language, Method and the Nature of International Law" (1971) 45 Brit. Y.B. Int'l L. 79

———, *Eunomia: New Order for a New World* (Oxford: Oxford University Press, 1990)

———, *The Health of Nations: Society and Law Beyond the State* (Cambridge: Cambridge University Press, 2002)

ALSTON, P., ed., *Human Rights Law* (New York: NYU Press, 1996)

ALSTON, P., & B. SIMMA, "Sources of Human Rights Law: Custom, *Jus Cogens* and General Principles" (1992) 12 Austrian Y.B. Int'l L. 82

ALTER, K., *Establishing the Supremacy of European Law: The Making of an International Rule of Law in Europe* (Oxford: Oxford University Press, 2001)

AMERICAN LAW INSTITUTE, *Restatement of Law (Second) Conflict of Laws* (St. Paul, MN: ALI Publishers, 1971)

AMERICAN LAW INSTITUTE, *Restatement of the Law (Third) of Foreign Relations Law of the United States* (St. Paul, MN: ALI Publishers, 1988)

AMLEY, E.A., "Sue and Be Recognized: Collecting § 1350 Judgments Abroad" (1998) 107 Yale L.J. 2177

ANDENAS, M., & D. FAIRGRIEVE, eds., *Judicial Review in International Perspective* (The Hague: Kluwer Law International, 2000)

ANGELL, N., *The Fruits of Victory: A Sequel to The Great Illusion* (London: Collins, 1921)

———, *The Great Illusion* (London: William Heinemann, 1911)

ARISTOTLE, *The Nichomachean Ethics*, translated by D. Ross (Oxford: Oxford University Press, 1998)

AUST, A., *Modern Treaty Law and Practice* (Cambridge: Cambridge University Press, 2000)

AVERY, C., "Business and Human Rights in a Time of Change" in M.T. Kamminga & S. Zia-Zarifi, eds., *Liability of Multinational Corporations under International Law* (The Hague: Kluwer Law International, 2000) 17

BAADE, H.W., "Legal Effects of Codes of Conduct for Multinational Enterprises" in N. Horn, ed., *Legal Problems for Codes of Conduct for Multinational Enterprises* (The Hague: Kluwer, 1980) 1

BADR, G., *State Immunity: An Analytical and Prognostic View* (The Hague: Martinus Nijhoff, 1984)

BAER, M., *Private International Law in Common Law Canada* (Toronto: Emond Montgomery, 1997)

BAHDI, R., "Globalization of Judgment: Transjudicialism and the Five Faces of International Law in Domestic Courts" (2002) 34 Geo. Wash. Int'l L. Rev. 555

BARCELO, J.J., & K.M. CLERMONT, eds., *A Global Law of Jurisdiction and Judgments: Lessons from The Hague* (The Hague: Kluwer Law International, 2002)

BAXI, U., "Geographies of Injustice: Human Rights at the Altar of Convenience" in C. Scott, ed., *Torture as Tort: Comparative Perspectives on the Development of Transnational Human Rights Litigation* (Oxford: Hart, 2001) 197

———, "Mass Torts, Multinational Enterprise Liability and Private International Law" (2000) 276 Rec. des Cours 305

BAYEFSKY, A.F., "International Human Rights Law in Canadian Courts" in B. Conforti & F. Francioni, eds., *Enforcing International Human Rights in Domestic Courts* (The Hague: Kluwer Law International, 1997) 295

BEATSON, J. & R. ZIMMERMANN, eds., *Jurists Uprooted: German-speaking Emigré Lawyers in Twentieth Century Britain* (Oxford: Oxford University Press, 2004)

BEATTY, D.M., *The Ultimate Rule of Law* (Oxford: Oxford University Press, 2004)

BEAULAC, S., "National Application of International Law: The Statutory Interpretation Perspective" (2003) 41 Can. Y.B. Int'l L. 225

BECKET, W.E., "The Exercise of Criminal Jurisdiction Over Foreigners" (1925) 6 Brit. Y.B. Int'l L. 44

BEDERMAN, D., *et al.*, "Brief of Amici Curiae in Support of Respondents" (1997) Hastings Int'l & Comp. L. Rev. 686

BELL, A.S., *Forum Shopping in Transational Litigation* (Oxford: Oxford University Press, 2003)

BENTHAM, J., *An Introduction to the Principles of Morals and Legislation* ed. by J.H. Burns & H.L.A. Hart (London: Athelone Press, 1970)

BERMAN, SIR F., "Jurisdiction: The State" in P. Capps *et al.*, eds., *Asserting Jurisdiction: International and European Legal Perspectives* (Oxford: Hart, 2003) 3

BERNSTEIN, A., "Conjoining International Human Rights Law with Enterprise Liability for Accidents" (2001) 40 Washburn L.J. 382

BETTAUER, R., "Germany Sues Italy at the International Court of Justice on Foreign Sovereign Immunity — Legal Underpinnings and Implications for U.S. Law" *American Society of International Law Insights* (19 November 2009) at 1

BIANCHI, A., "Denying State Immunity to Violators of Human Rights" (1994) 46 Aus. J. Pub. & Int'l L. 195

———, "International Law and US Courts: The Myth of Lohengrin Revisited" (2004) 15 E.J.I.L. 751

———, "Overcoming the Hurdle of State Immunity in the Domestic Enforcement of International Human Rights" in B. Conforti & F. Francioni, eds., *Enforcing International Human Rights in Domestic Courts* (The Hague: Kluwer Law International, 1997) 195

BINGHAM, LORD C.J., "The Future of the Common Law" (1999) 18 C.J.Q. 203

BLACK., V., & M. BRECHTEL, "*Muscutt v. Courcelles* Revisited: The Court of Appeal For Ontario Takes Another Look" (2009) 36 Advocates' Q. 35

BLACKMUN, H., "The Supreme Court and the Law of Nations: Owing a Decent Respect to the Opinions of Mankind" (1994) 88 ASIL Proceedings 383

BLACKSTONE, W., *Commentaries on the Laws of England*, 4 vols. (Oxford: Clarendon Press, 1765–69)

BLAIR, P., "The Doctrine of *Forum Non Conveniens* in Anglo-American Law" (1929) 29 Colum. L. Rev. 1

BLOM, J., & E. EDINGER, "The Chimera of the Real and Substantial Connection Test" (2005) 38 U.B.C. L. Rev. 373

BLUM, J., & R. STEINHARDT, "Federal Jurisdiction Over International Human Rights Claims: The *Alien Tort Claims Act* after *Filártiga v. Peña-Irala*" (1981) 22 Harv. Int'l L.J. 53

BORN, G., & D. WESTIN, *International Civil Litigation in United States Courts: Commentary & Materials*, 2d ed. (Deventer: Kluwer Law & Taxation Publishers, 1994)

BOYD, K., "The Inconvenience of Victims: Abolishing *Forum Non Conveniens* in U.S. Human Rights Litigation" (1998) 39 Va. J. Int'l L. 41

———, "Universal Jurisdiction and Structural Reasonableness" (2004) 40 Tex. Int'l L.J. 1

BOWETT, D.W., "Jurisdiction: Changing Patterns of Authority over Activities and Resources" (1983) 53 Brit. Y.B. Int'l L. 26

BRADLEY, C.A., "The *Alien Tort Statute* and Article III" (2002) 42 Va. J. Int'l L. 587

———, "The Charming Betsy Canon and Separation of Powers: Rethinking the Interpretive Role of International Law" (1998) 85 Geo. L.J. 479

———, "The Cost of International Human Rights Litigation" (2001) 2 Chicago J. Int'l L. 457

———, "Universal Jurisdiction and U.S. Law" (2001) U. Chicago Legal F. 323

BRADLEY, C.A., & J.L. GOLDSMITH, "The Current Illegitimacy of International Human Rights Litigation" (1997) 66 Fordham L. Rev. 319

———, "Customary International Law as Federal Common Law: A Critique of the Modern Position" (1997) 110 Harv. L. Rev. 815

BRADLEY, C.A. *et al.*, "*Sosa*, Customary International Law and the Continuing Relevance of *Erie*" (2007) 120 Harvard L. Rev. 869

BRAV, E.J., "Opening the Courtroom Doors to Non-Citizens: Cautiously Affirming *Filartíga* for the *Alien Tort Statute* (2005) 46 Harv. Int'l L.J. 265

BRILMAYER, L., *Conflict of Laws: Foundations and Future Directions* (Boston: Little Brown, 1991)

———, *Justifying International Acts* (Ithaca: Cornell University Press, 1989)

BRÖHMER, J., *State Immunity and the Violation of Human Rights* (The Hague: Martinus Nijhoff, 1997)

BROWNLIE, I., *Principles of Public International Law*, 6th ed. (Oxford: Oxford University Press, 2003)

BRUNNÉ, J., & S. TOOPE, "A Hesitant Embrace: The Application of International Law by Canadian Courts" (2002) 40 Can. Y.B. Int'l L. 3

BÜHLER, M., "The Myth of Act of State in Anglo-Canadian Law" in C. Scott, ed., *Torture as Tort: Comparative Perspectives on the Development of Transnational Human Rights Litigation* (Oxford: Hart, 2001) 343

BURLEY, A.-M., "The *Alien Tort Statute* and the *Judiciary Act of 1789*: A Badge of Honor" (1989) 83 A.J.I.L. 461

BYERS, M., *Custom, Power and the Power of Rules: International Relations and Customary International Law* (Cambridge: Cambridge University Press, 1999)

———, "Decisions of British Courts during 1996" (1996) 62 Brit. Y.B. Int'l L. 537

———, "Decisions of British Courts during 1999" (1999) 70 Brit. Y.B. Int'l L. 276

———, "English Courts and Serious Human Rights Violations Abroad: A Preliminary Assessment" in M.T. Kamminga & S. Zia-Zarifi, eds., *Liability of Multinational Corporations under International Law* (The Hague: Kluwer Law International, 2000) 241

BYRNES, A., "Civil Remedy for Torture Committed Abroad: An Obligation under the *Convention Against Torture*" in C. Scott, ed., *Torture as Tort* (Oxford: Hart, 2001) 537

ĆAPETA, T., *The Judiciary of the European Union: National Courts as European Courts* (Zagreb: IMO, 2002)

CAPPELLETTI, M., *The Judicial Process in Comparative Perspective* (New York: Oxford University Press, 1989)

CAPPS, P., M. EVANS, & S. KONSTADINIDIS, eds., *Asserting Jurisdiction: International and European Legal Perspectives* (Oxford: Hart, 2003)

CASSESE, A., *Human Rights in a Changing World* (Cambridge: Polity Press, 1990)

———, *International Criminal Law* (Oxford: Oxford University Press, 2003)

CASSESE, A., *et al.*, eds., *The Rome Statute of the International Criminal Court: A Commentary* (Oxford: Oxford University Press, 2002)

CASTEL, J.-G., "Back to the Future! Is the 'New' Rigid Choice of Law Rule for Interprovincial Torts Constitutionally Mandated?" (1995) 33 Osgoode Hall L.J. 35

———, *Canadian Conflict of Laws*, 3d ed. (Toronto: Butterworths, 1994)

———, "The Proof of Foreign Law" (1972) 22 U.T.L.J. 33

———, "The Uncertainty Factor in Canadian Private International Law" (2007) 52 McGill L.J. 555

CASTO, W.R., "The Federal Court's Protective Jurisdiction over Torts Committed in Violation of the Law of Nations" (1986) 18 Conn. L. Rev. 467

CARTER, P.B., "Public Policy in English Private International Law" (1993) 42 I.C.L.Q. 1

CHARNEY, J., "Transnational Corporations and Developing Public International Law" [1983] Duke L.J. 748

CHAYES, A., "The Role of the Judge in Public Law Litigation" (1976) 89 Harv. L. Rev. 1281

CHIBUNDU, M.O., "Making Customary International Law through Municipal Adjudication: A Structural Inquiry" (1999) 39 Va. J. Int'l L. 1069

CLAPHAM, A., *Human Rights Obligations of Non-State Actors* (Oxford: Oxford University Press, 2006)

CLAPHAM, A., & S. JERBI, "Categories of Corporate Complicity in Human Rights Abuses" (2001) 24 Hastings Int'l & Comp. L. Rev. 339

COFFEE, J.C., "No Soul to Damn, No Body to Kick: An Unscandalized Inquiry into the Problem of Corporate Punishment" (1980) 79 Mich. L. Rev. 386

COKE, SIR E., *Selected Writings and Speeches*, ed. by S. Sheppard (Indianapolis: Liberty Fund, 2003)

COLE, D., *et al.*, "Interpreting the *Alien Tort Statute*: *Amicus Curiae* Memorandum of International Scholars and Practitioners in *Trajano v. Marcos*" (1988) 12 Hastings Int'l & Comp. L. Rev. 1

COLLIER, J.G., *Conflict of Laws*, 3d ed. (Cambridge: Cambridge University Press, 2001)

CONFORTI, B., & F. FRANCIONI, eds., *Enforcing International Human Rights in Domestic Courts* (The Hague: Kluwer Law International, 1997)

CONFORTI, B., "National Courts and the International Law of Human Rights" in B. Conforti & F. Francioni, eds., *Enforcing International Human Rights in Domestic Courts* (The Hague: Kluwer Law International, 1997) 3

CORWIN, E.S.,"The Establishment of Judicial Review, Part 1" (1911) 9 Mich. L. Rev. 102

———, "The Establishment of Judicial Review, Part 2" (1911) 9 Mich. L. Rev. 283

———, "The 'Higher Law' Background of American Constitutional Law" (1928) 42 Harv. L. Rev. 149

———, "*Marbury v. Madison* and the Doctrine of Judicial Review" (1914) 12 Mich. L. Rev. 538

COWLES, W.B., "Universality of Jurisdiction Over War Crimes" (1945) 33 Cal. L. Rev. 177

CRANDALL, S.B., *Treaties: Their Making and Enforcement*, 2d ed. (Washington, DC: John Byrne & Co., 1916)

CRAWFORD, J., "The Contribution of Professor D.P. O'Connell to the Discipline of International Law" (1980) 51 Brit. Y.B. Int'l L. 1

———, "Decisions of British Courts during 1976–1977" (1977) 48 Brit. Y.B. Int'l L. 333

———, "International Law and Foreign Sovereigns: Distinguishing Immune Transactions" (1983) 54 Brit. Y.B. Int'l L. 75

———, *The International Law Commission's Articles on State Responsibility: Introduction, Text and Commentaries* (Cambridge: Cambridge University Press, 2002)

———, "*Marbury v. Madison* at the International Level" (2004) 36 Geo. Wash. Int'l L. Rev. 505

———, "Public International Law in Twentieth-century England" in J. Beatson & R. Zimmermann, eds., *Jurists Uprooted: German-speaking Emigré Lawyers in Twentieth Century Britain* (Oxford: Oxford University Press, 2004) 681

CROSSKEY, W.W., *Politics and the Constitution in the History of the United States* (Chicago: Chicago University Press, 1953)

CURRIE, J., *Public International Law*, 2d ed. (Toronto: Irwin Law, 2008)

DALTON, R., "Participation in Treaty Regimes: Putting the Constitutional and Legal Issues in Historical Perspective" in T. Franck, ed., *Delegating State Powers: The Effect of Treaty Regimes on Democracy and Sovereignty* (New York: Transnational, 2000) 19

D'AMATO, A., "The *Alien Tort Statute* and the Founding of the Constitution" (1988) 82 A.J.I.L. 62

———, "What Does *Tel-Oren* Tell Lawyers?: Judge Bork's Concept of the Law of Nations is Seriously Mistaken" (1985) 79 A.J.I.L. 92

D'AMORE, C.A., "*Sosa v. Alvarez-Machain* and the *Alien Tort Statute*: How Wide Has the Door to Human Rights Litigation Been Left Open?" (2006) 39 Akron L. Rev. 593

DAVIDSON, C., "*Tort au Canadien*: A proposal for Canadian Tort Legislation on Gross Violations of International Human Rights and Humanitarian Law" (2005) 38 Vand. J. Transnat'l L. 1403

DAVIDSON, W.L., *The Logic of Definition Explained and Applied* (London: Longmans, 1885)

DEVA, S., "Human Rights Violations by Multinational Corporations and International Law: Where from Here?" (2003) 19 Conn. J. Int'l L. 1

DICEY, A.V., & J.H.C. MORRIS, *Conflict of Laws*, 13th ed. (London: Sweet & Maxwell, 2000)

DICKINSON, E., "Changing Concepts and the Doctrine of Incorporation" (1932) 26 A.J.I.L. 239

———, "The Law of Nations as Part of the National Law of the United States" (1952) 101 U. Pa. L. Rev. 26

DODGE, W., "The Historical Origins of the *Alien Tort Statute*: A Response to Originalist" (1996) 19 Hastings Int'l & Comp. L. Rev. 221

———, "Which Torts in Violation of the Law of Nations?" (2001) 24 Hastings Int'l & Comp. L. Rev. 351.

DONOVAN, D.F., & A. ROBERTS, "The Emerging Recognition of Universal Civil Jurisdiction" (2006) 100 A.J.I.L. 142

DRIEDGER, E.M., *Driedger on the Construction of Statutes*, 3d ed. by R. Sullivan (Toronto: Butterworths, 1994)

DRINAN, R.F., & T.T. KUO, "Putting the World's Oppressors on Trial: The *Torture Victim Protection Act*" (1993) 15 Hum. Rts. Q. 605

DUNCAN, G., & D.O. DYKES, *Principles of Civil Jurisdiction* (Edinburgh: William Green & Sons, 1911)

DUNNING, J.H., *The Multinational Enterprise* (New York: Praeger, 1970)

DUPUY, P.-M., "L'unité de l'ordre juridique international: Cours general de droit international public" (2002) 297 R.C.A.D.I. 105

EDINGER, E., "New British Columbia Legislation: The *Court Jurisdiction and Proceedings Transfer Act*" (2006) 39 U.B.C. L. Rev. 407

ELLIOTT, M., *The Constitutional Foundations of Judicial Review* (Oxford: Hart, 2001)

ELLIS, J.J., *Founding Brothers: The Revolutionary Generation* (London: Faber & Faber, 2002)

ESTREICHER, S., "Rethinking the Binding Effect of Customary International Law" (2003) 44 Va. J. Int'l L. 5

EVANS, M.D., "Getting to Grips with Torture" (2002) 51 I.C.L.Q. 365

EVANS, M.D., ed., *International Law* (Oxford: Oxford University Press, 2003)

EVANS, M.D., & R. MORGAN, "Torture: Prevention versus Punishment" in C. Scott, ed., *Torture as Tort: Comparative Perspectives on the Development of Transnational Human Rights Litigation* (Oxford: Hart, 2001) 135

FALK, R., *Law in an Emerging Global Village* (New York: Transnational, 1998)

———, *The Role of Domestic Courts in the International Legal Order* (Syracuse, NY: Syracuse University Press, 1964)

FARRAND, M., *The Records of the Federal Convention of 1787*, 4 vols. (New Haven: Yale University Press, 1966)

FARROW, T.C.W., "Globalization, International Human Rights, and Civil Procedure" (2003) 41 Alta. L. Rev. 671

FATIMA, S., *Using International Law in Domestic Courts* (Oxford: Hart, 2005)

FELDMAN, N., "The Voidness of Repugnant Statutes: Another Look at the Meaning of *Marbury*" (2004) 148 APS Proceedings 1

FITZGERALD, O.E., ed., *The Globalized Rule of Law: Relationships between International and Domestic Law* (Toronto: Irwin Law, 2006)

FORCESE, C., "*ATCA*'s Achilles Heel: Corporate Complicity, International Law and the *Alien Tort Claims Act*" (2001) 26 Yale J. Int'l L. 487

———, "Deterring 'Militarized Commerce': The Prospect of Liability for 'Privatized' Human Rights Abuses" (2000) 31 Ottawa L. Rev. 171

FORSYTH, C., *Judicial Review and the Constitution* (Oxford: Hart, 2000)

FOX, H., "Approaches of Domestic Court to the Assertion of International Jurisdiction" in P. Capps, M. Evans, & S.V. Konstadinidis, eds., *Asserting Jurisdiction: International and European Legal Perspectives* (Oxford: Hart, 2003) 175

———, *The Law of State Immunity* (Oxford: Oxford University Press, 2002)

FRANCK, T., ed., *Delegating State Powers: The Effect of Treaty Regimes on Democracy and Sovereignty* (New York: Transnational, 2000)

FRANCK, T., *The Empowered Self* (Oxford: Oxford University Press, 1999)

———, *The Structure of Impartiality: Toward the Organization of World Law* (New York: MacMillan, 1968)

FREY, B.A., "The Legal and Ethical Responsibilities of Transnational Corporations in the Protection of International Human Rights" (1997) 6 Minn. J. Global Trade 153

FUKS, I., "*Sosa v. Alvarez-Machain* and the Future of *ATCA* Litigation: Examining Bonded Labour Claims and Corporate Liability" (2006) 106 Colum. L. Rev. 112

GARNETT, R., "The Defence of State Immunity for Acts of Torture" (1997) Australian Y.B. Int'l L. 97

GATTINI, A., "To What Extent Are State Immunity and Non-Justiciability Major Hurdles to Individuals' Claims for War Damages?" (2003) 1 J.I.C.J. 343

———, "War Crimes and State Immunity in the *Ferini* Decision" (2005) 3 J.I.C.J. 224

GIBNEY, M., K. TOMAŠEVSKI, & J. VEDSTED-HANSEN, "Transnational State Responsibility for Violations of Human Rights" (1999) 12 Harv. Hum. Rts. J. 267

GLENN, H.P., "Persuasive Authority" (1987) 32 McGill L.J. 262

GOFF, LORD, "The Future of the Common Law" (1997) 46 I.C.L.Q. 745

GOODMAN, R., "Congressional Support for Customary Human Rights as Federal Common Law" (1998) 4 ILSA J. Int'l & Comp. L. 455

HABERSTROH, J., "Comment: *In re World War II Era Japanese Forced Labor Litigation* and Obstacles to International Human Rights Claims in U.S. Courts" (2003) 10 Asian L.J. 253

HAFFKE, C., "The *Torture Victim Protection Act*: More Symbol Than Substance" (1994) 37 Emory L.J. 1467

Halsbury's Laws of England, 4th ed. (London: Butterworths, 1977)

HAMBURGER, P., "Law and Judicial Duty" (2003) 72 Geo. Wash. L. Rev. 1

HAMILTON, A., J. MADISON, & J. JAY, *The Federalist Papers* (New York: Oxford University Press, 2008)

Harvard Research Draft Convention on Jurisdiction with Respect to Crime by E. Dickinson, Rapp. (1935) 29 A.J.I.L. Supp. 429

HELFER, L.R., "Overlegalizing Human Rights: International Relations Theory and the Commonwealth Caribbean Backlash against Human Rights Regimes" (2002) 102 Colum. L. Rev. 1832

HENKIN, L. "John Marshall Globalized" (2004) 148 APS Proceedings 1

———, "International Law as Law in the United States" (1984) 82 Mich. L. Rev. 1555

———, "Is there a 'Political Question Doctrine'?" (1976) Yale L.J. 597

HIGGINS, R., "Dualism in the Face of a Changing Legal Culture" in M. Andenas & D. Fairgrieve, eds., *Judicial Review in International Perspective* (The Hague: Kluwer Law International, 2000) 9

———, *Problems and Process: International Law and How We Use It* (Oxford: Clarendon Press, 1994)

HIRSCHL, R., "Resituating the Judicialization of Politics: *Bush v. Gore* as a Global Trend" (2002) Can. J.L. & Jur. 191

HOLDSWORTH, SIR W., *A History of English Law*, 7th ed., 16 vols. (London: Sweet & Maxwell, 1956)

HORN, N., ed., *Legal Problems for Codes of Conduct for Multinational Enterprises* (The Hague: Kluwer, 1980)

HUTCHINSON, G., *The Admiralty Jurisdiction and Practice of the High Court of Justice* (London: Sweet & Maxwell, 1931)

HYDE. J., "Economic Development Agreements" (1962-I) 105 Rec. des Cours 267

JACKSON, J., "United States" in F.G. Jacobs, ed., *The Effect of Treaties in Domestic Law* (London: Sweet & Maxwell, 1987) 141

JACOBS, F.G., ed., *The Effect of Treaties in Domestic Law* (London: Sweet & Maxwell, 1987)

JÄGERS, N., *Corporate Human Rights Obligations: In Search of Accountability* (Antwerp: Intersentia, 2002)

JANIS, M.W., "Jeremy Bentham and the Fashioning of International Law" (1984) 78 A.J.I.L. 405

JAY, S., "The Status of the Law of Nations in Early American Law" (1989) 42 Vand. L. Rev. 819

JESSUP, P., "The Doctrine of *Erie Railroad v. Tompkins* Applied to International Law" (1939) 33 A.J.I.L. 740

JESSUP, P., *Transnational Law* (New Haven: Yale University Press, 1956)

JEWETT, M.L., & H.L. MOLOT, "*State Immunity Act*: Basic Principles" (1983) 61 Can. Bar Rev. 843

JOHNSON, J., *The Making of International Agreements: Congress Confronts the Executive* (New York: NYU Press, 1984)

JOSEPH, S., *Corporations and Transnational Human Rights Litigation* (Oxford: Hart, 2004)

———, "An Overview of Human Rights Accountability of Multinational Enterprises" in M.T. Kamminga & S. Zia-Zarifi, eds., *Liability of Multinational Corporations under International Law* (The Hague: Kluwer Law International, 2000) 75

JUENGER, F.K., "Mass Disasters and the Conflict of Laws" [1989] U. Ill. L. Rev. 105

KAHN, Z.S., "How Far is the 'Door Ajar'?: Whether Rape as Torture is Actionable under the *Alien Tort Statute* after *Sosa*" (2006) 12 Cardozo J.L. & Gender 685

KAMMINGA, M.T., & S. ZIA-ZARIFI, eds., *Liability of Multinational Corporations under International Law* (The Hague: Kluwer Law International, 2000)

KINDRED, H., "The Use and Abuse of International Legal Sources by Canadian Courts: Searching for a Principled Approach" in O. Fitzgerald, ed., *The Globalized Rule of Law: Relationships between International and Domestic Law* (Toronto: Irwin Law, 2006) 5

KINLEY, D., & J. TADAKI, "From Talk to Walk: The Emergence of Human Rights Responsibilities for Corporations at International Law" (2004) 44 Va. J. Int'l L. 931

KLABBERS, J., "Doing the Right Thing? Foreign Tort Law and Human Rights" in C. Scott, ed., *Torture as Tort: Comparative Perspectives on the Development of Transnational Human Rights Litigation* (Oxford: Hart, 2001) 553

KLEFFNER, J.K., "The Impact of Complementarity on National Implementation of Substantive International Criminal Law" (2003) 1 J.I.C.J. 86

KLUMM, M., "International Law in National Courts: The International Rule of Law and the Limits of the Internationalist Model" (2003) 44 Va. J. Int'l L. 19

KNOP, K., "Here and There: International Law in Domestic Courts" (2000) 32 N.Y.U. J. Int'l L. & Pol. 501

KOH, H., "Is International Law Really State Law?" (1997) 111 Harv. L. Rev. 1824

———, "Transnational Public Law Litigation" (1991) 100 Yale L.J. 2347

KONTOROVICH, E., "The Piracy Analogy: Modern Universal Jurisdiction's Hollow Foundation" (2004) 45 Harv. Int'l L.J. 183

KOSKENNIEMI, M., *From Apology to Utopia: The Structure of International Legal Argument* (Helsinki: Lakimiesliiton Kustannus, 1989)

———, *The Gentle Civilizer of Nations* (Cambridge: Cambridge University Press, 2001)

———, "International Law in a Post Realist Era" (1996) 16 Australian Y.B. Int'l L. 1

———, "The Pull of the Mainstream" (1990) 88 Mich. L. Rev. 1946

L'HEUREUX-DUBÉ, THE HON. JUSTICE C., "The Importance of Dialogue: Globalization and the International Impact of the Renquist Court" (1998) 34 Tulsa L.J. 15

LA FOREST, THE HON. JUSTICE G.V., "The Expanding Role of the Supreme Court of Canada in International Law Issues" (1996) 34 Can. Y.B. Int'l L. 89

LANG, D.G., *Foreign Policy in the Early Republic* (Baton Rouge, LA: Louisiana State University Press, 1985)

LAROCQUE, F., "*Bouzari v. Iran*: Testing the Limits of State Immunity in Canadian Courts" (2003) 41 Can. Y.B. Int'l L. 343

———, "Case and Comment: *Alien Tort Statute* Survives the Supreme Court" (2004) 63 Cambridge L.J. 532

———, "Civil Remedies for Terrorism" in C. Forcese & N. LaViolette, eds., *The Human Rights of Anti-Terrorism* (Toronto: Irwin Law, 2008) 425

———, "Le délit transnational de la torture" in S. Rogers, R. Ruparelia, & L. Bélanger-Hardy, eds., *Critical Torts* (Toronto: LexisNexis Canada, 2009) 263

———, "Recent Developments in Transnational Human Rights Litigation: A Postscript to *Torture as Tort*" (2008) 46:3 Osgoode Hall L.J. 605

———, "The Tort of Torture" (2009) 17:3 Tort Law Review 158

LAROCQUE, F., & M. KREUSER, "L'incorporation de la coutume internationale en common law canadienne" (2007) 45 Can. Y.B. Int'l L. 173

LAUTERPACHT, E., ed., *The Collected Papers of Hersch Lauterpacht*, 4 vols. (Cambridge: Cambridge University Press, 1970–1978)

LAUTERPACHT, H., "Allegiance, Diplomatic Protection and Criminal Jurisdiction Over Aliens" (1945–47) 9 Camb. L.J. 330

———, "Is International Law Part of the Law of England?" in E. Lauterpacht, ed., *The Collected Papers of Hersch Lauterpacht* (Cambridge: Cambridge University Press, 1975) vol. 2 at 537

———, "The Problem of Jurisdictional Immunities of Foreign States" (1951) 28 Brit. Y.B. Int'l L. 220

LeBel, The Hon. Justice L., & G. Chao, "The Rise of International Law in Canadian Constitutional Litigation: Fugue or Fusion?" (2002) 16 Sup. Ct. L. Rev. (2d) 23

Leclair, J., "Judicial Review in Canadian Constitutional Law: A Brief Overview" (2004) 36 Geo. Wash. Int'l L. Rev. 543

Lillich, R.B., "Damages for Gross Violations of International Human Rights Awarded by U.S. Courts" (1993) 15 Hum. Rts. Q. 207

———, "The Proper Role of Domestic Courts in the International Legal Order" (1970) 11 Va. J. Int'l L. 9

Linden, A., *Canadian Tort Law*, 6th ed. (Toronto: Butterworths, 2001)

———, "Tort Law as Ombudsman" (1973) 52 Can. Bar Rev. 155

Lipscomb, A., ed., *The Writings of Thomas Jefferson* (Washington, DC: The Thomas Jefferson Memorial Association, 1903)

Lowe, V., "Jurisdiction" in M. Evans, ed., *International Law* (Oxford: Oxford University Press, 2003) 329.

Macdonald, R. St. J., & D.M. Johnston, eds., *The Structure and Process of International Law: Essays in Legal Philosophy, Doctrine and Theory* (The Hague: Martinus Nijhoff, 1983)

Maier, H.G., "Extraterritorial Jurisdiction at a Crossroads: an Intersection between Public and Private International Law" (1982) 76 A.J.I.L. 280

———, "Jurisdictional Rules in Customary International Law" in K.M. Meessen, ed., *Extraterritorial Jurisdiction in Theory and Practice* (The Hague: Kluwer Law International, 1996) 64

Mann, F.A., "The Doctrine of Jurisdiction in International Law" (1964-I) 111 Rev. des Cours 1

Matheson, M.J., "Judicial Review in International Organizations: ICJ Review of Security Council Decisions" (2004) 36 Geo. Wash. Int'l L. Rev. 615

McConville, A.C., "Taking Jurisdiction in Transnational Human Rights Tort Litigation: Universality Jurisdiction's Relationship to *Ex Juris* Service, *Forum Non Conveniens* and the Presumption of Territoriality" in C. Scott, ed., *Torture as Tort: Comparative Perspectives on the Development of Transnational Human Rights Litigation* (Oxford: Hart, 2001) 157

McGregor, L., "Torture and State Immunity: Deflecting Impunity, Distorting Sovereignty" (2008) 18 E.J.I.L. 903

Meeran, R., "Liability of Multinational Corporations: A Critical Stage in the UK" in M.T. Kamminga & S. Zia-Zarifi, eds., *Liability of Multinational Corporations under International Law* (The Hague: Kluwer Law International, 2000) 251

MEESSEN, K.M., ed., *Extraterritorial Jurisdiction in Theory and Practice* (The Hague: Kluwer Law International, 1996)

MELVIN, V.A., "*Tel-Oren v. Libyan Arab Republic*: Redefining the *Alien Tort Claims Act*" (1985) 70 Minn. L. Rev. 211

MERON, T., *Human Rights and Humanitarian Norms as Customary Law* (Oxford: Clarendon Press, 1989)

MILLETT, RT. HON. THE LORD, "The *Pinochet* Case — Some Personal Reflections" in M. Evans, ed., *International Law* (Oxford: Oxford University Press, 2003) 7

MOLOT, H.L., & M.L. JEWETT, "The *State Immunity Act* of Canada" (1982) Can. Y.B. Int'l L. 79

MONESTIER, T., "A Real and Substantial Mess: The Law of Jurisdiction in Canada" (2007) 33 Queen's L.J. 179

MONTESQUIEU, C.L. DE S., *De l'esprit des lois*, 2 vols. (Paris: GF-Flammarion, 1979)

MOORE, J.N., ed., *Civil Litigation against Terrorism* (Durham, NC: Carolina Academic Press, 2004)

MORAN, M., "An Uncivil Action: The Tort of Torture and Cosmopolitan Private Law" in C. Scott, ed., *Torture as Tort: Comparative Perspectives on the Development of Transnational Human Rights Litigation* (Oxford: Hart, 2001) 661

MORSE, C.G.J., *Torts in Private International Law* (Amsterdam: North Holland, 1978)

MUCHLINSKI, P.T., "Attempts to Extend the Accountability of Transnational Corporation: The Role of UNCTAD" in M.T. Kamminga & S. Zia-Zarifi, eds., *Liability of Multinational Corporations under International Law* (The Hague: Kluwer Law International, 2000) 97

———, "Corporations in International Litigation: Problems of Jurisdiction and the United Kingdom Asbestos Cases" (2001) 50 I.C.L.Q. 1

MURPHY, J.F., "Civil Liability for the Commission of International Crimes as an Alternative to Criminal Prosecution" (1999) 12 Harv. Hum. Rts. J. 1

NAGAN, W.P., & L. ATKINS, "The International Law of Torture: From Universal Proscription to Effective Application and Enforcement" (2001) 14 Harv. Hum. Rts. J. 87

NOLAN, D.R., "Sir William Blackstone and the New Republic: A Study of Intellectual Impact" (1976) 51 N.Y.U.L. Rev. 731

NORBERG, N., "The US Supreme Court Affirms the *Filartiga* Paradigm" (2005) 3 J.I.C.J. 1

NOWAK, M., & E. MCARTHUR, *The United Nations* Convention Against Torture: *A Commentary* (Oxford: Oxford University Press, 2008)

O'KEEFE, R., "Customary International Crimes in English Courts" (2001) 72 Brit. Y.B. Int'l L. 293

———, "Decisions of British Courts during 2004" (2004) 75 Brit. Y.B. Int'l L. 407

OLDHAM, J., *The Mansfield Manuscripts and the Growth of English Law in the Eighteenth Century* (Chapel Hill, NC: University of North Carolina Press, 1992)

OPPENHEIM, L.F.L., *International Law: A Treatise* (London: Longman, 1905)

———, *Oppenheim's International Law*, 9th ed. by R. Jennings & A. Watts (London: Longman, 1992)

ORAKHELASHVILI, A., "State Immunity and the Hierarchy of Norms: Why the House of Lords Got it Wrong" (2007) 18:5 E.J.I.L 955

———, "State Immunity and International Law: Three Recent Cases before the European Court of Human Rights" (2002) 15 Leiden J. Int'l L. 703

———, "State Immunity and International Public Order" (2002) 45 Ger. Y.B. Int'l L. 227

———, *The Effects of Peremptory Norms in International Law* (Ph.D. Thesis, University of Cambridge, 2004)

———, *The Effects of Peremptory Norms in International Law* (Oxford: Oxford University Press, 2006)

ORANGE, J., "Torture, Tort Choice of Law and *Tolofson*" in C. Scott, ed., *Torture as Tort: Comparative Perspectives on the Development of Transnational Human Rights Litigation* (Oxford: Hart, 2001) at 292

PARLETT, K., "Universal Civil Jurisdiction for Torture" (2007) 4 Eur. H.R.L. Rev. 385

PAUST, J.J., "Federal Jurisdiction Over Extraterritorial Acts of Terrorism and Nonimmunity for Foreign Violators of International Law under the *FSIA* and the Act of State Doctrine" (1983) 23 Va. J. Int'l L. 191

———, "The History, Nature and Reach of the *Alien Tort Claims Act*" (2004) 16 Fla. J. Int'l L. 249

PINGEL-LENUZZA, I., *Les immunités des états en droit international* (Bruxelles: Éditions Bruylant, 1998)

PITEL, S., "Reformulating a Real and Substantial Connection" (2010) 60 U.N.B.L.J. 177

PITEL, S., & C. DUSTEN, "Lost in Transition: Answering the Questions Raised by the Supreme Court of Canada's New Approach to Jurisdiction" (2006) 85 Can. Bar Rev. 61

POLLAK, L.H., "*Marbury v. Madison:* What did John Marshall Decide and Why?" (2004) 148 Proceedings of the American Philosophical Society 1

PUDER, M.G., "Supremacy of the Law and Judicial Review in the European Union: Celebrating *Marbury v. Madison* with *Costa v. Enel*" (2004) 36 Geo. Wash. Int'l L. Rev. 567

RANDALL, K.C., "Federal Jurisdiction over International Law Claims: Inquiries into the *Alien Tort Statute*" (1985) 18 N.Y.U. J. Int'l L. & Pol. 1

———, "Universal Jurisdiction under International Law" (1988) 66 Tex. L. Rev. 785

———, *Federal Courts and the International Human Rights Paradigm* (Durham, NC: Duke University Press, 1990)

RANDELZHOFER, A., & C. TOMUSCHAT, eds., *State Responsibility and the Individual* (The Hague: Martinus Nijhoff, 1999)

RE, JUDGE E.D., "The Universal Declaration of Human Rights: Effective Remedies and the Domestic Courts" (2003) 33 Cal. W. Int'l L.J. 137

REECE K., & J. SMALL, "Human Rights and State Immunity: Is there Immunity from Civil Liability for Torture?" (2003) 1 Netherlands International Law Review 1

REEVES, P., "The Influence of the Law of Nature upon International Law in the United States" (1909) 3 A.J.I.L. 547

REIMANN, M., "A Human Rights Exception to Sovereign Immunity: Some Thoughts on *Princz v. Federal Republic of Germany*" (1995) 16 Mich. J. Int'l L. 403

REISMAN, M., & M. HAKIMI, "Illusion and Reality in the Compensation of Victims of International Terrorism" (2003) 54 Ala. L. Rev. 561

REYDAMS, L., *Universal Jurisdiction: International and Municipal Legal Perspectives* (Oxford: Oxford University Press, 2003)

RIDENOUR, A., "Apples and Oranges: Why Courts Should Use International Standards to Determine Liability for Violation of the Law of Nations Under the *Alien Tort Claims Act*" (2001) 9 Tul. J. Int'l & Comp. L. 581

ROSCOE, E.S., *A History of the English Prize Court* (London: Lloyd's, 1924)

SARKAR, L., "The Proper Law of Crime in International Law" (1962) 11 I.C.L.Q. 446

SAUMIER, G., "Judicial Jurisdiction in International Cases" (1995) 18 Dal. L.J. 447

SCELLE, G., *Précis de droit des gens* (Paris: Recueil Sirey, 1932)

SCHACTER, O., "Human Dignity as a Normative Concept" (1983) 77 A.J.I.L. 848

———, "International Law in Theory and Practice: General Course in Public International Law" (1982-V) 178 Rec. des Cours 21

SCHREUER, C.H., *State Immunity: Some Recent Developments* (Cambridge: Grotius, 1988)

SCOTT, C., "Remarks: The *Alien Tort Claims Act* under Attack" (2004) 98 A.S.I.L. Proceedings 58

SCOTT, C., ed., *Torture as Tort: Comparative Perspectives on the Development of Transnational Human Rights Litigation* (Oxford: Hart, 2001)

SHAW, M., *International Law* (Cambridge: Cambridge University Press, 2003)

SINCLAIR, SIR I., "The Law of Sovereign Immunity: Recent Developments" (1980-II) 167 Rec. des Cours 113

SLAUGHTER, A.-M., "Judicial Globalization" (2000) 40 Va. J. Int'l L. 1103

———, "A Typology of Transjudicial Communication" (1994) 29 U. Rich. L. Rev. 99

STEINERTE, E., & R.M.M. WALLACE, "Case Note: *Jones v. Ministry of Interior of the Kingdom of Saudi Arabia*" (2006) 100:4 A.J.I.L. 901

STEINHARDT, R.G., "International Humanitarian Law in the Courts of the United States" (2004) 36 Geo. Wash. Int'l L. Rev. 1

———, "Laying One Bankrupt Critique to Rest: *Sosa v. Alvarez-Machain* and the Future of International Human Rights Litigation in US Courts" (2004) 57 Vand. L. Rev. 2241

STEPHENS, B., "The Amorality of Profit: Transnational Corporations and Human Rights" (2002) 20 Berkeley J. Int'l L. 45

———, "Corporate Accountability: International Human Rights Litigation against Corporations in US Courts" in M.T. Kamminga & S. Zia-Zarifi, eds., *Liability of Multinational Corporations under International Law* (The Hague: Kluwer Law International, 2000) 209

———, "Individuals Enforcing International Law: The Comparative and Historical Context" (2002) 52 DePaul L. Rev. 433

———, "The Law of Our Land: Customary International Law as Federal Law after *Erie*" (1997) 66 Fordham L. Rev. 393

———, "Responding to Rogue Regimes" (2002) 36 New Eng. L. Rev. 919

———, "*Sosa v. Alvarez-Machain*: The Door Is Still Ajar for Human Rights Litigation in U.S. Courts" (2004) 70 Brook. L. Rev. 533

———, "Taking Pride in International Human Rights Litigation" (2001) 2 Chi. J. Int'l L. 485

———, "Translating *Filártiga*: A Comparative and International Law Analysis of Domestic Remedies for International Human Rights Violations" (2002) 27 Yale J. Int'l L. 1

STEPHENS, B., *et al.*, *International Human Rights Litigation in US Courts*, 2d ed. (Leiden: Martinus Nijhoff, 2008)

STORY, J., *Commentaries on the Conflict of Laws* (Boston: Little, Brown, 1883)

SUCHARITKUL, S., "Immunities of Foreign States before National Authorities" (1976-I) 149 Rev. des Cours 89

SWAN, M., "International Human Rights Tort Claims and the Experience of United States Courts: An Introduction to the US Case Law, Key Statutes and Doctrines" in C. Scott, ed., *Torture as Tort: Comparative Perspectives on the Development of Transnational Human Rights Litigation* (Oxford: Hart, 2001) 65

SWEENEY, J.M., "A Tort Only in Violation of the Law of Nations" (1995) 18 Hastings Int'l & Comp. L. Rev. 445

TALPIS, J.A., & J.-G. CASTEL, "Interpreting the Rules of Private International Law" in *Reform of the Civil Code* (Montréal: Barreau du Québec, 1993) vol. 5B, Private International Law

TALPIS, J.A., & S.L. KATH, "The Exceptional as Commonplace in Quebec *Forum Non Conveniens* Law: *Cambior*, a Case in Point" (2000) 34 R.J.T. 761

TAYLOR, A., "Another Front in the War on Terrorism? Problems with Recent Changes to the *Foreign Sovereign Immunities Act*" (2003) 45 Ariz. L. Rev. 533

TERRY, J., "Taking *Filártiga* on the Road: Why Courts Outside the United States Should Accept Jurisdiction over Actions Involving Torture Committed Abroad" in C. Scott, ed., *Torture as Tort: Comparative Perspectives on the Development of Transnational Human Rights Litigation* (Oxford: Hart, 2001) 125

TESON, F., "International Human Rights and Cultural Relativism" (1985) 25 Va. J. Int'l L. 869

TETLEY, W., "Current Developments in Canadian Private International Law" (1999) 78 Can. Bar Rev. 152

TOCQUEVILLE, A. DE, *De la démocratie en Amérique* (Paris: Vrin, 1990)

TOMUSCHAT, C., "Individual Reparation Claims in Instances of Grave Human Rights Violations: The Position under General International Law" in A. Randelzhofer & C. Tomuschat, eds., *State Responsibility and the Individual* (The Hague: Martinus Nijhoff, 1999) 1

———, "Reparation for Victims of Grave Human Rights Violations" (2002) 10 Tulane J. Int'l & Comp. L. 157

TOOPE, S., "The Uses of Metaphor: International Law and the Supreme Court of Canada" (2001) 80 Can. Bar Rev. 534

TREMBLAY, L., "*Marbury v. Madison* and Canadian Constitutionalism: Rhetoric and Practice" (2004) 36 Geo. Wash. Int'l L. Rev. 515

TROOBOFF, P.D., "Foreign State Immunity: Emerging Consensus on Principles" (1986-V) 200 Rec. des Cours 245.

VAGTS, D.F., "The Multinational Enterprise: A New Challenge for Transnational Law" (1970) 83 Harv. L. Rev. 739

VAN ALEBEEK, R., "The *Pinochet* Case: International Human Rights Law on Trial" (2000) 71 Brit. Y.B. Int'l L. 29

VAN ERT, G., "The Admissibility of International Legal Evidence" (2005) 84 Can. Bar L. Rev. 31

———, "Judicial Notice and Reception Theory: Thoughts on the Contribution of Roland St. John MacDonald" (2002) Can. Y.B. Int'l L. 251

———, *Using International Law in Canadian Courts*, 2d ed. (Toronto: Irwin Law, 2008)

VAN SCHAACK, B., "In Defense of Civil Redress: The Domestic Enforcement of Human Rights Norms in the Context of Proposed Hague Judgments Convention" (2001) 42 Harv. J. Int'l L. 141

VATTEL, E., *Le Droit des gens ou Principes de la loi naturelle*, 3 vols. (Paris: Librairie de Guillaumin et Cie, 1863)

VAZQUEZ, C., "Direct vs. Indirect Obligations of Corporations under International Law" (2005) 43 Colum. J. Transant'l L. 927

VIRGO, G., "Characterisation, Choice of Law and Human Rights" in C. Scott, ed., *Torture as Tort: Comparative Perspectives on the Development of Transnational Human Rights Litigation* (Oxford: Hart, 2001) 325

WALKER, J., "*Muscutt* Misplaced: The Future of Forum of Necessity in Canada" (2009) 48 Can. Bus. L.J. 135

WARD, H., "Securing Transnational Corporate Accountability through National Courts: Implications and Policy Options" (2001) 24 Hastings Int'l & Comp. L. Rev. 451

WARNER LA FOREST, A., "Evidence and International and Comparative Law" in O. Fitzgerald, ed., *The Globalized Rule of Law* (Toronto, Irwin Law, 2006) 367

WARREN, C., "New Light on the History of the *Federal Judiciary Act of 1789*" (1923) 37 Harv. L. Rev. 49

WATERMAN, J.S., "Thomas Jefferson and Blackstone's Commentaries" (1933) 27 Ill. L. Rev. 629

WEINBERG, L., "Our *Marbury*" (2003) 89 Va. L. Rev. 1235

WEINRIB, E., "Aristotle's Forms of Justice" (1989) 2 Ratio Juris 211

WESTLAKE, J., "Is International Law a Part of the Law of England" (1906) 22 Law Q. Rev. 14

WHITE, G.E., "The Constitutional Journey of *Marbury v. Madison*" (2003) 89 Va. L. Rev. 1463

WRONKA, J., *Human Rights and Social Policy in the 21st Century* (New York: University Press of America, 1998)

YANG, X., "State Immunity in the European Court of Human Rights: Reaffirmations and Misconceptions" (2003) 74 Brit. Y.B. Int'l L. 333

———, "Universal Tort Jurisdiction Overt Torture?" (2005) 61 Cambridge L.J. 1

YNTEMA, E., "The Comity Doctrine" (1966) 65 Mich. L. Rev. 1

Briefs, Reports, and Resolutions

Basic Principles and Guidelines on the Right to a Remedy and Reparation for Victims of Gross Violations of International Human Rights Law and Serious Violations of International Humanitarian Law, adopted by the United Nations General Assembly, 26 March 2006, A/RES/60/147

Brief of *Amicus Curiae* European Commission in *Sosa v. Alvarez-Machain*, 2004 WL 177036

Brief of *Amicus Curiae* United States in *Filartíga v. Peña-Irala*, (1980) 19 I.L.M. 585

Charter of the Organization of Supreme Courts of the Americas (1996) 40 St. Louis U.L.J. 1131

Commentary of the *Draft Articles on Jurisdictional Immunities of States and Their Property*, in Report of the ILC on the works of its 43rd session, 1991, A/46/10(Supp)

Commission on Human Rights, The right to restitution, compensation and rehabilitation for victims of gross violations of human rights and fundamental freedoms, Special Rapporteur C. Bassiouni, E/CN.4/2000/62, 18 January 2000

Congressional Research Service, *Suits Against Terrorist States by Victims of Terrorism*, Order Code RL31258, Library of Congress, 2005

Draft Articles on the Responsibility of States for Internationally Wrongful Acts, UN GAOR, 56th Sess, Supp No 10, p. 43, UN Doc A/56/10 (2001)

Institut de droit international, Resolutions, 1891 Hamburg Sessions (J. Westlake, L. von Bar, & A. Hartmann Rapps.), *Projet de règlement international sur la compétence des tribunaux dans les procès contre les Etats, souverains ou chefs d'Etat étrangers*

Institut de droit international, Resolutions, 1931 Cambridge Session (A. Mercier Rapp.), *Le conflit des lois pénales en matière de compétence*

Institut de droit International, Resolutions, 1993 Milan Session (B. Conforti Rapp.), *The Activities of National Judges and the International Relations of their States*

International Law Association, Committee on International Human Rights Law and Practice, Rapp. M.T. Kamminga, "Report on the Exercise of Universal Jurisdiction in Respect of Gross Human Rights Offences" (London: International Law Association, 2000)

International Law Association, Committee on International Human Rights Law and Practice, "Report on Civil Actions in the English Courts for Serious Human Rights Violations Abroad" [2001] 2 Eur. H.R.L. Rev. 129

L'immunité de juridiction et d'exécution des états: À propos du projet de Convention du Conseil de l'Europe, Actes du Colloque conjoint des 30 et 31 janvier 1969 (Bruxelles: Éditions de l'Institut de Sociologie, 1971)

O'Connor, Hon. Justice D., *New Review Mechanisms for the RCMP's National Security Activities*, Report of the Commission of Inquiry in the Actions of Canadian Officials in Relation to Maher Arar, Ottawa, 2006, online: www.ararcommission.ca

Torture Victim Protection Act, House of Representatives Judicial Committee Report, reprinted in B. Stephens & M. Ratner, *International Human Rights Litigation in US Courts* (New York: Transnational, 1996) at 255

Torture Victim Protection Act, Senate Judicial Committee Report, S. Rep. No. 249, 102d Cong., 1st Sess. (1991), reprinted in B. Stephens & M. Ratner, *International Human Rights Litigation in US Court* (New York: Transnational, 1996) at 255

Table of Cases

Index

About the Author

François Larocque is vice-dean and associate professor at the Faculty of Law, University of Ottawa, where he teaches tort law. He has also taught history and theory of the common law, public law, and constitutional law. His research and legal practice relate mainly to transnational human rights litigation and language rights. Prior to joining the law school, he clerked at the Supreme Court of Canada and the Ontario Court of Appeal. François completed his Ph.D. in law at the University of Cambridge after completing his B.A. in philosophy and LL.B. at the University of Ottawa. He is a member of Law Society of Upper Canada.

Printed and bound by CPI Group (UK) Ltd, Croydon, CR0 4YY

15/09/2026

14962400-0004